Pr

I came to *The Diary of Sabine Baring-(   )   per
understanding of the life and perso   My
expectation had been that I would spe   ord
Office and there transcribe a selection   uld
address specific questions and provide support for my views on particular issues. I
soon realised however that to use the diary in this way would be to do less than
justice to an important document. What I found myself dipping into was a twenty-
year journal of the life and times of an intelligent, well informed, acutely observant
and energetic man of many interests. All these attributes were evident in all I read.
Patently this document would answer many more questions than I had been
intending to pose. This diary is a lively and, on the whole, superbly written
commentary on the social life and mores of Victorian gentry. Furthermore it gives
insights into the process of novel writing; detailed observations on the Victorian
restoration of a 17th century manor house; invaluable information on the
architecture of several Devon country houses; details of numerous Devon churches
before the 19th century 'restoration'; contemporary accounts of the attitudes and
behaviour of Victorian Devon clergy. It is undoubtedly the source of much of the
anecdotal, folklore and other material to be found in many of Sabine Baring-
Gould's publications, but especially his two volumes of *Reminiscences*.

The more I read the more excited I became and could not wait to share my
enthusiasm with Dr. Merriol Almond, the great granddaughter of Sabine Baring-
Gould and owner of the diary. Until then Dr Almond had not been aware that the
diary existed. She first mooted the possibility of transcribing it in its entirety. By
this time I had already come to the conclusion that one approach to understanding
how and why Sabine reacted to the events in his life as he did, would be by
following his own contemporary commentary on it over a considerable period of
time. The diary provided just such an opportunity. Used in this way the whole
document would be far more valuable than the sum of its parts and therefore must
at some stage be transcribed. It was a short step from this realisation to taking a
deep breath and offering to carry out the task.

Ron Wawman
4 June 2009.

Acknowledgements

I am indebted to many people for helping me to make, interpret and publish this transcription. Merriol Almond for her enthusiasm, encouragement and permission to borrow the diary from the Devon Record Office; also for her permission to publish the diary, letters and Family Bible entries. John Draisey for his support, advice on publication and the revelation of an almost totally erased passage through the use of ultraviolet light. Keith Lister for alerting me to the diary, the bible entries and other important sources including, of course, his own biography; also for clues in the mystery of what became of the marriage of Sabine's sister, Margaret. David Shacklock for presentational advice. The Rev. John and Mrs Pam Hunwicke for their clerical, classical, armorial and many other areas of scholarship, in particular the translation of Latin and obscure Greek, invaluable comment on Victorian mores, editing suggestions and a keen eye for an 'indecipherable' word. Albert Spry and Arthur Perkin for local history and dialect. Sybil Tope for her encouragement and the loan of books with which to check continental and Devon place and family names. Susanne Clayton for putting me on the track of *The Lamerton Hunt Song*. Graham Yeo for identifying the prisoner of 'Orchard'. Hazel Harvey for pinning down the Colleton Crescent household and knowledge of ice-skating on the R. Exe. Moira Harris for her knowledge of personalities associated with *Red Spider*, the opera. Roger Bristow for his inestimable bibliography, help with little known published work and the considerable time and effort he put into the production of all the maps accompanying this transcription. Ian Maxted for tracking down *Deutches Familienblatt*. Andrew Dakyns and Jonathan Morgan for their efforts to trace *Zitta* in Germany. Kingsley Rickard for his advice on obscure prescriptions for coughs and strains. Elizabeth Goldsworthy for her encouragement and for the identification of Devon family and place names. Alan Payne for French transcription and editing advice. Elizabeth Dickinson for access to family letters, permission to quote from them and her knowledge of the Dickinson family. Martin and Shan Graebe for support at a difficult time, for time consuming but invaluable editing assistance, for the definitive transcription of a letter from the Rev. Fleetwood Sheppard, for help with lachrymatories/urinals, Schubert's *Der Lindenbaum as well as* Gladstone and *The Turk and the Tory;* also for many other items of knowledge about Sabine. Carol Matthews for permission to publish a letter to Polly Davey. Becky Smith for pointing me in the direction of Arthur's unpublished biography and for the tenacious primary source research that confirmed 1875 as the year *Willy went out of his mind.* Ray Canfield for his IT skills and excellent photographs of Sabine's sketches. Toni Kemeny for permission to use her evocative sketch of a 19th century bell buoy. Charlotte Yeo for her thoughtful and striking portrait of Sabine after Melton Fisher. Penny Yeo for her meticulous editing and proof reading. Above all, Margaret for the initial proof reading of the raw transcription but mostly, like Grace, for putting up with my Sabine-like pre-occupations for far too long.

Ron Wawman
June 2009.

Contents

Illustrations

Introduction

Introduction

The Search for Sabine Baring-Gould

The Rev. Sabine Baring-Gould (Hereafter referred to as Sabine) has been variously described as an antiquarian, ecclesiastical historian, biographer, hagiographer, theologian, folklorist, travel writer, archaeologist, medievalist, collector of folk songs, hymn writer, novelist and author of a vast number of short stories and more than 1000 articles on a wide range of subjects.[1] Books and popular articles about Sabine have often promoted the assumptions that he was eccentric and averse to social contact and these assumptions have been repeated from work to work. One important feature of this diary is that it enables us to test these prejudices against primary evidence.

There is much to suggest that Sabine's difficult relationship with his parents during childhood led to a natural reticence about his private life and inner thoughts. His half brother, Arthur, although 31 years younger, became his curate in 1895 and in many ways knew Sabine well. He nevertheless wrote the following:

> *The one thing he would never talk about was his inner life, his spiritual struggles, what doubts or difficulties he had conquered, how he had been led to take Orders, and what his thoughts were on his ordination.* [2]

Sabine revealed only certain aspects of himself in his two volumes of biographical *Reminiscences* [3] [4] and wrote:

> *others will remonstrate at my digressions, yet, if I digress, it is precisely for the sake of avoiding to talk of self.* [5]

Avoidance of talking of self left a partial vacuum for others to fill and made the task of his biographers more difficult. This goes some way to explaining why the four published biographies do not always give totally convincing insights into how or why Sabine achieved what he did. The first, by William Purcell,[6] published in 1957, although in many ways a balanced and informative account of the life of Sabine, was limited by a heavy reliance on published work by or about him. The second, published in 1970, by the Rev. Bickford Dickinson,[7] third son of Sabine's eldest child, Mary, is a warm, well-written and insightful account of his grandfather. However, his closeness to his subject and other family members meant that he drew selectively, and sometimes with bias, on family anecdote, personal knowledge and family correspondence. The third biography by the Rev. Harold Kirk-Smith,[8] published in 1997, drew substantially on published material and contributed critiques of much of Sabine's work including his more successful novels. Kirk-Smith gave particular emphasis to ecclesiastical matters and wrote at some length on the Catholic Revival in the Anglican Church and Sabine's place in it. He made limited use of primary source material and although he quoted selectively from what he described as letters written by Sabine to a friend during his last five years, [9]it is now known that he only had access to typed and selectively edited transcriptions of these letters made by Sabine's correspondent. The most recent biography, by Keith Lister,[10] published in 2002, made better use of primary source material but was principally concerned with the life of Sabine's wife Grace and her relationship with her husband. Lister assimilated much new material about Grace's early life and about Sabine's years in Yorkshire but was not as successful in his search for a better understanding of the personality of Grace and her relationship with Sabine.

The biographies make limited use of letters and only the most recent, by Keith Lister, mentioned and quoted from a diary.[11] Until that biography, *Half My Life*, was published in 2002, rjw had assumed, like Sabine's half-brother, Arthur Baring-Gould,[12] that there was neither diary nor much in the way of significant personal letters on which to draw. In *Further Reminiscences*[13] Sabine quotes from an 1862 diary but whether that diary still exists and, if it does exist, where it is located is not known. But Arthur Baring-Gould was mistaken; there is a significant body of correspondence and one substantial diary from which much can be learned about the life, times and thoughts of Sabine Baring-Gould.

Unsupported by other sources, the entries in a time-limited diary cannot give a complete picture of Sabine Baring-Gould. What they will do is correct some false assumptions and fill some gaps in what was previously known about the man before the diary was transcribed.

The Structure of the Diary

The diary that has eluded all previous writers apart from Keith Lister is but one item in the Baring-Gould archive held in box 5203 at the Devon Record Office. It is to be found in an old, fragile and well-thumbed ledger book, the dimensions of which are 9 by 7 by 1.25 inches.

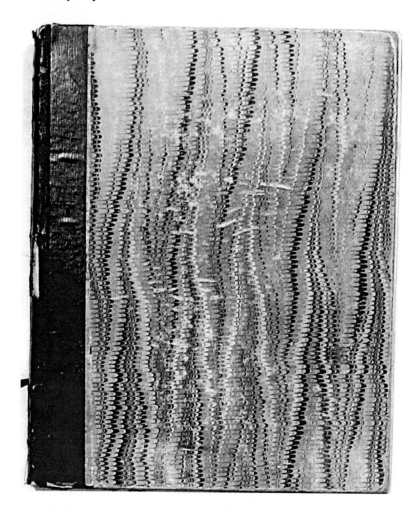

Fig. 1: *The Diary*

At the top of the first page appears, in Sabine's own handwriting, the words:

The Diary of Sabine Baring-Gould.

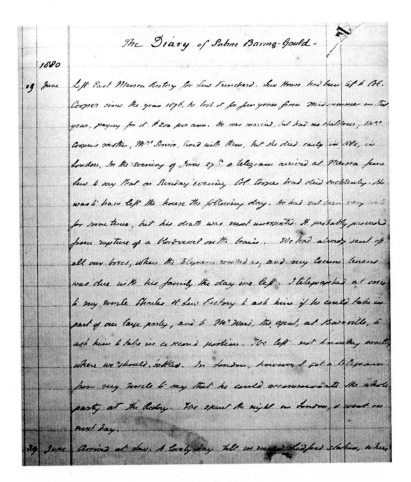

Fig. 2 Title Page

This heading is followed by page after page of closely written cramped handwriting, interspersed by occasional pen and ink or pencil drawings.

On the whole the diary unfolds as a well-written and readable document that covers numerous and diverse topics and events. In the process, the diary throws light on a personality which, although previously well known in a superficial sense, has kept many of its secrets hidden.

The diary covers the period June 1880 to November 1899 but the coverage varies hugely from one year to another. The reader will discover that different parts of the diary have a subtly different character. Therefore, to make it more manageable for the reader, the transcriber has chosen to present it in four roughly equal parts, each part covering a period of residence in a different place. The first part covers a mere four months living at Lew House between leases. The second part covers 11 months when Sabine and his family were resident at Freiburg. The third part covers his 4 years living in the rectory as rector of Lew Trenchard. The final part covers his first 14 years living in Lew House as the squire and rector (squarson) of Lew Trenchard. Lew House, nowadays usually referred to as Lew Trenchard Manor, is the seat of the Baring-Gould family and, as such, features prominently in the diary.

It is only possible to speculate on what might have been the purpose of this diary. It probably had several uses and these changed over time. At its simplest it was a record of events beginning in 1880 when Sabine and his family embarked on a fifteen-month adventure and ending abruptly in 1899 for no apparent reason.

It was certainly a repository for numerous accounts of events and anecdotes that were used at a later time in his publications. The early pages include a great deal of family history, as if one intention was the provision of a family record that could be made available, in the course of time, not only for Sabine's own use, but also that of others. If he knew and intended or even merely anticipated that, at some date in the future, members of his family at least would read his diary it would explain such features as the attempt to erase most of a derogatory entry concerning Daniel Radford.[14]

Sabine used extracts from diary entries extensively in many of his publications but especially the two volumes of Reminiscences written in his old age.[15] [16] Here they were published, sometimes much as written, but often appropriately edited and occasionally embellished. More than 180 references to incidents, family history and anecdotes recorded in the diary have been identified in a selection of Sabine's published work. There were undoubtedly more. Often the same anecdote is to be found in different publications. Sometimes, especially when describing local events or notorious family figures, he gave the characters false names and altered the geographical setting. Not infrequently he unintentionally gave the wrong dates in his publications for significant events, occasionally with unfortunate results. The simple reason for this is that the year of an entry in the diary is often not easy to find. Thus his absence from home when his wife Grace moved the family and effects from Lew Trenchard Rectory to Lew House, was for a brief four days so that he could officiate at the wedding of his cousin in Paris. He was not also on a long sojourn in Germany as he described in *Further Reminiscences*[17] and in the *1862 Family Bible*.[18]

Many of the anecdotes reproduced in the Reminiscences were freshly written in the diary on the day he heard them in the course of what was, evidently, a busy social life. Several times he wrote introductions like: *heard a good story today* or *heard a rich story today*. This is particularly true in the first five years of the diary where he described, and evidently enjoyed, much social coming and going. It is impossible to avoid the conclusion that he was drawn to social contact with others and delighted in gossip. This is a strong rebuttal of suggestions that Sabine was a loner who disliked socialising.

The diary was certainly used as a notebook in which to record for future use such things as Sabine's architectural and armorial findings in the grand houses of Devon but particularly during his extensive renovation of Lew House. Sabine often railed against the destructive church renovations perpetrated in Devon during the early 19th century. He joined earlier antiquaries such as Richard Symonds[19] and the Rev. Dr. Jeremiah Milles[20] in recording valuable evidence of the contents of Devon churches before 'ecclesiastical restoration' took hold. Sabine's evidence even stretched back to reminiscences of what, as an archeologically minded boy, he had seen in the 1840s.

Towards its end, the diary became a scrapbook; a receptacle for a variety of items, such as a letter from the Rev. Fleetwood Sheppard, who was a close associate of Sabine in the process of collecting folk songs,[21][22] pasted in along side completely unrelated entries on 15 August 1894. There is also an almost illegible record of roses planted in the greenhouses and garden[23] and an obscure page of Greek.[24]

Entries in the diary often relate to singular, problematic or contentious issues. Those personal aspects of his life, that fitted him comfortably and unremarkably, appear less frequently and with little comment. Thus it is that while there are many vivid pen pictures of unusual and often unpleasant people, his wife, Grace, remained in the shadows, despite being mentioned in the diary more often than anyone else. Sometimes Sabine used the diary to reflect at length on his mixed feelings towards his father and his mother [25][26] and he dwelt in some detail on the tensions with his father over his choice of career and his uncertainty over whether or not he would inherit Lew House and the estate. Understanding these events and the extent of Sabine's distress has been aided by the subsequent transcription of significant letters between Sabine and his parents. [27]

There are numerous references to the writing of novels, particularly the dates on which these were started or finished, as well as repeated comments on how much he was, or was not, paid for them. Those keen to discover where, when and with whom he stayed when researching the novels may not find these questions answered but they will find his passionate views on novel writing and novel readers. To his diary he confided an intense dislike of both![28]

There is ample evidence both in the diary and elsewhere that Sabine was very conscious of his origins, the Gould family pedigree and his social position. There is also much to suggest from this diary that living in, restoring and passing Lew House on to his heirs was a major, if not the major, object of this period in his life. If so then it could well be that the diary was intended as an apologia for that preoccupation as well as an heirloom for his successors.

The Challenges of Transcription

As those who have worked on his manuscripts know only too well, Sabine's handwriting is at times difficult to decipher. It is fortunate for the transcriber of the diary that he took some care with entries over the first few years and it was only towards the end of the diary, as entries became shorter and less frequent, that he sometimes descended into a hurried scrawl.

Sabine was inclined to use every available line on a page and every bit of space on a line. As the end of a line approached he tended to try to fit long words into small spaces. This did not help the process of transcription!

Several subjects are often covered in the entries for one day and this creates problems for the reader because, although he always started a new subject on a fresh line, the beginning of a new paragraph is rarely immediately apparent and it is difficult for the casual reader to pick out where one item ends and another begins.

The transcription is unabridged, apart from the omission of newspaper cuttings referring to the weddings of daughter Mary and Sabine's half-sister Leila.[29] In general the diary is presented here as written, even where the order is at times confusing, as when the occasional item is pasted into the diary out of context. Where several different items are covered on a single day, paragraph breaks are used in the transcription both to separate items and to make a long page of unbroken, but related, text easier to follow.

Being entered in a ledger, the dates in the diary had to be written by hand and, although Sabine generally entered both the day and the month, it was usually only in the first entry in any year that he identified the year. This undoubtedly often caused Sabine to make mistakes when he used the diary as a source of events described in his published work. Therefore, to avoid confusing modern readers, in the transcription the year has been added in italics for all other entries. Occasionally, particularly towards the end of the document, dates were sometimes omitted altogether. Sabine invariably entered the date on the same line in the ledger on which the related entry began. For clarity in the transcription the date of an entry has been given its own line and entered in bold.

Spaces often occur in the narrative. Presumably these were there because Sabine did not know or could not remember such things as names, dates and measurements. Sometimes he returned and inserted the missing item at a later date. Often he did not. Some of his corrections or brief comments may have been made long after the original entry. A small number of gaps represent a failure on the part of the transcriber to decipher a word—most often the name of a place or person. To distinguish these gaps a question mark in italics and square brackets has been inserted alongside them thus: *[?]* Similar, italicised, question marks have been inserted alongside transcribed words the accuracy of which is uncertain—again most often the name of a place or person. Any question mark not in italics and brackets belongs to Sabine, not the transcriber.

Sabine frequently resorted to the use of an ampersand. The transcriber could detect no pattern to this usage and has therefore invariably transcribed these using the word 'and.'

Much time has been taken up wrestling with uncertain words and phrases. Most, but not all, of these have yielded to a combination of lateral thinking; good lighting; magnifying glass; enlargement of photographs on a computer; English, French and German dictionaries; a range of maps; internet search engines; travel guidebooks; Sabine's publications; letters and a bibliography.[30] The process of transcription and analysis has also been greatly aided by the scholarship of others.

One of the most time-consuming, amusing, but not untypical challenge, was the phrase *a magnificent pue of the skirrets of the purest rénaissance* which was written of the church at Peter Tavy on 1 February 1882. 'Pue' was easy. It appears more than once in the dtyuhjbniary and, despite not being an accepted modern spelling of the word, is patently what is usually known as a 'pew'. For some weeks the word 'skirret' resisted interpretation. The dictionary definitions were either an *architect's instrument* or a *water parsnip*, but neither of these made sense. Eventually a scholastic friend realised that the pew was that of the *Skiret* family of Peter Tavy! The capital 'S' in 'Skirret' had not been obvious.

The following late addition to the text written on 4 July 1880 only became clear when it had been photographed and the digital image enlarged on a computer screen.

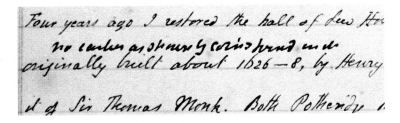

Fig. 3 Handwriting example

This transcribes as: *Four years ago I restored the hall of Lew House. The house was originally built about 1626 – 8, by Henry Gould (no earlier as shown by coins found in it) who purchased it of Sir Thomas Monk.*

Sabine's attempt to score out a derogatory entry made on 22 July 1880 concerning his good friend, Daniel Radford was eventually overcome through the use of ultraviolet light.

Throughout the diary, the transcriber has added brief editing comments. These always appear in italics and square brackets. References to where, in Sabine's publications, many events and anecdotes can also be found, appear as footnotes. More detailed notes are given as 'Explanatory Endnotes' in appendix A.

Despite these attempts to make the diary easy to follow, the reader would still have difficulty finding particular items of interest without further assistance. A comprehensive 'where to find' subject index is provided at appendix B to assist in the search for entries relating to such things as Sabine's work as a writer; the Gould family history; the immediate family; the renovation of Lew House; financial problems; folk lore, anecdotes, etc.

For ease of reference the appendices also include indexes of the names of people and places mentioned in the diary. Maps are provided at appendix D to show the itinerary of continental tours and assist in the location of West Country places mentioned in the diary.

All entries made by Sabine in the 1862 family bible[31] have been added to aid the comparison of events and dates and to help set the diary in its historical context. It is possible that entries were first made in this bible around the time the diary began and that Sabine copied earlier family and personal events from other records.

Finally, to assist the unravelling of the concentrated family pedigrees to be found in the early pages of the diary, the family trees of the Goulds, the Baring-Goulds of Lew Trenchard and the Monks of Potheridge are given at appendix C.

A word of warning—the family history recorded in some of the earliest entries in the diary does not make easy reading. The reader should not let this put him off the diary. Skip the history and follow the narrative. Only return to the family history if and when this is thought to be essential.

A Journey Through The Journal

What follows is an exposition of the four parts of the diary highlighting the significant events, attitudes and memoirs to be found in each of them.

Part I: Sabbatical at Lew, June to October 1880

1880. 29 June: Left East Mersea Rectory for Lew Trenchard. Lew House had been let to Col Cooper since the year 1876; he took it for four years from midsummer in that year, paying for it £200 per ann.

It is no co-incidence that the diary begins at the start of what was to become a 15 month sabbatical during which, having left his friend, the Rev. J. M. Gatrill, behind as his locum in East Mersea, Sabine lived the life of a leisured country gentleman firstly at Lew and then in Freiburg. Sabine was not, however, the wealthy landowner this might suggest. He had inherited Lew House and its estate eight years previously but these were difficult times for farmers and the net income from the estate was almost nothing. As a result, he could not afford to live at Lew House on a permanent basis. He was only able to finance this brief stay at Lew between leases, by drawing on income derived from leasing out the house over the previous eight years and through the expedient of borrowing £1000 from an aunt.

This was to be a very full and satisfying 4 months much of which was spent entertaining and visiting family, friends and various members of the Devon clergy and gentry—hardly the actions of a recluse. From this intense social activity Sabine derived a stream of anecdotes that he recorded in his diary. From the nature of the anecdotes it is difficult to avoid the conclusion that he enjoyed gossip and was not averse to hearing and recording scandal. He also relished stories about social upstarts and inferior pedigrees.

While living and working as the rector of East Mersea he had indulged a keen interest in his family history and pedigree by frequently taking the train to London and Somerset House where he explored the family records. Now, within days of starting the diary, he embarked on a detailed pedigree of the Monk and Gould families and their links with Lew House. He supplemented this review of family history by studying the memorials and registers in several parishes in South Devon but particularly at Staverton, the ancient seat of the Devon Goulds.

Sabine also gave time to the study of antiquities on Dartmoor and, under the direction of the Rev W. Lukis, an antiquarian, who was a guest at Lew House, re-erected the menhir that had been found in the wall of the leat at Lew Mill.

The most revealing and dramatic entry in this section of the diary is to be found on 12 September when news of the death of the Rev. Charles Lowder, his early Anglo-catholic mentor, triggered an account of the ten years that followed his coming down from Cambridge in 1857. These included the brief sojourn at Pimlico with Lowder, the eight happy years at St John's Middle School, Hurstpierpoint, and his first two years as a curate at Horbury, Yorkshire. The strained relationships with his parents that resulted from his father's implacable opposition to Sabine's determination to take Holy Orders overshadowed the whole of this period.

Sabine described how in 1866, after two years as a curate at Horbury, Yorkshire, he visited Lew. At the time he was unaware that his brother Willy was experiencing the early signs of the mental and physical illness that finally killed him. Sabine completely misconstrued Willy's rudeness to himself as well as his father's concerned attention for Willy. He concluded that his father had finally made up his mind to leave Lew House and Estate to his brother, Willy. In the diary he wrote how, as an angry reaction to this presumed disinheritance:

> *I made up my mind to go as a missionary to British Columbia and entered into a correspondence with the SPG[32] about a mission there vacant. Then I proposed to dear Grace and was accepted.*

It can be deduced from this entry that one important result of his decision to give up any pretensions to the squirearchy and its social obligations was that he, at the age of 32, now felt free to propose to Grace Taylor, a young mill girl, half his age. He never did become a missionary and eventually he did inherit, but he also did marry Grace. Some indication of the intensity of his feelings towards his parents at the time of the events he was recording many years later is revealed in a letter written to his mother while he was at Pimlico.[33]

Undoubtedly the most significant achievement chronicled in the diary in this brief four months was the completion by Sabine of the second phase of his rebuild of Lew House. It is difficult to contemplate quite how he was able to demolish the old, dilapidated and largely abandoned original staircase wing in the time available between leases and then erect a new, bigger and far grander staircase wing. Plans must have been carefully laid, building material assembled and a skilled workforce recruited well in advance of his arrival at Lew. Although Sabine left behind in his diary an outline record of what he found and what was built in its place, he gave no account of the planning, preparation and organisation. He eschewed the use of architects and preferred to rely on his own plans and to use local craftsmen, but the extent to which others were involved in the organisation of this ambitious project is not known. This cannot have been other than a very expensive project and Sabine was never again financially in a position to proceed with his plans at such pace. Another 31 years and several periods of financial embarrassment would pass, before the rebuild of the house finally came to a halt in 1911.[34]

PART 2: Sabbatical in Freiburg:
October 1880 to September 1881

Sabine did not want to leave Lew House after four months but believed he had no option.

I should not have let it so soon, but have spent the winter at Lew, but that this year, as last, the farmers cannot pay their rents in full. I allowed off 10% last year, and this, but still several are behind, unable to pay at all.....Now, by letting the house for 5 years I hope to make a thousand pounds and by economy abroad to save some money, at the same time that I am getting the children educated well and cheaply.

On 22 October the family left Lew and began their journey to Freiburg and *economy abroad*. The family knew Freiburg well, having previously spent the winter of 1877/8 there, and the children were able to look forward to a reunion with two elderly ladies who had been their teachers there. Sabine looked forward to cheap lodgings and to renewing the friendship he had forged in 1877 with Frau Wilhelmine Hillern, a German authoress of some repute.[35] The diary chronicled the development of a working relationship between the two authors that soon degenerated into an acrimonious legal dispute, the end of their friendship and the insightful comment:

I am very much like a buoy. Every wave goes over me, and yet I am never completely submerged. The condition is not a happy one, but there are others that are worse.

The eleven months in Freiburg led to a further store of amusing anecdotes gleaned from those he met. These give an insightful account of an expatriate community of relatively impecunious English 'gentry' living well but cheaply and mixing with the local German community.

Reminiscences were recorded of early-married life, of his father's death, of the mental illness of Willy and of the personalities of significant family members. Some of these accounts, suitably edited, appeared in his published Reminiscences.

Sabine described excursions into the Black Forest and to the Alps with various groups of relatives and friends, and wrote proudly of the behaviour of his children at a local fair.

For the first time the diary reveals a commitment to novel writing. Sabine recorded the receipt of a bundle of criticisms of his recently published novel *Mehalah*. Some critics had objected to the unpleasantness of the characters in the novel; this prompted an explanation from Sabine:

I admit that Mehalah is unpleasant and bitter. I wrote it when greatly depressed and embittered by two most ungentlemanly reviews of my "Germany"..........The first was offensive and insulting to the last degree, there were other reviews most unfair and captious, accusing me of blunders I had not made.

Sabine was also commissioned by a Berlin publisher to write a novel in German, to which he gave the title *Zitta*. This was eventually published in Brussels under the name *Etelka*.[36] On 2 August the family moved from the busy town of Freiburg to stay for a month at a favourite haunt in the quiet village of Laufenburg on the Rhine. Here, day in and day out, Sabine retired to his room to write this novel while the rest of the family enjoyed the summer. This pattern of behaviour anticipated, in a small way, the self-denying treadmill Sabine eventually came to endure while he financed the remainder of the rebuild of Lew House.

It is not known how long Sabine intended to reside in Freiburg but early during his time there his uncle, the Rev. Charles Baring-Gould, who was the incumbent at Lew Trenchard, died. Although Sabine made no comment to this effect in the diary, it can be deduced that it was his uncle's death that at last made a return to Lew financially viable and led directly to his decision to present himself to the living of Lew Trenchard.

PART 3: Rector of Lew Trenchard: September 1881 to October 1885

The third part of the diary commences with the return of Sabine to Lew Trenchard as rector. Because there were still four years of the lease on Lew House to run, Sabine was unable to re-commence the re-build of the house and had to bide his time in the rectory. Unperturbed, he continued to draw rent on Lew House at the same time as he threw himself into work about the estate. He moved a road, presumably so that the site of the house would have room to accommodate an anticipated North wing. This wing was not added until 1895; this is clear evidence that Sabine was from the beginning working to a plan. Sabine also beautified the derelict lime quarry by repeatedly planting the waste, or 'ramps' with trees, by erecting a romantic cottage there and by turning the quarry into a picturesque lake. In the garden he built a pixie well, erected two greenhouses, added a statue of Andromeda and the Dolphin, and planted rose beds. Throughout the estate he spent time and money improving existing cottages and farms.

Sabine also gave time to working with Colonel Vivian who was compiling and editing a new edition of the 1620 *Visitation of Devon*.[37] This task involved visiting old houses and churches throughout the county and busying himself with registers and memorials. In the diary he described and sketched coats of arms and features of the places he visited. Often he railed against the unsympathetic restoration of West Country churches that had been carried out earlier in the century. He was, like so many members of the Victorian lesser gentry, at pains for his pedigree to be seen in as good a light as possible. The much-expanded coverage given to the Goulds in the 1895 edition of the Visitation reflected the special attention Sabine had given to his own pedigree. So it was that what, in the original manuscript, had been barely a page became fifteen pages of closely detailed genealogical description. It is also evident from the diary that Sabine did not hesitate to put others in what he thought was their genealogical place!

Writing took up much of Sabine's time during his four years at the rectory and this is reflected in diary entries. He found time to write several of his best novels during this Period. *John Herring,*[38] *Margery of Quether,*[39] *Court Royal,*[40] *Red Spider,*[41] *The Gaverocks*[42] and *Eve*[43] were all written then and a pattern was established of entering in the diary the date he started writing, the date he finished, the date he sent the novel off to the publisher and what he was paid for it. From time to time he reviewed his earnings from publications in the diary.

All this activity did not curtail Sabine's social life and the steady collection of anecdote and folklore.

A pattern of spending several months writing a novel is discernable. During the time Sabine was writing a novel other entries in the diary are less in evidence. This is probably indicative of the intense mental pre-occupation required by him in the process of novel writing. As such, this once more anticipated the treadmill he was soon to find himself on when he was compelled to write novels incessantly as the only way to finance the rebuild of Lew House.

During this period Sabine made two trips to the continent with his friend, the Rev. J M Gatrill, one in 1883 and one in 1884 (not 1885 as he claimed in *Further Reminiscences*). He gave a brief itinerary in each case and was very proud to demonstrate how frugally he lived.

In 1885, after four years living in the rectory, Lew House finally became vacant and, on 29 September, the family moved in. It is well known that Sabine was absent on the continent when the move took place because that is what he wrote in *Further Reminiscences*. Some have been critical of this absence at such a busy time for his wife, Grace. However Sabine was not away for several weeks that summer as it would seem from his published account,[44] but for a mere 4 days so that he could officiate at the wedding of his cousin, Alex Baring, in Paris. It is highly unlikely that he would have wanted to be away from Lew when the most momentous move of his life was taking place and he was probably faced by an unavoidable clash of dates. In 1885, to go from Lewdown to Paris, officiate at a wedding and return in 4 days was probably the best that anyone could have achieved. Sabine is known to have been impractical about the house,[45] [46] and it is likely that Grace was only too pleased to have him out from under her feet while she, by all accounts a capable woman, expertly managed the move of children, staff and household effects. Whatever the truth, this is what Sabine wrote on his arrival home two days after the move:

> *1 Oct 1885: The last change made till the great one of all. I slipped in without anyone seeing me, left the carriage and came by the garden, that I might on crossing the threshold of my dear house, say a prayer to God to bless me in the home of my ancestors to which I have come at last to make it a home, and to enable me to remain in it; I shall have difficulty as times are so bad, and my income is reduced. Grace is truly marvellous. The way in which she managed the moving, organised everything shows real genius.........No hitch, all worked on wheels, thanks to dear Grace. She is a general in the house.*

PART 4: The Squarson of Lew Trenchard:
October 1885 to November 1899

The last part of the diary covered 14 years and the entries were dominated by three inter-related factors: The restoration of Lew House, money, or the lack of it, and writing novels. Entries became briefer, with longer gaps between them, and there were fewer reports of social interaction and anecdotes. Instead there were long and detailed accounts of the rebuild of Lew House and Sabine's discoveries concerning its past structure. Sketches accompany several entries. Between 1885 and 1887 his work on the house included the restoration of drawing and dining rooms and the extensive rebuild of the library and East staircase wing. He then proceeded to build a completely new kitchen in an extended east wing. A new north wing was constructed to accommodate pantry, dairy and coalhouse. These essentially utilitarian structures were concealed behind a delightful cloister. In the process he created a courtyard. A letter to his daughter, Mary,[47] reveals that it was already Sabine's intention that, at some future date, the main entrance to the house would be through this courtyard. This would have finally come to pass had the First World War not have aborted his construction of a gatehouse.[48] Having built a new kitchen he was at last able to demolish the old kitchen and, in its place build, his grand ballroom. The ballroom was completed in 1897.

The process of rebuilding was far from smooth. A revealing cry of anguish was written on 24 August 1886:

> *A grievous discouragement to me is that I can find no sale for any of my historical and mythological articles… …The editors always say 'send us a story' And here I protest that I write novels with anger and heat because they take me off my proper course of study, history, especially ecclesiastical, and mythology which is my favourite study. I write only because I cannot build and restore this house, I can not live on the estate, without supplementing my income from my pen. When I have finished a novel, I regard it with loathing and bitterness against it, as having engaged my time and thought which might have been better employed… …*

Another cry of anguish came on 21 Jan 1890 as Sabine left Lew Trenchard en route for Italy in the middle of an influenza epidemic:

> *No building done to Lew House in 1889. In 1888 I built the gallery to E… …I have been unable to complete more than the walls of this gallery, as my funds were very low. I had in Jan 1889 to borrow £500 from the City bank Exeter, and deposited there as security, the Deed of resettlement of estate and my affidavit relative to the policies on my own and my wife's lives.*

It seems likely that Sabine was particularly low in spirits as he continued:

> *Should I not return from abroad, having succumbed to my bronchitis,*
> *then I should like Edward, when able, to complete Lew House according*
> *to my plan, or as near as he can at his convenience.*

The creation of the gallery was not completed until 1911 presumably because this was an ambitious project that, apart from being very expensive was, as evidenced by several letters to his daughter Mary, particularly disruptive of everyday life in the house.

Family health is often referred to throughout the diary but particularly in this final section. Sabine frequently mentioned his own susceptibility to the family failing — bronchitis—and it was his efforts to escape from this regular winter visitor that eventually led to a pattern of taking off for the continent in January of most years and not returning until the late spring. Nothing, other than his own health, seems to have been allowed to get in the way of this migration. He had the robust attitude to women's matters common to the Victorian gentry. Thus on 4 February 1889, just 20 days **after** the birth of his daughter Cicely and 6 days **before** her baptism,[49] he wrote: *Left Lew for Italy*, although if his account of this visit to Italy in *Further Reminiscences* is accurate he was actually running away from an influenza outbreak that occurred when he was staying with his cousin Francis Baring-Gould at Merrow Grange, Guildford.[50]

Sabine's continental trips were used for research into the numerous travel books he wrote, but in his diary he simply entered the itinerary and never described the places he visited. There is no indication that he ever took the diary with him during these journeys away from home. Details of the places he visited were presumably recorded elsewhere, probably in notebooks.

Throughout the whole diary there are frequent references to members of Sabine's immediate family, although two of his fifteen children, Cicely and Joan, never receive a mention. A simple explanation for these omissions could be that these younger children were either never seriously ill, or never responsible for behaviour remarkable enough for comment. Or could it be that, as his granddaughter, Cicely Briggs,[51] believed, he simply had favourites and her mother, Cicely, was not fortunate enough to be one.

The transcriber's first impression was that Sabine wrote very little in the diary about Grace, but when, in the process of transcription, he turned to the creation of an index of names it emerged that Grace was mentioned in 25 entries – more than any one else. This finding could mean that, although Grace was closely involved with much that occupied Sabine's time, his feelings towards her were such that he felt no need to paint the pen pictures that make the personalities of his father, mother, uncles and aunts stand out.

This final section of the diary chronicled some of the struggles Sabine had with his maturing family. On unspecified dates in 1893 he wrote of the engagement of his daughter, Mary, to Harvey Dickinson, and this was soon followed by a detailed description of their wedding, but not before he had written of his alarm at Harvey Dickinson's plans to sell off the Dickinson's renowned ancestral home at Dunsland, near Holsworthy, and his suspicions that a marriage settlement was being drawn up that would be unfavourable to his daughter. A recent personal communication[52] suggests he had good grounds for his concerns.

There are two interesting copies or drafts of 'put down' letters to suitors for the hand of his daughter Daisy, one in 1889 and the other in 1891.

It is evident from several entries that Sabine's eldest son, Edward, was expected to take on his father's mantle in due course and was therefore regarded as someone special. On 15 Oct 1889 he wrote as Edward (then aged 18) departed for the United States of America:

> *Dear Edward left us … …*
> *Edward is a very dear boy, everyone loves him, so perfectly gentlemanly in his manner, so upright in mind, and with such a true sense of honour, I doubt not also with deep true love and fear of God in his heart. It is time he should go, as Alex Baring is about to leave the firm of financiers into which Edward goes, and also because he has learned all he can at the school at Tavistock, ...*

In case the reader might begin to see Edward as a paragon Sabine continued

> *.....and is liable to be spoiled by his sisters and others who make a great deal of him. He has no small opinion of himself, and cannot endure contradiction.*

Towards the end the diary became less well organised and more in the nature of a notebook or scrapbook with songs and verses, letters, an obscure page of Greek, various newspaper cuttings all pasted in, sometimes out of context, alongside sporadic every day entries.

On 4 Nov 1899 he wrote: *Laurence Burnard asked me for Barbara,* then aged 19.

10 Nov 1899:

> *My answer.*
> *I have delayed writing to you till my return from the Potteries that I might well think over what you said to me on Saturday. It seems to me from what Barbara tells me, that you would not be in a position to marry for some 18 months. Now B. is really in her ways and mind so much of a child still that I think it very advisable, in so important a matter, that she should not engage herself, till she has had time to decide whether she is in earnest or not. She is such a butterfly that is thoughtless when to alight, that I think for the happiness and security of all, it is … … ....*

This was written at the bottom of a right hand page. The reader will turn the page expecting to see the rest of this draft or copy only to find—nothing. The diary comes to an end. Why the letter was not completed and why the diary ends at this point is not known. Perhaps Barbara persuaded her father not to send such a critical letter, but to meet with Laurence and resolve any doubts that way. Perhaps Sabine decided to discuss the situation with Laurence's father, Robert Burnard, his close friend and associate in archaeological work on Dartmoor. Perhaps Sabine had grown tired of keeping a diary. Perhaps these and many other questions will remain unanswered.

In April 1901 Barbara did marry Lawrence Burnard and, by January 1902, Sabine had completely and favourably changed his opinions of Barbara.[53]

Introduction References

[1] Bristow C. R. *SBGAS Newsletter 50*. Feb 2006 pp 4—10

[2] Baring-Gould, Arthur. An unpublished biography of Sabine Baring-Gould, p9

[3] Baring-Gould S. *Early Reminiscences*, 1923, London, Bodley Head

[4] Baring-Gould S. *Further Reminiscences*, 1925, London, Bodley Head

[5] Baring-Gould S. *Early Reminiscences*, p343

[6] Purcell W E. *Onward Christian Soldier*, 1957, London, Longmans

[7] Dickinson B H C. *Sabine Baring-Gould*, 1970, Newton Abbot, David and Charles

[8] Kirk-Smith H. *Now The Day Is Over*, 1997, Boston Lincs, Kay

[9] Baring-Gould S. Evelyn Healey Letters, M. Almond

[10] Lister K. *Half My Life*, 2002, Charnwood, Wakefield

[11] Lister K. *Half My Life*, p90

[12] Baring-Gould, Arthur. An unpublished biography of Sabine Baring-Gould, p9

[13] Baring-Gould S. *Further Reminiscences*, p109.

[14] Baring-Gould S. Diary. 1880 Jul 22

[15] Baring-Gould S. *Early Reminiscences*

[16] Baring-Gould S. *Further Reminiscences*

[17] Baring-Gould S. *Further Reminiscences* chap. 12

[18] Baring-Gould S. Entries in 1862 Bible. W Country Studies Library. Baring Family File.

[19] Symonds Richard. Additional MS 17062, British Library

[20] Milles, The Rev. Dr. Jeremiah, *Parochial History of Devon* MS Top. Devon. C.9—11

[21] Baring-Gould S. *Further Reminiscences*, Chap. 15.

[22] Baring-Gould S. Diary 1894 Aug 15

[23] Baring-Gould S. Diary 1885 Jan 06

[24] Baring-Gould S. Diary 1893 undated

[25] Baring-Gould S. Diary 1881 Jan 03

[26] Baring-Gould S. Diary 1881 Jan 24

[27] Baring-Gould The Rev. S. Archive Deposit Box 5203, Devon Record Office Box 25 Family letters

[28] Baring-Gould S. Diary 1886 Aug 24

[29] Baring-Gould S. Diary 1893 undated

[30] Bristow C R. *A Bibliography of the Works of S. Baring-Gould*, 2005. Available From the author

[31] Baring-Gould S. Entries in 1862 Bible.

[32] SPG: Society for the Propagation of the Gospel

[33] **Baring-Gould S. Letter to his mother, spring 1857, see Explanatory endnote 17:**

[34] Baring-Gould S. Entries in 1862 Bible. 1911-12

[35] Baring-Gould S. Diary 1881 Mar 04

[36] Premilly J de, *Baring-Gould (Le Révérend Sabine) Tablettes Biographiques des Hommes du Temp*, Société de Gens de Lettres, 1885 Paris

[37] *Visitation of the County of Devon comprising the Heralds Visitations of 1531, 1564 and 1620 with additions* by Lt. Col. Vivian printed 1895, Eland, Exeter.

[38] Baring-Gould S. *John Herring*, 1883, London, Smith Elder and Co,

[39] Baring-Gould S. *Margery of Quether*, 1884, London, Cornhill Magazine

[40] Baring-Gould S. *Court Royal*, 1885-6, London, Cornhill Magazine

[41] Baring-Gould S. *Red Spider*, 1887, London, Temple Bar,

[42] Baring-Gould S. *The Gaverocks*, 1887, London, Cornhill Magazine

[43] Baring-Gould S. *Eve*, 1887-8, London, Longman's Magazine

[44] Baring-Gould S. *Further Reminiscences*, Chap. 12

[45] Baring-Gould S. *Further Reminiscences*, p.24

[46] Dickinson B H C. *Sabine Baring-Gould*, p. 58

[47] Baring-Gould S. Letter to daughter Mary 1895 May 10. Elizabeth Dickinson

[48] Wawman R J. *The House that Sabine Built part III, Cloister, Gallery and Gatehouse*, Newsletter SBGAS 58, October 2008, pp 2-4

[49] Baring-Gould S. *Baring-Gould of Lewtrenchard, Co. Devon.* Undated family pedigree. DRO Box 5203

[50] Baring-Gould S. *Further Reminiscences*, p.216

[51] Briggs C. *The Mana of Lew*, 1993, Praxis p.20

[52] Dickinson Elizabeth, personal communication

[53] **Barbara and Laurence Burnard: Explanatory endnote 70**

The Diary of Sabine Baring-Gould
1880 to 1899

Part 1. Lew Trenchard: June to October 1880

1880. **29 June**

Left East Mersea Rectory for Lew Trenchard. Lew House had been let to Col Cooper since the year 1876; he took it for four years from midsummer in that year, paying for it £200 per ann. He was married, but had no children; Mrs Cooper's mother, Mrs Senior, lived with them, but she died early in 1880, in London. In the evening of June 27th a telegram arrived at Mersea from Lew to say that on Sunday evening Col. Cooper had died suddenly. He was to have left the house the following day. He had not been very well for some time, but his death was most unexpected. It probably proceeded from rupture of a blood vessel on the brain. We had already sent off all our boxes, when the telegram reached us; and my locum tenens was due with his family the day we left. I telegraphed at once to my uncle Charles at Lew Rectory[1] to ask him if he could take in part of our large party, and to Mr. Ward[2], the agent, at Burnville, to ask him to take in a second portion. We left not knowing exactly where we should settle. In London, however, I got a telegram from my uncle to say that he could accommodate the whole party at the Rectory. We spent the night in London, and went on next day.

1880 **30 June**

Arrived at Lew. A lovely day till we reached Lidford[3] station, where my carriage and that from the Rectory awaited us. Then it came on to pour, and we had a drenching before we reached the Rectory. Our party was not complete. We were obliged to leave Daisy[4] behind, with the governess, Miss Biggs, at Mersea. Daisy had been ill with congestion of the lungs and bronchitis followed by congestion of the brain. She was unconscious and wandering an entire week, and we left her having taken a decided turn for the better, but not strong enough to be moved. In the evening, late, I walked down to Lew House, and saw Col. Farewell, who had married a sister of Mrs. Cooper. The body of Col. Cooper had been moved that day to Bath where Mrs. Cooper wished him to be buried. She was to leave the following morning for London.

1880 **1 July**

Mrs. Cooper left. The servants do not depart till tomorrow.

1880 **3 July**

Got into Lew House. Found that the cook of the Coopers had laid her hands on everything she could carry off in the kitchen. We were therefore short of various necessary articles, however we make shift for a few days.

---

[1] Now known as Coombe Trenchard
[2] Mr Frank Ward of Ward and Chowen, then agents to the estate.
[3] Lydford: Frequently spelt Lidford in the 19th century
[4] Margaret: Sabine's second child, known as Daisy, b. 9 August 1870, then aged 10

1880 **Sunday 4 July**

Four years ago I restored the hall of Lew House. The house was originally built about 1626 —8, by Henry Gould *[Later annotation by Sabine:* No earlier as shown by the coins found in it*][1]* who purchased it of Sir Thomas Monk.

Both Potheridge,[2] the family place of the Monks and Lew Trenchard had been mortgaged to the Goulds in 1626, early in the year 1627 (marriage licence dated 23 Dec. 1626) Mary Gould eldest daughter of William Gould of Hayes married Thomas Monk eldest son and Heir of Sir Thomas Monk, and, as her dowery *[sic]* William Gould restored Potheridge unencumbered to the Monks.

Old Sir Thomas died however shortly after, and was buried 7 July 1627 at S. Thomas Church by Exeter, but whether in the jail as a debtor, or at the house of Hayes I do not know. Thomas Monk had five children by his wife Mary of these two were sons Thomas and George. Thomas died in 1631/2 and was buried at S. Thomas Feb. 7. George died in 1659. Of the daughters, Elizabeth (bap. 3 Feb 1628/9 at S. Thomas) married Thomas Pride who was knighted by Cromwell in 1657. His will was proved 20 Nov. 1658, and is a curious document. He entitles himself therein Thomas Lord Pride. Of Mary, bap. 2 May 1630, at S Thomas, I know nothing. Frances third daughter married John Le Neve Esq. and died in her confinement, of smallpox, and was buried in Westminster Abbey 12 May, 1677. Her child, Mary lived only 24 hours. John Le Neve was buried in the Abbey 2 Aug. 1693. Through the failure of issue, and early death of Thomas Monk, Potheridge came to George Monk, Duke of Albemarle; the great general, and king restorer. The Duchess of Albemarle was the daughter of a blacksmith, one Clarges, a woman without education and beauty.[3] The Duke obtained a baronetcy for her brother — I believe I am right in the relationships – Sir Walter Clarges, and he married Lady Elizabeth Wymonsell, widow of Sir Robert Wymonsel *[sic]* Bart. of Putney. She was the daughter of Sir Thomas Gould Kt. and Alderman of London, eldest son of John Gould of Clapham Esq, brother of Mary Gould who married Thomas Monk[4].

But to return to Lew Trenchard. By deed dated 1 Nov. 1626 Sir Thomas Monk and the lady Elizabeth, his wife conveyed to Henry Gould the manor and advowson[5] of Lew Trenchard. ~~I presume that Lew House was begun about then, and built next year.~~ Henry Gould died Aug. 31, 1636 at his house of Floyers Hayes near Exeter and was buried at S. Thomas Sept. 6. His wife, Anne, daughter of Zachary Wills of Bottus *[sic]* Fleming[6] and S. Mary Arches, Exeter, probably came to reside at Lew during her widowhood. Her eldest son Henry, born in 1621 was buried 9 April,

---

[1] Problems of transcription: See *Introduction to the Diary* p xvii, fig 3
[2] Potheridge, near Great Torrington, Devon
[3] Ann Clarges: See explanatory endnote 1.
[4] Thomas Monk: See appendix C. The Monk Family Tree
[5] Advowson: The right of presentation to a church benefice
[6] Botus Fleming: NW of Saltash, Cornwall

1639, at S. Thomas; the second son, Zachary, bap. 22 Sept, 1622 at S. Thomas, died and was buried at Lew between 1636 and 1649, Edward, the third son then entered on the estate. He married Elizabeth, dau. of William Searle of Exeter in January 1654/5. In 1664 he built Lew Mill House as Dower House, a picturesque building, three stories high. In November 1667 his mother Anne fell ill and died – apparently of the plague. Edward proved her will on Nov. 9th. and died —also of the plague, a few days later. He was ill when he proved her will and accordingly wrote his will the same day. His will was proved by his widow on Nov. 27, twenty days later. Edward Gould had three sisters — besides one who died young. These were Elizabeth born in 1620, who died unmarried before 1652, Anne married William Symons of Hatt in Bottus Fleming, and Alice who married Hugh Jones Esq. of Penrose in Sennen.[1] Edward Gould left by his wife, Elizabeth, a son Henry and two daughters. Henry was born in 1657

The year after the death of Edward Gould, his widow married Francis Edgcumbe gent. of Lamerton[2] (mar. lic.[3] 8 Dec. 1668). Henry was matriculated at Oxford from Exeter College 11 May 1676, on his way to the university he seems to have stayed with Mr. Francis Jones, merchant, in London, probably the second son of Hugh Jones of Penrose, his first cousin, and there he met his ward, Elizabeth Legatt, a girl of sixteen. He fell in love with her, and next year when he was 20, and she 17, they were married. The licence is dated 1 Oct. 1677. His sister Sarah died unmarried and was buried at Lew Trenchard 13 Mch. 1728/9. He died between 1703 and 1706. His wife survived him and was alive in 1718. By his wife Elizabeth, Henry Gould had three sons. William, the eldest, Moses, and Henry. I have an old bible in which the three boys have scribbled their names. Henry went to sea and died off Lisbon in H.M. ship "York" in 1707. His will was proved in 1710. Of Moses I know nothing save that he was alive in 1724, when Sir Edward Gould of Highgate left his property in default of issue marem,[4] to him. On the granite door of Waddlestone[5] is cut M.G. and I think it possible that he may have taken this farm under his brother, and built the house. He was alive certainly in 1724. Waddlestone was purchased in   , it had belonged to the Worths, but a Worth was insane and an Act of Parliament was passed for the sale of his property , and then it was purchased.

Henry Gould and Elizabeth, his wife had two daughters, Anne and Susanna. Anne married the Rev. Joseph Jane M.A. Rector of Truro, son of Joseph Jane of Liskeard and nephew of Dr. William Jane, Regius Professor of Divinity at Oxford and Dean of Gloucester. They were married at Lew 6 October 1713, and had a son Rev. Joseph

---

[1] Sennen, near Lands End, Cornwall.

[2] Lamerton, near Tavistock, Devon

[3] Mar. lic: marriage licence.

[4] Default of issue marem: Default of male issue

[5] Waddlestone: Also known as Warson. Farmstead S of Lew Trenchard. The doorway with the initials was incorporated in the tower when this was erected in 1886.

Jane, tutor of Christ Church Oxford and rector of Iron Acton, Gloucestershire, a very eccentric man. The second daughter Susanna married Peter Truscott son of the Revd. John Truscott, Rector of Lew Trenchard. Henry Gould entertained a great dislike for the rector, and the marriage was greatly against his wishes. It took place on 19 March 1729 at Lew. There is a dim tradition that he refused to be present, that after the marriage in the church Susanna returned to Lew House, and died suddenly, of heart complaint, a virgin bride. Certain it is that she was buried four days later 23 Mch 1729. Peter Truscott married again, and was buried at Lew 21 April 1758, having survived his second wife, Alice, who was bur. 3 Nov. 1755. It is very probable that the White Lady who is said to haunt Lew House was this Susanna, in her bridal white.[1] Later tradn. has made it Margaret Gould who died in 1796, sixty seven years later.[2] William Gould, who was born about 1679 married Elizabeth daughter of Philip Drake of Sprats Hayes in Littleham[3] and Mary, his wife, daughter of William Green of Topsham. They were married at Topsham 20 Sep. 1718. She was baptized at Littleham 29 July, 1694. William Gould was buried 24 June, 1735, and Elizabeth his wife Aug. 6, 1727, both at Lew Trenchard. They had but one son, William Drake Gould who was born 23 Nov. 1719 in his grandfather's house at Topsham. In 1736 died Edward Gould Esq. of Pridhamsleigh and Coombe in Staverton,[4] the last of the Staverton branch. He was the son of Edward Gould of Staverton, and his second wife Alice daughter of Humphrey Gayer of Plymouth, and sister of......wife of......Calmady of Leawood[5]. Edward Gould had met her on a visit to Lew in the Christmas of 1663, and he married her early in 1664. Of his sons Edward, John, William, Humphrey and Walter, only Edward had survived and he never married. He left all his estates in Staverton[6] to William Drake Gould, who forthwith moved to Pridhamsleigh which was a handsome house. Probably then it was that Lew House was part pulled down. At the same time Lew Mill Dower House was lowered a storey, and turned into the miller's house. Lew House was converted into the Dower House.

In restoring the Hall I found traces of the walls being turned for a porch, and the porch I purpose rebuilding. Cut granite stones which originally, in all probability belonged to it, I remember forming an entrance to the "shipping"[7] near the stables. My father pulled these down and I have hitherto been unable to discover them. That Lew Mill Dower House was lowered a storey is evident from the division walls of rooms with doors in them now in the roof, cut off by the rafters and slate. The house extended originally also further East, making a longer South front, but

---

[1] Susanna Gould: The story told in full in *Further Reminiscences* p 104; *A Book of Folk Lore* chapter 4.

[2] The haunting of Margaret Gould, Old Madam, *Early Reminiscences* p 163-4

[3] Littleham, Exmouth, Devon

[4] Edward Gould of Staverton, *Early Reminiscences* p ix; *Further Reminiscences* p 77

[5] Leawood: An estate at Bridestowe, Devon

[6] Staverton, near Totnes, Devon, seat of the Devon Goulds

[7] Shipping. Presumably Sabine was referring to a shippon or cowshed.

that portion has been pulled down probably at the time when the Staverton
property fell to William Drake Gould. In 1740 William Drake Gould married
Margaret, daughter of John Belfield of Dartington. She was born 2 Dec. 1711, and
must have been a singularly beautiful woman.[1] By her he had a son Edward, born
27 Dec.1740, baptised at Buckfastleigh 1 Feb. 1741, and a daughter Margaret bap.
25 May 1743 also at Buckfastleigh.

William Drake Gould died 29 Oct, and was buried 7 Nov. 1766 at Lew Trenchard,
whereupon Edward, his son came in for the Staverton Estate, at the age of 26.
Edward was a cavalry officer, a dashing fellow and a gambler. In a few years he ran
through all his property. There is still alive an old woman, a farmer's widow, at
Staverton, aged over 90; last summer when I was at Staverton, she said to the vicar
"Does Mr. Gould know how his family lost their estates here? I believe the story is
all but forgotten, so I will tell you and you can tell him" Her story was this. Edward
Gould had been gambling one night, and had lost a great amount of money, and was
nigh ruined. Desperate, he left the house, mounted his horse, put on a black mask,
and waylaid the man who had won so much money of him. When the fellow came
up he challenged him as a highwayman, with "Your money, Sir, or your life" "Oh,
Edward Gould, Edward Gould!" exclaimed the man —recognising him by his voice
— "I did not expect this of you" "You know me" answered Edward, and shot him
through the heart. For this murder he was tried. He engaged John Dunning of
Ashburton as his counsel, and Dunning managed to get him off but Edward was
obliged to make over what remained of the estate to Dunning in payment of costs.
What corroborates this story is that Coombe certainly did fall into the hands of
Dunning, Lord Ashburton; and it is now the property of Lord Ashburton (—Baring).
It went from Dunning to the Barings.[2] Be this story true or false, one thing is certain,
Edward Gould ran through all the property that had fallen to him, and Lew would
have gone also if he could have got hold of it, but it had been made the dower of his
mother, and he could not touch it. She died at Lew House. The present best bedroom
was her drawing room. The Hall was then one large room with open granite
fireplace.[3] The present drawing room was the dining room. It was in this room that
she died. To return to Edward Gould. Several stories are told of him. He was a
famous rider, Astley was in his troop, and he taught him to ride.[4] He was wont to
fling a crown on the ground, spur his horse to full gallop, and then swing himself
down, as he passed the spot, pick up the crown and recover his seat, without
dismounting. He was in a battle, —Minden, I believe —, he had a favourite dog. He
passed his glove under the collar of the dog, and swore to follow where the dog led.

---

[1] Margaret Gould, née Belfield, *Early Reminiscences*, p. 101-2
[2] Edward Gould and John Dunning: This account is to be found in *Further
Reminiscences* p 77-8; *Old Country Life* (with the name St. Pierre substituted for
Gould) p 78-81; *A Book of Devon*, p 254.
[3] The Hall: Sabine's father, Edward, had partitioned the hall in 1850 to make a
billiard room. Sabine recreated the Hall as one large room in 1876. 1874 plan of
Lew House drawn by Sabine. Deposit Box 5203 Devon R O.
[4] **Philip Astley: See Explanatory endnote 2.**

The dog dashed in among the enemy. Edward followed, cut his way through, captured a standard, found his dog killed with a sabre cut, took his glove, and cut his way back. He died in Bristol, in 1780, I do not know the date of his burial, nor where it took place. He was never married.

When Staverton property was lost, the story is told that madam Gould, his mother, sat silent in her high backed chair musing what to do. Should she, as she felt inclined, go to Bath, and spend the evening of her days in card playing, or should she strive to recover the ruined fortunes of the family. She sat all night irresolute, but when the grey morning shone in on her through the window in the hall, she had made up he mind. She would trust God, and do her best to recover the shattered fortunes of the family. She stuck to her purpose, and lived at Lew the rest of her days.[1] She farmed a good deal of land herself, and superintended all that had to be done. Sir John Coleridge used to tell of his having come to Lew to see her. He stopped to ask at a rick of corn of some harvester his way to Lew House, and to Madam Gould. "I am Madam Gould" said a voice from the top of the rick, and looking up he saw the old lady there. She had a famous black bull which the Duke of Bedford was very desirous to possess. He sent her several handsome offers for it, but she refused to sell the bull. At last he sent — "Tell Madam, that if she will let me have the bull, I will strike spurs into my horse, and gallop down Lew Hill, without saddle or bridle." She at once sent him the bull as a present. This was the old steep road from the school room to the cross[2] by the church.[3]

Lady Northcote and Lady Young[4] came to Lew to stay with their grandmother. They wore kid shoes. "What do you mean by coming here with gloves on your feet?" she asked. She had a glass of cold water brought her every night to the foot of the stairs, and drank it before going to her room to bed. One day she was riding on the Bridestowe road, when overtaken by the carriage of the Harris' of Hayne. Both stopped, and she asked where Mr. and Mrs. Harris were going. "To Exeter." "I will ride with you." She did so. On the way Mr. Harris asked what she was carrying in her saddle bags. "Money" she replied, "I have all my rents here. "Good God, Madam! Are you not afraid of highwaymen?" "They have rather reason to fear me" she answered, pulling forth a loaded pistol. [5] She was often heard to say extending her lap that her son Edward had cost her as much gold as she could carry in her lap. In 1790 she purchased Orchard[6] and added it to her estate. Her daughter Margaret married Charles Baring of Courtland near Exmouth, on 6 Sept. 1767 at S. Leonard's church near Exeter, in which parish Larkbeare is situated where the

---

[1] Old Madam's resolve: *Early Reminiscences* p 102; *Old Country Life* p 51-2

[2] Cross: crossroads. Lew Hill is now a public footpath known locally as 'ragged lane'

[3] The Duke of Bedford and Old Madam's bull: *Early Reminiscences* p 154

[4] Lady Jacquetta Northcote and Lady Emily Young, daughters of Charles and Margaret Baring. Kid shoes: *Early Reminiscences* p 154

[5] Old Madam and her loaded pistol: *Early Reminiscences*, p 153

[6] **Orchard, old manor house, Thrushelton, Devon. See Explanatory endnote 3**

Barings then lived. There must have been some suspicion of the ~~legality~~ validity of the marriage, probably doubt as to the orders of the parson who celebrated it, for the marriage was repeated in the same church 5 May 1768, before the birth of the first child. Madam was present on both occasions, but the other witnesses were different.

Charles Baring had peculiar religious views, and he built a chapel at Gallaford in Lympstone parish in which he put a Levite [1] to preach his doctrines, which were Unitarian in some points, peculiarly his own in others. He obliged his wife to attend this chapel. She was a gentle, meek, sweet person, unable to oppose his domineering spirit. He was a disagreeable man by all accounts. Madam Gould was invited to stay with them at Courtland. On Sunday the carriage conveyed the party to Gallaford chapel. Madam sat through the service with a grim countenance, and neither stirred nor responded. She did not speak in the carriage on the way back; but when she reached the house she sharply rang the bell, and ordered her carriage at once. Mr. Baring and her daughter expressed their surprise and distress at the abrupt leaving, and asked how they had offended her. She vouchsafed no answer. She refused even to dine with them, and when the carriage came round, as she entered it, she turned to Charles Baring, and said "Lew shall never be yours, and never, if I can help it, shall you set foot within the door of Lew House. For William it shall always be a home, to William [2] it shall go on my death, —to you —not an acre. Good bye. You shall never see my face again." And she kept her word. [3]

When she was dying she sent a servant with pillion [4] to Exmouth to fetch her daughter — "I don't want to see Mr. Baring." So Margaret came on a pillion to say farewell to her mother, but Charles Baring did not venture to come. Madam died 10 April 1796 and left Lew Trenchard to her grandson William Baring, subject to the condition that he should assume the name of Gould. She was a strict and devout Churchwoman. In her time she and her clerk were almost the only persons who could read, and in giving out the psalm, the clerk was wont to say "Let Madam and me sing to the praise and glory of God." [5]

1880 **Monday 5 July:**
Went to Plymouth. My cousin, Sir George Young [6] is contesting the borough. He has tried several times, but failed at each election. He had tried before at Chipenham *[sic]* and failed, beaten by Goldney. At Plymouth he was beaten last election by Bates. Unfortunately the second Liberal candidate, Macliver [7] got in by

---

[1] **Levite: See Explanatory endnote 4**
[2] William Baring-Gould, Sabine's grandfather known as 'The Devonshire Adonis'
[3] Old madam's resolve: *Early Reminiscences* p 101-2; *Church Revival* p 73
[4] Pillion: cushion behind a horseman for a second rider
[5] Old madam in church: *Early Reminiscences* p 155
[6] Sir George Young Bt: descended from his paternal great grandmother, Lady Young, née Emily Baring, sister of Sabine's grandfather, William Baring-Gould
[7] Peter Stewart Macliver, Liberal MP, elected first of two members April and July 1880

4 votes ahead of Sir George, to everyone's surprise and Young's infinite disappointment. He and the Liberal committee had been so certain of Sir George getting in that they had given Macliver the votes of the cabmen employed by them. Macliver, moreover, being a man of wealth, had bribed extensively but knowingly.

A petition against Sir Edmund *[sic]* Bates[1] was got up and the Judge, ------*[?]*[2], came to Plymouth to try the case. The judgement was against Bates, who was unseated, and Clarke stood as his nominee. The bribery by Bates has been very extensive, and Plymouth constituency has been thoroughly demoralised by gifts of blankets, and coals, and money. Sir George wished me to be at Plymouth and on the platform with him when he gave his address to the electors, and I was glad to go and show my sympathy. I dined with Sir George and Lady Young and her sister Constance Kennedy: Mr. Hicks, the chairman of the Liberal Committee, a jovial, vulgar, kindly wine merchant of Plymouth, was there, and also Mr. Collier. Not much hope, for the judgement has roused all the lovers of bribes to vote for Bates. Sir George, moreover, is of a cold disposition, he is an intellectual man living much in the world of ideas, with great self-respect and dignity, and the pettiness and meanness of canvassing are so repulsive to him that he shrinks from it, and canvasses with a reluctance which is manifest.

This is put down to pride, it is not common pride, but sense of dignity; hints for bribes he cannot endure; he is too conscientious to bribe, whereas Macliver, on a hint walks up to the chimneypiece, says "That's a pretty bit of china, I will give you a guinea for it," and buys a bit of rubbish which he pitches away outside the door. Or observing a bit of crystals of quartz says "I suspect this stone is auriferous" and slips a sovereign under it when the intelligent voter observes "Well I suppose it does mean brass." Lady Young declares that in a tumult, an excited Conservative mother, unable to restrain her feelings, and unable to find any other missile at hand appropriate to fling, caught up a small boy and flung him at Sir George's head. The child was caught by one of Sir George's supporters and was not hurt, nor did he hit Sir George. The story is true, I believe. It comes from the man who caught the boy in his flight. Lady Young is a charming person, pretty, bright, full of Irish elasticity of spirits. She cheers Sir George up, he is disposed to droop. He has been much tried by disappointments. I slept at Nelson Villa, — Mrs. Glennie's —a cousin —distant —of my dear mother. Harriet, her eldest daughter I have always regarded as a cousin, but I believe the relationship is distant.

1880 **Wednesday 7 July:**
Returned to Lew Trenchard from Plymouth, and brought Harriet Glennie with me. A lovely day.

---

[1] Sir Edward Bates Bt: MP for Plymouth 1871 to 1880 and 1885 to 1892
[2] It has proved impossible to transcribe and identify the name of this judge

1880 **8 July:**

The Plymouth election. Drove to the station & waited to hear the result by telegram. Sir George defeated by 144. Telegraphed my sympathy with his disappointment, and begged him to come here as soon as he could get away.

1880 **9 July:**

Sir George and Lady Young came. He looks much depressed. The election has cost him three thousand pounds —money he had made by work for Government —sitting on commissaries etc and which he had put aside for the purpose. He has been offered one or two things but refuses permanent work as he hopes to make another push to get in when a vacancy offers.

1880 **Sunday 11 July:**

Barbara[1] baptised in the afternoon by Uncle Charles. Sir George Young Godfather, Lady Young and Harriet Glennie Godmothers. Barbara christened in christening robes of Mrs Petty[2]—some 150 years old and looked like a child come out of an old Vandyke portrait.

1880 **12 July:**

Began to pull down the wing where I erect the new staircase. This wing has long been in a ruinous condition. My father would not allow a fire to be lighted in the chimney. The wall leaned out and the roof was hardly kept together. The room above served as a servant's bedroom. In former times it had been Uncle Charles room when a boy. The room under was used as china and glass closets, and the fireplace blocked up. A curious discovery was made directly. This wing, and probably the whole house, had once been a storey higher. There were in the gable two granite one light windows with their heads knocked off to allow of the roof when lowered cutting them across. No attic room could possibly exist as constructed now. The room above was no doubt only an attic room, but the walls must have been higher, and the gable steeper. At the same time we found a circular staircase in the wall leading originally from the room below to this attic. When the house was lowered the rubbish was thrown in completely choking the staircase up to the top. In this rubbish we found a coin of Charles II, worn, and so probably dropped by the masons in or shortly after 1736, when Lew was partly demolished. Presently we made further discoveries. In the servant's bedroom there had formerly been a two light granite window, looking north. The wall below it had been taken out, and the window let down to the level of the floor, the mullion knocked away, and then a chimney had been built outside, so as to convert the window into a fireplace; or the floor had been raised to the level of the window, I could not make out which, but I think the latter was the case, and what confirms me in this believe *[sic]* is, that the door into the stair case was cut across by the floor. The north gable had originally the appearance and plan

---

[1] Barbara: Sabine's 8th child. b. 12 March 1880
[2] Mrs Petty: Diana Amelia, b. 1746, d. of Col. John Sabine, m. 1766 John Petty esq.

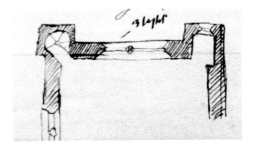

Fig. 4 North gable, Lew House

On the left the staircase, on the right a cupboard or closet with a small granite window in it. Between them a two light window. Now, when the window was converted into a fireplace, a chimney was built out to a level with the projecting staircase and cupboard, and, as the gable would have looked odd with three projections in it, the masons filled across and made one flat wall. Consequently the wall there was 8 ft. thick, in part consisting of two 4 ft. walls. But this was not the only change that had been made. At some time the staircase perhaps descended to the lower storey. There it also had been converted into a privy, blocked up above, and a drain cut away, below. Then this also had been abandoned & walled up. We found in the lower side of the fireplace an ounce weight stamped

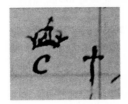

Fig. 5 Charles I ounce weight stamp, Staircase wing fireplace, Lew House probably of Charles I.

Inscription:
? three light

Inscription:
three light
window below I
think

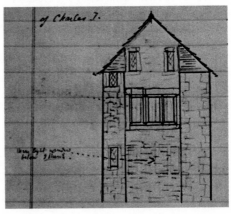

Fig. 6 Staircase wing, Lew House. North elevation

The staircase was not lighted by windows to the North like the cupboard, but by windows to the West. In the sketch the arrangement of roof to these two projections is conjectural. I suppose them to have been lean-too. *[sic]*

I am not certain that the newel staircase did descend to the lower storey. It had been so altered below that it was impossible to make out, but perhaps there had been originally a privy there. As there was no fireplace originally in this gable, my impression is that the whole wing was originally a great staircase, with a landing from which issued the newel staircase leading to servant's bedrooms in the attic. Consequently, as I am reconverting this wing into staircase I am restoring it to its original destination; moreover I am building the W. closet where the old privy stood. The walls throughout are in so bad a condition, having been laid simply on the earth without foundation, that I must take these down and rebuild.

1880 **14 July:**
Sir George and Lady Young left. I drove them to Lidford *[sic]* in a deluge of rain. Lady Young obliged to go into the waiting room of the station and change her clothes. The rain came down in a sheet, "solid water" as a boatman at Mersea described a day of continuous downpour.

1880 **16 July:**
The Keelings arrived. Mr. Keeling is a retired lawyer at Colchester. His mother was a Miss Hillerdon, a Devon family, connected with the Bulteels of Fleet. *[sic]*[1] His first wife was a cousin, related to the Bulteels, and his second wife a Miss Neeshaw, whose mother was a Bulteel. He is very full of his Devonshire relationships and likes to consider himself a Devon man; His father's family have been respectable Colchester solicitors for some generations. He is a man of some means and lives very comfortably. Mrs. Keeling is a very bright, pleasant person, pretty with her silvery grey hair and delicate complexion. Her face full of vivacity and her eyes sparkling —dancing with mirth.

1880 **17 July:** Drove the Keelings over to Sydenham to see the old house.[2] Daisy arrived today from Mersea, looking very delicate, and still with a little cough, very excited with delight at seeing Mary[3] again. Mary has been ill ever since her arrival, and has spent several days in bed.

1880 **Sunday 18 July:**
The picture of General Monk, Duke of Albermarle, was bought by me in London, and did not originally belong to the house. I have had it examined, and the face is said to have been repainted. It is possible that the picture may not originally have

---

[1] Bulteel: A Huguenot family of Flete House, Holbeton, near Ivybridge, Devon
[2] Sydenham: An Elizabethan house, south of Lewdown. Much admired by Sabine who copied some of its features in Lew House. eg the arcades in the drawing room panelling.
[3] Mary: Sabine's eldest child, then aged 11.

been intended for Monk. I am much annoyed. I do not however like to have the new paint removed, for the painting, as it stands, is a likeness of Monk.[1]

1880 **19 July:**
As Mr Keeling and I were sitting talking in the hall about 11 o'clock last night, everyone else gone to bed, he on one side of the fireplace and I on the other, we both suddenly heard a sound as of someone in a stiff satin dress slowly walking through the Hall. We both ceased speaking, and heard the drag of the satin on the floor with its peculiar stiff rustle. Keeling said "Good God, what is that?" I started up and answered "I cannot tell unless it be a sweep of rain against the window" and I ran out of the front door but it was not raining. The moon shone through a silvery haze and the flags under the hall window were perfectly dry. I confess when Keeling said he would go to bed I did not remain many minutes behind in the Hall.[2]

A very remarkable circumstance happened four years ago when Beatrice died. She was suffering from whooping cough and cutting back teeth at the same time. The irritation produced diarhoea *[sic]* and dissentry, *[sic]* but neither Grace nor I thought her life was in danger. So little did we suspect it, that we went to Launceston to call on Miss Pierce the day before she died, and did not see the doctor when he came. However, as we had not an intelligent nurse, Grace was sleeping in the nursery — the room on the right at the head of the stairs, with Beatrice. I was in the best bedroom, Madam's old drawing room. About 12 o'clock or 1 o'clock, I was woke by Grace coming to my bedside in a very nervous state. She said "I cannot sleep in the room alone. There are such strange noises. I have heard feet passing the door as though carrying something heavy down the front staircase." I tried to soothe her, and said it was imagination, but she persisted. Beatrice had her eyes wide open, as though looking at something, she said. While she spoke there came a heavy blow struck at the party wall, between the bedroom and the dressing room, quickly followed by a second. I started up in bed, and then there came a third. The blows were quite distinct and loud, and shook the room. It was as though they had been struck by a fist. Next morning Beatrice died. She had been dressed and taken down to the library, and in the forenoon was on her mother's lap, whilst I was writing in the drawing room, when I heard a cry from Grace, and the nurse ran in to call me. The little girl had died in her mother's arms, on her heart, the little light had gone out like an expiring flame. She was a dear little girl, very gentle and sweet with a thorough Sabine face, blue eyes and a Sabine mouth.[3]

The Monument to her in the church was carved by Knittel of Freiburg 1/3 modelled from Veronica.[4] It is very like Vera and the likeness is not close to

---

[1] **General George Monk: See explanatory endnote 5**
[2] Ghost story: *Early Reminiscences*, p 160. Here the date is incorrectly given as 1877
[3] Beatrice: Sabine's 4th child b. 7 January 1874, d. 25 March 1876. Death: *Early Reminiscences* p 159. *Further Reminiscences* p 145
[4] Veronica: Sabine's 5th child, b. 14 August 1875, familiar name Vera

Beatrice. Beatrice had a mug with 'Think on Me' given by Susan Pengelly, the coachman's wife. She always drank out of this, so I have had it represented on the monument as upset with the last drop distilling from it. It is curious that the next tramp of feet down the stairs carrying a weight was that of the bearers with her coffin. She was laid in the cedar room.[1]

1880 **20 July:**

After the death of Margaret Gould[2] my grandfather did not reside at Lew. He travelled a great deal, was in Spain, Italy, France, Dalmatia, Germany, Austria, and Russia. Besides Lew House he had Ivy House at Teignmouth, and there his wife lived. It was only long after, when he had lost a great deal of money through bad speculations, that Ivy House was sold, and then the family moved to Lew. My grandmother never liked Lew. She was fond of society, and had been the head of society at Teignmouth; she detested the dullness of the country, and was not happy at Lew. The losses of my grandfather, and banishment to Lew embittered her, and she became querulous. My grandfather was a very handsome man.*[3]*

He was called the Adonis of Exeter when he lived at Larkbeare.[4] Besides his bright blue eyes and fair complexion, he had the most charming of manners, perfect polish of manner, and the kindest of hearts. General Edward Sabine has said to me, in his old age — he is 91 —"If I was God and made a world, I would make all the men like William Gould, and then it would be quite a perfect world." I asked him — "What about the Eves? — Should they be like your sister Emily?" In his quick way the dear old man answered: - "She had too sharp a tongue. There would be no paradise then."[5]

One sad loss was Pridhamslee *[sic]* House. This alone remained of the Staverton property. It was an encumbrance as the house needed much repair, but there was a farm attached to it. This house, as far as I can ascertain, was built by Edward Gould of Coomb, about 1650-60, and formed a quadrangle. It was entailed and so Captain Edward Gould the gambler could not sell it. My grandfather, however, with my father's consent, sold Pridhamsleigh. It went to Lord Cranstone *[Cranstown]* and is now held for life by two ladies said to be his illegitimate daughters. It will be sold some day and I will strain every nerve to buy it back again. It is a beautiful old mansion, but has had two sides of the quadrangle pulled down. The grand staircase which was of oak has been burnt, as the farmer's wife told me, who now lives there. It served them as firing for a many a day.[6]

---

[1] The location of the Cedar room is not known.
[2] Margaret Gould: Old Madam
[3] William Baring-Gould: *Early Reminiscences,* pp 97-8
[4] Larkbeare: Residence of the Baring family in Exeter, now mostly demolished
[5] General Sir Edward Sabine, brother of Sabine's paternal grandmother, Diana Amelia. Polar explorer, geophysicist and President of the Royal Society. For his opinion on his sister see *Early Reminiscences*, p 97.
[6] Pridhamsleigh: *Further Reminiscences*, p 79. See also entry for 19 Sept 1880

In the summer of 1877, I removed all the monuments of the Goulds from Staverton Church to Lew Trenchard. In a former restoration of the church some, which were of marble and which had stood against the walls, were thrown down and used for pavement.[1] This had so injured them that two — one of Henry Gould and one of Joan Gould have had to be entirely recut. The former was broken, the latter was in several pieces. Another of Joan Gould, — a later Joan — was not hurt seriously and I had the letters deepened, nothing more done to it. The vault had already been filled with concrete as the pillars were leaning. The stone of Edward Gould 1607 and Elizabeth Thuell has lost a portion of it. I have the original brass of Margaret Gould "a Pearle in Gold right netely [sic] set" here.[2] A copy is left at Staverton

1880 **22 July:**
The Keelings left. I took them to the Ravine at Lidford, but Mr. Keeling was quite unable to go along it. He turned giddy and I had much difficulty in getting him back. When I was a boy the Ravine could not be explored. A few years ago a Mr. Radford, a London Coalmerchant, a relation/cousin of Radford the Linendraper at Plymouth, bought a bit of land above it, along with the ravine itself, built a house there, 1875, and established himself there. He cut walks about the ravine and made it accessible. After some hesitation the Hamlyns called and invited Mr and Mrs Radford to **[lunch. They came but he was so coarse and vulgar that they have dropped them again. He was himself so offensive with his bad manners that no one else in the neighbourhood ventured to call after the experience of the Hamlyns]**[3] We shall want to go to the ravine, and take friends to see it so have called, Mr Radford was **[fortunately]**[4] out fishing. Mrs Radford, his second wife, is a very sweet looking and pleasant person. She is said to be gradually licking her bear into shape.[5]

Much of the land about the Ravine and waterfall belongs to Mr. Newton of Millaton[6] in Bridestowe, but he was declared a bankrupt last winter and the land is advertised for sale. Mr. Newton's father was a portjobber during the European war, with Napoleon, and he took contract for pork for the navy. As soon as he got a little money he invested it in land often mortgaging the land for two thirds, and finding one third. The land he bought was nearly all poor clay land or coppice and rock. He was a drunken, vulgar old dog, so drunken and disreputable that when he died, the rector of Bridestowe refused to read the burial service over him. The Newtons appealed to the Bishop who ordered the

---

[1] Staverton Monuments: *Further Reminiscences*, p 84
[2] The brass is prominently displayed in St Peter's church. Sabine's transcription of the last phrase is inaccurate: It should read: *Death Dartes at all spares not a Margaret although a Pearle in Gould most neetly set.*
[3] Here 5 lines of text had been scored out. Under normal light only a few words can be made out. With ultraviolet light it is evident that Sabine had made a very derogatory comment about Daniel Radford. The scored out words are shown in square brackets and bold type
[4] Here the word 'fortunately' is scored out but was revealed by ultraviolet light.
[5] **Daniel Radford: See Explanatory endnote 6.**
[6] Millaton House, Bridestowe, Devon.

rector, Mr. Hinds Howell, to perform the service; and he was obliged to do so. The old fellow foolishly did not give his son a decent education, and young Newton became a country squire without the manners and mind for association with the class to which he belonged by position. Feeling himself unfit to associate with gentlemen, he took refuge in the kitchen with his maids, and with gardeners, and workmen. The Hamlyns have done their best to draw him out and introduce him into a better world, but he is shy, uncouth, and frightened, and returned to his maids and men as more congenial company. He talks broad Devonshire; is very good natured, and harmless. He has never married. The property was so heavily encumbered with mortgages, and with an unreasonable legacy he had to pay his sister, that all heart has been taken out of him. He saw no chance of clearing the estate, and could not make up his mind to sell. Now that we have had bad seasons, and rents not paid, the mortgagees have foreclosed, pronounced Mr. Newton a bankrupt, and are going to sell the property. The only advantage will be that his sister —a coarse, vulgar woman, who ignores her H —will not succeed him at Millaton.

Another squire who has failed and gone in this neighbourhood, has been Captain Luxmore of Witherdon, in Germansweek. His story is very sad. He married young and inconsiderately, a person with whom he soon found it was impossible to live. She left him, or disappeared, when he was on one of his voyages and he could find no trace of her. After some time supposing her to be dead he married one of the handsome daughters of Mr. Carpenter, rector of Germansweek. After having had several children, to his discomfiture one day, the original wife turned up. His second wife was therefore not his lawful wife, nor his children legitimate. He paid the woman a round sum to pack her off to America, and disposed of Witheridge *[sic. Presumably this should read Witherdon]* which he had built, and has gone with his 2nd wife and children —I know not where, in hopes of getting away from the chance of pursuit by his first wife.

1880 24 July:
Pulling down done and rebuilding begun. Edward Sabine[1] laid the foundation stone of the staircase wing. Only a halfpenny put under it. This wing will look somewhat out of proportion till the rest is built.

Daisy ill again, and in bed with her cough. Mary better.

1880 Sunday 25 July:
S. James Day. I have done a good deal of planting here each year. 600 Bird cherries and 600 Maples in Lew Wood. The ramps again and again in spite of disappointment. Now the young larch and Scotch have taken, most of the rhododendrons have died, and most of the Scotch planted on the top. Planted orchard by the Black Valley[2], and Raddon Wood. The latter failed eaten by rabbits.

---

[1] Edward Sabine: Sabine's third child and eldest son, then aged 9
[2] The location of Black Valley is not known

1880 **26 July:**
Went to Staverton and stayed in the Vicarage. Made large extracts from the
register. The reredos to the church I gave, it was carved in Freiburg copied from
one in the Cathedral, but without the group of figures in the niche. It wants that.

1880 **27 July:**
Walked to Dartington. Lunched with Mr. Champernowne. Made extracts from the
register. In the afternoon to Broadhempston. I copied the following queer monument. No
date on it; so probably put up by Mr. Eales in his lifetime.

"To the Memory of Edward Eles of Beeston. Gent. who dyed….day, in the year…
Here lies a Body clothed with a stone// Whose clay steed Parts could scarce be
found in one//His soule (the Diamond of ye Body) now// Triumphs in Bliss Where
thronging pleasuers grow// To Boust her: wherefore conclude it strange// If wife or
child should grieve for such a change// Natuers Bond is cancelled, his fate
contented// Before he dyed (with Leave) Ye Heavens lamented."

A slab in the chancel has a coat on a chevron bet. 3 lions passant, 3 fleur de lis,
impaled with —an oak tree proper. Tinctures not indicated.
"To the Memory of Robert Warrying Gent and Ellinor his wife.

Fig. 7 *Warrying memorial, 'hands clasped'*

"Under this stone two corps of them abide// What lived and lov'd together and so
dyed// Wedlock and Death hath with Ye Grave agreed// To make for them an
everlasting marriage bed// Where in repose mixed dust doth lye// Their souls gone
up both hand in hand on high."

Another coat with label of 3 points for eldest son on the Warrying arms. Impaled with it
between and fess wavy, 6 cross crosslets AD 1656. To the memory of Mary Warrying,
wife of Avis Warrying dau. of Robert Warrying the younger, Gent. "Mother and daughter
each within this tomb// Enwrapped do lye in one earth's common womb// Expect the day
when twins in one new birth. // A resurrection shall bring them forth." AD 1654

1880 **28 July:**
Was all day in Totnes examining the Register[1]

---

[1] *A Book of Devon*, p 319: "The registers of Totnes are very early and of great
interest, as containing much information concerning the old merchant families and
the landed gentry…"

1880 **29 July:**
At Ashburton doing the same

1880 **30 July:**
Returned to Lew. Charlie and Fritz Hall[1] at Lew. Boys are nuisance.

1880 **Sunday 1 Aug:**
Preached on St. Peter's chains, it being Lammas Day[2]

1880 **7 August:**
Revd. W. Lukis, Rector of Wath[3] arrived. He had been engaged this summer and last in planning the prehistoric remains on Dartmoor. They are being so ruthlessly destroyed that it is very necessary that this should be done, and the Royal Soc. of Antiquaries has made a grant to him to carry out this important work.

1880 **Sunday 8 August:**
Walked with Lukis in the evening to Eastcot Beacon,[4] showed him cairn or tumulus on Galford Down, and returned by Lew Mill. There I showed him a long, and curious stone — granite — that has been recently taken out of the mill leat, where it has formed one wall of the leat for — I suppose — 100 years. The stone is.... high, for eighteen inches it is rough, above that it shows tokens of rude drawing at the base and the angles are smoothed off. The width of the stone at base is....., the narrow face is .... It somewhat tapers towards the top where the measures are .... and ..... The base shows distinctly the depth to which it was originally planted.[5] But the most remarkable feature of the stone is a cup like depression 4 inches deep and .... in. in diameter; at the apex, but not exactly in the centre. That the stone originally stood upright; and so stood for long ages is shown by the fact of the water from this cup having dribbled over one side of the stone and furrowed a line down it of more than a foot. Perhaps the stone was not originally exactly upright, and this determined the side of the overflow; but that the overflow of so small a hole should have cut itself a groove down the granite column shows that it must have stood upright for an enormous length of time. The stone was probably thrown down when the mill was made. This was probably before 1664 when the Dower House was built. The mill is spoken of in a marriage settlement of 1654. Had the stone been available ten years later, it would no doubt have been used up for the granite lintels or sills of the windows of the Dower House. But in all probability it had been thrown down and used for the wall of the

---

[1] The identities of Charlie and Fritz Hall are not known.
[2] The Lammas Feast is of pagan origin and celebrates the first day of the harvest. The Christian feast of St Peter's Chains, also on 1 August, celebrates St Peter's deliverance from Herod's bondage.
[3] The Rev W Lukis of Wath, Yorkshire: A renowned Victorian antiquarian.
[4] Eastcot Beacon, Coryton, south of Lewtrenchard
[5] Missing dimensions: Presumably Sabine intended to insert measurements but never did.

leat long before that, and from being constantly under water was not seen and thought of. It was taken up because the water oozed out below it, and a proper wall had to be built. It was then flung on one side. Mr. Lukis unhesitatingly pronounced it a prehistoric monument and advised its re-erection on the spot where found, and where probably it stood until flung down on the construction of the leat.[1]

It is curious that he has noticed and measured very similar cup like holes bored in stones on Dartmoor, but these have not been at the apex, but on the sides of long or round stones. The discovery of this hole gives him reason to suspect that there may have been originally similar holes on the menhirs of Brittany. These he has not paid attention to. Many of them have crucifixes let into their summit, and he has taken it for granted that the holes into which the bases of these crucifixes were let were bored for the purpose. But is it not more probable that the holes being there already had been utilised for the insertion of the crosses? It would be a difficult job to bore a suitable hole in the top of such a stone as the Pierre de Champs Dolent at Dol[2] when upright for the insertion of the crucifix. But if the hole were already there, the fixing of the cross in it would be an easy matter.

It is remarkable that one of the superstitions condemned by the Council of Nantes in ...... ,[3] was the veneration for stones on the top of which oil had been poured. Can these have been the consecrate stones, and the cup like hollow have contained the oil?

1880 9 August:
Began to rebuild the porch. Went with Lukis to Belstone Tor and showed him the Nine Maidens circle. It is in reality the base of a cairn, but it has one peculiarity about it. The stones alternately at right angles to each other, the only example I know. There are more than nine stones, some fifteen in all. According to tradition they dance at noon. Mary and Sabine[4] very eager to see them dance, but were disappointed. Arthur my half brother was with us.[5] The East Okement glen is most picturesque.

1880 10 August:
Went with Lukis to Prince's Town.[6] Lovely weather.

---

[1] The Lewtrenchard menhir: In *A Book of Folklore*, chapter 4, Sabine claimed that the menhir was thrown down by his grandfather, William Baring-Gould, to stop superstitious farmers getting their cattle to rub against it to increase the yield of milk.
[2] Menhir du Champs Dolent, Mont Dol, Brittany
[3] **Council of Nantes AD658: See Explanatory endnote 7**
[4] Sabine: Sabine was referring to his eldest son, Edward Sabine.
[5] Arthur Baring-Gould, then aged 14 years; son of Edward Baring-Gould and his second wife, Lavinia.
[6] Princes Town: usually known as Princetown, Dartmoor

1880 **11 August:**
Planned the line of stones on Down Tor. This is some 1175 ft. long and begins
from a circle and cairn. The first two stones, the largest 12 ft. high have been
recently thrown down, the marks of the quarrymen's bars are there showing that it
is the work of this spring. A sketch by Spence Bate taken last year shows them
standing. This year also the quoit of the cromlech at Merrivale Bridge has been
broken in three by the quarrymen.[1]

1880 **12 August:**
Returned to Lew to superintend the building.

1880 **14 August:**
Lukis returned, and Canon Thynne of Kilkhampton[2] arrived. The latter had some
good stories of old Jack Radford of Lapford and Froude of Knowstone.[3]

The story told in "The Maid of Sker"[4] of Froude having the road dug up and filled
with peat water, and laid lightly over with road dust to intercept the Bishop[5] on his
way to Knowstone is true, the bishop's carriage was upset in it. But what is also
true is that the Bishop persevered and did get to Knowstone. Froude received him
in his hall or dining room and shoved a bottle of brandy across the table to him.
"No thank you, Mr. Froude." "Ah, my Lord. You may do without it, mebbe, to
Exeter, but in these parts we must drink a lot or perish of dullness." After a while
the Bishop said "Mr. Froude, I have heard some very queer and unsatisfactory
stories of you." "I dare say you have my Lord. Now look 'ee here. When I've been
to Torrington or Bideford, I've, times out of mind, heard vokes talk a lot of very
queer, fishy tales about yu. Now my Lord, bless 'ee, I know very well what is
proper between gentle vokes, I don't believe a bit of them, I say. They's all a pack
of damn lies. And when you next hear any of these queer tales about me, my Lord,
just you stan' up for me, and say, Damn your eyes. I know old Froude out at
Knowstone, and I'll swear they's all a parcel of lies."

One day Froude came down stairs smartly dressed. "Where be yu going today?"
asked his housekeeper. "That's no concern of yours but I'll tell 'ee. I'm going to be
married." Thou'rt not going to be such a vule as that." Exclaimed Sally. "Ah, but I
am though." replied Froude and departed. At about 1 o'clock Froude returned
alone, and sat down composedly, and ordered some dinner. "But where is the
wife?" asked Sally. Have 'ee been married then?" "Married I have been, though."

---

[1] At Down Tor with the Rev W Lukis, Dartmoor: *A Book of Dartmoor*, p. 230
[2] Kilkhampton, North Cornwall. Canon Thynne, who also provided Sabine with
material of his biography of Parson Hawker, impresses as a prodigious if
unreliable gossip.
[3] **John Froude and Jack Radford: Two notorious Devon clerics. With Jack
Russell, see explanatory endnote 8.**
[4] The *Maid of Sker* by R D Blackmore
[5] Bishop Phillpotts of Exeter

"Then where is Mrs. Froude" "I tell 'ee, Sally, Mrs. Froude is at the public house some three miles from here. Her zed to me 'I beg leave to differ vrom thee on that point' Some point you know I was talking of. So I lukes her in the vace and sez, 'Mrs Froude, I never allow anyone outside my house to differ from me and not everlastingly repeat it after. Zometimes their stacks get fired, sometimes their cows are lamed. Sometimes they themselves get a shot. And I win't allow anyone inside my house to differ from me. So you remain here and turn it over in your mind. If you intend to have no will and no opinion different from mine, you can come on at your leisure to Knowstone. If not yu can turn back and go home to where yu came vrom. Nobody wants yu at Knowstone and yu are heartily welcome to keep away.' So serve the dinner Sally and if her is agreeable her'll come, if her isn't her can go home and be damned.

The following is on the authority of Jack Russell, vicar of Swimbridge[1] who told it himself. He called at Knowstone parsonage one day, and found Froude sitting over his fire smoking, and Mrs. Froude sitting in a corner, against the wall at the further end of the room. Froude had his back to her, Russell was uneasy, and made some remark, —asked whether Mrs. Froude was unwell. Froude turned his head over his shoulder and said to her "Mrs. Froude. Be yu satisfied or be yu not. Yu knows the agreement we made. If yu be not satisfied, yu can go home to your family whenever yu like, and I won't hinder yu, and I may tell 'ee I don't care a damn whether yu stays or whether yu goes. Are you satisfied" "Yes" answered the lady faintly. "Her's satisfied" said Froude. "And now have a drop of zider, Jack"

Froude and Radford were both very wicked men. There is strong suspicion that Froude caused the death of certain persons who were obnoxious to him; he had men in Knowstone, who did whatever he told them; and there are nearly as bad stories told of ~~Russell~~ Radford. The difference between the men was that Radford was brutal and Froude fiendish. A young woman was found drowned in Lapford, and Radford took good care to be out of the way until after the inquest, but there was reason enough to suspect that he had seduced and then murdered her, or had driven her to suicide. Jack Radford was an immensely strong man; and he loved nothing better than a fight. The bishop heard of this and said to him once, "Mr. Radford, I hear that you make men drunk in your rectory and then set them to fight." "Dearee no," answered ~~Russell~~ Radford "Who ever told you such lies, my Lord! Why, when they begins to fight in my parlour, I take them by the scruff of the neck and turn them out into the Churchyard."

One day he said to his groom "Come on Bill, will you go and take a rise out of old Newton Fellowes" afterwards Lord Portsmouth. So they smutted their faces, and disguised themselves in cast off clothes, and went to the lodge at Eggesford.[2] They were denied admittance, but forced their way in and walked up the drive. Presently

---

[1] **The Rev. John Russell, see explanatory endnote 8**
[2] Eggesford House, Eggesford, N. Devon, seat of Lord Portsmouth, built 1820-1830. Derelict since 1911.

the lodge keeper came after them and attacked the groom, who turned and fought him. Then from the shrubbery burst a couple of gamekeepers. "Leave them alone. It's a beautiful sight, don't interfere and spoil sport," said Radford. But one of the men rushed at the groom. "Oh, thee will, will thee" said Jack Radford and caught him with his great hand, and in a moment had flung him on the ground. The other man then attacked him and was speedily thrown. The groom had demolished his man, and so he and Jack Russell *[sic, read Jack Radford]* sauntered on up the drive to the front of the house. Radford went up to the door and was about to ring when Newton Fellowes appeared, and angrily enquired what they wanted there, in front of the house. "Work your Honour!" said Jack Radford pulling a forelock. "Work is it you want?" asked Fellowes, "but did not my keepers stop you coming up this way" "They tried it, but they couldn't du it" answered Radford, "There they come skulking up, the blackguards," said Radford, pointing to the three men who now appeared. "They could not stop you?" asked Fellowes. "We flung them all three on the road" said Radford, "and now we'll ax your Honour for something to drink your Honour's health." Newton Fellowes gave Radford a crown, and dismissed the three keepers their places.

This was scarce fair, for Radford was the best wrestler and one of the strongest men in England. He was only beat once, and that was when he was drunk, in Exeter. He had gone up to Exeter for a spree and in some low public met a Welshman and had a fight with him and was horribly beat about the head and body and mauled. Next day, when sober ~~Russell~~ Radford followed the man by train to Bristol, and thence to some small place in Wales. He knocked at his door and called him out, and fought him, and utterly thrashed him, and when the man could scarce speak, and was unable to hold up, "There," said the Devonshire parson, "Now take care how you lay a finger on Jack Radford again when he is drunk. If you wish to have another bout with him when sober, call when you will at Lapford parsonage, and he is at your service."

Some years ago Heenan[1] or Sayers[2] or some other great prize fighter went about England and was exhibited. He came to Taunton, but was there taken ill, and could not be shown, so the manager wrote or telegraphed to Jack Radford to come and supply his place. Radford went at once, and was exhibited, stripped, showing his muscles and mode of hitting, —as the advertised well known pugilist. The Taunton people would have been none the wiser, but as it happened, Lord Portsmouth was in the tent, and Radford saw him. He supposed that Lord Portsmouth recognised him, so he went up to him, called him aside, and whispered, "My Lord, the second best man in England is laid on the shelf, — so they had to telegraph for the best man to take his place." Lord Portsmouth told the story afterwards, but said nothing at the time. I heard the story from a farmer in Lapford, who was in the train with me last year. He knew also Jack Russell, vicar of Swimbridge, another sporting parson, but Russell is a very different man. As the farmer said, "Russell is a

---

[1] John Carmel Heenan, 1833-1873, American bare knuckle fighter
[2] Tom Sayers, 1826-1865, English prize fighter

gentleman and a Christian, Radford was a blackguard and a heathen." Russell is a very kind hearted, good man, and though great in the hunting field, he is also an eloquent preacher. The farmer told me something he himself had witnessed of Radford's proceedings which showed what an unredeemable brute he was. [1]

1880 **Sunday 15 August:**
Heard a good story from Thynne. His coachman went a Sunday or two ago to a Primitive Methodist chapel.[2] He told his master afterwards the sermon he had heard. The preacher took for his text "Awake up my Glory, awake psaltery and harp." 'King David,' said he, woke up airly *[sic]* in the morning, just as the sun was rising. So he opened his window, and he leaned his two elbows on the sill, and he smelt the beautiful fresh air, and saw the sun come a peeping up over the Eastern hill, like a spark of gold. So, says David, there he comes, the glorious sun to liven up the long day, wake up my Glory! My beautiful shining luminary and give us a long bright day, for we want it sore, for the hay harvest; And then, my brethren, he made another re-mark; and that was addressed to his possle-tree. Now I don't pre-tend *[sic]* to know exactly what sort of tree a possle-tree is, but travellers, and them that have journeyed in the East, and commentators on Holy Scriptures du inform us, that it is a sort of a plant that turns its face to the sun whichiver *[sic]* way the sun be. In short, it is a sort of convolvulus. Now, David saw the convolvulus drooping, with its blossom full of dew, and says he, Possle tree! says he, my hearty, wake up! The glorious sun is woke and shining, and it becomes you to wake up too, and look at thicky sun vull in the face, as is your nature to"

1880 **16 August:**
As I suspected the wing I have taken down proved to have contained originally the principal staircase of the house, this was of wood to the first storey, and then, from the landing, a winding stair in the wall, lighted by a granite window looking into the back court (west) gave access to the attic rooms. There was apparently no well, the ascent was from the left then a landing then to the right, and by a gallery over the lower stage to the door leading to the newel stairs. I fancy that the cupboard with the window in it was a later addition — at least above, as it could not have been used, when the stairs were up. It may have been on the first landing, and also in the attic, but was inaccessible from the principal landing at the head of the stairs, this also explains why this window did not range with the two light window, but was high up above the ceiling of the bedroom which had been constructed out of the stair landing. The flooring of this room was in two parts, one formed the old gallery and was very rotten, the oak ~~joists~~ rafters reduced to snuff, the other part of deal.

---

[1] Radford and Russell: Throughout this account almost all the references to Radford are written over the name Russell. It seems likely the corrections were made at a later date – possibly when he was quoting the stories in various publications
[2] **Primitive Methodists: See explanatory endnote 9.**

Canon Thynne left, and I went again to Prince's town and assisted Lukis in planning the avenue on Harter Tor, *[Hart Tor]* just below Black Tor. Examined a pit hut but found nothing though we dug down 6 feet, believe these depressions are not huts but shafts for tin descending some 12 ft. with radiating levels of no great length, the smaller pits "smelting places" for tin[1]

1880 **17 August:**
Returned to Lew

1880 **19 August:**
Engaged all morning re-erecting the menhir at Lew Mill, to Lukis' great delight. It really is an imposing stone.

In the afternoon went to an afternoon tea dance at the Arundells at Lifton. Grace and Evelyn[2] with me. Met Mrs. Kelly[3] for the first time. Reginald is High Sheriff this year. Lukis left to stay with Poole at Slade[4] and plan in that neighbourhood.

1880 **27 August:**
Called at Kelly. Reginald has two female swans devotedly attached to each other, each lays several eggs — about 6 — in the spring, and the two birds sit side by side on them with no result. Pitying their condition Reginald sent to Tancock's's[5] for a male swan. It arrived but quite failed to ingratiate himself with either. And this spring again these virginal birds laid their unfertilised eggs and drove off the male bird with fury when he made his advances towards them. Again the eggs are addled.

1880 **28 August:**
This is from an American Religious paper:
> "To the memory of Mistress Maguire
> Who attempted to kindle a fire
> But the faggots were green
> So she tried kerosene—
> Now she's gone where the fuel is drier."

Heard from Lukis. "In a dense fog on Wednesday. I measured the whole length of the line of stones from the circle on Staldon *[Stall]* Moor, past the ring at Erme pound, and terminating at a kistvaen in the direction of Erme Head. The length of the first portion which extends to the river bank at Erme pound is 3,966 ft. After

---

[1] Black Tor: *A Book of Dartmoor*, p 270.
[2] Evelyn: The identity of Evelyn has not been established. Possibly Evelyn Marshall, see the entry for 1 Jan 1882
[3] Mr and Mrs Reginald Kelly, of Kelly House, Kelly, near Lifton
[4] Slade: Near Cornwood, S Devon
[5] Tancocks's: The identity of this establishment has not been established.

passing the river, and at a point about 200 ft. from the N.W. corner of the pound the line resumes its course and stretches for 6,873 feet to the kistvaen.[1]

Supposing therefore that these two portions belong to one and the same line (which I do not doubt) the entire length from circle to kistvaen is 10,839 feet! The Down Tor line is a pygmy to it. We have had a succession of dense fogs and yesterday Mr. Poole and I went to Coryndon *[Corringdon]* Ball to look for the 7 lines of stones mentioned in Murray on the authority of Spence Bate.[2] We left S. Brent station about 8 a.m. and it was not until 2.30 p.m. that we found the lines. The whole of this time we were persecuting a most fatiguing search —circulating the hilltops, and trying to avoid the bogs. When at length we returned to the gate of the moor where we had commenced the search —then the lines were under our very noses. The stones are very small, many have muck to their tops, and some are invisible. We had time to measure two of the lines, which we shall probably take in hand tomorrow.

I hope you will give orders to some one at Lew Mill to put a charge of buckshot into the billsticker's legs if he should desecrate the monolith while you are abroad.

On a window at Beaumaris[3] an old vicar had himself delineated in stained glass some two hundred years ago, with the inscription under it. "nunc primum transparui" No man is ever, or can be ever, perfectly seen through. That was perhaps his idea, but there is a higher truth, we do not see the beauty, colour, goodness of man till the day reveals him to us, and he becomes transparent. There is more of good in man than we suspect or give him credit for.

1880 **Sunday, 29 August:**
Took morning duty at Stowford[4] church. When I was a boy the people in this church were wont to bow at the Glorias. I noticed today that none did this. In twenty or thirty years the custom has died out. In Lew church the men on entering used to touch their foreheads with their hands and make a bob of the head – whether to the parson, the squire, or the altar I do not know. This has died out also. In my father's time, as in my grandfather's, the wagon roof of the church had the ribs painted blue and yellow, the altar was also draped in blue and yellow, and so were pulpit, reading desk and our pue, *[sic]* as these were the colour of our arms. The Gould livery was blue and yellow. My grandfather adopted the Baring livery of claret colour, with striped red and white waistcoat. My father had no footman as in my grandfather's time, and the coachman was given a green coat with red and white striped waistcoat, and such Pengelly still wears. Buttons gold.

---

[1] Stone Row and Kistvaen at Staldon or Stall Moor: *Book of Dartmoor*, p 213
[2] C. Spence Bate: dentist, zoologist and writer on prehistoric antiquities on Dartmoor
[3] Beaumaris, Anglesey
[4] Stowford, northwest of Lewdown

Maria Beere, —our old servant, — a girl when Margaret[1] was a girl and we were boys, came over to see us. She told me of old Mr. Parker of Luffincot[2] whom my father and mother knew. He is a learned man, well read in patristic theology.[3] I remember years ago there was some talk of his marrying. "Why Parker" said West of Tetcott[4] — "There will be a change —instead of thy fathers thou shall have children" However, he did not marry. He has kept up his daily service for …… years, at seven every morning; never failing. He is now aged 75, never eats meat, and throughout Lent takes only bread and water. A hidden saint of whom the world knows nothing.[5] Next parish is Mr. West, he has a surpliced choir and a bright Catholic service. His little church is crowded. Today is his last Sunday service. He has been for some time suffering from cancer — and today he says his farewell mass, and retires from work to die. Another saintly man unknown outside his immediate neighbourhood!

1880 **30 August:**
What curious coincidences occur. I was driving Grace back from a call at Eversfield (Old Culmpit) when descending Lew Hill, I said, "One of the first things I can remember was when we lived at Culmpit, my father was driving my mother to Lew, and I was in the gig, when down went the horse, just here, and he and my mother were thrown out." At that moment, and in the same spot down went the horse I was driving and over on his side, breaking a shaft, but fortunately not cutting his knees. He had trod on a loose stone worked out of the road in the hot dry weather.[6]

Another coincidence happened some years ago at Mersea. Capt. Bruce of the Coastguard drove over from West Mersea to carry off Mary to go with his wife's children in his yacht. They had not left the rectory five minutes, when Capt. Bruce returned running. At a gate leading into the road from the glebe field the wheel of the carriage had gone to pieces, and the carriage had fallen on one side. My man was obliged to help him and me to get the carriage back into my coach house, and I lent Capt. Bruce mine to drive home with. A few hours later whilst sitting
at tea we heard a horse tearing along the road, and much shouting. Fearing there was an accident I ran out of the house, down the drive and into the road, and there, - in the identical spot where Capt. Bruce's carriage wheel had broken lay an upset tax cart,[7] one of its wheels had gone to pieces and thrown the driver out.

---

[1] Margaret: Sabine was referring to his sister Margaret
[2] Luffincot: A small village in West Devon
[3] Patristic Theology: Knowledge of the Fathers of the Church
[4] Tetcott: a small village neighbouring Luffincot in West Devon
[5] The Rev. Frank Parker of Luffincot: *The Catholic Revival*, p 73
[6] Falling horses: *Early Reminiscences*, p 149. Part of Sabine's childhood was spent at Eversfield, Bratton Clovelly.
[7] Tax cart: A light spring-cart —so named because originally it attracted lower taxation.

During the ten years I have been at Mersea, these are the only two accidents of the kind that have happened in the parish, and both took place in the same day, and in the same spot.

1880 **31 August:**
Dawe[1], the carpenter, is full of an odd story. He says he saw it in the paper, and it must be true, "Someone in America has changed her sect" "Not an unusual thing, surely Dawe" said I "women are given to change in religious matters as in others" "Well sir", said Dawe, scratching his head, "I never myself experienced anything of the sort! I don't see that religion has much to do with it. It was this — so it stood in the paper. There was a woman — and she married and had a family, and then she changed her sect; she grew a black beard and moustache and became a regular man. Then she got married to a young maid, and by her had another family, and the queer part of it is, she was mother of one family and father of the other."[2]

1880 **1 September:**
Not a bad story of last election. Mr. Stern of German (Jewish) extraction contested in Kent in the Liberal interest. At a public meeting when addressing the electors, someone shouted out, "Pray, who are you?"
"Whom am I?" answered Mr. Stern. "I am a naturalised Englishman. My father was a Baron, my Grandfather was a Baron —" "Pity your mother and grandmother weren't barren too" shouted a voice from the crowd. [3]

Mr. Newton's property to be sold on the 16th. It consists of 8,000 acres. He owes £150,000. There is a rumour that is *[sic]* sister married to a doctor —Ashford — at Torquay will buy it. I hope not —a vulgar lot.

Another election story — not very choice. Chambers was the Liberal candidate for Middlesex. There is an antiquarian shop in Tottenham Court Road, and the shop keeper had recently received a consignment of Roman lacrymatories, *[sic]*. slim necked vessels, and these filled his window. Being a zealous Liberal, above these in the simplicity of his heart and enthusiasm of his convictions, he had pasted the appeal in large letters "Chambers for Middlesex."[4]

1880 **2 September:**
The monument to Beatrice in Lew church was modelled from Veronica[5] by Knittel of Freiburg two years ago. It is very like Vera now. The butterfly on the

---

[1] Samuel Dawe lived at Hollycot, Thrushelton. He made Sabine's desk
[2] A sex change: This story is repeated in *A Book of Folklore*, chapter 3 although here the carpenter tells the story of a Cornish *man* who after fathering a family, changed his sex, married again and had another family. Why did Sabine change the gender?
[3] Election story: Repeated in *Early Reminiscences* p 54.
[4] Roman Lachrymatories: These were slim necked bottles used for the collection of tears. They were not unlike small male urinals!
[5] Beatrice and Veronica: See also footnotes 2 and 3, 19 July 1880.

arm had the wing broken by the mason in putting it up. In Lew church the East end was formerly occupied by a two light window high up. Under this the whole wall was covered with painted tabernacle work, a figure of S. Michael[1] and the corresponding figure on the other side uncertain. This was discovered before I can remember, my Uncle Alexander[2] told me of it. When the monument to my mother was put up, there were the traces of a S. Christopher found on the plaster. That I saw, but every portion was demolished when my father renovated the church the year he died. I was absent and unable to take tracings.

1880 **3 September:**
The present dining room was made by my father. He rebuilt the wall, and turned the fireplace. It was formerly open to the stairs and used as a passage, the floor painted in squares, black and white. There was a passage or corridor above stairs with latticed windows. My grandmother blocked off the passage and converted it into two bedrooms back to back, then the only means of passing from one end of the house to the other was through the best bedroom. My father broke through the wall and reconstructed the passage, narrower, keeping two bedrooms which he was able to do by widening the dining room below about 3 ft.

1880 **4 September:**
Mr. Spenser,[3] *[sic]* headmaster of the Tavistock Grammar School came over and called. He was a great friend of my father. He had not been here since my father's death.

1880 **Sunday, 5 September:**
Took duty at Stowford church in the forenoon. Mr. Blackburn waited and introduced himself to me after service. A little awkward, as the neighbourhood does not visit. A few years ago he became too intimate with a girl on Lew Down, whereupon Mrs. Blackburn left Haine, and her daughter went with her. She has not returned but a daughter now resides with him off and on. The neighbourhood keeps aloof, no one visits Haine. Laura, the youngest daughter is married to Mr. John Wollocombe's eldest son.[4]

A few years ago I brought an architect down to advise about restoring Lew House or building a new mansion in Down House field above the woods and away from those cancers – the quarries. "You must have other — Delabole[5]—slate for the roof" said he. "But" I observed "I have my own slate quarry a rifle shot off, and the Lew slate is far more durable than that of Delabole." "It is a bad colour. It will never do." "But really," said I, "It seems absurd to send carts to Delabole for slate

---

[1] St Michael: This might indicate that the original dedication of the church could have been to St Michael. Personal communication from the Rev. John Hunwicke
[2] Uncle Alexander: The Rev. Alexander Baring-Gould, paternal uncle.
[3] The Rev. Edward Spencer, headmaster of Tavistock Grammar School.
[4] The Rev. John Wollocombe, rector of Stowford. See explanatory endnote 10
[5] Delabole Slate Quarries, near Tintagel, N. Devon. Still active. 'The largest man made hole in Europe'

— two days journey there and two days back, when we have a superior slate at hand." "Of course if you persist in this" said he, "it must be. But the slate is a bad colour and will spoil the house." That afternoon we were walking in the lane to Lew Mill, when I said passing the slate quarry ramp, "Do look at that magnificent crimson and yellow dock leaf." "Stay a bit," said the architect, "allow me to find out the leaf, for I am <u>colour blind</u> and am curious to know if I can distinguish between a crimson leaf and one that is green." He selected the wrong leaf. "Oh, my friend," thought I, "how valuable must be your opinion on the colour of slates when you cannot distinguish crimson from green." I told him that I intended putting in the old granite windows, that the old stable quoins were made of window jambs, and that there were any number of sills, and mullions used to prop stacks. "No that won't do. You must have fresh cut windows, you cannot use the old ones after they have been displaced." I paid him for his trouble and dismissed him back to London and thenceforth have done without an architect.[1]

Mr. Saville's house at Oaklands[2] and Lord Portsmouth's at Eggesford were building at the same time. Oaklands near Dartmoor, Eggesford near Exmoor. It is said that the same architect was employed for both but of that I am not sure.

The architect said to Lord Portsmouth, "My Lord, you must build of grey Dartmoor granite not of this red stone of Exmoor — and make the house look as though of brick. The soft silvery grey of Dartmoor granite is unsurpassed for beauty." To Mr. Saville, said the architect, "My dear sir, you must not think of building of Dartmoor granite, every cottage is built up of that, it is crude in colour, cold and bleak. You must have the warm rosy red granite of Exmoor." So day after day the wagons of Lord Portsmouth and of Mr. Saville passed each other, the former conveying grey granite to the neighbourhood of Exmoor, the latter red granite to the outskirts of Dartmoor.

The old motto of the family[3] was either "Toujours son tache" or "Gold bydeth ever Bright." Both have the same meaning, referring to the untarnishing nature of gold, but I like the first rendering best. James Gould, mayor of Exeter, chose a different motto, perhaps in reference to his defiant royalism: "Spernit pericula virtus"[4]. My grandfather only used the Baring motto, and my father the same by preference. "Probitate et Labore,"[5] for this he had a great liking.

James Gould, mayor of Exeter in 1649, died in 1659. He is said to have saved the Cathedral from ruin by buying the lead roof and the bells, and not removing them.

---

[1] **Sabine and architects: See explanatory endnote 11; See *A Book of Devon* p 31.**
[2] Oaklands, Okehampton: *A Book of Devon* p 212.
[3] Gould family motto translates: *Always without stain*
[4] James Gould's motto translates: *Virtue spurns danger*
[5] Baring motto translates: *With integrity and work*

This incident is not in Prince's Worthies of Devon,[1] but was told me by Edward Gould of Colneford[2] his lineal descendant, — he showed me some letters of his grandfather to the Dean of Exeter referring to this as a tradition in the family. James Gould had two sons, Sir Edward Gould Knight; who lived at Highgate, a very wealthy man, and James, a merchant. Sir Edward had no children so he left his property to the sons of James, but he *[sic. Read 'they'?]* was not to come into it for 60 years, during which time the money was to accumulate. James Gould went to China, and there got himself modelled in China clay in Mandarin costume. He was amused at the proceedings, and the modeller took him smile and all. On his return to England he gave the figure to his wife. He died in 1680 and was buried at Islington (June 11th). His son Edward — born 1677 died on board the "Montagne" in the East Indies in 1720, his portrait by Sir Geoffrey Kneller is now in the possession of Edward Gould of Colneford. I have a copy of it here at Lew.[3] He did not come in for Sir Edward's property. Edward was married to Jane daughter of Sir Francis Pemberton, and by her had thirteen children, of these two sons lived, Edward, the eldest, who married Mary daughter of Robert Thoroton of Screveton, and the Revd. William Gould, Rector of Hoxne.[4] Edward came into Sir Edward's property as well as his grandfather's and bought a large estate at Mansfield Woodhouse.[5] His son, Edwin Thoroton Gould who eloped with Lady Barbara Yelverton, sole child of the Earl of Sussex, and his heiress, was a handsome spendthrift. He ran through every penny of old Sir Edward's and old James Gould's monies, had to sell Mansfield Woodhouse, and died in Paris, unable to come to England on account of his debts. Curiously of all that was left of Sir Edward and James Gould, nothing remained but the clay model of James Gould made in China, together with the Chinese hat, the shoes, one of the padded silk stockings, and the creese,[6] which he wore when modelled. Besides these the only relic is a Chinese bronze puzzle he brought home with him, — but the secret how to open it has been lost. These are now all in the possession of Edward Gould of Colneford.[7]

I sent an artist to copy the head of old James Gould. The rough sketch is capital, but the picture he has made from it is execrable. It is now at Lew

1880 **7 Sept**:
Revd. Edmund Field,[8] chaplain of Lancing[1] arrived to spend a few days with me, also the Hon. C. Lindley Wood, eldest son of Lord Halifax, who married Lady

---

[1] Worthies of Devon: by John Prince, 1701. See also *Further Reminiscences* p 79
[2] Colneford, Essex
[3] Edward Gould's Portrait. *Further Reminiscences* facing p 82
[4] Hoxne, Suffolk
[5] Both Screveton and Mansfield Woodhouse are in Nottinghamshire.
[6] Creese or Kris: A Malay dagger with a scalloped edge.
[7] Gould History: See *Further Reminiscences* pp 81-2
[8] The Rev. Edmund Field: *Early Reminiscences* p 283-4 *a most excellent man, kind, good, very much in earnest, but, oh, such a talker!*

Agnes Courtney. I have not seen him for some four or five years, when I stayed with him at Powderham. I driving him from Lidford station the horse fell and cut his knees badly.

The Baroness Burdett Coutts is engaged to be married to Mr......... Bartlett, she is aged 67 and he 25; she has brought him up; and he has persuaded her that he loves her, and as there is no fool like an old fool she believes him. But here come the crux. She has inherited old Coutt's money through the Duchess of S. Alban's, and the Duchess by codicil in the will has left it to the baroness ~~only~~ so that it will be forfeited should she marry an alien. Mr. Bartlett is an American. Legal opinion has been sought to decide this knotty point whether he be an alien or not. His grandfather fought on the British side in the war in America for independence. Consequently he was not an American. The baroness is very much put out at the objections made by her relations to the marriage. Old Coutts the Banker left the bulk of his fortune and share in the Bank to Miss Meller the actress, with whom the old fellow was enamoured. The Duke of S Albans, not much to his credit, married her. She on her death, left the greater part of the money and shares in the bank to Miss Burdett, daughter of Francis Burdett and his wife who was a Coutts, but with the aforenamed proviso and Miss Burdett assumed the name of Coutts, and has been created a baroness in her own right.[2]

1880 8 Sept:

Pouring rain. The other day Lord Percy was at Torquay and there encountered young Palk, a prig. What did Mr. Palk do, but advance to him with the salutation "Glad to make your acquaintence! A Palk ought to know a Percy." The original Palk was carrier between Dawlish and Exeter. His son went to India, where he amassed a considerable fortune, and invested it all in land. He bought the land now covered by Torquay for £40,000. He or his son, I forget which — was created Baronet (1782) and the conservative government, before going out; had given the title of Baron Haldon to the descendants of the old carrier whose wagons were wont to traverse Haldon.[3]

1880 9 Sept:

Took Wood and Field in the morning to see Sydenham, and in the afternoon to Lydford falls, the ravine, and Kitts' steps.[4]

On the day of the Duke of Wellington's funeral, on the balcony of Old Burlington House[1] was my uncle, Gen. Sabine, then president of R. Society, my aunt, her mother,

---

[1] Lancing College, Sussex, the senior school of the Woodard Foundation.

[2] **Baroness Burdett-Coutts: See explanatory endnote 12: With Rajah Brook of Sheepstor, *Book of Dartmoor* p 229.**

[3] The Palks: See *A Book of Devon*, pp 289-293 for a full and honourable account of the Palk family, which begins *A cloud of dust has been stirred up to disguise the humble, but respectable, origins of the family.*

[4] **Kitts' Steps: A waterfall on the R. Lyd, Dartmoor. See explanatory endnote 13**

Mrs Leeves,[2] a gentleman, my uncle had invited —   , and Tennyson, the poet
laureate, also invited. It was a very cold day, raw with a sharp wind. On the windy side
was a projecting screen at the balcony end, and a chair against it, naturally the place for
Mrs. Leeves, then a very old lady. But Tennyson on coming out on the balcony, looked
about, and finding this the only sheltered spot made for it, seized on the chair, wrapped
his plaid round him, and leaning over the balcony rail remained the whole time silent,
and steeped in thought, quite unconscious of the annoyance he had caused, and how
indignant with him others were for his rudeness. Afterwards appeared his poem on the
event. The inspiration came on him in that sheltered nook. Who can say? Had he not
been screened, the world would have been deprived of the poem, or had had but an
inferior copy of verses. Field recalled this to me.

1880 **10 Sept:**
Heard a good story of Lord Dufferin's from Wood. He was in the train one day
with a lady. No one else in the same carriage. The train rushed into a tunnel. Lord
Dufferin in the dark crept under the seat and completely secreted himself. When
the train came out into the light he was not to be seen. The lady, in great agitation
ran to the window on the further side and looked out, and, by her manner was
evidently in great alarm. Shortly after, the train dived into another tunnel,
whereupon Lord Dufferin crept out, and reseated himself composedly where he
had been before. When the train emerged into the light, the lady to her unspeakable
terror found him there, calmly reading a newspaper. At the next station she darted
out of the carriage to get into another, firmly persuaded that he was the devil.

I remember a capital story I heard in Tyrol a couple of years ago. An English
gentleman was travelling to Brindisi from London, via München, Innsbruck, and
the Brenner. He had been travelling night and day and was accordingly soiled and
uncomfortable with dust. As the train entered a tunnel he asked its length. "Ein
stund." 'A stund! That is an hour. In an hour of darkness I can easily change my
shirt" He proceeded at once to divest himself, and had got the dirty shirt off, and
had not yet got the clean one on, when whish! The train dashed into broad
daylight. The compartment was occupied by other travellers. Ein stund has the
double significance of an Hour and a (German) mile.[3]

1880 **11 Sept:**
Went with Wood and Field to Tavy Cleave and ascended Lynx Tor[4]. In the
evening they left. A lovely day. Found a piece of white heath — a sign of good

---

[1] **The Royal Society and Old Burlington House. There are problems with
Edmund Field's story. See explanatory endnote 14.**
[2] **Mrs Leeves and a ménage à trois: The mother-in-law and wife of General Sir
Edward Sabine. See explanatory endnote 15**
[3] Stripping off in a railway tunnel: This story is repeated in *Further Reminiscences*
pp 68-9 but somewhat elaborated.
[4] Tavy Cleave and Lynx (or Links) Tor: Dartmoor features: *A Book of Dartmoor*, p
141-2

luck— and brought it home to Grace. The heather brown, pink, rich yellow and amber of Millais' picture, "Over the hills and far away". Had tea and plenty of cream in the "Dartmoor Inn." Found built into one of the walls of Lidford a stone such as Lukis has seen great numbers of on the moors, with a circular cup cut into it, perhaps a mould for tin. These are also found in Cornwall. They are however always circular, and sometimes perforate the stone. They are in large slabs or long stones, in the flat surface. My idea is that gates were hung between them, and these holes served as sockets in which the gate post revolved. As such they are used in Guernsey.[1]

1880 **12 Sep:**
Took duty again at Stowford. John Wollocombe's very reluctant to return and no wonder. A fresh scandal at Haine. Mr Blackburn had his second son, Mr Arthur B. (The eldest is in an asylum) and his wife and children staying at Haine. A disreputable affair came out, in which Mr. Arthur B. figured as his father had done five years before.[2] Mrs. A. B. on charging her husband with his infidelities was knocked down by him. They were to have been at the Arundell's dance at Lifton, but while we were there a note came from Mrs. A. B. "Circumstances have occurred which require me to leave Haine. We are packing and depart at once." The note was commented on, but the explanation only came out later. It is said that she intends to sue for divorce. I saw Mr. A. B. at Lidford station yesterday, taking his departure.

Daisy was found crying after service on Trinity Sunday. When asked the reason for her tears, she replied that she did not want to go to heaven, for Papa has just read in the epistle that there were four beasts there full of eyes, before and behind, and she was afraid that they would be always staring at her.[3]

Saw in the papers of the death of Revd C F Lowder of St Peters London Docks. The name awakened a train of thought and recollection. When I took my degree at Cambridge I went to him and asked him if he could find me some church work to do. My father had wished me to go to the Grammar School, Marlborough to my uncle Fred. Bond and help him till something was settled. I declined to do this as my uncle had no sympathy whatever with the Catholic cause, and work in his school was not what I wanted. Lowder was the curate at S Barnabas,[4] London. He took me into the college, gave me a little bedroom in the attics and there I spent a month or two. My father had no idea where I was, but I was doing some parochial visiting and teaching the choirboys. Every now and then I appeared at General Sabine's[5] that my existence might be known but neither my uncle nor my father

---

[1] Swinging Gates at Lydford: This story is repeated in *A Book of Dartmoor*, p 133.
[2] Mr Blackburn of Haine: See the account for Sunday 5 September 1880
[3] **The epistle of Trinity Sunday Mass. See explanatory endnote 16**
[4] St Barnabas church, Pimlico: The first Anglo-Catholic Church to be built in London
[5] General Sir Edward Sabine then held the rank of colonel

knew where I was.[1] At last, after Easter,[2] a peremptory letter came from my father
ordering me at once to go to Marlborough and my father refused to allow me any
money whatever until I left London and had satisfied him of my whereabouts.[3]

I showed this letter to Lowder who recommended me to go to Shoreham to Mr
Woodard, the provost of St Nicholas College and he would give me some work.
Accordingly I went there. Mr. Branthwaite was then master of the school. I
remained there some weeks but found that my classics were not equal to the
teaching in this school nor was I satisfied that it was the place for me. [4]

Then I was sent to St John's College, Hurstpierpoint,[5] a school for the middle
classes, to educate them in Church principles. There I was satisfied I had found the
work and place I wanted. I was given £20 per annum for the first two years —the
salary was afterwards raised. I was very hard worked for the first two or three
years, so hard that I had scarce any time to myself for not only did I teach in the
school all day but I was required to teach the servitors[6] in the evening. I believe the
headmaster[7] thought I was an enthusiast and he would prove me by hard work. I
stood it and the work was made lighter afterwards. I was very happy at
Hurstpierpoint. At Danny Hall in the parish lived the Campions. Mrs. Campion
was a relative through the Barings, and I saw a good deal of them and met at
Danny the Dowager Marchioness of Bath, and the bishop of Durham (Baring).[8]

After eight years spent there, my friend Joseph Fowler was offered the vacant
chaplaincy. He came down to Hurst. He was very anxious to take it. I was most
anxious to secure him for the place, as I feared the church tone was declining, and
Dr. Lowe, the Headmaster, was striving to alter in other ways the character of the
school, he introduced Greek into the curriculum of necessary studies and was
trying to make of the school a nursery for the universities. Which was not what
some of us conceived was wanted. Lewin Pennell, one of the masters was also out
of heart at the change, and afterwards left to join the S. African mission, and died

---

[1] **To compare this matter of fact account with an emotional account written in
a letter to Sabine's mother at the time, see explanatory endnote 17**
[2] Cambridge: The date Sabine came down from Cambridge is uncertain. The
relevant records at Clare College are missing but this diary entry suggests Sabine
took his degree and came down in the New Year, probably of 1857.
[3] **The Rev. Charles Lowder: see explanatory endnote 18.** See also Wawman R J,
Sabine and the Ministry of the Keys, Transactions SBGAS volume 8, p 34-48
[4] Sabine at Lancing College: *Early Reminiscences*, p 270
[5] Shoreham and Hurstpierpoint are both in Sussex
[6] Servitor: an assistant schoolmaster
[7] Headmaster at St John's College: Edward Lowe, Woodard's close friend and
associate.
[8] Bishop Charles Baring: *Early Reminiscences,* p 271 *one of the narrowest bishops
the church produced at that period.*

at Zanzibar.'[1] I believe he never would have left Hurst had it maintained its character. Fowler said he could not take the chaplaincy as he was engaged to go to Horbury to be curate to Revd. John Sharp.[2]

On a sudden inspiration of enthusiasm I said "I will go and take your place if Mr Sharp will have me in deacon's orders in your room." Fowler wrote, Mr. Sharp consented to the substitution, and gave me a title for orders.[3] I had long desired to take orders but my father and mother had constantly refused me permission and I did not like to go against them in so important a matter. They just endured me being at Hurst in a position they thought very unsuitable.

My father put it plainly before me as his determination, if I went into orders I could not hope to inherit Lew. The property was entailed on a son, but not on an eldest son, or so he informed me. The living was destined for one son, the estate for the other. If I took orders I must be content to be only rector at Lew, and Willy should be squire.
Before my mother died, she withdrew her opposition and asked my father not to refuse his consent should I again solicit it.[4]

When I had finally made up my mind, I wrote to him, to ask his consent. He gave it but again let me understand that I was cut off from the succession to the property. I felt this very keenly and there was a coldness between us. I went direct from Hurst to Ripon and was ordained there, deacon, on Whitsunday 18....*[1864]* Next day I went to ~~Hurst~~ Horbury, and saw it, and Mr. Sharpe for the first time. The first year I acted as a curate in the parish generally, but after I was ordained priest I was given the district of Horbury Bridge and there I worked until I had got a chapel built, which would serve eventually for a school.[5]

I went home to Lew for a month about this time, the chapel was built and my father asked to see me whilst my brother William was at Lew. Poor Willy had sometime previous had a bad attack of brain fever at Doncaster when engineering a new line thence with Lincolnshire.[6] This had left results which only after some years showed how serious disorganisation of his brain had been. He behaved very badly during that visit — I believe now because his brain was disturbed. I knew nothing of the brain fever and attributed it to a motive. I saw he was much with my father with whom he had tastes in common, and, at table, and before my father he

---

[1] Richard Lewin Pennell: *Early Reminiscences,* p 284. Son of the squire of Cheriton Bishop and *one of the dearest and most saintly of men I ever knew*
[2] **The Rev. John Sharp: See explanatory endnote 19**
[3] The Rev. J T Fowler: *Early Reminiscences*, p 336
[4] Opposition to Ordination, *Early Reminiscences,* p 297
[5] Horbury Bridge: *Further Reminiscences*, chapter 1.
[6] **Brother Willy's mental breakdown described as *'mental overstrain'*: Early Reminiscences, p 220. Explanatory endnote 26 for the true nature of this illness.**

behaved to me with studied rudeness. I was very angry, and returned to Horbury before the expiration of my holiday. My father said not a word about the property and I concluded that he held by his purpose and had communicated this to Willy, who was elated with the prospect of stepping into my shoes. I ought perhaps to have come to an open explanation with my father, but as he never broached the subject, I did not like to begin it. Of one thing I was certain, I would not take the living, with my younger brother at Lew House as squire. I felt that a wrong was done me and that it would rankle in me and daily distress me at Lew and cause a lasting bitterness between Willy and me.

I made up my mind to go as a missionary to British Columbia and entered in a correspondence with the SPG[1] about a mission there vacant. Then I proposed to dear Grace and was accepted. She had nothing but would make a good wife in the New World. The mission in British Columbia was filled. There was a vacancy in Honolulu. I applied for that and wrote to the bishop of Honolulu. He declined my services as he had filled the vacancy and there were not funds available to support more clergy. Then Lady Downe offered me Dalton[2] and I went there for the epiphany 18–. *[1867]*

1880 **13 Sept:**
Sir Walter Carew's only son Capt. Walter Carew was excitable and odd. He was engaged to Miss Daniels, his second cousin. The original Daniels sold dried fish about the streets of Bath, and getting together by degrees some money invested it in West Indian Plantations, at a time when these were greatly depreciated. His son went out to the W. Indies and realised a very large fortune. Old Daniels bought Stoodley[3] of the Fitzackerleys, an estate of some 6000 acres. Mr. Daniels the father of the lady who married Captain Carew, and a grandson of the fishman, married a Miss Carew. Captain Carew one day when engaged to Miss Daniels saw a farmer's son in church looking at her very attentively. After service he went up to him and knocked him down. Sir Walter gave the father £100 not to bring an action against his son, which would have led to his being struck off the roll of magistrates. After the marriage, indeed at once on return from honeymoon, Mrs. Walter Carew suddenly left her husband and would never again be persuaded to live with him. She went to Collypriest[4] to her mother and lived with her there.

After this Captain Carew went completely out of his mind. He ran about the streets of Tiverton with a drawn sword. He tried to drown himself, but was fished out of the hole in the river into which he had thrown himself, before he was dead. Sir Walter then sent for Dr. Fox, and Captain Carew allowed himself to be removed without resistance to his establishment near Bath, but was found there next morning with his throat cut. He had somehow managed to escape the vigilance of Dr. Fox and the keeper and secreted a knife about his person. The

---

[1] SPG: Society for the Propagation of the Gospel
[2] Dalton, near Thirsk, Yorkshire
[3] Stoodley: Stoodleigh. near Tiverton, Devon
[4] Collypriest, near Tiverton, Devon

next brother of Sir Walter had died childless, the third of the brothers, Mr. ~~Peter~~ Henry Carew had married a milliner at Bath, Susan Syms, a woman of bad character, and she had a son, but whether by ~~Peter~~ Henry Carew is doubtful. Mr. ~~Peter~~ Henry Carew is dead, and now that Sir Walter is dead this child in whom it is very questionable whether any Carew blood flows, is the baronet and heir to Haccombe[1] and the magnificent Carew estates. The woman has recently married again, and has had the impudence to insert in the papers that ~~three~~ two Miss Carews acted as her bridesmaids, an absolute lie. It is a sad addition to the story that Mr. Tom Daniels of Stoodley, grandson of the old fish hawker, who married Miss Carew has also cut his throat.

1880 **14 Sept:**
The late Lord Devon when old, married a young thing. A few weeks after the marriage, very early in the morning he turned up at Mamhead parsonage,[2] and asked his son, Mr. Courtney to take him in. "But father" said Mr. Courtney, "What is the matter with your face, it is scratched and bruised and discoloured." Lord Devon had to admit that Lady Devon had done this with her nails and fists. He never lived with her afterwards.

1880 **15 Sept:**
The Harvest Festival. Gave brass chandelier to the church and it was put up for the first time. This chandelier I bought at Mecklin'[3] some years ago. It came from the church of S. Jacques, and was taken out, I believe, when gas was introduced. It has on it our Lady and Child in a halo of glory, and 18 sconces for lights.

A pouring rainy day. The Revd. I. K. Hughes, vicar of Staverton preached the sermon. He stayed with us.

1880 **16 Sept:**
Mr. Hughes left. Planted the newest piece of ramps with larch and Scottish fir. The top is not yet in condition for planting, I have holes made in the slopes, fill these with earth let down in boxes, and then insert the young trees.

1880 **17 Sept:**
An unfortunate affair has taken place at Plymouth. The incumbent of Trinity Church is a little man, who is a great light in the Evangelical world, at least the little world of Plymouth. Recently an American woman has been lecturing on Electro Biology at Plymouth, and the vicar foolishly went up on the platform and allowed her to practice upon him. Evangelical pastors are as a rule much like the conies,[4] a feeble folk — intellectually and spiritually, and the vicar of Trinity

---

[1] Haccombe: Haccombe House, Near Newton Abbot, Devon
[2] Mamhead: West of Starcross, Devon.
[3] Mecklin: Mechelin, Belgium. This fine chandelier was stolen from St Peter's Church, Lewtrenchard in recent years
[4] **Conies: See explanatory endnote 20.**

Church is very feeble. The charlatan obtained complete mastery over him, made him stutter and adhere to his chair, forget his name, and finally dance on the platform. She put him through the paces in polka, waltz, and jig, and finally made him dance the vulgar buffoon performance called the "Perfect Cure" jigging, capering and going through the stages of tipsyness. Of course, since this his influence is at an end, and he is become such an object of ridicule, that his friends sincerely urge his changing his living to some place where the noise of his antics have not attained.

It is a very unfortunate thing that Dr. Temple, Bishop of Exeter, is not a gentleman in manner and speech. He has a harsh hard voice and strong Devonshire twang. He is marvellously unsympathetic with his clergy, and has I believe none in the diocese who entertain the smallest affection for him. I heard an instance of his want of breeding the other day. He invited the Mayor and Mayoress of Exeter to dinner, a few weeks ago, as well as some other persons. Among the latter were Reginald and Elizabeth Downall, the son and daughter of the late archdeacon. The bishop and Mrs. Temple were not in the room to receive their guests, who waited and talked among one and other until the dinner bell rang, when the bishop and Mrs Temple came in, and having just noticed his guests, he gave his arm to Miss Downall, and Mrs. Temple made Reginald give her his, and quietly ignored the Mayor or Mayoress. Elizabeth Downall was very uncomfortable and distressed at this insult to the chief magnate of the city, but, of course, could no nothing. She told Mr. Field afterwards that she never before felt so ashamed of the bishop.

The late vicar of Dartmouth, Mr Forster,[1] *[sic]* got into some squabble with his parishioners about trifles, and the bishop sent for him to Exeter. When Mr. Forster arrived, he was shown into the Bishop's study. Dr. Temple gave him a curt nod and went on writing letters without further noticing him. Mr. Forster waited, swelling with indignation; at last it burst forth, "My Lord" he said "I have come up from Dartmouth at your request, and you have received me with impertinence. I am vicar *[of]* Dartmouth, and I have not been accustomed, nor will I allow myself, to be treated like a sixth form boy at Rugby, You have kept me standing, My Lord, a quarter of an hour, without noticing me, or offering me a seat. If you wish to speak to me, do so, at once, or I shall leave a house the master of which seems not to know the first duties of a gentleman."

He has had some other sharp lessons, but there is no making of silk purses out of sow's ears.[2]

1880 **Sunday 19th Sept:**
I understand from my uncle that my father agreed to allow my grandfather to sell the remains of the Staverton properties — I fancy it was Pridhamsleigh House and

---

[1] Mr Foster, vicar of Dartmouth: *Further Reminiscences*, p 116
[2] **Archbishop Frederick Temple: See explanatory endnote 21: See also *Further Reminiscences*, Chapter 10.**

the home farm — and my grandfather undertook to pay him £300 per ann. for allowing this.[1] With some of the money the alternate presentation to Lew Trenchard was bought of Mr. Tremaine, (and two fields near the school.) The rest was lost in ruining speculation. My father wanted my grandfather to buy Coryton then for sale, but he preferred risking it in mines and lost all of it.

1880 **20 Sept:** Planting the top of the new ramps of the Lime Quarry with larch, beech, birch, and Scottish fir. The slopes to the North, facing the house I had planted two years ago. I have however now put in a hundred lilaacs, *[sic]* and a number of rhododendrons of good sorts my father had planted in the avenue where they had not thrived under the drip of the oaks, I have moved to the slopes of the quarry. Put in also a few sycamore and some seringas, *[sic]* ribes, perriwinkle *[sic]* and spiraea.

1880 **24 Sept:**
Went to Plymouth with Grace and the nurse with little Barbara to pay a visit to the Glennies. Mrs Glennie is a relative of the Bonds through the Blighs, and so they are distant cousins —very distant indeed.

1880 **25 Sept:**
Lunched with Aunt Emily Baring-Gould, she tells me that when my grandfather lived in Teignmouth, the family only came to Lew for six weeks every summer, they did not settle at Lew till my grandfather's embarrassment began.[2] She tells me the ~~Scottish fir~~ Austriaca[3] planted on the ramps were put in by my grandfather in 1846 the year before he died.

1880 **Sunday, 26 Sept:**
Baby[4] very unwell

1880 **27 Sept:**
Returned to Lew. My aunts, Fanny and Emily Bond[5] came. Streatham House[6] near Exeter adjoining Belmont where my great aunts, the Misses Snow lived, was the property of Mr. Thornton West. He was the illegitimate son of old Dick Thornton the millionaire, a man who from sweeping out offices rose by successful speculations to die worth two million of money, which he left to his so-termed nephew, Thornton West, who it is believed was his son. Mr. Thornton West gave Tom Snow[7] £17,500 for Belmont —standing in 30 acres of land, as it adjoined his place, intending to throw the house down and join the grounds to his

---

[1] Pridhamsleigh: *Further Reminiscences* p 79. See also entry for 20 July 1880.
[2] Grandfather William's financial embarrassment: *Early Reminiscences*, pp 37-98
[3] Austriaca: Austrian black pine
[4] Baby: Barbara, then 6 months old
[5] **Maternal aunts, Fanny, Emily and Kate Bond: See explanatory endnote 22**
[6] Streatham Hall, not House
[7] Tom Snow: father of Lavinia Baring-Gould, Sabine's stepmother

own, but he died, leaving a young son, and Belmont still stands. Mr. Thornton West married the daughter of a solicitor at Uffculme, second rate people.

1880 **28 Sept:**
Sent petition for licence of non-residence to the Bishop of S. Alban's.
Aunts Fanny and Emily Bond seem highly delighted with being once more at Lew. Neither has been here since my mother's death.

1880 **29 Sept:**
Mr. Bird, vicar of Launceston and his wife came to lunch, they are friends of the Bonds. In Launceston churchyard on a tombstone is the inscription

> "Vengeance is not prepared for me,
> This cup of wrath was drinked by Thee,
> Then, O my soule forbear to frown,
> And suck this milder mixture down."

1880 **30 Sept:**
Mrs. Glennie and Mary Glennie arrived. We have had this week the loveliest Michaelmas Summer

1880 **2 Oct:**
The Bonds and Glennies left. Livy[1] and Leila[2] arrived in rain.

Planted some apple trees in the orchard below the walled gardens. I cut down an old tree and told William Ball to put a young one in its place. "Near it, but not where it stood," said he, "My father used to say, a young man rarely thrives in an old man's shoes."

1880 **6 Oct:**
Carrie Buller arrived at the Rectory, she is the daughter of Mrs. Buller who was daughter of Mrs. Coney.[3] She is like the picture of Mrs. Redhead as Eleanor Baring.

1880 **9 Oct:**
Hard at work all week getting ready for our departure. I asked Edward at tea how he liked the prospect of leaving Lew. Down went his head and he could scarce swallow his meal for tears. The children have been as happy as the day is long here.

---

[1] Livy: Stepmother Lavinia's familiar name
[2] Leila: Lavinia's daughter, Sabine's half-sister
[3] Mrs William Coney: daughter of Caroline Baring who was a sister of Sabine's paternal grandfather

Part 2: Freiburg, October 1880 to September 1881

1880 **22 Oct:**

Left England. We departed from Lew on Tuesday, the 12th, a lovely day, but we were all in sad spirits at leaving the dear old place, which is let now for five years to Mr. Reginald Morshead, at £200 per annum.[1]

I should not have let it so soon, but have spent the winter at Lew, but that this year, as last, the farmers cannot pay their rents in full. I allowed off 10 per cent last year, and this, but still several are behind, unable to pay at all. Reckoning my receipts and balancing against them the necessary outs, i.e. the annuities, mortgage and the work done on the property, up to midsummer the property yielded me £2.0.0 for the half year! Aunt Fanny Bond has very kindly lent me a thousand pounds at 3 percent and with this I have lived and built this summer. Now, by letting the house for five years I hope to make a thousand pounds and by economy abroad to save some money, at the same time that I am getting the children educated well and cheaply.[2]

From Lew we went to town and hired lodgings in Keppel St. for ten days where we might leave the children, whilst Grace and I went on to Mersea and packed winter clothes, and got the house ready for Mr. Gatrill who will be my locum tenens. We got off on 22nd. Oct., and crossed by Dover and Calais. The passage was rough and everyone of the party was ill. Unfortunately our engine broke down near Tournai, and we did not arrive in Brussels till two hours after we were due. The children bore the journey and deprivation of regular meals better than might have been expected. On reaching Brussels we found that our luggage was left behind with the train at Tournai. We had got into a train sent to the rescue when our engine failed, but the luggage had not been forwarded with the passengers,

1880 **23 Oct:**

After much trouble got the luggage and started by the night train for Strassburg.*[sic]* Daisy ill with bronchitis and choking. We were seriously uneasy, but the carriage was heated almost to suffocation by pipes from the engine, and the hot dry air suited her, and she got better during the night.

1880 **Sunday 24 Oct:**

At Strassburg where we arrived early. Most of the children coughing or with head colds. Had breakfast and then I went off to High Mass at the Cathedral. A bitter raw day with East winds blowing. The bells dancing in the great gallery built for their reception between the west towers. Again, as on every previous occasion the effect of that west front on me was overpowering, and when I entered that beautiful nave the procession was mounting the stairs to the choir singing the introit. The effect was more than I could bear, and tears filled my eyes. It is

---

[1] Lew House let to Mr Reginald Morshead: *Further Reminiscences*, p 101

[2] **Fanny and Kate Bond, maternal aunts: see explanatory endnote 22**

strange, but this is the effect this Cathedral always has on me, the same as some marvellously beautiful scene in the Alps, or some exquisite piece of music. Last time I was here with Gatrill and another I expected them to share my enthusiasm, but found they did not, they both preferred Metz. Now Metz to me is beautiful, but it does not move the soul like Strassburg. I am quite untouched by Cologne.[1]

1880 **25 Oct:**
In glorious sunlight, with the Black Forest Mountains radiant in their autumnal tints, beautiful beyond description, we arrived at Freiburg. The same sort of day exactly as that on which we arrived three years ago. Then, in my admiration of the colouring I spoke to the kellner[2] at the inn about it. "Ah yes" said he, "Our mountains are fossil rainbows."[3]

1880 **26 Oct:**
Next door to us is a Schnell-laufer,[4] a man who is running for a wager next Sunday against a horse 46 times in an hour. He is with his wife, and sundry animals, a squirrel, a cat, and some birds. The children are very excited about him. Freiburg is full and we can hear of no furnished lodgings to let. One of the Princes of Reuss[5] was here last week, looking for some, and unable to get any went away. I have asked at two or three hotels at what price they will take us in, en pension, but the terms are beyond my reach.

1880 **29 Oct:**
Saw an advertisement of four rooms to let, furnished, with pension, I went, saw, and engaged them. It will be inconvenient having so few rooms, only one sitting room but nothing else is to be got. Terms moderate, a pound per diem, exclusive of wine, fuel and paraffin, but inclusive of every thing else besides.

1880 **3 Nov:**
Shall be very glad to get into our new quarters, Daisy's bronchitis is bad, and Barbara has a bad bronchial cough. I fear it foreshadows trouble to her through life from that family weakness. My grandfather suffered from it, so did his sister, Lady Northcote, my uncle Charles has not taken duty for some 15 years on account of it, and I suffer also every winter.

1880 **6 Nov:**
Enter our house No. 17 Katherina Strasse today.

1880 **Sunday, 7 Nov:**
Misty cold day. Very comfortable in our house.

---

[1] Strassburg and Cologne cathedrals: *Further Reminiscences*, pp 67-8.
[2] Kellner: German for waiter
[3] Fossil rainbows: *Further Reminiscences*, p 85.
[4] Schnell-laufer: German for a runner
[5] Reuss: the smallest states in the German Confederation

1880 **8 Nov:**
The children began their schooling, Mary, Daisy, Edward and Veronica[1] go to two old
maiden ladies, the Fräulein von Reichenstein who tenant a little house not far from here
and teach young children. The eldest is rather prim, the second Fräulein Ertrich is
hunchbacked and dwarfish, but with the most kindly loving heart. The poor ladies have
the portraits of their ancestors round their little sitting room, one or two large oil
paintings —a number of miniatures. They seem really delighted to see the children
again. The three eldest remember them well and are fond of them, and bothered me
every day to be allowed to go and see their old mistresses of three winters ago, and so I
gave them leave one day and off they rushed. But when the ladies saw and recognized
them and kissed and hugged them, communication was ended for they could speak no
English and the children could not express themselves in German.

1880 **16 Nov:**
The fair is in full swing. Whirligigs and shows and stalls, and the children are in wild
delight. Last time we were here in 1877, Edward went all round the fair studying what
he could buy, and objected to laying out money first in this, then in that, till he found a
purse, and he spent half his money on that, in order that he might be able to preserve
the rest in it safely. The same dislike to spending money appears now when he is nine.
He would not go into the show of Zulus because that was expensive 15 pfennigs, nor
witness the achievement of the Industrious Fleas, because entrance was 10 pfennigs;
and though all the rest down to Julian spent their money in rides on the whirligigs,
Edward would not, dearly as he loves a ride, it would be waste of money. However all
at once he saw a little perambulator for a doll. Vera had been for some days clamouring
for one. At once his purse opened and he bought it, as a present for her, and alas! In
getting out his money for it, dropped and lost 50 pfennigs. He has been very
disconsolate since at his loss; and refuses to receive the sum from Mary however much
she urges it on him, because she is richest and can best afford it.

1880 **17 Nov:**
Today, Edward's birthday, Mary has made him accept 50 pf. as a birthday present.
His mother has also given him a mark, and I am to treat him and the others this
afternoon at the fair to merry-go-rounds and shows.

1880 **18 Nov:**
At the fair again Edward has spent the 50 pf. Mary gave him in purchasing a box
of bricks as a present for her.

1880 **19 Nov:**
The arrangements of this house are rather amusing. Our landlady the Frau
Deiekterin[2] belongs to an old Basle patrician family, she has however married a

---

[1] Ages of Baring-Gould children at school: Mary aged 11, Daisy 10, Edward
almost 9, and Veronica 5.
[2] Deiekterin: The nearest modern German words to Deiekterin and deiektor are
dichterin and dichter: an authoress and author, writer, poet.

German of bürgeslichter[1] origin of the parasitic name of Wucherer (usurer). She
occupies a neat snug room upstairs, has her stove heated, and a hot bottle carried
up to her every evening to warm her toes, but the poor Deiektor - a Deiektor once
but of what is not known, - is consigned to a sort of lumber room at a distance
where uncared for and in cold he sleeps among broken furniture and old clothes.
He does not, I fancy, enjoy a stove, for he sits on the stairs smoking and reading
the Tagblatt, a daily sheet of local advertisements. Every morning a nice tray with
napkin and white roll and cup of coffee and milk is taken up to the Deiekterin's
room for her breakfast, and a cup of coffee without milk and a scrap of bread is put
on the staircase window sill for the husband. The children declare that he cleans
the boots in the morning. The wife sleeps with a coat of arms —his arms —at the
foot of her bed, and spends her leisure in art and literature. She is always trim and
nicely dressed and eager for artistic gossip — I have lent her "Selections from
Ruskin," which she is going to translate — He crawls about slipshod and depressed
and untidy, and shares I fancy little of his wife's comforts and few of her favours.
When she is out he steals down to the kitchen to have a chat with the maids, but
they pack him off with scant ceremony, and he creeps back disconsolate to his
dusthole in the attics.

1880 **20 Nov:**
There has been a very curious exhibition at the fair, which I visited. A man
stripped save for a pair of drawers and a ~~short~~ sleeveless armless jersey, who called
himself the Modern Pluto performed with red hot irons in a manner I cannot
understand. I was close to him and saw that there was no deception. He first got a
sort of iron scraper about the size of a hoe iron, which was heated red hot in a fire
of charcoal burning at my feet, and in which were glowing several irons, and with
these he raked his arms and legs, and then both his cheeks and neck. The white ash
fluttered about from the hot iron and some fell on my sleeve. Then he took a
glowing red hot poker and continued to lick it with his tongue till it was cooled. To
make quite sure that there was no deception I tried to touch it; and had to draw
away my hand pretty sharply, and an English friend standing by me lit his cigar at
the iron after it had touched his tongue. Then he took a thin flat iron bar, red hot,
and worked at it with his teeth till he had bitten off a piece about ¾ inch, which he
threw down with his teeth. Next he trod on red hot plates of iron, but I do not think
so much of this, as he only drew his feet over them one after the other, without
resting his weight on them, and probably only touched the glowing iron with the
horny portions of the heel and sole. Lastly he swallowed a couple of teaspoons of
boiling oil. This seemed to be a greater effort than the rest and in performing the
feat his face turned purple and the drops of sweat burst out on his brow. I was too
close to the man —I could touch him with my hand, for any deception to have
been practiced. How he managed is to me a marvel. This, moreover, went on all
day for eight days from eleven o'clock in the morning till late at night. I was told
he went through the performance 20 times in one day, the principal day of the fair.[2]

---

[1] Bürgeslichter: equivalent to 'bourgeoisie'
[2] **Pluto: When did Sabine see this performance? See explanatory endnote 23**

1880 **21 Nov:**

The chaplain here Rev. Neville Lawrence is married to a 1ˢᵗ. cousin of Mrs. Lloyd Jones, who was a Miss Worth of Worth in N. Devon. The story of the Worth family is a sad one. The Worth family must have had large possessions at one time in the county, Holdstrong and Waddleston[1] *[sic]* once belonged to them, but a Worth became lunatic and an act of parliament was passed to enable some of his property to be sold for the payment of his creditors. Then it was that one of my ancestors —which of the Goulds I forget, bought the two farms. At that time much of the family property passed into other hands. However the family was still well off, and Worth House was built in the Georgian period, and is big and handsome in its way. The grandmother of Mrs. Lloyd Jones, and of Reginald Worth the last squire, her brother, dead this year, ran away with the butler to Paris, and carried off all the family jewels, and they were never recovered. The father ran away twice from his wife, once with a married lady, Mrs.------ and secondly with a Bristol barmaid. Mrs. Worth thus deserted lived rather fast, she was a handsome dashing woman, and queer stories are told of her, not much to her credit. The son, Reginald, was forced to take orders that he might enter a family living, as the finances of the family through two generations of spendthrifts, were at a low ebb. He took to drinking, and lived with women of bad character in Exeter, and ruined his constitution. The last few years he has been better, but he died this year, having worn himself out prematurely by his excesses. The property now goes to Mrs. Lloyd Jones for life, her husband, my dear old college friend, the Revd. W. Lloyd Jones, rector of Washfield,[2] drops the name of Jones and assumes that of Worth, and then it passes to his eldest son, who will bear only the name of Worth. It is to be hoped that the vein of bad and reckless blood has dried up.

1880 **1 Dec:**

One night when I was at Dalton,[3] my Persian cat came to my door and gave signals that he wanted to go out. So I slipped on my trousers and shoes, and came down and unlocked the door. The moon was shining, and as I opened the door I saw a figure move in the garden. I had for some time missed fruit and vegetable, and I now had the thief in the act. I caught up a stick and dashed across the cabbage beds after the man, who fled, and dived into a dark corner, where was a deep dry ditch overhung by thorn bushes. I went after him and progged with my stick into the ditch, till I came on flesh. I presume I progged too lustily for it to be a pleasant bed for the man, as he plunged out, and ran through the orchard, and I ran after him. It was dark in the shadows of the apple trees, but nevertheless I gained on the fellow, and he finding that took a header into a dense forest of sting nettles that grew nearly to the shoulders in robust

---

[1] Holdstrong and Waddlestone (also known as Warson): Both at one time farmsteads on the Lewtrenchard Estate
[2] Washfield, a village near Tiverton, Devon
[3] Dalton, near Thirsk Yorkshire, often referred to by Sabine as Dalton i' t' Muck. He served there as perpetual curate from 1867 to 1871. *Further Reminiscences*, chapter 2.

luxuriance. I beat down the nettles and cut my way after the man, till at last I got one foot on either side of him. He lay very still. "Now then" said I "I have you, and I insist on knowing your name. My stick has got lead in the handle, and unless you tell me who you are, I will catch you such a crack on the skull with it that you will lie quiet till I can get a lanthorn and examine your face." The prostrate creature then struggled to its feet, then a bald head emerged into a patch of moon light. "I beg your pardon Sir!" "Oh! Willy Jakes" —! In fact it was my gardener! Next morning he came, very crestfallen, much bruised, and with his face and bald head a mass of sting nettle spots to apologize. I found in the ditch sundry cabbages, cauliflowers etc he had been collecting to carry off.

We had a curious adventure there — at Dalton, just before Daisy was born.[1] In the evening Grace went to her looking glass in the window to brush her hair, when a gun was discharged close by and the shot smashed the glass above her head. I was downstairs, and hearing the discharge of the gun rushed forth, but was unable to find who had fired, and then I ran upstairs and found Grace in great alarm. I went off to the police, but nothing came out for some time. At last I discovered that a young man working in the adjoining farm had been paying his addresses to our servant girl, a very pretty proud girl she was, and she had met his advances with such contempt, that to revenge himself, he had, lain in waiting in my garden, till he saw her, as he supposed go to the window to draw the curtains for the night, as was her wont when arranging the bedrooms, when he fired; whether he intended to hurt or only to alarm I never knew for he ran away from his place and what became of him I could not ascertain.

When Grace and I were first married, we neither of us knew very much about housekeeping. She sent me into Thirsk one day, to order some meat, and whether she told me the amount and kind of meat I was to order I cannot tell, but by the time I got to Thirsk I had clean forgotten everything about the meat except that meat was to be sent. I went to the butcher and ordered some. "Of what sort?" "A round of beef" said I boldly. "A large one or a little one?" "Oh! a good sized one". The butcher no doubt thought we were going to have harvest home so next day an immense round of beef arrived. The servant came, hardly able to control her laughter, into the drawing room and my wife went out. In another moment she darted back "What have you done? Just come and see" she explained with a face the picture of dismay. I followed, sneakingly, into the kitchen; there, on the floor, lay a huge mass of red beef —40lbs —it weighed, and the butcher's man stood there wiping his forehead, he had sweated so, bringing it up from the cart. Well, we had that great mass boiled in the copper, and we ate it hot, then we ate it cold, —for dinner, for breakfast, for supper. We were a whole month working our way through that round of beef and then we had not come out at the other side, for we were only three in the house then. Grace, myself, and the maid. We loathed it, and,

---

[1] Daisy: (Margaret) Sabine's 2nd child.

unable to go on any longer, we gave a picnic to the choir on the Hambledon Hills and fed them thereat with the remains of the round of beef.[1]

Before I was married there was an old dragon of a housekeeper who managed for me, a woman with a hard plastered false front of hair and a grim face. But she was a good-hearted woman and she remained with us for a month till I had engaged another servant, a younger woman. There was an interim of a week between the going of the older woman and the arrival of the young one, and Grace undertook to manage for the time. We got Mrs Warne's cookery book[2] after breakfast and pitched on the receipts which were to be executed for dinner, and the results were satisfactory. But the first evening I proposed green pea soup for supper, so we got the green peas and shelled them, in the kitchen, and put them in the pot about 9 pm and sat on, I reading aloud and Grace sitting knitting and looking in the pot every now and then. The peas remained as hard as bullets. However we sat on till near midnight before the soup was ready, and were in a state of ravenous hunger then so we could have digested them raw. We generally supped at nine or half past and were in bed by ten. That was the last time we attempted green pea soup for supper.

Dalton was a very dreary and depressing place but not so dreary and depressing as East Mersea.[3] At neither place are there pretty walks, lanes and woods. But then Dalton was near a railway station and within three miles of Thirsk. Moreover the pretty Hambledon Hills were visible from it and accessible by train. If we had had a pony carriage we might have got about and seen pretty bits of country, but we were obliged to walk; the curacy was £150 and a house, and the expenses of the church and services fell entirely on me. I cannot say that I was happy at Dalton. At Mersea I have been very happy, though nothing can be more dreary and uninteresting than the place. Still I have now a library and pretty furniture and pictures, and in summer, have always friends staying with us, and in winter, I run up continually to town. At Dalton I was so completely isolated from friends and relatives that I felt more utterly dull and desolate than at Mersea.

1880 **5 Dec:**
Had a call today from Herr and Frau von Hillern[4] and their two daughters Hermine and Charlotte. Frau v. Hillern is just returned from Mannheim where her "Geier Wally" has been produced for the first time on the stage. She wrote the drama herself, adapting it from her own novel. It has been received enthusiastically, she was called three times on to the stage to receive the applause of the audience. She is a very clever woman certainly, of immense power but that power is sometimes

---

[1] A round of beef: *Further Reminiscences*, p 24-5.
[2] Warne's *Every Day Cookery* by Mary Jewry.
[3] East Mersea. Sabine was appointed rector to the crown living of East Mersea, 1871 and remained the incumbent there until 1881.
[4] Frau Wilhelmine von Hillern: Explanatory endnote 24. See *Further Reminiscences*, p 85-6

very unpleasantly used. Her last story "Sie Kommt doch" is odious. Poor thing! Three or four years ago she was thrown from her horse and her ankle and arm broken in several places. She will never be able to do other than hobble with a stick, and walk more than across a room, and her arm is twisted and bent out of all shape. But her spirit is vigorous as ever. She is a very plain woman with an ugly mouth, hair now nearly white piled on top of her head and white eyelashes which give a rather wild and uncanny look to her eyes. Hermine is exactly like her mother, has all her cleverness, and is better looking. A nice, good hearted girl, but when crossed her eyes glare like those of a tigress, and a look comes over her face as though she were going to spring at your throat and strangle you.

1880 **6 Dec:**
The Revd. W. K. W. Chafy-Chafy of Rous Lench Court[1] has just left after staying in Freiburg three months. When we were at Lew four years ago he was curate of Lydford. He is a man of large fortune, and when at Lydford he threw about his money freely. Since then he has bought Rous Lench a fine old place, the house plaster and oak, with magnificent gardens. At Lydford he built the stables of the Rectory to serve if needed, as a school and did much to the house. He restored the church and supplied it with complete sets of vestments and altar covers of the richest quality. He furnished the Rectory sumptuously, the drawing room with blue silk curtains, — and after remaining curate in charge there for three or four years, went away and left the furniture of Church and Rectory to Mr. Fuller the Rector as a present. One instance of his way of proceeding he told me himself. Mr. Fuller asked him to preach one day at Prince's Town, where he, Fuller, lived and had charge of the chapel. Chafy-Chafy, puzzled how to proceed, telegraphed to Eaton Square, — his town house, — for his coachman, large carriage and pair of horses, to come down at once to Lydford to take him thence to Prince's Town. Accordingly they came, and Chafy-Chafy started, but as the coachman knew nothing of the road, and had not, indeed, been to the county before, they lost their way, and did not arrive at Prince's Town till the service was over. Never for one moment did it occur to him to take the train to Tavistock, and hire a trap from the Bedford. I find him now in very low spirits. He has invested a very large sum in the property he has bought; and that presumably on the eve of a fall in the value of land, and the failure of farmers right and left. One large farm that paid him £800 per ann. has been since last year tenantless, and is untilled and left to go to rack and ruin. The same with a smaller farm of a value to him of £300 a year. Other farms are only held on a rental half of what was formerly paid.

Under these circumstances he has been forced to come abroad to retrench He does this by bringing with him two English nurses to his three children, and an English footman —not a courier, a man who cannot speak a word of any other language than his native Northamptonshire, and is absolutely useless, for Chafy-Chafy has been en pension at the principal, most expensive, and least comfortable inn here, and now he is off to Florence to spend the winter in a grand hotel there. The footman has nothing to do but eat his head off. I have no doubt whatever that

---

[1] **The Rev. Chafy-Chafy and Rous Lench Court: Explanatory endnote 25.**

Chafy-Chafy has been unsparingly pillaged at the Zöhringen Hof here. Unless one knew to the contrary, one would suppose that he had never been abroad before, so utterly unable is he to manage for himself and accommodate himself to circumstances.

I tremble to think what his wood bill will amount to, as he refuses to use the German stoves in the manner employed in the country, by firing up twice a day, and turning off the damper when they are out, so as to convert the stove into a great hot air vessel. He will burn fuel in it all day long in all his rooms; no gain, as in these stoves one cannot see the fire, and as wood is exceedingly expensive, he will have to pay a pretty penny for this fancy. Advantage there is none, as no greater heat is obtained in the room, indeed one gets more warmth by shutting the damper than by heaping on fuel. We have here in our sitting room a stove adapted for coals. The fire is made up at 8 a.m., and by 9.25 it is out. Then the damper is turned, and we have not yet had occasion to light the fire again all day. After dinner we open the windows for half an hour and thoroughly change the air in the room. No sooner are the windows shut again, than the stove begins again to pour out heat, and rapidly restores the temperature to what it was before.

1880 **7 Dec:**
My little aunt Harriet[1] — born in the year 1---- was one of the smallest, quaintest, most delicate little beings I remember to have seen. She was not, and never can have been beautiful. She had the Sabine features exaggerated, was very like the picture of Mrs. Petty[2] on the stairs, in white satin, and like also to Frances Sabine[3] (by Hogarth) I do not remember her at that youthful age, but Aunt Emily[4] says she was like her as she could stare at 21. I suspect that she was not given enough to eat when a growing girl. As I remember her, she wore a white frilly cap with lilaac *[sic]* ribbons in it, very large and elaborate about her wizen little face, and small grey curls. She dressed in white with puffed, old fashioned sleeves, tightening about the arm below the elbow, adorned with lilaac *[sic]* satin bows. She was always chilly, and sat crouched into the fire, with her dress turned over her knees, lest it should scorch, and her petticoats singeing with proximity to the fire. Her sister said her poor little shins were always red and roasted. She spread out her delicate hands, very delicate and transparent fingers, over the fire and then closed them over her knees and then opened them again, like a piece of mechanism. She was not clever, read a good deal, but remembered nothing. The Literary Gazette was her journal, and all the bound volumes at Lew were hers.

---

[1] Aunt Harriet Baring-Gould 1801-1857: First child of William and Diana Amelia Baring-Gould. Unmarried. *Early Reminiscences* p 109-110
[2] Mrs John Petty, b 1747, d of Colonel John and Mrs Susanna Sabine. Portrait, *Early Reminiscences*, p 103.
[3] Frances Sabine, unmarried sister of Field Marshal Sir Joseph Sabine
[4] Emily Sabine Baring-Gould b 1812, 3rd child of William and Diana Amelia Baring-Gould, unmarried.

She had not much to say for herself, but her voice was pleasant, tremulous and weak, but with that old cultured intonation which is now almost lost, but which went with Chinese vases and the odour of pot-pourri. Poor little Aunt Harriet, she could not go out of doors in a strong wind. She could not stand against it but was fairly carried off her feet. One day at Bude she was on the pier, when a gust actually swept her off, like a feather and carried her off into the water, the wave swept her back, and my father who had darted after her, caught her before she struck the stones. She was dreadfully frightened, and her little voice rose in a shrill cackle above all the expressions of sympathy. She was hurried off, undressed and put to bed, and never ventured on the breakwater again.

1880 **8 Dec:**
My uncle Alexander[1] was in the E. India Service, and a dashing young Lieutenant. I have heard a story of him. He had a very capital horse, in India, and excellent jumper. At Mess one day the possibility was mooted of getting across a certain gully, at a leap. Some said no horse could do it, others said it was feasible. A bet was made that it could not be done, and my uncle Alexander, took it. He rode his horse at the gap, and the horse with a tremendous effort reached the further side. He was at once bet that he could not do it a second time, and he foolhardily took it. The horse refused the leap several times, reared, swerved, and evidently had no heart for it, but he spurred and lashed the poor animal, till he drove it desperately at the gash. The horse just reached the further side with a supreme effort, and then went down, on the ground and never rose again. My uncle won the bet but lost a most valuable horse.

He married in India Margaret Ireland, she was no beauty, and somewhat older than himself, a bony hard Scottish woman, gone out to India on the chance of catching a husband, there, as there was not the remotest possibility of her getting one in England. She must have been a woman of some force of character for she completely colonised and accidulated *[sic]* his cheerful and suggary *[sic]* life. She so completely "converted" him that he sold his commission, and went to Cambridge to study for Orders. My grandfather was very angry, and would not help him; but he managed by what he had realised from the sale of his commission, to get through his university course, and obtain orders and a curacy. He was sometime, I believe, at Hull, and began to shine as a very keen and eloquent Calvinistic preacher, just at a time when the old Evangelical supply was running short; consequently he has ever since had the pick of any livings he chose to accept from Puritanical patrons and sinecurite *[sic]* trustees. He was for some time at S Marks, Wolverhampton, and   there I visited him just before I entered at Cambridge, and never spent a more detestable fortnight in my life. I had brought Shakespeare with me, and this caused scandal. My cousin, Baring,[2] went to his

---

[1] Alexander Baring-Gould, b 1814, 5th child of William Baring-Gould. *Early Reminiscences*, pp 230-2
[2] Baring Baring-Gould, b 1842, only child of Uncle Alexander, later of vicar St Michaels, Blackheath

mother, after looking over my shoulder and said "What do you think! Sabine is reading a play!" "My son" said Aunt Margaret "If sinners entice thee, consort not with them". My sister Margaret was staying there at the same time, and if we were at all merry together, in the evening at prayers, in the extempore effusion of my uncle, we were prayed for before several maids and any visitor who had stopped to supper, that we might be delivered from the unseemly spirit of levity.[1]

He has since had Ellacombe by Torquay, and now, a church at Winchester. My Aunt Margaret has been as deaf as a post for years. My uncle Alexander has so completely dissociated himself from the rest of the family that he never comes to Lew to the rectory, or writes; and I believe now that none of the party there have met him for some years. Even though he was near Torquay, in the county, he showed no disposition to keep up family association. The fact is, he is surrounded by a circle of puritanical old women who hang on his lips and burn incense under his nose, and he cannot endure to be outside this ring of planets revolving round this sun and source of light. He has grown narrower, sourer, and less genial than his wife, and the cousins at Lew Rectory are much more disposed to feel kindly towards her than him. He is not pleasant looking. He has the Sabine mouth and sharp face with that self conscious smirk, and unreal expression, that utter absence of all frankness of eye, which so generally characterises a man of the school to which he belongs. You see a mask and not a face, through which a pair of suspicious eyes peep at you and then turn hastily away or fall.

He is sincere, most earnestly so, but one never feels when one hears him speak, that you are listening to a real man, and that a human heart is beating behind the black waistcoat. Perhaps it is for this reason, that, old and white haired as he has become, age and a snowy head do not make him venerable. The white hairs are to some a crown of glory, to others a fool's cap. The finger of time softens and sweetens hard faces, when left to nature, but pinches, sharpens and makes disagreeable those that have become artificial. I do not for a moment believe that the man plays a part consciously, but I believe that his Calvinism is so unnatural, so inhuman a religion, that it has disturbed him mentally, morally, and physically.

My father's face which was once hard and stern and showed little gentleness in its reserved severity, in old age became wonderfully soft and sweet and loveable. I remember when we — Grace, Mary and I were at Lew just before my father's death. That afternoon Grace said to me "I could hardly resist kissing his hand as he put it in mine" No one would feel the like desire to touch my uncle Alexander's hand.

1880 **10 Dec:**
Grace and I were at Lew only a very short time before my father's death. We were going abroad, to spend a fortnight on the ~~Moselle~~ Meuse and to be rejoined at

---

[1] Prayers for unseemly levity: this story appeared anonymously as '*a letter from a friend*' in *The Church Revival*, p 102.

Brussels by Emily and Sophie,[1] who were to go with us to the Tyrol and the
Dolomites. My father was then unusually well and very happy. We dropped Mary
at Mersea and went on via Harwich to Antwerp, and thence by Brussels to Namur
and Dinant and dawdled about on the Meuse enjoying the lovely weather. We
returned to Brussels on ~~Friday~~ Thursday evening fully expecting to meet the
cousins on Saturday, spend the Sunday in Brussels and push on the Monday. On
Friday morning I went to the post office to ask for letters and found there a
telegram and letter awaiting me which were over a week old saying that my father
had died suddenly by a stroke. We were too late then to catch the morning train, so
we got off by the evening train to Ostend and Dover and got to London on
Saturday morning. Unfortunately the Prince of Wales crossed from Calais the same
morning or rather, night, and we could not get our portmanteau passed [sic] the
customs till his train had been disposed of. This made us miss the first train down
to Devon, we however got off by the next and arrived at Lew just a couple of hours
after my father's funeral. Telegrams had been sent to the police at Brussels to
enquire after us, and to Spa but none had reached us until too late, on our return to
Brussels.

Willy was at Lew; he had come from town, and then the cousins noticed the first
evidence of his mind going. He was quite unable to arrange or direct anything
about the funeral. Poor Willy! What finally upset him was a journey to Algiers. He
had taken it into his head that the climate in Algiers would set him up in health.
The aunts'[2] and I helped him with money and he came to me to discuss the
arrangements for departure. I was naturally eager and excited, and said how
delighted I should be to go, and went in heart and soul, with his plans and arranged
his trains from a foreign Bradshawe. I thought him dreadfully downcast and ready
to raise a thousand objections. Grace told me after she had noticed that he was
crying all the while, the tears were running down his cheeks. I knew at the same
time that there really was no necessity for his going to Algiers, he was perfectly
sound in lungs and all he complained of was indigestion now and then and a
numbness, which I supposed came from it, in his hands.

He did finally start, and arrived in Algiers. One letter I got from him thence, a most
strange one, he wrote that he could not sleep, the dogs howled all night, and the
Arabs fought and cut each other, and there was blood, blood, everywhere. A week
later the aunts got a letter from his landlady, a kind good French woman, to say
that Monsieur was very excited and distressed, and insisted on leaving, but there
was no real occasion, still seeing how excited he was, she felt that he ought not
travel alone, and would try and persuade him to stay. He was very nervous and
fanciful about himself and had made up his mind that if he stayed in Algiers he
would die there.

---

[1] Sabine's cousins Emily, b 25 April 1838 and Sophie, b. 12 May 1846, daughters
of the Rev. Charles Baring-Gould.
[2] **Aunts: Almost certainly aunts Frances and Marianne Kate Bond. See
explanatory endnote 22**

A few days after I got a telegram from Exeter, urging me to hurry down there at once as Willy had arrived at Colleton Crescent[1] in a most extraordinary and alarming condition. I went down at once and found that he had taken to his bed and could not be induced to leave it. He said that he had run away from Algiers as his landlady had attempted to poison him, and he did not dare to eat anything she gave him. He had got to Paris and had gone to an hotel. There, he said, he obtained a room au troisième and had locked the door, but in the night he had heard the servants of the hotel whispering in the passage and trying his door, and that he was convinced they intended to murder him and he had rushed out on the balcony and screamed for the police. From that point his story was confused, how he got to London and on to Exeter we never ascertained, and he never was able to tell us. He was in mortal terror of being robbed and would let no-one touch his handbag containing his money. At Colleton Crescent he kept it under his pillow. His impression was that everyone was bent on robbing him, and he charged poor Crabbe, the manservant,[2] with having stolen his clothes, because, I suppose, he saw him take them away to be brushed. With great difficulty and only by being very peremptory with him, could I persuade him to get up and dress and come out and walk with me. I stayed several days with him in Exeter, took him to the skating rink and to the theatre to see 'Richelieu' but nothing could draw him out of his state of nervous alarm and unrest. The medical man called in thought very seriously of the case. At last Drake[3] came down and saw him, and we both tried to rouse him, but ineffectually; then I resolved on taking him with me to London, getting him examined there by a physician who was experienced in mental affections and then take him on with me to Mersea. The opinion given in town was sanguine, the doctor said that his nervous condition seemed to have received a great shock or overstrain, that it was a condition not unlike a condition what he had found persons in after a railway accident, and that with quiet he would in all probability recover. Unfortunately I did not then know all I learned afterwards, that he had been attacked with brain fever at Doncaster and that he had gone to Lew on his recovery. Dr Willis[4] had told my father plainly that Willy would end his days in an asylum. My father, perhaps naturally, had not hinted anything of the sort to me, and I scarce even knew that he had been ill at Doncaster. I took him home with me to Mersea, and he remained with me some time, and a very trying time it proved, he gradually became more troublesome and caused me daily greater alarm. I did not know what might happen. He sank into the deepest gloom and had the strangest fancies. One day I drove him over to West Mersea, and called at the Vicarage. The vicar talking of all sorts of things said something to me of a great fish that had been caught by the boatmen. When we came away, Willy said to me, "You heard how all the conversation turned on me. That great fish meant me." It was so at our table, every subject of conversation he took as directed personally against himself. I found

---

[1] Colleton Crescent: 4, Colleton Crescent, Exeter was the home of the Bond aunts.

[2] Thomas Crabbe, manservant at 4 Colleton Crescent, 1881 census.

[3] Edward Drake Baring-Gould, 1851-1887, Sabine's younger brother.

[4] Dr J H Willis: Known to have been practising in Lewdown in the 1850s and 1860s

he walked into Colchester and back without telling me, so that sometimes he was absent for a day, and I had no idea what had become of him.

One evening I came in the dusk into my library and found him sitting brooding in my chair, he started up, and said to me "I want five pounds that you owe me for the turning lathe I gave my father" My dear Willy" I said, "You have had the money and I have your receipt for it". He gave a scream, beat his head, and cried out "all the world is conspiring to rob me". Then he drew his knife, opened it, and rushed at me knife in hand, screaming "Give me five pounds or I will kill you" I started back, went into the hall, took a heavy stick, and returning, with a firm tone, bade him at once lay the knife down. He cried out that he was a ruined man, gave up the knife and began to weep and tear his hair. I put the knife away, took away the razors from his room and some gunpowder which was there with a pistol, and telegraphed at once to Witham, to Dr Tomkins, who kept a private asylum, to send a man at once, by next train. I telegraphed also to a doctor at Colchester, and sent to our nearest surgeon, to be at the Rectory next day at early dinner, and see my brother. Next morning the keeper arrived, the medical men at once examined poor Willy, and signed the requisite papers, and the day after I went with Willy and the keeper to Witham, where, dear fellow he remained for five years. Paralysis gradually stole up from his feet to vital parts. His tongue was soon affected and after the first year he could no longer speak.

With all his delusions, which were very painful, and infirmities, he never ceased to be quite a gentleman, indeed, to the very last the gentlemanly instinct remained in him, and whenever Mrs Tomkins, or Grace, or any lady entered the room, he always put on a bright smile, and struggled to rise from his chair. His brain fever was brought on by overwork. He and another were engineering the N Lincolnshire line and it had to be done by a certain day. His compadre fell ill and the whole work and responsibility fell on Willy. The strain was too great and he fell ill with it, and that attack sowed the seeds of his final malady.[1]

1880 **12 Dec:**
Received 2 great bundles of reviews of my "Mehalah" from the publisher, most say that it is clever, but repulsive, one says that it is a study of Ouida.[2] I have never read a line of her's. Another that the end is copied from Mr Black.[3] I have never read one of his novels. What is true is that there is a resemblance between Elijah Rebow and "Heathcliffe" in "Wuthering Heights", but not intentional, though I have read Emily Bronte's wonderful novel, which, by the by, I could not follow until I had drawn out the pedigree of the family of Heathcliffe's Katie for constant reference. I admit that Mehalah is unpleasant and bitter. I wrote it when greatly

---

[1] **The true nature of the illness of Sabine's brother William: See explanatory endnote 26. See also *Early Reminiscences* p 220**
[2] Ouida: the pen name of Marie Louise de la Ramée, 1839-1908, successful novelist.
[3] Black: Possibly William Black, 1841-1898, a Scottish novelist who was immensely popular during his lifetime

depressed and embittered by two most ungentlemanly reviews of my "Germany"[1] in the Academy and the Saturday. The first was offensive and insulting to the last degree, there were other reviews most unfair and captious, accusing me of blunders I had not made.

I think it was "The Bookseller" which contained this wise critique, that my book contained no information which was not familiar to everyone except that Barons in Germany are plentiful, and that the sewage of the towns is not carried away by water, but spread over the fields. Another reviewer sneered at the book which could contain such statements as that Mont Blanc is visible from the Hohentwiel– a statement made in Baedeker. As if Mont Blanc was not in the panorama from the Hochenschwand printed in Schnart's "Schwartzwald" I had taken such pains over my book, and am convinced it really did contain so much information. – blunders some there were I was ready to acknowledge – that I was hurt more than I can express by the attitude of the reviewers. Moreover they spoiled the sale of the book, at the very time when I was sore distressed for money, as the farmers could not pay their rent at Lew nor those at Mersea their tithe. In the bitterness of my spirit I wrote Mehalah very quickly in a month, without a pause, and poured out in it my wrath and bile. Then I was better. Kegan Paul refused the novel. Smith and Elder gave me £50 for the copyright. I got a little over £100 for my Germany. I had calculated on £300 for the latter.

1880 **15 Dec:**
Saw "Geier Wally" performed at the theatre here. Frau von Hillern has adapted her own novel to the stage very cleverly. It was performed for the first time last week at Mannheim, with great applause, she was called on three times, the enthusiasm was so great. The same "Wally" —Frau Rosa Keller from the Mannheim theatre took the part here as did Ernst the "Joseph". Frau Keller was wonderful, it was superb acting of a very powerful part. The play wants some alterations I think to make one act lead up to the other, it is at present too disjointed and rugged in construction.[2]

1880 **25 Dec:**
Christmas day in pouring rain. We all dined — down to Julian —with Frau von Hillern; Herr von Hillern is Öberpresident des Gerichtskammer, Head judge,'[3] he cannot speak a word of English, and Grace no German. He had to take her into dinner and I suspect found dinner rather dull. The children behaved very well. The von Hillern's provided some horribly sanguine beef —German beef is a very different thing from English —and plum pudding to make an English Christmas dinner.

---

[1] Baring-Gould S. *Germany Past and Present*, 1879, C Kegan Paul
[2] *Geier Wally*: 'The Vulture maiden' Frau von Hillern's dramatisation of her novel of the same name. See *Further Reminiscences*, pp 85-6
[3] Öberpresident des Gerichtskammer: Head judge of the local courthouse

I have written to London about the production of "Geier Wally" on the English stage and have already half completed the translation and adaptation. One act, the fourth (English), third (German), I have completely recast and rewritten, and I flatter myself improved. I think Miss Linda Dietz[1] will take the character of Wally.

1880 **26 Dec:**
I see to my astonishment that my "Mehalah" is advertised to come out in the "Deutsches Familien Blatt"[2] as a novel by a well known Gelehrter[3] I have given no leave for the translation to be made. I suspect it is done by Miss von Hillern, if so, it is cool to do it without leave or offer to share profits. I gave Frau v. Hillern half of what I received for the translation of her "Arzt der Seele" — Ernestine — not much, the share of each was £4.2.0[4]

1880 **27 Dec:**
At a party the other evening at a retired German officer's, Major von Baumbach, his son Lieut. von B. dressed up in a very light red gown, with frizzled hair, and stalked through the room, and then recited some verses composed by Hermann, a comic actor at the theatre about Miss Festing, the daughter of Capt. Festing, an English gentleman staying here. She dresses in red and in the present English fashion, and goes by the nickname among the Germans of "the stick of sealing wax" —be it noted, she is tall and very thin. She is a nice modest girl, but looks here most extraordinary in this fashion of dress, and the Germans cannot understand it at all. The party of the von Baumbach's was given in honour of the newly appointed General to the Garrison here, and there were numerous officers present. Some of these are intimate with the English, and were highly indignant at the jest. One we know. Baron von Renzl wrote next day to Lieut. von Baumbach and told him that till there was some explanation of this unseemly jest and caricature of a lady, a visitor in the place, —he must decline his acquaintence.

Young von B. wrote back at once to say how sorry he was that he had done this, it was not done proprio motu,[5] but he was pressed to do it —in fact it was, there can be no doubt, his father's doing, and that he felt all along that he was not acting quite right. The thing has made a stir here; the English knowing the Baumbachs, have ceased to visit there, or know them in the street. Curiously enough Capt. and Mrs. Festing are almost the only persons who do not know of the affair. He is an impetuous man, and if he did he would write at once to the General in command about it, and should he not take the matter up, apply to the chargé d'affaires at Darmstadt who acts for Baden as well as Hesse. This might be very unpleasant for

---

[1] **Linda Dietz: English actress. See explanatory endnote 27**
[2] *Deutschesfamilienblatt* **and Mehalah: See explanatory endnote 28**.
[3] Gelehrter: German for 'scholar.'
[4] *Ein Artz der Seele*: novel by Frau von Hillern, translated into English by Sabine as *Ernestine*, published, 1879, by de la Rue. *Further Reminiscences*, p 86
[5] Proprio motu: *by his own will*

the Baumbachs, as the act was not only grossly ungentlemanly but contrary to military discipline.[1]

Hermann, the comedian, was going to recite his verses on the stage in the theatre, but fortunately Herr von Geyling who is one of the committee managing the theatre heard of it, - he is a gentleman, an old noble —and he at once saw Hermann and told him he would fine him 300 marks should he sing his song or make any allusion to the "stick of sealing wax"

1881 1 Jan:
The court at Lew in Nov. brought in £560, of this £300 went at once in annuities and £200 for expenses on property and Lew House. So my receipt amounted to £60. This is an advance on the Court in May, which brought me in £2.10.0. I should not have been able to get through this year at all if Aunt Fanny had not lent me a Thousand pounds at 3 per cent. The whole of some of the flocks have been swept off by disease and in 1879 the harvest was nought. Things were better in 1880 but the losses by the destruction of sheep by rot cannot be repaired in a year. The arrears now amount to £1000 and I shall see none of this. Besides I must lower the rent of Down House and Orchard[2] £20 or £25 each, which will be permanent reduction of income I shall feel as an inconvenience.

1881 2 Jan:
Heard a good story of the father of a Mr. Browne I knew, — old Browne was the parson-squire of Batcombe in Somerset, and he had a neighbour, parson again, Mr. Lear of Compton Abbas.[3] They were old port wine drinking jolly old fellows, and Mr. Browne by his expensive living had brought himself down into straits. One cold winter night old Browne of Batcombe was dining with old Lear of Compton Abbas; after dinner, Browne made ready to depart, and the great yellow family coach was ordered to come round for him. Lear saw him into his greatcoat and mufflers in the hall, and wanted to attend him to the door. "Don't come to the door" said Browne, "You may catch cold, old friend." However Lear insisted, and then went down the steps, in spite of Browne's remonstrances. Then to his surprise he saw Browne ascend the box. "Why, good heavens, man! What makes you go on the box instead of riding inside?" "I like it, I prefer it, and the cold braces me up after a heavy dinner." "But, nonsense, Browne, this will never do! Come down and jump inside at once." Lear opened the chariot door, — and found the carriage full of hay. Browne had run short of hay for his horses at Batcombe, and short of money to purchase any, he had told his coachman to fill the coach with as much hay as he could take from parson Lear's stable. I have met the son of this Browne, he is an old clergyman living at Beckenham, and is a great friend of the dowager Lady Young. The Lears are an old Somersetshire family and, I believe, are still

---

[1] Major Festing and Prince William von Bismarck: For Major Festing's reaction to Prussian insults see *Further Reminiscences*, pp 87-8
[2] Down House and Orchard: Two farms then part of the Lew Trenchard Estate.
[3] Compton Abbas, Dorset.

resident in the county. No relation of the Lears at Salisbury. I heard this story from
Capt. Festing.

1881 **3 Jan:**
My father was a very fine tall man, six feet high exactly, and looking every inch a
soldier. His hair very light and his eyes blue. When courting my mother, he went
by the nickname of 'The Silver Poplar', among her sisters, a capital name which
combines indications of his height and upright carriage, and the almost white
paleness of his hair. I believe also that his complexion was originally very delicate
and fair. He was a very decided man, and had all the Gould obstinacy about him. If
he once said a thing he stuck to it. He was certainly cold in temperament, and
showed little or no warmth of feeling: we respected him, as children, but dreaded
rather than loved him. Indeed when playing, if we thought he was coming, we
would run and hide away. He was a strict disciplinarian, and severe in punishing
us, and many a tremendous beating I have had from him. I know that as a boy, and
even up to the time when I went to college I have sometimes been burning at heart
with a sense of wrong, at some harshness or bitter speech which I had incurred,
because I did not follow in the line he had chalked out for me. His theory was that
all children's minds were blanks and that their character and destinies were fixed
by the education given them, and the impression fixed on them by their parents.[1]

He had made up his mind that I was to go into the army, and Willy into the
Church, and our studies were given that direction. However when I had arrived at
the age when I must enter Woolwich I fell ill and my lungs persisting in a delicate
condition, it was found necessary that I should be taken for a winter or two to the
south of France. I remained thus delicate till I was too old for the army. This was a
great disappointment to my father; and he did not quite know what to make of me.

He was very strong in his religious prejudices, and from the moment I went to
college I was attracted by High Church principles. This angered him greatly and
alienated us from one and other. Then our tastes were wholly uncongenial. He was
fond of mechanics for which I had not a particle of taste, and he disliked and
despised the Arts other than painting, and in this latter, he had little or no sense of
colour, but a strong eye for form. He did not care much for music, and not at all for
any literature except books of travel. The only poet he could endure was Crabbe.[2]
He was, in fact, wholly unimaginative. It was a grievous disappointment to him
when I chose the Church and Willy positively refused to read for Orders, but it was
a great mitigation of his disappointment when Willy took to Engineering as his
profession. My father was a strictly just man, and was the soul of honour; I think as
scrupulously conscientious a man as well could be, of an upright and blameless
life. He had formed a bitter view of men, and regarded all as self seeking, or fools,

---

[1] For Edward Baring-Gould's views on education see *Early Reminiscences* p 104-5
[2] George Crabbe, 1754-1832: A poet of some renown in his day. Described by
Byron as *nature's sternest painter, yet the best*. It was perhaps the realistic
portrayal of rural life that attracted Edward

and was shy, so that he would not go into society. Even when we had parties at Lew, he just showed, and then retired to the library for the rest of the evening. There was no getting him to go out to any of the neighbours. He said it was not worth the waste of time, they could talk of nothing but Board of Guardians or parochial squabbles. If he stayed at home, from a book he could get more in ten minutes than in ten hours among the parsons and squires of the neighbourhood.

1881 **5 Jan:**
~~Heard~~ Have heard a couple of curious ghost stories both at first hand. Our landlady Frau Wucherer, a Swiss lady of family but married here told me that she had visited several times at a parsonage in the Black Forest, staying with the Pfarzer[1] and his wife who were old family friends. The first time she stayed there, she was very uncomfortable in the room that had been given her, for at night she was conscious of someone walking up and down the room sighing and moaning low, and it seemed to her as though the person were a female wringing her hands and pacing in great distress of mind. She did not like to complain of what she had heard though it kept her awake, and after the recurrence next night she made some excuse and cut her visit short. A few years after she revisited the same parsonage and was again put in the same room. The first night she heard precisely the same pacing to and fro, with low moans and sighs, and could not sleep a wink. Next morning she plucked up spirit to mention the circumstances to her hostess, who thereupon gave her another room, downstairs, and she was no more troubled with the noises. Before she left, she heard that the room in which she had been disturbed had been occupied by the sister, or sister-in-law of the preceding pastor, who had long been in great trouble of mind about some family matter, and had destroyed herself. The hostess would not, however, tell her this before she left the house, lest it should excite and disturb her.

The other story I heard from Mrs. Mills, a widow lady living here. She was staying with the Youngs of Puslinch along with her husband, a clergyman; they were both on a first visit to Puslinch.[2] In the night Mrs. Mills woke, and was startled to see a skeleton standing at the foot of the bed. She remained still, hardly breathing, when she felt that her husband was trembling, and holding his breath: —that in fact, he was not asleep. Then she whispered to him, in a low tone "Do you see that figure?" "Yes" he answered, in a low voice, "I have been watching it for some time, and was afraid of your waking and seeing it also."

The deathwatch I know very well is only an insect; but I remember a curious coincidence connected with it. I have very rarely heard it; except before my mother's death. Then, when she was sitting in the hall, it ticked loudly and distinctly. Aunt Kate was there with us, attending to her, and she ordered the fire to be made in the drawing room and her chair to be moved there, to avoid the ominous sound. But next day as we were sitting in the drawing room, the

---

[1] Pfarzer: Of uncertain meaning. Possibly pfarrer, a priest
[2] Puslinch: a manor house near Newton Ferrers, Devon

deathwatch began to tick there, by the fireplace, as it had in the hall. My mother looked round, and said "I know what that means, it is telling me that my minutes are numbered."[1]

The following story I heard from my mother. She was sitting one evening late alone – I think at Culmpit Bratton.[2]—reading her Bible before going to bed, when, on looking up, she distinctly saw her brother Frank standing opposite her, at the other side of the table, in his midshipman's uniform. She looked at him steadily, without the figure fading and then she thought to herself "I know what this means" and having a pencil in her hand, she noted down in her Bible On the flyleaf, the date "_____ saw Frank" It was not for two months that the news reached the family that he had died off Ascension that same night.[3]

He was on board Sir Edward Belcher's vessel; there had been some oversight, or neglect of duty, and Sir Edward, — then Captain Belcher, had punished him by putting him under a hencoop, on deck, under the tropical sun, to subject him to humiliation as well as punishment. Captain Belcher was a brutal man, hated by all the crew, and all who had to do with him. Either the sun, or distress of mind, or both combined, brought on brain fever, and the poor lad died at sea, as near as can be judged, at the very time that my mother saw him.[4]

I was at Lew to my sister's marriage —unfortunate marriage[5] — with T H Marsh, and then I returned to Hurstpierpoint where I was a master at the time. A few days after, something occurred to me and I wanted particularly to communicate with her. I sat up deliberating in my mind what I had better do, I thought that if I wrote home for her address it would cause a delay, as she was on her wedding tour, and I was moreover very doubtful whether my mother knew where exactly they would be. The next day I got a letter from my sister "Do write to me, Dear Sabine, and tell me what you want, or whether you are ill. Last night you came to my bedside, drew the curtain, and said 'Margaret, write, I must say something to you' And now I want to know what you have to say, for the incident has made such an impression upon me, that I cannot shake it off' In the meantime I had made up my mind not to consult her in the matter, and therefore wrote back, that I had nothing to say to her, except that I wished her every happiness.

My father and mother went to Manchester, the year of the Art exhibition there,[6] to be with Willy, then working at Whitworth's.[7] They were not satisfied that he was

---

[1] Marianne (Kate) Bond and the death-watch beetle at her sister, Sophia's death, *Early Reminiscences*, p 314.
[2] Culmpit: The house at Culmpit, Bratton Clovelly is now known as Eversfield
[3] Actual words: *saw Henry, January 3, 1840. Early Reminiscences* p.24
[4] **Admiral Sir Edward Belcher: See explanatory endnote 29.**
[5] **Margaret's unfortunate marriage: See explanatory endnote 30**
[6] The Manchester Art Treasures Exhibition, 1857
[7] **Joseph Whitworth: see explanatory endnote 31.**

among steady young men, and afraid he would be drawn into idleness and folly, and therefore they thought best to go there and make a home for him. While there an urgent letter came from Aunt Emily Baring-Gould to call my father down to Devonshire as his mother was dangerously ill and sinking. My mother urged him to go off at once, but he said he would wait for another letter. That he had received was so urgent, that my mother could not understand his delay. At last he said — and was all the time ashamed of admitting it —that he had dreamed the night before that he was coming out of Lew Church with his mother on his arm, when she said to him "Edward, I must go to the vault". He turned with her towards it, when her hand checked him, on his arm, and she said "No, Edward, not this time, another and later day". This had so impressed him that when the letter came, he was convinced it was a false alarm. And so it proved. Next day brought news that the old lady had rallied, and that immediate apprehensions were passed, I heard him tell this himself: He was a most unimaginative man, and had no patience with stories of the supernatural, and would wax quite wroth when he heard of appearances of Old Madam, or reports of her having been seen. But he was quite convinced that this dream was more than a coincidence. Indeed, had not the impression made on him been very strong, he would at once have started for Teignmouth.

It is curious that it is precisely the most matter of fact, unimaginative persons who "see visions and dream dreams". My Aunt Lavinia Snow was a very stout, amiable old lady, of the most prosaic mind. Indeed, so much so, that I never found a point of contact with it, —whereas I always did with her sisters Juliana and Marianne.[1] One morning she came down to breakfast at Belmont, when my Aunt Fanny and my mother had walked out from Exeter to Breakfast with them, this they often did on bright mornings. When my Aunt Lavinia came in, she said, "My dears, I have had the oddest dream, last night, and marvellously distinct; so that I seemed to see everything transacted before me like real life. I thought I saw the Dawlish coach attacked on Haldon by highwaymen with black handkerchiefs over their faces, and I thought they took the mail and let the coach go on, and they carried off the mails to an old flint and gravel pit and examined them there, and when they had taken what they wanted, they left the bags there". Towards the middle of the day, the news came into Exeter that the Dawlish coach had been robbed, the preceding night, on Haldon, and the mails stolen. It was not until some days later that the mails were found in an old flint pit. I have heard the story both from my mother, and my Aunt Juliana.

There was another occasion, when a robbery was committed in Exeter when Aunt Livy saw it take place in a dream, and, if I am not mistaken, was able to inform the police where the stolen property was secreted. But I do not distinctly remember the circumstances, so will not relate them.

---

[1] Great aunts Lavinia, Juliana and Marianne Snow, sisters of Tom Snow who was the father of Sabine's stepmother, Lavinia

I have heard one or two curious stories from Pengelly.[1] When we were abroad he was once or twice put into the house to keep it aired. He and Susan occupied the library. They have both told me that sometimes, at night, they have heard the wildest racket going on in the drawing room and hall, sometimes as though several persons were pacing up and down there, with the communicating doors open, which were slammed, then as though scuffles were taking place.

He and Susan have listened at the doors leading from the dining room into these rooms to the racket going on within, and have gone round outside and listened to it through the windows; but when they ventured to open the doors, all was silent. He says that one night, it was exactly as though the table was being rolled round the room, and the chairs flung about, and when, after some hesitation, he went in, expecting to find the furniture in some disorder and broken everything was in its place. Here, I have no doubt, the rats were at work and occasioned the noises.

Another of his stories is different in character. When he was a boy he was sent once or twice a year to Exeter with a waggon *[sic]* to bring down groceries for the house. On such occasions he started very early in the morning, about 3 a.m. so as to reach Exeter by evening. One morning he had started, as usual, it was in autumn or early winter, and the stars were bright, and there was just a feeling of frost in the air. He was within the waggon, with his lanthorn, rather drowsy, when just by Coombow *[sic]* the two horses stopped abruptly. He whipped them, and shouted to them to move on, but they would not stir. Then he jumped out, and found them standing with their heads down, snorting, and evidently terrified. He supposed that they saw something lying in the road, and he took his lanthorn from the waggon and began to look. He saw nothing whatever. Puzzled, he lashed the horses again, but they trembled and sweated, and would not stir. He lashed them furiously, and then, all at once, both horses leaped as though to clear some obstruction, and then dashed ahead at a gallop, and then did not stop until they had got some way up the hill beyond Coombow. Then they seemed as exhausted as if they had been driven hard to Okehampton. What frightened them he never could tell. The singular part of the story is both were simultaneously alarmed, and both leaped at the same time. That they saw something, and would not tread on it, Pengelly is convinced, but what that was he is unable to conjecture.[2]

A curious circumstance happened when we were at Dalton. Just outside Topcliffe is the house of a Mr. Tetley, a yeoman, and Baptist preacher; he a very worthy harmless man, of some means, and with a rather nice house. A sort of avenue leads to it. Mrs. Tetley was a very bitter Baptist, a woman with a sharp and rancorous tongue, a nuisance to Mr. Hawkins the Vicar, as she was persistent in her efforts to injure the church, —in every conceivable way, by malignant insinuations, and underhand attacks. If he were trying to get young people together for confirmation, she would get at the girls and by sneers and persuasion induce them to withdraw.

---

[1] William Pengelly: coachman to both Sabine and his father.
[2] Pengelly and the wagon: *Further Reminiscences*, p 26.

This wretched old creature was ill, very ill; and one day Mitchell the doctor drove to the door to make a visit, having his brother and wife in the dog-cart. He left them at the door, and his dog was under the trap, playing with some straw, and jumping after the whip's end, which Charles Mitchell teased him with.

Then Charlie left off playing with the dog and began to talk to his sister in law, and after a while to grumble at his brother Tom staying so long in the house. Suddenly the dog arrested their attention, he was playing with straw, when, instantaneously, he started back from the drive, his hair bristled over his body, he uttered a wild scared howl, and crouched further back into the hedge, with his eyes starting out of his head, then he dashed off at a furious pace, tore once or twice round the house, howling in the same wild unnatural way, and then scowered[1] down the drive as hard as he could race, and was lost to sight, though the howls were still audible. At this moment Mr. Mitchell came out of the house, looking grave, and mounting the trap and taking the reins, said, "It is all over. The old lady has just died." Then he heard about what happened to the dog, and listened to its distant yelps. He drove home at once, got his gun, and went after the dog, a great favourite, and found it at last in a hedge, backing into it and looking like a possessed being rather than a dog —so altered that he would not have known his dog again but for what he had heard. He spoke with it, but the beast only glared and barked at him, without showing a sign of recognition; and he shot it though the head. Then he went home and drove over at once with his wife and brother, and told me what had happened. The three were in a state of liveliest excitement, but he entreated me not to mention the circumstances, lest it should work round to Mr. Tetley's ears and distress him. As Mrs. Mitchell said, the dog seemed, in the midst of its play, suddenly to have seen a horrible sight which drove it mad with terror. And the appearance of the dog, as seen by Mr. Mitchell when he shot it, was of an animal scared out of its senses by some terrible fear. I heard these particulars within one hour of the occurrence, and by the three who saw it.[2]

Now for one more story and that of a different nature; but it is one about which I do not know what to say. Not long after our marriage, Grace startled me by saying she had seen a little green man about ~~a foot~~ 6 inches high sitting in a hedge. She had seen this when she was about ~~twelve~~ ten years old. She was with her brother John at the time, but he was on the other side of the hedge which was thick, and did not see it. They were blackberrying, when, all at once she saw, standing on a leaf or twig, a distinctly formed man in a green suit, with little twinkling eyes, looking at her. She screamed to John, and he broke through the hedge, and came to her, but by this time the little green man was gone. Now, whilst writing this I have questioned Grace again about it, and she adheres to her statement. She is positive she saw it. I suggested a large green grasshopper but she repudiates the notion and

---

[1] This word does not appear in a dictionary. Perhaps Sabine meant 'scowdered' ie 'scorched down the road

[2] A Dog possessed: *Further Reminiscences*, p 25.

persists that it was a little man in green she saw, quite unlike a grasshopper. I give the tale as told to me, and make no comments.[1]

1881 **23 Jan. Sunday:**

Have been much engaged for a fortnight with translating and arranging "Geier Wally" from Frau v. Hillern's play, and have been in correspondence for its production in England. A Miss Dietz is to take the part of Wally, and buy the play. Frau v. Hillern asks, I think an exorbitant sum for the play, £1,500 for the exclusive right to it in England and America. Whatever she gets she will give me a third for my trouble in the matter. I have had to run to and fro between the von Hillern's and here and the telegraph office arranging for Miss Dietz to go to Mannheim or come here when the "Geier Wally" is acted so that she may see the piece with Frau Rosa Keller in it. Miss Dietz was ill and unable to come last week when we had got Frau Keller to come here and take the Geier Wally.

So now I suppose we will have to go to Mannheim to settle the affair. Last week, moreover, we have had a sick house, all the family ill, Barbara and Daisy seriously so, with Bronchitis, the old enemy again. I have also had a bad cold and a cough. However, thank God, all are better now. On Friday night I heard from Miss Dietz and ran off with the letter at once to the von Hillern's. The old judge was in bed, so I had to go into his bedroom and there his wife and daughters and I sat and discussed the terms of the agreement. He had a great white night cap on with white lappets over the ears, and a white tassel at the top of the cone, and as he talked this bobbed first over his forehead, and then flopped back over his neck. Frau v. Hillern was in a blue dressing gown, and I suspect was only very partially dressed. The old man wanted us to have supper in his bedroom, and Frau v. Hillern and I were quite content, but the girls interfered, and we adjourned to the dining room, but not till we had promised to return to the bedroom after supper to conclude the arrangements. The old judge is very rapacious and wants not only £1,500 but one pound per evening for each performance of the "Geier Wally". This will never do, and his wife and daughters agree with me. So I have said nothing about this in the letter.[2]

1881 **24 Jan:**

My dear mother was one of the most charming and sweetest persons imaginable. I can quite remember, as a little fellow, watching her, and thinking "What a lovely mother I have got". She had a wonderfully pure and delicate complexion, dark brown hair, and brown eyes. Her features were finely cut; but what was most striking about her was the sweetness of her expression. She had that marvellously fascinating gift of ready sympathy, and was able at once to put everyone at ease who spoke with her, and enter thoroughly into his interests, so that gentlemen and

---

[1] **Grace and the little green man:** *Early Reminiscences*, **p.19. See also explanatory endnote 51**

[2] **Frau Wilhelmine von Hillern: Explanatory endnote 24. See also Diary 15-26 December 1880 with footnotes.**

ladies alike loved her and delighted in her society. She was also such a perfect lady in feeling, tone and manner, with quiet dignity like a halo round her. She was a very devout woman, and spent much time in prayer, and she had a yearning for love and sympathy which did not meet with much response from my father, who was of a naturally reserved and cold disposition and never allowed his feelings to be seen. My poor dear mother had her failings, she was utterly unpunctual and unsystematic, whereas my father was precise to a moment and orderly to admiration. My mother was always losing her keys, or forgetting to answer a letter till it was past time, and then detaining the postboy and making him miss the post, when my father had letters of importance written six hours before, in the bag to go. I have inherited my mother's want of tidiness.

Then we used to get such interminable pious talks from her. Dear soul, I never got an idea from one of them, they were very good, but very colour and matter less, and all I could do was look up into her sweet angel face, and stroke her delicate hand, and let the pious talk flow over me like a warm stream of water, which soothed and lulled to sleep, but was utterly unstimulating to mind or soul, and did anything rather than brace up the religious sense. The only impression these interminable lectures produced in me was that my mother was goodness, piety, holiness itself. She never said an unkind word of anyone, but had always an excuse for everyone of whom she had heard an evil report.[1]

1881 **12 Feb:**
I received a telegram from Emily to say that her father[2] was very ill and not expected to live, and begging me to return immediately to England. I could not return that day as there is no boat on Sunday across, moreover I must arrange with Fr. v. Hillern about Miss Dietz and the play, as Miss D. is to be in Freiburg during the ensuing week. I saw Fr. v. Hillern same night and told her that I must be away, but left the conduct of the matter wholly in her hands, trusting her to see that our agreement was carried out.

1881 **Sunday 13 Feb:**
Saw Frau v. Hillern again, spent the greater part of the morning with her making final arrangements. She empowered me to assure Miss D. that she would not publish the play if she objected to it. Fr. v. Hillern wished to telegraph to this effect, but I stopped this as I said I should be in town on Monday and could see Miss Dietz and give her this assurance.

1881 **14 Feb:**
Arrived in London at 5.30 having left Freiburg the day before at 4.30 p.m. Miss Dietz and her mother met me at 6, Keppel St.[3] and we had a long interview. I

---

[1] Sabine's mother, Sophia, 1832-1863: *Early Reminiscences* pp 314-317.
[2] Cousin Emily's father, the Rev. Charles Baring-Gould
[3] 6, Keppel Street: Lodgings in London frequently used by Sabine. Off Gower Street and very convenient for the British museum and its library.

ascertained that by law, if the play were published Fr. v. Hillern would lose all her rights to its production on the stage. By slightly altering and adapting the play any director might then appropriate it. I heard also that Mr. Harris[1] the manager of Drury Lane had gone to Gotha to see a new play there. I knew that this was the "Geier Wally" to be performed at Gotha on that same evening. If he liked it he would take French leave with the play, appropriate it, and pay Fr. v. Hillern nothing. I wrote at once to her to warn her against publishing. Miss Dietz' lawyer advised her to quietly wait and let Fr. v. Hillern publish, and then get me to alter and adapt, and send the authoress £100, to take a right as she thought proper. Of course I would not hear of this, so I put Fr. v. Hillern on her guard.

1881 **15 Feb:**
Went down to Lew Trenchard. My uncle died on Saturday 12 February, the day Emily telegraphed. He had caught cold which had brought on an attack of pleurisy and when that was overcome by mustard plasters he had not strength to rally and speedily sank. The dear old man looked like a saintly statue, in his shell, his sweet gentle face rendered beautiful and angelic by the touch of Death.

He was a man in whom many of the gentler Christian graces were very conspicuous. None heard a harsh word from his lips, nor would he judge any man. His caution was carried to an excess, so that it was impossible to obtain from him a decided opinion on any point. If asked for an opinion he stated both sides farely *[sic]* and left the interrogator to make his choice. My father was impetuous and passionate, but my uncle Charles was neither, placid, patient, and never put out. Nothing can have been more beautiful than his tender care and forbearance with Charlie, his eldest son, who has been part paralysed and not quite right in his head for the last fourteen years.
He has cared for him like a child, borne with all the waywardness, and disagreeable habits with really marvellous patience. Now that his father is dead, Charlie has put himself forward as head of the house. That is intolerable, as he has not self control or mind to order anything. I have telegraphed to a doctor at Totnes whom I saw in the summer to arrange that he should be removed next week. His mother cannot bear the nervous strain of having him in the house. He ran after her with his stick raised to strike her today, and since then she has kept her room. He has also threatened Sophie. Aunt Marianne[2] is completely overcome at the prospect of losing him, but sees that it is inevitable.[3]

1881 **16 Feb:**
Dear Lew though in winter garb showing signs of spring. The rooks noisy and busy about their nests. The crocus out in the avenue and in the flower beds. Below the lawn the daffodils swelling and ready to shake out their golden fringes. A day of brilliant beauty, clear sky and sunshine, but an East wind blowing cold from the

---

[1] **Sir Arthur Harris: See explanatory endnote 32.**
[2] Sophie was one of the Rev. Charles' daughters; Marianne his wife
[3] The Rev. Charles Baring-Gould, *Further Reminiscences*, pp 100-1

moor. Alas for the great elm, the largest tree on the property that stood near Lew House by the drive. In the storm last week it was blown down. The trunk sawn through just above the roots is 8 ft in diameter. It was a magnificent tree, one of the noblest elms I have ever seen. It was rotten in the core at the root, and last summer did not leaf as vigorously as of old. Another noble tree that went was a beech just above the quarry at the foot of the little Barn park.[1]

1881 **19 Feb:**
My uncle was buried today at half past twelve. The coffin was of polished oak with handsome brass mountings. It was covered with wreathes and crosses of white flowers. There was a large attendance of the neighbourhood and of farmers and the parish generally. The day was lovely, balmy, and sunny. At his own request he is laid near his daughter Caroline. I had a double grave made, so that Aunt Marianne may lie by him on the other side. My uncle Alexander came to the funeral and my Aunt Emily from Plymouth

1881 **23 Feb:**
Came to Exeter and met with Frank Bond and his bride just returned from Paris where they have been for their honeymoon. She is very well shaped and pleasant looking, but hardly pretty, with an almost Jewish look in her eyes and cast of nose. She is very self confident and perfectly at ease, a nice contented happy person, rather disposed, I suspect to look to be surrounded by comforts and disinclined to rough it. She was a Miss Vivian daughter of -------------. They have had a comfortable time of it in Paris. She happens to know Christine Nilsen the soprano, who has a house in Paris, and Miss Nilsen, most kindly and generously placed it, her carriage and servants at their disposal, saw that they were provided with tickets for whatever they wanted to see, and were lodged and fed luxuriously. And the young couple seem most thoroughly to have enjoyed Paris, and not yet to be tired of each other.

Frank is a very nice fellow. Clever, straightforward, the ideal of a young man, a fellow one cannot see without loving and trusting. When we go to Lew we must manage to get them there, and weave closer cousinly ties. His aunts are proud of him and justly. I hope his wife is worthy of him. He deserves the best of women.

1881 **25 Feb:**
Came to town in hopes of finding Miss Dietz returned from Freiburg and ready with her suggestions for the emendation of the Geier Wally.

1881 **Sunday 27 Feb:**
Miss Dietz arrived this morning.

1881 **28 Feb:**
At work all day on the play. Dined in evening at Dietz's and read the new scenes and recastings, which were approved.

---

[1] Little Barn Park: The location of this field is not now known locally.

1881 **1 March:**

Finished the play. Took it to Miss Dietz and dined at her house. Met Mr. Bailey the stage manager, a Devonshire man, a very nice bright, gentlemanly fellow. Miss D., her mother, Mrs. Hallock,[1] and Mr. Bailey are charmed with Freiburg, but hope they may never have any more dealings with Fr. v. Hillern who haggled with them, in Mr. Bailey's words, "like a Billingsgate fishwoman," and seemed lost to all sense of decency and justice in the rapacity of her demands. She tried to get Miss D. to undertake that the right to the play should lapse back to the authoress in the event of her death, and certainly at the end of ten years. Finally she screwed £1,250 out of Miss D., and threw me wholly overboard —made no stipulations for me at all, and left me to receive whatever Miss D. liked to give me. Miss Dietz proposes to give me £250. Of that £100 down and the rest in instalments as money comes in; but she expects that Fr. v. Hillern, on her side will give me £250 so as to make the £500 covenanted between us. Miss D. did not conceal from me however that Fr. v. Hillern demurred to this wholly and spoke of keeping the entire sum to herself. I thereupon wrote Fr. v. H. a cool and somewhat cutting letter on the subject. Her conduct is scurvy to the last degree, if she be really determined to give me nothing

1881 **4 Mch:**

This is my case. Immediately after the 1st performances of the "Geier Wally" in the theatre at Freiburg on Jan. 4th and 5th I called on Frau v. Hillern, and told her that I was ready to obtain the production of the play in England, that I knew of a person who, I believe, was the only actress in England capable of doing justice to the leading part, and who, I had no doubt would be ready to come to an arrangement for the purchase of the play. On Jan. 5th I wrote to Miss Dietz about the play and gave her an idea of it, to sound her in the matter.

Frau von Hillern on Jan. 6th told me that if I would make this arrangement for her, she would give me half the sum she received. She made this offer because I had translated her "Arzt der Seele" and published it, and had, on 13 Dec. 1880 placed in her hands half of my profits though I was not bound to give her anything, ten years having elapsed since the German publication. Frau v. Hillern accordingly offered me the same terms that I had given her. But these I declined as unfair to the authoress, and told her I should be perfectly content with one third of the sum realised by the sale of "Geier Wally". On Jan. 9th I dined with Fr. v. Hillern and this arrangement was finally agreed on between us.

On Jan 16 I wrote to Miss Dietz "For the first time today I have had a plain discussion of terms with Frau v. Hillern, after reading your letter to her, and this is what she says:— She has no wish to sell the right for a sum down; if she does it will be for a high sum. She gets 10% of the take in all German theatres that makes her £15 to £20 per night. She thinks that an arrangement had better be come to direct with her and she will arrange with me, I will take1/3; she offers me 1/2, but I am ready to take 1/3." To this Miss Dietz answered that she would rather pay a

---

[1] Mrs Hallock: The accuracy of the transcription of this name is dubious

sum down, but would like to know what the "high sum" asked would be. On Jan 22nd I wrote a letter to Miss Dietz in Fr. v. Hillern's room, at her dictation, and on her paper with coronet and monogram. "Frau von Hillern has sent for me this morning and has come to this decision: —She is ready to give you the entire and exclusive right to "Eagle Wally", for representation in England and America for the sum of £1,500; (one third of which comes to me) paid down at once."

Miss Dietz wrote again making some demur to paying so large a sum down, but agreeing to the main terms. On Sat. 29 Jan. I wrote in Fr. v. Hillern's room at her dictation. "Fr. v. Hillern says – and this is her final decision. 1. You shall have the play for a sum of £1,500 of which £750 is to be paid down at once, and the other half seven hundred and fifty, on 1st June next. 2. If you agree to this, please at once get an agreement drawn out to this effect – a three cornered agreement, that of this sum the authoress shall have 2/3rd and I 1/3rd, and that for this sum you will have absolute right to the play in England and America to keep or dispose of (i.e. the English edition)." To this letter Fr. v. Hillern appended a postscript in her own hand. "Hoping that it will not be long before you come to the agreement proposed by me – which I have done my utmost to meet you."

Miss Dietz letter of Jan. 27th was "It is certainly true that Frau v. Hillern's terms for "Eagle Wally" are very high, but, as she says, when everything is considered, they are not perhaps excessive. I am at all events prepared to accept them subject to certain details the nature of which it will be impossible for me to explain fully or satisfactorily in writing. I did not expect Fifteen hundred pounds is a very large sum to be paid down at once and I know very few actresses or managers who would not be greatly troubled to do it.

It is of course at a considerable sacrifice that I manage at all to buy a play, and I did not expect to have to realize so large a sum all at once. I am determined to strain every point however, and trust Frau v. Hillern will not be unmerciful in the matter. Do you not think that she might be persuaded to take a third of the whole amount and give me a little time to realize the rest. I am <u>sure</u> to have it only it will be <u>very</u> inconvenient to find at once, and would probably cost more of a sacrifice than I have any right to make, as I am obliged to consider my people as well as myself. I am willing to pay at the least five hundred pound down with the promise to pay the rest within a stated time, or to forfeit the first payment and all rights to the play."

On receipt of this I again went to Fr. v. Hillern but could obtain from her no further concession than this: —I wrote on the paper with the coronet and monogram in her room, "I have carried your letter directly on receiving it to Frau v. Hillern and she has given me her terms – not for America, but for England. She says that she will dispose to you of the sole right to the play the "Eagle Wally" for £750 for the first 100 representations, the sum to be paid before hand, after that, each representation is to be paid for by a royalty of £5. Of this arrangement one third is to come to me as translator etc. With regard to America a fresh arrangement will have to be made. I write this in haste to catch the post, as you want an immediate answer, and I write now from Frau v. Hillern's house, on her and Herr v. Hillern's dictation of terms."

To this Frau v. Hillern added a postscript and signed it containing merely an expression of compliment and pleasure at her play falling into good hands.

On Feb 12. I received a telegram from England recalling me to my uncle's deathbed. I at once went to Frau v. Hillern and told her I must return to England. Miss Dietz was to come to Freiburg the following week to conclude the contract. I should therefore be away, and I must leave the matter with Fr. v. Hillern to arrange according to our verbal contract. Fr. v. Hillern had in the meantime taken steps to register her play at Stationer's Hall. I saw Fr. v. Hillern again on Sunday morning Feb. 13 and told her that I was forced by circumstances to leave my interests in her hands. I then left Freiburg on same afternoon. On evening of Feb. 14th I met Miss Dietz and her mother Mrs. Hallock *[?]* and I learnt from them that in the event of the play being published, Fr. v Hillern would lose all her rights over it. The lawyer proposed to allow her to publish and then give her £100 which would be ample payment, and Miss Dietz could then arrange with me for an English version. I immediately wrote to Frau v. Hillern on no account to publish, and warned her of the consequences. On my return to London from Lew on Feb. 28th I called on Miss Dietz and learned to my surprise that Frau v. Hillern had demanded and obtained from her £1,250, and when Miss Dietz said that of this, of course, £250 would go to me, Frau v. Hillern had shown a determination to repudiate her agreement. Miss Dietz was ready to pay me £250 for the work I did for her, but she supposed as a matter of course that Frau v. Hillern would pay me the other £250

1881 **18 Mch:** Fr.
v. Hillern has made no movement so far. I met her in the Kaiserstrasse outside her house going out with the judge for an airing as he is ill. She turned a dead white and then came up to me and held out her hand. I received it coldly and then she began to talk very fast and said that she was not satisfied with having signed the agreement in my absence, for had I been there, — she is convinced I might have made better terms for <u>her</u>!!! and much to the effect that she had not got as much out of Miss Dietz as she might, then when I began to allude to my own demands she flew off saying that she could not leave her sick husband, but hoped we would be friends again. I have therefore written to her a plain statement of the facts and of my demand. We shall see how she will act. But I much doubt her paying me anything unless being forced to do so. She hopes to smother me with words and professions of friendship.

1881 **19 Mch:**
Received £35 from Smith and Elder. They paid me originally £50 for the copyright. They have sold right of reproduction by Tauchnitz for £15, of translation into French and German for £10 each. I believe that they had a right to keep these sums, but they waived it and passed the money over to me. The sale of Mehalah has not been good and the publishers say they have lost £50 by it, but hope to recover somewhat by 'The Railway' cheap edition and by sales in the colonies.

I have heard today from Schorer, publisher of 'Deutsches Familien Blatt' who is publishing the translation of Mehalah. The story is exciting interest and attracting attention in Germany.[1] I propose writing a Schwartzwald story, and Schorer purports coming to Freiburg in April to see me about it. I have also had an offer from Skeffington's for two vols. of sermons for which he will pay £100. I have likewise to write a sort of physical geography of Germany for the series edited by Mr Pullen for which I am to receive something like £35

1881 **22 Mch:**
Really Fr. v. Hillern is a very clever woman. I find that she has been to a Jew lawyer with my letter to ascertain from him whether it is not possible for her to bring an action against me for some expressions in it. It appears that by German law a private letter or private conversation may give rise to an action if one party in it thinks that something the other party has written or said reflects on his honour. The rich thing in the case is that Fr. v. Hillern is quite unscrupulous about acting dishonourably but most touchy about the hint that such a course if pushed by her is not straightforward and honourable. The lawyer has assured her that she can bring an action against me. Of course all she wants is to open up side issues to divert attention from the main issue; and she is desirous, if possible, of driving me from the place.

The point that she and her lawyer have hit upon is a side issue not affecting the main quarrel. It is in a postscript to my letter. In that I said that Messrs. Longmans were very angry about her conduct to them in the matter of Lady Wallace's translation of the "Geier Wally" in having accepted something from them, and simultaneously disposing of the story translated by Mrs. Bell to Touchnitz.[2] Longmans refused indignantly to take my translation of "Ein Arzt der Seele" because Fr. v. H. had behaved so badly to him in the matter of "Elsa and her Vulture". Fr. v. H. told me herself that she had received £25 from Lady Wallace, this came immediately from Longmans who thought Fr. v. H. had received their money for "Elsa and the Vulture." She had no right to dispose of the story to "Tauchnitz" and thereby spoil the sale of Elsa. Now because I mentioned this, and spoke of Fr. v. H. "having received something" from Longmans, she has me, as she received nothing <u>directly</u> from Longmans, only mediately through Lady Wallace. She has fastened on this quibble and is consulting with her lawyer to bring me into court for having in my private letter to her charged her with having received something from Longmans. This is very clever but infinitely disgraceful. Captain Malcolm has seen her and I think remonstrated with her, and the whole town is ringing with her conduct towards me, and I will not be surprised if for very shame she be brought to come to some terms with me.

---

[1] **Deutschesfamilienblatt and *Mehalah*: see explanatory endnote 28**
[2] Mrs Bell's translation of *Geier Wally* was published as *The Vulture Maiden* by Touchnitz in 1876

1881 **24 Mch:**

Heard the story of the life of Thoma the artist,[1] now living at Frankfurt but selling
his pictures in London as well as in Germany. He comes of a peasant family in
Bernau in the Black forest. His father died when he was young; but he had an
uncle, a maker of wooden spoons, a peasant with a strong musical turn. This man
made himself a violin and learned to play it. He strung five strings along the side
wall of his room, and as he composed a melody hung his spoons on the threads, to
represent notes, and played from them. He was wont in summer to take the young
people into the woods and tell them stories by the hour. A man of singular
intelligence and poetry and love of culture, he laboured to draw out the nobler and
aesthetic instincts in the souls of the peasant lads of his village. Thoma from early
boyhood longed to be a painter, without knowing exactly how to begin. His mother
told him she had a kinsman of Basel who was a painter, and she sent the lad to
him. But this man was a common housepainter, and whitewasher. Thoma was
employed in colouring the feet of stoves, he worked away for some weeks and then
said to his kinsman, "This is not quite the sort of painter I wanted to be." "Ah,"
said the house dauber, "It is the only sort you are likely to be, but if this is not to
your style, go to a decorator of clock fronts." So Thoma was apprenticed to a clock
face painter and there worked till he had saved a little money and attracted the
attention of a gentleman who helped him to study at Munich. There he fell in love
with a poor Italian workgirl with a very lovely face. He got his mother and sister to
receive her at Bernau and teach her to read and write, and he went on with his
studies. Then after two years he married the girl and got a few orders and painted
for his livelihood. He lived in an attic at Sechingen[2] for some time. Prosperity
came, and he took his mother and sister to live with him and now they all live
together at Frankfurt a/m. The sister though only a peasantess by birth and bringing
up writes letters and speaks as a woman of culture. The whole family live together
in the warmest attachment. I forgot to add to my account of the uncle that when his
wife scolded, he took his fiddle and played – like David before Saul – till the evil
spirit went out of her.

1881 **30 Mch:**

I heard a good story the other day. The Cayleys (a Lincolnshire family) were
giving a Christmas party last winter, and the children were to perform charades. By
special request, the children were to be allowed to invent and organise the charades
and carry them out unassisted by their elders. On the evening of the soirée all was
ready, and parents and guests equally in the dark as to the word that was to be
submitted to them for discovery, and the mode in which the component syllables
were to be dramatically represented. The bell rang, and the curtain rose. The scene
represented a church door. A young officer had just been married and he issued
from the sacred edifice with his bride, and her bridesmaids and his friends. At that
moment a telegram is brought him. War has been declared with Russia. The
officer's regiment is ordered to Kabul, he is required to present himself

---

[1] **Hans Thoma: see explanatory endnote 33**
[2] Sechingen: now known as Bad Säckingen

immediately at Portsmouth and take ship. The bride weeps and prays him to stay over the week. No, duty before all. He clasps her to his heart and tears himself away, without ever waiting for the wedding breakfast. Curtain falls as he dashes off exclaiming "duty calls" and the bride faints.

Second scene: —a room, at the back a green curtain. In the room sowing *[sic]* is the bride, now a wife of ten years standing. She laments her condition. Ten years ago; from the church door her bridegroom was torn from her to go India, and he has not returned — she has not seen his dear face since that day. Suddenly in dashes a splendid soldier, a General officer, his breast glittering with decorations. My own! I see you again! A cry and a rapturous embrace. Then an explanation. Says he, "My, darling, ten years have elapsed since you became mine, and we parted at the foot of the altar, never to see each other again until today. But, my dearest, Duty called and I obeyed, in those ten years I have won glory and I have earned these stars and orders. I have not been idle." "Nor I," answered the bride, "ten years have elapsed since our interrupted union, I also have done my duty, I have not been idle." Instantly the green curtains at the back fall away right and left, and disclose a nursery where are ranged ten cribs of varying size in which lie ten babies. Tableau: pride in the mother — admiration in the General officer — consternation in the general audience.

1881 31 Mch:
I find in looking over my papers that I have the draft of agreement between Fr. v. Hillern, Miss Dietz and myself, drawn up by Herr v. Hillern himself in his own handwriting, stating the agreement to be that Fr. v. Hillern is to receive £1,000 and I £500. This is dated Feb. 1st. and as she never hinted to me that she wished to go back from the bargain with me when I went to town, it seems clear that she is bound in honour to fulfil it.

1881 1 April:
I am very much like a buoy. Every wave goes over me, and yet I am never completely submerged. The condition is not a happy one, but there are others that are worse. I have an offer from Skeffington of £100 if I will write for him two vols. of village sermon sketches and one vol. of sermons for Saints' days. Also the offer from Samson Lowe of £-- for a volume on Germany – its physical geography. I am in treaty also with Schorer the publisher, Berlin for a German novel of the Black Forest, I will write it simultaneously of Dartmoor, for the English reader and of the Pyrenees for France.

1881 2 April:
I have made several purchases of china since I came here. A turin *[sic]* of Strasbourg faience, very beautifully painted with flowers, carnations, poppies and roses price 32/-. Unfortunately the legs are knocked off. The owner had one foot broken so he knocked off the other three to make it sit easily on the table. A pretty Strassburg faience covered vessel for pâté de foix gras painted with roses etc 6/-. Half a doz. common rudely painted Strasb. Plate 1/- each. A beautifully painted milk jug with cover sign ---------, —I presume Philip Hänurg *[?]* 20/-, and covered butter dish of Dresden marked *[small sketch of crossed swords]* in blue 20/-, a

Höchst cup and saucer painted with tulips etc. 4/-; two cups of Ludwigsburg china *[small sketch of crown etc mark]* with roses and forget me nots 10/- the pair. Fourteen plates beautifully painted with flowers, also Ludwigsburg 44/-, Three cups of Wedgeley *[?]* Berlin porcelain painted red house and trees; one doz. Worcester or Bow cup and saucers painted landscapes in blue, beehive and cottages, touched up by hand, 10/-. A Frankenthaler oval dish ribbed with flowery blue pattern, (Carl Theodore) 6/-, a ………… a Vienna porcelain cup and saucer with flowers 6/-, a set of Berlin coffee pot, sugar basin, milk jug and 4 cups and saucers very pretty painted with flowers all different, —of this century 15/, a creamy porcelain inkstand with bear fiddling on it seated between the ink pots 12/-.

1881 **4 April:**
Baron Bramwell's temper is not of the most amiable. With some difficulty his party got him to consent to a trip in the summer to the Alps. When in Switzerland he was most disagreeable. Nothing pleased him. He wanted his English comforts, and because he could not get them spoiled the enjoyment of his companions by incessant grumbling. At last the party arrived at a nice little inn situated on a high pasture, where in addition to beautiful scenery, pure air, and good cuisine, the baron found cleanliness and comfort. Almost for the first time his face relaxed and his temper cooled. He was pleased with his room. "Generally," he said, "there is no soap in the dish and no dish for the tooth brush. You pull out your hoarded soap and find it stuck all over with paper in which it was wrapped when wet; and then, in the morning, you have your tooth brush which has lain all night by the soap, tasting of it abominably. There is never a watch pocket, and you wake in the night with your timepiece, which you put under your pillow, lodged in the small of your back. Here, I am thankful to say, in my bedroom I discovered both soap and tooth brush; decent sized basins — not soup dishes, jugs not half pint bottles, — and a watch pocket above my bed. The Baron remained in an amiable mood all evening and the party he was with began to consider whether it might not be wise to make this little snuggery their headquarters. Next morning they met for breakfast and only awaited the Baron in hopes of seeing him genial as last night, and then to fall to at the bread and sweet butter and honey. Presently they heard a heavy step plunging down the stairs, the door burst open and Bramwell appeared with a face purple with passion, holding forth his gold repeater, and stammering with rage. "What do you think has taken place? Damn the place! There has been my precious repeater sopping all night in a bloody Holy water stoup above my bed — I took for a watch pocket and utterly spoiled. Damn it all!"[1]

Sir Henry Jackson recently appointed puisne Judge,[2] died — I think four days after. I have heard an anecdote about him. Lawrence the chaplain here met lady Jackson at dinner not long ago, — she said to him, "There is my daughter yonder,

---

[1] **Baron Bramwell's temper and Sabine's honeymoon tour: see explanatory endnote 34**
[2] Puisne judge: a junior judge.

there is my son — they are the only comforts I have in life— yonder is my
husband."

1881 **5 April:**
Lord Beckensfield *[sic]* is very ill. Evidently breaking up. I have heard a story of
Lady Beckensfield his wife. She always drove to the House with him when he was
Conservative leader in the House of Commons. One evening when some important
debate was coming on, in which he had to speak, she was with him in the carriage
as usual, when the footman in slamming the carriage door crushed her thumb. The
brave woman did not utter a cry or give the slightest hint of an accident for fear of
discomposing him and disturbing the train of his thoughts, she let him step out at
the House, and then —but not till then —fainted away, and the footman who had
let out Mr. Disraeli saw by then as he closed the door that she had swooned.

1881 **6 April:**
Frau Schorer wife of the proprietor of the Familien Blatt has been here to see me
about writing a novel for that magazine. It appears that a man in Berlin bought the
right to translate "Mehalah" of Smith and Elder, for £10, and sold the right to Herr
Schorer for 800 marks or £40, so that he pocketed £30 by the transaction. Schorer
has to pay extra for the translating. So we poor authors get the profits of our brain
work taken from us.

1881 **14 April:**
At last Frau v. Hillern shows signs of coming to terms, she has written to say that
she and Herr v. Hillern have placed the matter in the hands of their lawyer, Dr.
Noeff, — and she will be wholly and unreservedly guided by what he advises,
when he has heard both sides. Dr. Noeff is a keen old Jew who has acted for her
throughout. Today according to appointment I went to this lawyer, taking with me
Rev. N Lawrence as my witness to what passed, and stated the case, and my
demand for £250, i.e. 1/6 of £1250[1] the sum paid by Miss Dietz to Fr. v. Hillern, or
to be paid. I showed the lawyer the papers I had, and he urged me to reduce my
claim, but this I declined to do.

I then told him it was my intention to obtain an injunction against Miss Dietz
restraining her from paying the £750 still due to Fr. v. Hillern till the matter was
settled between me and Fr. v. Hillern in an English Court, and I told him that as Fr.
v. Hillern's agreement was not stamped its use for evidence in an English Court
was weakened, and she would have to pay a fine to stamp it before she could use
it.
The Jew was utterly staggered by my threat — and promised at once to
communicate with his clients. I am to be at his office again on Monday 18th when
there decision will be given.

---

[1] Sabine was no mathematician: £250 is 1/5th of £1250, not 1/6th!

1881 **18 April:** Been to Noeff's with Mr. Lawrence and had a long discussion. After much haggling I consented to resign £50 and reduce my claim to £200 i.e. 1/5 of £1,000 and I threatened that unless Fr. v. Hillern consented within six hours I would write to my lawyers in town to issue the injunction. Within a few hours I got a letter from him to say that Herr and Fr. v. Hillern consented, and to appoint me to meet her at his office on the ensuing Saturday to sign the agreement.

Here, pasted onto an unlined page of the diary left empty in the middle of the entry for 23 April 81, are two newspaper cuttings out of context and of later date. Both were annotated by Sabine:

1. From "The Times" of Aug. 26, 1881:

MEHALAH
      "Mehalah; A Story of the Salt-Marshes." Smith, Elder, and Co. 1880
"Mehalah" is a powerful but unpleasant story.
In wild conception, repulsive characters, and disagreeable incidents, it reminds us much of "Wuthering Heights;" but the dénouement, unlike Emily Brontë's remarkable novel, is strangely melancholic and tragic. It takes us back to end of last century, and the scenes are laid in the lonely salt-marshes on the Essex coast, between the mouth of the Colne and the Blackwater. The lawless manners of a rude amphibious population in a country rarely visited by strangers, no doubt gives the novelist's fancy considerable licence. Nor are we inclined to question that the general picture of the society in those parts and times may be as true as they are graphic.

There is humour, too, as well as sensation and pathos, in the descriptions of pauperised curates filling the places of rectors frightened away by fevers and agues, terrorized by their savage parishioners, and conniving at the practice of the smugglers; of farmers brutal in their manners, ignorant of religion, and reckless of morality; of farming men and fishermen still lower, if possible, in the scale of humanity; of unsexed women and all the rest of it. But even if we realize the possibilities in such a state of things, Elijah Rebow, who stands out most prominently through the pages, must be over-coloured and caricatured, unless we admit that truth is far stranger than fiction. Yet there is dramatic force in the conception of his truculent character, as there is hardly originality in the manner of his love-making. With all the tenacity of his iron will, he has set his heart on marrying Mehalah. In her savage beauty she has little of the softness of her sex, yet her strong character is dominated by his, and ultimately she almost turns to wax in his hands. He woos her by a succession of crimes, some of which are base and others atrocious. He cynically avows and exaggerates them to her. He hardly shows a single redeeming quality, save that faculty of concentrated devotion, which even survives her blinding him with vitriol in an outbreak of fury. Yet, monster as he is, the author succeeds so far in interesting us in him that, although the conventionalities of novel-writing must have been outraged, we consider that the end of the tale would have been more artistic had he been suffered to unite himself in peace to the girl he had sinned for, in place of involving her with himself in a terrible catastrophe.

2. By Algernon C Swinburne in the Athenaeum June 16, 1883:
A recent work of singular and admirable power, in which the freshness of humour is as real and vital as the fervour of passion, was at once on its appearance compared with Emily Brontë's now famous story. And certainly not without good cause; for in point of local colour 'Mehalah' is, as far as I know, the one other book which can compare and may challenge the comparison. Its pages, for one thing, reflect the sterile glitter and desolate fascination of the salt marshes, their minute splendours and barren beauties and multitudinous monotony of measureless expanse, with the same distinctive and unlaborious accuracy which brings all the moorland before us in a breath when we open any chapter of 'Wuthering Heights.' And the humour is even better; and the passion is not less genuine. But the accumulated horrors of the close, however possible in fact, are wanting in one quality which justifies and ennobles all admissible horror in fiction: they hardly seem inevitable; they lack the impression of logical and moral certitude. All the realism in the world will not suffice to convey this impression; and the work of art which wants it wants the one final and irreplaceable requisite of inner harmony. Now in 'Wuthering Heights' this one thing needful is as perfectly and triumphantly attained as in 'King Lear' or 'The Duchess of Malfi,' in 'The Bride of Lammermoor' or 'Notre Dame de Paris.'

1881 **23 April:**
Been to Noeff's and had another example of Fr. v. Hillern's duplicity and falsehood. She had had the agreement drawn out in duplicate and presented them to me to sign, according to our agreement made on the 18th; on reading them over, I found that she had reduced my demand to 1/5 of £750 the sum still due to her, hoping no doubt that this would escape my observation and gain for her another £50 reducing my claim in all to £100.[1] I was very indignant, so was Mr. Lawrence, who had heard the agreement made, and like me, saw in this another bit of duplicity. I was so angry and so disgusted that I signed the agreements, at the same time telling Fr. v. Hillern that I did so only to be wholly quit of all further transactions with her, as I felt I could no longer deal in any way with a person who so little understood what we regard in England as straightforwardness in transacting business. To my mind this final stroke was the most despicable of all. I find from English long resident in Germany, and intermarried with Germans, that Germans never trust one another in money transactions, and that no discredit attaches to the sharpest practice which would be regarded as utterly dishonourable in England.

What makes the matter worse in Fr. v. H's case is that we invited her daughters to visit us in England in 1879, and they spent between two and three months with us. We took them to town and showed them all the sights of London, and were

---

[1] Sabine's bad mathematics again: 1/5th of £750 is £150 not £100!

exceedingly kind to them. I went to Brussels to meet the girls and bring them to
Mersea, and took them back as far as Calais. They not only put us to considerable
expense, but also were an intolerable nuisance to us, from their rude and noisy
behaviour whilst with us. I shall never forget my dismay at a dinner party when
Miss v. Hillern, aged, I suppose, 20, after saying that she excelled neither in music,
nor in painting, nor in French, nor in English, added, "There is only one thing I can
do perfectly – I can hoot like an owl!" Then putting her hands together before her
mouth, she produced the loud and deafening hoots which boys make in the woods
to call one another —making the room ring with the noise —I think she repeated
again and again, till I, in an agony of shame touched her and implored her to desist.

On another occasion, when dining out, she took a great piece of meat on her fork,
and flung it <u>across</u> the table to a dog, to see if it would catch at that distance. The
villagers told our nurse, a German girl, that they knew these were not ladies, but
only shop girls, from their manners. They were not very perfect with their English
—and were rather fond of telling people what they did in Freiburg when they were
"on the streets" (auf der Strasse), till Grace warned them to use a different
preposition.

1881 **1 May:**
Made the acquaintance here of a Countess Kearney and her daughter, the
"Countess" Alice. The English here have kept aloof from them in suspicion from
their bearing the title. However in Walford's "Landed Gentry" I see "Kearney,
Robert Cecil (Count) of Ballivilla, Mayo; son of R. Kearney of Ballivilla by
Isabella dau. of Wm. Percival, C.B. Granddau. of I Kelly Esq. Of Liskelly
Galway: mar. Alice Florence dau. of Sir Wm. Palmer, Bart. *[of]* Kenmare and has
issue, Countess Alice; Count K. is Capt. 97th Regt. Residence is in Ballivilla,
Rome and Brighton." She is a very nice agreeable person and the daughter a bright,
pleasant, sensible girl. It is certainly odd that "Count" Kearney does not appear but
he is said to be in Ireland or England, during the present difficulties, trying to get
in his rents, and settle something with his tenants.

Have met some von Zieglers. Herr v. Z. is private secretary to the King of Bavaria,
and a queer time he has had of it with the crazy King. Often the King and he are
the sole audience to an opera, for the King has a horror of being seen, and insists of
an empty house when he attends. He does not show by day, and at night does all
that has to be done, convokes his ministers at 3 a.m., and transacts affairs of State
with them through Herr v. Ziegler, he in one room, the cabinet sitting in another.
One winter day he suddenly said to his secretary "Your wife and daughter would
like to walk in the palace garden. Let them come and walk there for one hour
tomorrow afternoon. I will have the snow shovelled away for them." Accordingly
next all forenoon men were employed digging out paths, through the snow to allow
of the two ladies to walk in the garden. They appeared and solemnly promenaded
between banks of snow three feet high, and after an hour retired. The King sent

them each a bouquet of flowers from the conservatory on the conclusion of their walk.[1]

Some years ago he made one attempt to get married but that failed ignominiously. He was in his box at the opera—he did appear in public then, when he observed a young lady —a cousin the Princess --------, in another box. He sent for her to come into his Royal box, and when she came, asked he if she would like to be Queen of Bavaria. Then he rose and announced to the theatre that he could present to the public their future Queen. However, the Princess did not bear an unsullied reputation, and it was contrived rapidly to marry her off to -------. Since then the King has not made another essay in love. When I was at Partenkirchen, I was told he spent all day in a cave of his hunting lodge near there, and only issued from it at night, when he rambled over the mountains accompanied only by his Jäger.[2] Although he goes to the neighbourhood of Partenkirchen, every summer, the inhabitants of the place have never seen him.

1881 **5 May:**
Kate Bond arrived via Brussels, where she had witnessed the fetes preceding the departure of the young Princess to be married to the Crown Prince Rudolf of Austria. Unfortunately K.B. arrived amidst clouds and drizzle, and did not receive a pleasant first impression of Freiburg.

1881 **7 May:**
Had a very pleasant excursion to the Kaiserstuhl, the Lawrences, Festing, Mills and other parties with us. We dined at Ihringen and filled the little room of the largest inn. Afterwards scattered in the woods picking lilies of the valley.[3]

1881 **12 May:**
Drove to S. Peters. Started in lovely weather, but by the time we reached the ascent, the clouds gathered and covered the sky. On reaching S. Peters snow came on, and we dined whilst it was falling. The weather cleared for our return by the beautiful Glotter Thal.

1881 **13 May:**
Drove to the Carthause and walked to S. Odilien and back through the woods. A lovely day and an exquisite walk.

1881 **14 May:**
Received the Diocesan surveyor's report and valuation of dilapidations at East Mersea, total estimate £263. Very moderate. I received for dilapidations £90 in

---

[1]Friedrich von Ziegler: Close friend to King Ludwig II and State Secretary of Bavaria
[2] Jäger: German for *huntsman*
[3] Excursion to the Kaiserstuhl; see map 1.

1861, *[sic]* but that included two cottages since pulled down, and that was just before the new act came into force.

1881 16 May:

Started with Grace, Kate Bond, and Mrs. Mills for a ramble in the Black Forest. A lovely day at starting, it held up till after we had entered the Höllen Thal, we dined at the Stern, and then the rain came down. However we pressed on, and we drove in closed carriage till we reached the Titisee, when the rain ceased. We baited at the Schluchsee, and there the sun came out. Prince Fürstenburg passed us, a fine looking man. It is always noticeable when we are in his domains as the woods are so well cared for, whereas the Crown domain woods and those of the commoners are in a condition of ragged neglect; arrived about 9.30 at Höchenschwand. I caught a heavy cold with the change of temperature spoiling my enjoyment.

1881 17 May:

Feverish and heavy with cold. Drove in rain to S. Blasien. The church in process of repair after the disastrous fire of 1867. Sun came out and we had a lovely drive down the Alb Thal. Dined at Alb-brüch. Returned another way to Höchenschwand.

1881 18 May:

Cold still very heavy on me. Saw the Alps with the sun on them as it rose, not the complete panorama, but the Jung Frau, Mönch, Eiger and Finsteraarhorn, and Titlis. Returned to Freiburg by Todnau and the mouth of the Wilhelm's Thal. Lovely view up this by evening light. Dined at Todnau where a new church, a miracle of hideousness is in the process of construction. Baited at Oberreid, saw the huge crucifix with human hair on the figure in the church. An old woman told us it grew and had occasionally to be cut, but that the hair of the beard does not grow. I shall use this Crucifix for my story in process of excogitation for the Familien Blatt.[1]

Daisy again ill with bronchitis, incessant cough.
The Countess Kearney gives me the following receipt for cough mixture given her by a famous doctor at Nice. Of chloroform Σ ii, syrup morphin ...., syrup Codeine, (?) *[Sabine's question mark]* Mucilag. gum arab. Aq. Lauro arab. Σ iii. Must take and sup occasionally, ...*[?]* 18 a 80. Pantaleoni, Nice.[2]

1881 Whitsunday 5 June:

Have been about for eleven days with Aunt Kate Bond. She was very desirous to see something of Tyrol, and unable to see it by herself as she speaks no German, so I undertook to accompany her. We went to Laufenburg and stayed at our old quarters at "der Krone". The old landlord and his daughter were delighted to see

---

[1] Black Forest and Freiburg excursions 12 to 18 May 1881: see map 1
[2] **Cough mixture: Explanatory endnote 35**

me again and hear about the children. Next day Ascension Day I went to the little church of Laufenburg (Baden side) and heard mass. In the afternoon we went on to Winterthur and were woefully disappointed to find a vulgar modern manufacturing town. On Friday to Romanshorn and crossed the lake of Constance to Lindau and thence by rail to Kempten, where we put up at the Post, dirty and expensive. Saturday by post coach in pouring rain to Füssen. Spent Sunday there in heavy rain. Rather amused in the train between Laufenburg and Waldshut, a young newly married pair got in and began endearments, pressing each other's hands, and as we passed through a tunnel, kissing. This was so shocking to Aunt Kate that she opened her parasol and held it (in the carriage) between her and the tender couple to screen the endearments from her chaste, old-maidish eye. Very harmless spooning it was though.

On Monday from Füssen to Reutte in the Lech Thal. Tuesday walked to the Plan See and Stuiben waterfall and, in the afternoon drove to Lermoos, where slept "Drei Mohren". A lovely day. Next day walked to Nassereith. There saw opposite the "Post Inn" a charming renaissance carved window, and hearing that at Imst is a good woodcarver I sought him out and told him to form an estimate of cost of copying it exactly for me. The man is clever and has an artistic eye full of enthusiasm and intelligence, his name "Johann Nessarich Grissemann" (Bildhauer[1]) My idea is to utilise this window for Lew House. It is a bay with two windows in it one above and the other below, and I purpose throwing out two such bays at the back of Lew House to the dining room and bedrooms over.[2] On to Landeck where slept. Next day crossed the Vorarlberg pass[3] to Bludenz by coach. ~~Saturday~~ Friday to Constance, and Saturday back to Freiburg. I saw in Reutte some nice brass locks and copied them, I shall get them made here for use in Lew House.[4]

1881 **10 June:**
Kate Bond left.

1881 **11 June:**
Began to write "Zitta" and my sermons outlines.

1881 **29 June:**
Sent to Bishop of Exeter my presentation of myself to Lew Trenchard. S. Peter's Day.

1881 **6 July:**
Left Freiburg for England to be instituted to Lew Trenchard.

---

[1] Bildhauer: *sculptor*
[2] Bay windows; Sabine did throw out superb bay windows in Lew House Dining Room and Gallery over, but they are in granite not wood.
[3] Vorarlberg pass: Arlberg pass
[4] Excursions in the Tyrol described on 5 June 1881: see map 2

1881 **19 July:**
Instituted by the Bishop of Exeter. [1]

1881 **20 July:**
Inducted by Revd. Grylls. Returned to Freiburg on July 28.

1881 **2 Aug:**
Left Freiburg for Laufenburg and have taken up our residence at the Crown[2] in Klein Laufenburg on the Baden side of the river.

1881 **22 August:**
Have finished my Sermons Outlines, 65 in all, and written and made a clean copy of 32 chapters of "Zitta". The children are as happy as the day is long. We have lovely weather, and the most picturesque of towns lying under our window across the Rhine.

1881 **3 Sept:**
Left Laufenburg. Finished and dispatched my "Village Sermons for Saints' Days". Returned to Freiburg and put up at the Alsace.

1881 **5 Sept:**
Finished "Zitta", and sent off the M.S. Have been working so hard at Laufenburg that I have not been out one day during my stay there till after tea, Sundays excepted. Since 11th June when I began the novel and the sermons, I have been working hard but was greatly interrupted by my visit to England in July. Today Mary and Daisy go to the Institut Wasmer, the school does not begin until next Monday, but I have thought it best that they should go there to sleep and have their meals, so as gradually to get accustomed to the great change when we leave them.

Sabine is a very independent young monkey, and will not, I fancy feel being left. He has taken a fancy to Herr Baader, with whom he is to live. Herr Baader is R.C. chaplain at the gaol, and is very highly spoken of. His house struck me as the cleanest I had seen in Freiburg. His sister lives with him. I was much pleased with what I saw of them, good, simple people, thoroughly honourable and kindhearted. Curiously enough Sabine has already taken a fancy to Herr Baader, and had made his acquaintence before I thought of sending him to him. Sabine has been engrossed all summer in butterfly, moth and beetle hunting.

I have sold the French translation of "Zitta" made by Countess Alice Kearney to a French paper to be issued en feuilleton[3] for £50. Of this sum she will receive half. She adapts the story to the neighbourhood of Monaco and Nice, it lends itself well to that.

---

[1] Institution By the Bishop of Exeter: *Further Reminiscences*, p 101
[2] The Crown: *der Krone.*
[3] En feuilleton: *serialised.*

Capt. Festing tells me that he always laid up his fields for hay on March 24th, not allowing a hoof on it after that day, and he almost always saved his hay in June. Our farmers have got in to the way of feeding off till end of April, the consequence is they do not make hay till in the S. Swithun's rains. He advises Jerusalem artichokes for feeding cattle and horses, they eat greedily the leaves and tubers, the stalks must be burnt to restore alkali to the soil. Potatoe *[sic]* disease almost always comes about 13th July. Vines to be pulled up the moment the speck appears. Plant strong eyes with good sprouts, turning purple, and not the whole potatoe. *[sic]* Feed in same field cattle, then turn on horses, last sheep. Horses eat what cows will not, and sheep what is left by both.

1881 **8 Sept:**
Arranged with Herr Bader *[sic]* for Sabine; his terms are 750 mks for the year and 250 for holidays, i.e. 1,000 mks or £50 per ann. For this the boy has lodging, food, fuel, lights, and general supervision. Schooling extra.

1881 **Saturday, 10 Sept:**
Left Freiburg. Poor Mary, Daisy and Sabine were on the platform and saw us off, the latter waving his butterfly net as long as we could see him. Vera cried all the way to Appenweier because she was parted from them. At Strassburg main station it was discovered that our perambulator had been put out at the Metzger Thor station. There was no time to recover it before leaving, and it could not be sent on till Sunday night when it would arrive too late in Brussels for me to recover it before proceeding; so I said to the clerk that it must be left, and that anyone of the porters who had babies was welcome to it. When I had left the office an employee came after me to know if I meant this seriously. "Perfectly." I said "I have got a large family" he replied. "Then take the perambulator." I said. "I cannot without formal authorisation." So I went back to the luggage office with him and there the clerk drew up a formal document assenting the transfer of the perambulator to Herr Otto, Öbersuperintendent of the Gepäck bureau, and authorising him to take it, when forwarded and use it as he saw fit. This created great merriment in the office and I had to shake hands all the way round, and as the express started the head clerk came running to the carriage door to say that he had been 20 years in the office and this was his first experience of the sort, and to beg that if I went back to Strassburg again I would call at the office to see how Herr Otto's babies got on in the kinderwagen.

1881 **Sunday 11 Sept:**
Spent Sunday in Brussels, bought another perambulator.

1881 **12 Sept:**
Arrived safely in London, at Lodgings 6 Keppel St.

1881 **15 Sept:**
Went to East Mersea to see luggage sent off.

Part 3. Lew Trenchard Rectory[1]
September 1881 to October 1885

1881 **Monday 20 Sept:**
Went to Lew

1881 **Sunday 25 September:**
Read myself in.

1881 **8 Oct:**
Grace, and the little ones arrived.

1881 **12 Oct:**
Heard a good story of Baron de Rothschild. The Emperor paid him a visit at his chateau of La Ferrières, and he was entertained with the most lavish prodigality. When the Emperor was leaving, he thanked the Jew banker for the hospitality he had shown and the pleasure the visit had afforded him. "Sire," replied the Baron, "J'en gardevoi toujours le mémoire" ("Sire, I shall ever keep the bill by me" instead of "la memoirè") "I shall never forget it"

1881 **29 Oct:**
Have been busy planting. On the Lime Quarry ramps in the place of those trees that failed which I had put in last year, and also on the slate quarry ramps, most sad. I have put in 130 silver pines, 50 pinus Douglassii, 50 Spanish chestnuts, and number of shrubs.

1881 **Monday 1 Nov:** All Saints:
A little daughter born at 12.45 a.m. The soft palate is split, and the child has great difficulty in swallowing. This will have to be sown *[sic]* up, a difficult operation, only to be performed when the child is some months older. The question of name is, shall she be Joan or "Diana Amelia"[2]

1881 **2 Nov:**
I bought in Tyrol a large umbrella, crimson with a wreath of flowers on it, blue, white and yellow. I used this umbrella at Mersea, about the psh. *[parish]* and people got accustomed to it. One snowy day I was driving into Colchester, Grace and I considered that we might venture to spread the red umbrella which would cover us both, and when we came near Colchester we could furl it. On our way we passed an umbrella-mender plodding through the snow with his head down, battling against the East wind and the driving sleet, and a bundle of umbrellas under his arm. As we passed, the man looked up, and the crimson umbrella blazed

---

[1] Lew Trenchard Rectory: Now no longer the rectory and, as a private house, known as Coombe Trenchard.
[2] Diana Amelia, Sabine's 9th child, familiar names: Emily as a child, Di in later life.

above him for a moment. That was a new experience, "a moment" as Hegel'[1] would term it, in his existence, an epoch making incident. Down in the snow went the umbrellas he was carrying and till we were out of sight he stood with eyes and mouth open, and hands extended, staring after us paralysed with astonishment. In all his umbrellaratic experience, he had never met with such a paraplui as this. I have brought the umbrella to Lew and we shall use it here.

1881 **3 Nov:**
Mr. Hamlyn said to me "My house[2] has cost me as much money as if I had built it new, and I may pride myself in the belief that I possess the ugliest mansion in Devon." He very foolishly gave it to a village plumber and painter to put to rights, and this man, a clever fellow in his own way, but without taste or knowledge of architecture has made of it a horrible sort of suburban villa.[3]

1881 **5 Nov:**
Kelly house was entered by burglars last night. In the afternoon the gardener saw two or three men, dressed as gentlemen, and smoking good cigars, sauntering round the house, and taking a look at the front, but thinking them gentlemen he did not interfere with them. At 8 P.M. however he saw one of them come hand over head sliding down the rain water shoot, so he went in and told Reginald Kelly who immediately sent to Lifton for a policeman. The sergeant of police came, and Kelly thinking the house was safe in his care went to bed. The butler sat up, gave the sergeant his supper, and then the policeman spent the night in walking round the house and the butler toasting his knees over the fire within. The burglars must have taken the measure of the country sergeant's foot, for they quietly went on with their work in cool indifference to his presence. They got up to a window on one another's shoulders, broke a plate glass, and with a centre bit bored a hole in the shutter, removed the bar, and entered. They examined every drawer and cupboard in the library, opening all the locks, but they only found £2 in money, and a pair of silver candlesticks, a gold watch and a fur cloak. They lighted wax candles and went to the pantry, but were unable to force the doors, and they left a silver inkstand behind, perhaps thinking it was plated, or perhaps disturbed.

1881 **6 Nov:**
Next night they broke into Bradstone Barton but found nothing there.

1881 **7 Nov:**
Last night they tried a farm in Lifton parish, but the farmer was roused and woke his sons and the robbers made off

---

[1] Georg W F Hegel, 1770-1831: influential German philosopher and one of the creators of German Idealism.

[2] Mr Hamlyn's House: Leawood, Bridestowe, Devon.

[3] The Plumber was Mr Rundle of Bridestowe: *My Last Few Words*, Chap. V. Mr Rundle also features in the disastrous painting of a bath, *Early Reminiscences*, p 248.

1881 **8 Nov:**

Three suspicious looking men were today about Lew House, they went round to the front, and then examined the little window of the small room (w.c.) under the great stairs. The coachman who had been watching came down on them and asked what they wanted, and they pretended that they had come to ask for a glass of water. He bade them be off, and followed them to Lew Down. They went into the Inn and remained there till half past ten when they left.

1881 **9 Nov:**

It turns out that the men after leaving the Inn went to my deserted cottage in the wood under the bank at Gallitrap.[1] They removed the door catch and fixed it inside, and made up a roaring fire. Some men passing along the road saw flames coming out of the chimney and thought the cottage was on fire, so went down to it, but it was fastened on the inside and they could not get in. This morning the men went to Stowford and examined Mr. Wollacombe's house pretty minutely, they were so evidently making examination, that Mr. W. sent for the policeman. Before he came they departed. The policeman tells me that these three are not supposed to be the actual burglars, but the avant-couriers who examine the lie of the land for them, make notes and communicate with them what they have seen. The attempt may not be made for another year or two; when suspicion is lulled.

1881 **12 Nov:**

Had a call from Miss Harris, she is in great excitement because she hears I am examining Registers for the new edition of the Visitation of Devon by Col. Vivian.[2] The family have lately claimed to call themselves Mohun-Harris, and pretend that the heiress of Mohun married in to the Harris of Haine family. This was not the case. Cordelia Mohun did marry John Harris of Haine, but his son died without issue, and the estates devolved on his nephew, so that no Mohun blood flows in the Harris veins. They pretend however that John Harris of Haine and his wife Cordelia had a dau. Cordelia who married her cousin and that their son inherited Haine. This contradicts their pedigree as established by monuments and register.

I have had a letter from Christopher Arthur Harris in which he asserts that the Donithornes were anciently Bonithornes. This is not true. The Donithornes were day labourers in the parish of ----------. Then they became tinners, and made their money so. They can be perfectly well traced by the register. Mr. Harris asserts that the last Lord Mohun died intestate, and that his estates at Okehampton passed to the Harris family as heirs at law. This is not true, the 4th Lord Mohun, killed in a duel, left a will, dated, 23 Mch 1710, proved in the Consistory Court Canterbury 6 Mch 1713, in which he leaves everything to his wife and a thousand pounds "to my pretended daughter by my first wife."

---

[1] **Gallitrap: see explanatory endnote 36**
[2] Visitation of the County of Devon: Originally published 1620, later edition with additions by Col J L Vivian 1895.

1881 **13 Nov:**
Witherden has been bought of Capt. Luxmore by the guardians of a lad, for him, he is the **[illegitimate son of]**[1]

1881 **14 Nov:**
Herr Schorer of Berlin buys of me "Zitta" for 4,000 mks or £200. I retain a right to publish a French version next year, en feuiliton, but I must not publish in England or France till 1 Jan. 1883. The French version by the Countess Alice Kearney is disposed of to Capt. Deresne for £50[2]

1882 1 Jan:
Capt. Deresne[3] refuses the translation of Ct.ess. Alice; and she wants to force me to pay her £25 for her trouble.

Have been engaged on draining and have nearly finished several fields.

Baby received into Church today. Godfather Edward S.B.G;[4] Godmothers, Aunt Emily B.G. and Evelyn Marshall.

Aunt Emily tells me she remembers the present drawing room panelled throughout, and a handsome chimneypiece in the Grinling Gibbons style with wreaths of fruit and flowers. The panelling had been painted white, and the flowers and fruit picked out with gold. My grandfather took down the panelling to hang the room with paper, and the chimneypiece was destroyed to make way for that in black marble now there. I can dimly recall the old chimneypiece which I suspect remained after the panelling was torn away. If I remember right there were little pillars on the mantelpiece[5]

For Christmas have put up an oak altar table and hangings on the walls, and furnished the altar with a wooden cross and two candlesticks, and a brass alms dish.

1882 **1 Feb:**
Have been to Peter Tavy and seen the havoc wrought there by the architect St. Aubin,[6] *[sic]* that curse to the West of England. I remember the old church unrestored. There

---

[1] The phrase in square brackets and bold had been scored out by Sabine but has been rendered visible to the transcriber with the aid of ultraviolet light. It is not known why the father's name was never entered but it seems likely that the erasure occurred many years after the original entry by which time the boy would have matured and perhaps become an accepted member of the local community.
[2] **Zitta: See explanatory endnote 37**
[3] Capt. Deresne: Presumably a French publisher but no trace has been found of him.
[4] Edward Sabine Baring-Gould, b 4 April 1843, son of Uncle Charles Baring-Gould.
[5] Decorative chimneypiece panelling: see the entry for 31 May 1896
[6] **James Piers St Aubyn, architect: see explanatory endnote 38**

was in it in the n. aisle a magnificent pue *[sic]* of the Skirrets[1] of the purest renaissance, Henry VII age of oak black with age and richly carved. It had pillars at the corners, with heraldic animals on them, the pue was large and square. It has gone, only a few scraps have been worked into a screen at the w. end, and a bit of the beautiful over cornice used as a desk for the music books on the organ. I am told that a couple of cartloads of carved oak was left to rot in the churchyard. This was done when Mr. Gibbons was incumbent about ten years ago. I knew nothing of it or would gladly have secured the precious work. Bridestowe Church has been defaced even more recently, there the screen was taken down and the tracery sawn through and then plastered on the deal bench ends.[2] Whitchurch has been conscientiously done, not in good taste, but without destruction of anything of interest. The screen in N. Aisle is from Moreton Hampstead, it was given by Lord Devon.

Virginstowe has been rebuilt some 15 years ago. Several cartloads of rich bench ends and screen work were carted away and destroyed. O! if I had only been in this neighbourhood during the last twenty years what I might have saved and secured. I remember a rich lower portion of screen gilt and painted with saints at Dunterton. Mr. John Wollocombe repaired the church a good number of years ago in the most hideous fashion, and then this screen was destroyed. But perhaps the worst case of all is Jacobstow, this was done up four years ago by Miss Pierce. She only restored the church on the condition that the screen should be destroyed. It was quite perfect and very rich, with parcloses.[3] I was at Lew at the time, but knew nothing of this till too late to secure it. Maristowe has been horribly defaced. The screen formerly crossed the N. Aisle and a parclose cut off the N. chapel from the chancel. The parclose is gone, and only a portion of the screen remains under the tower. In Broadwood Widger the remains of old stained glass of the crucifixion in the E. window of the N. transept chapel have been destroyed. Of this I have a sketch taken when I was a boy. At Morwenstowe last summer during the deformation by St. Aubin, it was found that the walls were painted throughout with subjects, very rich, all were scraped away.

On Jan. 20th I began the new road, or rather turning the old one, behind Lew House.[4]

1882 **20 Feb:**
Walked with Mr. John Northmore of Cleve[5] to Trecarrel,[6] interesting ruins, the hall very fine, the little chapel threatening a fall, all built out of cut granite blocks. The

---

[1] Skirrets: a Peter Tavy family. For the pew see *A Book of Dartmoor* p 137.
[2] Bridestowe restoration, *A Book of Dartmoor* p 138
[3] Parclose: a screen or rail enclosing an altar or tomb, or separating a chapel from the main body of a church
[4] Turning the road: The road behind Lew House was moved a few yards north in anticipation of the creation of the North wing and cloisters in 1896
[5] Cleve: Cleve House, Exwick, Devon
[6] Trecarell: Trecarell, near Trebullett, southwest of Launceston. The chapel is now restored. See *A Book of Cornwall,* p 88

old oak panelled screen in the hall remains but the wall panelling has disappeared, the screen is Jacobean and not good. Indeed the architecture of Trecarrel is bad, coarse and clumsy. But it is nevertheless a most interesting place. The great gate of entrance has been thrown down and lies scattered about in the orchard, bits in the farmyard and some built into the garden wall.

Mr. N. told me a curious story. He says that the Coleridges derive from the illegitimate son of Mr. ~~Thos.~~ William Northmore of Cleve by a woman named Coleridge of —I believe Morchard Bishop where the entry in the register is to be found, this son was John Coleridge, Vicar of Ottery and master of Ottery school b. 21 Jan. 1719. Wm. Northmore lost his wife Anne in 1717. His mother was told this by Revd. Edward Coleridge, Vicar of Mapledurham. Mr. Northmore wrote afterwards to Mr. E. Coleridge to ascertain the facts more particularly, but Mr. E.C. gave an evasive reply[1]

1882 **27 Feb:**
Went to Cheriton Bishop to stay with Mr. Pennell at Medland. This is an old Q. Anne brick mansion that belonged to the Davyes, the heiress married Fawke who ran through a great deal of money and sold it. The Grandfather of the present Edward Pennell bought it, together with much land in Cheriton.[2] Unfortunately the father left the property to be divided among his children, consequently all has been sold except Medland, which Mr. Pennell retains. In the park are some superb trees. The house is now only partially occupied and almost ruinous. Some of the windows boarded up. A farmer occupies the portion that was of old, the servant's suite, and Mr. Pennell has put the drawing room, library and a couple of bedrooms in to order for himself. He is a bachelor and a cripple with both legs bent, so that he gets on only with the assistance of sticks. The farmer's family cook and cater for him. The front stairs are ruinous, the balustrade broken and the front hall is hung round with horse gear, the handsome ceilings are falling, the chimney piece in the dining room has been torn down, the cornice and chimney piece in the drawing room are very beautiful work of the period. My bedroom opened into two other rooms, with no keys in the locks, and one of these rooms was at the head of an unused, mouldering back stair. The truckle bed in it was heaped up with female garments. A fire was lighted in my grate but there was no fireguard and the hot embers of flaming coals rolled out during the night on the floor and I was forced to jump out of bed and throw them off the oak boards under the hearth. In the big adjoining room the windows were broken and partly boarded up and the wind moaned mournfully through it all night long. On getting into bed I found that there was only an upper sheet, blanket beneath —and I could not sleep well, what with the blanket and the moaning winds shaking the doors, and the coals avalanching at intervals into the room.

---

[1] **John Coleridge, father of S T Coleridge. Explanatory endnote 39**
[2] Mr Pennell of Medland, Cheriton Bishop: *Early Reminiscences*, p 288

The last of the Davies married a Fawke, who squandered the property. It is curious that in the Visitation of Devon of 1620 the arms of the Davys of Medland is given, az. 3 cinquefoils pierced, or, on a chief of the second a lion passant gules; whereas on all the Davys monuments in the church the arms are those of the Davyes of Elberly and Beauford, argent 2 chevronels sable betw. 3 mullets gules. One of the monuments in the church has a curious inscription on Andrew Davie of Medland Esq. who d. 2 Dec. 1669, aged 30. The arms are Davye impaled with Drewe, under which is written Pompa mortis majus terret quam mors ipsa.[1] The lines that are curious are:-

> "Defunctus videor vivo tamen auspior *[auspice]* Christo
> Mors est *[in]* terris vivere, vita mori
> Vita quid Exsilium, quid Mors translatio: coelum
> Patria: et exuto *[for exuto, exuta?]* carne, superstes ero."[2]

The present Sir Henry Robert Ferguson-Davies, is the son of a gentleman named Ferguson of Raith and lady Elgin with whom he ran away, she was divorced afterwards by Lord Elgin. He was rapidly advanced in the army, and on his marriage with Frances Juliana, only surviving sister of Sir John Davies, Bart. Of Creedy Park,[3] was created a Baronet, with the name of Davies assumed in addition to that of his mother to which he has no right. Foster's Baronetage is silent wholly about his parentage, it gives his birth in 1798, but does not name his father and mother. He quarters the Davies coat along with az. 3 cinquefoils, or, on a chief of the last, a lion passant gules, the coat of the Medland Davys family. For Ferguson he bears nothing.

I heard a good story of the Bishop.[4] His pronunciation is very unpleasant, being a mixture of Cornish and Cockney. God is Gad, Lord, Lard, train is trine, voice, vice, noise, nize. A little while ago he sent for Hanson, the curate of Axminster, and said to him, "You must leave, I shall withdraw your licence." "Why, my Lord?"
"Never mind why, I choose it. You must go."
"But I ask the reason." "I will not give you the reason. It is sufficient if I say Go."
"My Lord," said Hanson, "I have a right to know it: And I also have a right of appeal to the Archbishop, if you refuse to tell me."
"If you will know," said the Bishop, "It's your <u>vice</u>." (voice)
"Excuse me, my Lord, if I tell you a story," said Hanson coolly, "The week before last I took a friend to the Cathedral where you were to preach. When I came out I asked my friend how he liked your Lordship's sermon. He replied 'It was an

---

[1] Translation: *A procession of death terrifies more than death itself*
[2] Translation: *I seem dead but I live with Christ as my patron.*
                  Death is to live on Earth, life is to die.
                  What is life but exile, what death but translation to heaven?
                  My flesh has been stripped away but still I survive.

[3] Creedy Park, near Crediton, Devon
[4] **Archbishop Frederick Temple: see explanatory endnote 21**

uncommonly able sermon, and the man would be a good preacher but for his abominable vice' —and now my Lord, seeing that we are both tarred with the same brush, had we not both better leave the diocese together." "Get along with you," said the Bishop very angry. Hanson has just been appointed to Throwleigh — but <u>not</u> by the Bishop.

Poor old Angell the late organist was asked by the precentor to correct the pronunciation of the choristers in the matter of their Rs and Us. "Really Mr. Precentor, said Angell, "I am an old man, and I am getting so bewildered about the modern pronunciation of words, that I do not know what is right and what is wrong. I <u>did</u> believe G.O.D spelled God, but we have it on the highest ecclesiastical authority that it spells <u>Gad</u>. What am I to do?" [1]

1882 **28 Feb:**
Returned to Lew. Pengelly tells me that he remembers the parlour at Lew Mill,[2] when it was panelled with dark polished oak, and had a beautiful plaster ceiling, far richer than that in the large room. My grandfather destroyed this, and broke out a door where a window stood, and made a cottage of this part. The parlour was on the left of the entrance door, it had two windows in it. One is left, but every trace of the original beauty of the room is gone. The amount of destruction he wrought at Orchard is piteous to think of, the tower gate house torn down, the whole house lowered a storey, the panelling destroyed.[3] I have seen recently Collacombe,[4] and havoc has been wrought there quite lately. A parlour opens out of the hall, originally part of it, the granite window has this winter been taken out, and replaced by a vulgar sash window. I remember the hall panelled, this has all been burnt. One wing of the house was taken down some time ago

1882 **1 Mch:**
More havock; *[sic]* I have just seen S. James' church in Okehampton. When last I saw it, the old bench ends were in situ. Now they have all been swept away with the exception of three on each side near the door. I have recovered what I believe to have been four of the old bench ends from Staverton church, removed at the restoration (so called) some thirty years ago. They have since lain in a china shop, one, —the book desk has on it our early arms, a chevron between 3 roses, the colours not indicated. Another end has on it two Cornish choughs. The Knapmans bore choughs on their arms, but I do not think had any property in Staverton. I do not know for certain that these came from Staverton, but I cannot conjecture in what other church our arms could be.[5]

---

[1] These stories of Archbishop Temple are told in *Further Reminiscences* p 115-6
[2] For Lew Mill, here and elsewhere in the diary, read as 'Lew Mill Dower House'
[3] There is current evidence that at least part of *Orchard* was indeed lowered by a storey but as yet no traces of a gatehouse have been found there.
[4] Collacombe, Lamerton, Devon.
[5] **Staverton Bench Ends: Restored and used at St. Peter's Church, Lewtrenchard. Explanatory endnote 40**

1882 **4 Apr:**
Went to Exeter and was made a magistrate.

1882 **1 May**:
Began the cottage on the Lime Quarry ramps.[1] Nearly all the trees I planted on the ramps two years ago are dead, I have put in a few more this Spring to take their places, and these are doing well, but almost every larch then planted is dead. Went to Staverton.

1882 **7 May**:
Preached for the Idiots Asylum at Starcross. Stayed with uncle Edward C Bond.

1882 **8 May:**
Returned to Staverton. Saw at the East Ogwell Rectory the portrait of Elizabeth Reynell, da. of James Gould of Exeter and Mr. Taylor to whom it belongs informs me that his brother has the portrait of Sir Edward Gould her brother. The Taylors are lineal descendants of the Reynells of Ogwell, the heiress having married a Taylor. Mr. Taylor has sold Ogwell house and all the property to Mr. Scratton. I have asked to be allowed to have the two portraits copied.

1882 **17 May:**
Heard today from Mr. Pierce Taylor who was of Ogwell but has sold it. He tells me that he has the portrait of Sir Edward Gould, and writes "I can have no objection to you having a copy of Sir Ed. Gould's portrait made, nor to its being taken at my house, in the event of the copyist being a respectable character. He should, however, be a first rate workman, as the picture is <u>very good</u>, and I should say hard to copy well. It represents a man of, perhaps, about 30, or less, very peculiar looking, but rather <u>weirdly</u> handsome, one of those of whom one would say, that he must have had a beautiful mother. He is small of stature, with singularly large eyes, black eyebrows, and a proud, haughty mouth; good complexion and brown hair, which appears to have been his own, though curled about his head and shoulders. He is very handsomely dressed, in black velvet with a fine lace steinkirk[2] and ruffles, tied with red ribbands, painted with great spirit. His right hand holds a letter, and a small gold watch lies near it. The hand is remarkably well painted. The back-ground is dark, and the hair shadows and others melt with it, <u>à la Corregio</u>. Taking it altogether it is a fine half-length, and one that will tax all the copyists savoire faire to reproduce. I have always heard that it was painted in Italy, and by the well known <u>Carlo Maratti</u>. That painter died in 1713 aged 87. Sir Edward is 30 years old, or less, when the portrait was taken, must have sat to him when his reputation was at the highest. I find however that Marath sometimes painted portraits.[3] "besides this, I have one of a lady, who, I was always

---

[1] This cottage was known by Sabine as *Rampenstein*.
[2] Steinkirk: a cravat with long laces
[3] James Gould of Exeter, Sir Edward Gould and Carlo Maratti: *Further Reminiscences*, p 81-2

told, was his sister, though the name, Hall, which was given her, does not appear in the genealogy of your family, as I have seen it. The picture, a half-length also, is not a bad one, though inferior to that of her alleged brother. She is very décolleté, and a blond, with a good looking face and fine eyes, though light."

This lady was Mary, da. of Edward Gould of Mansfield who m. Urban Hall of Mansfield Woodhouse in 1764 and d. 1787. *There follows an undated afternote by Sabine:* It is not of Mrs. Hall but is Frances da. Sir F. Pemberton who mar. Edwd. Gould, I am almost sure.

At Upcot in Broadwood Widger in the parlour window is this coat of arms in stained glass. per pale or. and sa. 3 sinister hands couped at wrist counterchanged impaled with Southcote. What marriage does this represent.[1]

Fig. 8 Coat of Arms, Upcot, Broadwood

1882 **10 June:**
Returned from Boscastle where I have been staying with Ernest Hammick[2] He has some of the bench ends of the old church used up to make an altar and credence[3] and sedilia.[4] The figures on them are very singular[5] The first is evidently a characature *[sic]* of the new fashionable importation of earthenware commodes from Bristol and the sculptor pours scorn on those apes of high society who use them instead of going out behind a hedge 'more patrum'[6] The second is a bird diving into the waves, with another bird hovering over them, and the third is a rabbit with one bunny looking out of its hole and another darting into it. Another has two ducks running, another a cock and hen.

---

[1] Upcott, Broadwoodwidger, northwest of Lewdown, *Old Country Life*, p 66
[2] Ernest Hammick: The Rev. Sir St. Vincent
[3] Credence: a small table by the altar for the bread and wine
[4] Sedilia: seats for officiating clergy
[5] **Boscastle bench ends: See also the entry for 1 March 1882. The birds and rabbits were at some point copied by Sabine onto two of the Staverton bench ends at St Peters. See explanatory endnote 40**
[6] More patrum: in the ancestral way

Fig.9 Bench ends at Boscastle

Mr. H. has two, very curious from S. Juliot, on one shield is IHS. On the other a hand (the inside)

Fig. 10 *Rolle Crest, Boscastle*

[After note in pencil: Rolle crest*]* couped at the wrist, and without thumb, and with something like a bit of stick lying across the palm. The second bench end from S. Juliot has IHS on one shield, and on the other a mysterious knot or coil.

Davidstowe which I saw has been wrecked. There was a good and very perfect screen with parcloses, each parclose different. The screen has been destroyed, a bit of one parclose is used for the tower arch, and the tracery has been sawn in half and plastered on to the bench front in the chancel. This was done quite recently 3 years ago.

Heard a rich story. Mrs. R.B.[1] is a great screw, although the family is very well off. She gave a lunch the other day; during it there occurred a pause in the conversation; then the governess (who was leaving next day) exclaimed so that everyone at the table could hear "O! I beg your pardon Mrs. B! I quite forgot that you had forbidden me ever to take the cream when it is passed round, and I have helped myself to some! What shall I do? I am so sorry. Shall I leave it in my plate or <u>may</u> I eat it as it is here."

Mr. Kinsman of ~~Boscastle~~ Tintagel told me he was receiving a child in to the church which had been privately baptized, and he asked the mother, "With what matter was this child baptized." "Please Sir, with matter out of Mrs. Tregella's baby's arm —it's reckoned a very healthy child."

---

[1] Mrs R.B: Mrs Bryant. See the entry for 24 June 1882

When Mr. Kitson came to Anthony he saw, on looking through his register only boys' names among the baptized, so he said to his clerk, "Why then is this? Are only boys born in Anthony?" "No, Sir, but only boys is brought to be christened, 'taint no good for girls as them is not taken into the Dockyard."[1]

At Dalton I had a blacksmith named Joseph Whiteoak, who had seven little girls. At last a son was born. He came to me and asked to have the child baptized next Sunday. "Yes, if you like, Joseph," I said, "but on Thursday after that the new church will be opened and then you can have your little boy baptized the first in the new font and new church." Joseph shrugged his shoulders and answered with a grin, "I'd as lief not, Sir; folk say that fust child as is baptized i' a new font is sure to dee. Na' this is a lad. If it had been a lass, it wouldn't ha' mattered and you'd ha' been welcome, but as it's a lad I wi'n't risk it."

I do not know if this is an old story, but it was told me as having actually occurred at table d'hote at Mentone[2] A commercial traveller there swore a great deal, and presently noticing that a clergyman was by him, he apologised, "Beg pardon, Sir, but I am a plain man and always call a spade a spade." "I should not have supposed that from the tenor of your previous conversation," answered the parson, "I should have thought you would have designated a spade — a damned shovel."

The Archbishop of Cantab. was dining the other day at the Duke of Westminster's, when suddenly his face grew ghastly, and he laid down his ~~knife and~~ fork, and said in an agitated tone. "It has come at last, as I feared. Excuse me, but I have for some time been dreading a stroke, and as I have been feeling strange I have repeatedly pinched my leg under the table, and – I am unable to feel it - so I know that I am having a seizure." "Console yourself," said the Duchess of Sutherland, who sat beside him, "It is not your leg but mine you have been pinching under the table."[3]

Heard a rich story when at Staverton of how the living of S. Brent was sold. The incumbent, the Revd. ---- Cole was the proprietor and he had been in treaty for the sale but put a price on the living which was too high. One day the candidate for the purchase got a telegram from Cole's lawyer in Totnes to come down by next train. He did so, and was told that Mr. Cole was very ill and had been prayed for in church and was not expected to live. The lawyer accompanied the purchaser to the rectory where he was admitted and entreated to make as little noise as possible and stay as short a time as he could in the dying man's room. He and the lawyer went up and saw the old man in bed so prostrate as to be scarce able to speak. No demur as to the price was now made and the contract of sale was rapidly drawn and signed, and a deposit paid. Then the purchaser went down and walked about the grounds and glebe, there was an hour or two to

---

[1] Baptism at Anthony, Cornwall: *Old Country Life*, p 147-8
[2] Mentone: On the French Riviera
[3] Archbishop Tait: *Further Reminiscences*, p. 120

spare before the train could reconduct him to town. Presently Mrs. Cole came out to him in the garden and begged him to come in and have some dinner. He declined as, under the circumstances, he did not wish to trouble the house. "Not at all," answered Mrs. Cole, "Mr. Cole would be delighted of your society." "Mr. Cole?" "I forgot to add," said the lady, "The crisis is happily passed and Mr. Cole is risen, dressed, and impatient for his dinner."[1]

1882 **24 June:**
Dined last night at Kelly College, met old Price Mitchell of Halwell.[2] He told a good story of old Commodore Williams whom I remember, when I was a boy; he was a great hunting man, and he and Mitchell had been out one day and Mr. Trelawny, now Sir Jno. *[John]* asked them to dine with him at Hallwood.[3] The Commodore had suffered from a spill and his corduroy breeches were beplastered with mud; Mr. Trelawny offered him a suit of his own, but the Commodore found that he was far too stout to get into them, so — he turned his breeches, and as the buttons did not come right; pinned them down the front and so came down in turned breeches and his hunting coat and dined with the ladies. This 40 years ago, would not be possible now.

This is the structure of the old door at Hurdwick.[4]

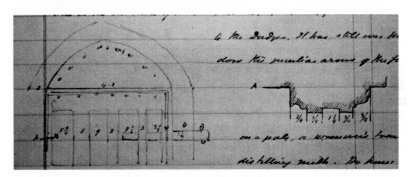

Fig. 11 Old door at Hurdwick

This house belonged to the Doidges. It has still over the door the peculiar arms of the family, on a pale, a woman's breast distilling milk. The house is small, with some magnificent chestnuts by it; a porch with granite doorway, and a little court with one arch of granite thrown across the entrance. There was a drawing room built out in the 18th cent. With its panelling partly in situ. Upstairs an old chimneypiece of same date with a landscape in panel in the middle, a chimneypiece much like that at Lew Mill. This and the entire house are going to rack and ruin.

---

[1] The Living of Mr 'Baker' for sale: *The Church Revival*, p 118
[2] Halwell: village in Devon between Totnes and Dartmouth
[3] Hallwood, at Petrockstow, near Hatherleigh, Devon.
[4] Hurdwick, north of Tavistock, Devon.

I saw today Wringworthy in Mary Tavy the house of the Cake family, a family not even named in the Visitation of 1620 and yet which was certainly of some local significance. The head of the family put down as Gent. in the register in 1602. The house and land now belong to Mr. Carpenter Garnier.

The house plan is this.

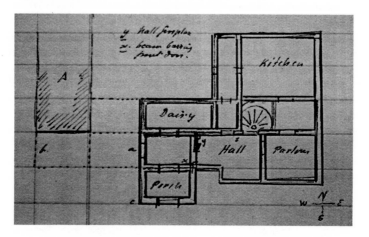

Fig. 12 Wringworthy House plan, Mary Tavy

A: is an outhouse with early windows cut in Brent tor stone. The staircase is a newel. The Hall was panelled with fine linen pattern but has been cut down and only one side preserved and that not perfect. The fireplace is destroyed. I am not clear about the plan of the kitchen portion. I suspect there was a door at (a) with a portion of the house destroyed a-b, but no traces remain, the wall a-c was rebuilt a few years ago. Then the dairy was probably a passage connecting the house with A. The house is slated in front, none of the windows are of stone, and no granite is used only Brent tor stone. At x is a beam of oak with a ring at the end slipping back in the depth of the wall, which pulls out and bars the front door so that it cannot be opened from the outside. The date of the house is Henry VII reign. The pannels *[sic]* with linen pattern are 2 ft. 5" by 1 ft.; at z between the two doors is the huge skull of a bull with hair on, and immense horns. The dairy is a lean to. The hill has been dug into on the East to allow the house to nestle into it.

When at Boscastle I saw an interesting house that belonged to the Tinks, and was built by one Baldwin Tink, whose marriage appears in the Trevalgar[1] Register. The house is Well Town. The plan is peculiar, the fireplace is in the wall adjoining the porch and principal window. The divisions of the rooms inside have been so changed that the plan is not easily made out; and the old staircase is gone.

---

[1] Trevalgar: Near Boscastle.

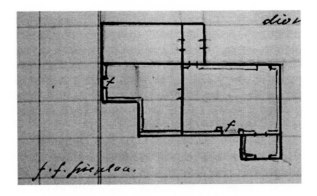

Fig. 13 Well Town, Boscastle, plan

The exterior of the house is eminently picturesque. In the room over the porch a madman was detained for some years till the magistrates interfered, when he was removed to Exeter, where he speedily recovered.

We had a much worse case here, within my memory, at Orchard. In the little dark room without window between the parlour and cider cellar and barn was kept the brother of old Mrs. Yeo for – if I remember right – 16 years, in a state of nakedness and filth.

Mr. Yeo - who is still alive, a kind hearted man was not conscious that he was acting cruelly. Nicholson Vowles was then in Lew House as we were abroad and he took the case up, and Mr. Yeo was sent to prison and the poor wretch removed to Exeter Asylum.[1]

But to return to Well Town. On the ~~drip ends~~ spandrels of the door are the initials B.T.

Fig. 14 Welltown, Boscastle, front elevation

On Saturday last we called at the Bryant's at Peter Tavy. Mr. Bryant is rector and his wife is da. of Mr. Abrahall a great scholar and tutor. Mrs. B. is a good Greek, Latin and Hebrew scholar, but knows nothing of housekeeping. He has some three

---

[1] **The Prisoner of Orchard: Explanatory endnote 41.**

thousand a year, at the least, but lived at the rate of £150, and squalidly at that. No servants will remain in the house, and when we came the one German slut they have had recently was leaving. The dirt is indescribable. They had tea in for us, and Mrs B. to do honour to my wife took down a china cup from the cabinet where it had stood for months, and poured the tea into it, floating the dust and cobwebs to the top. She took in a dress of her daughter's to the Bakers in Tavistock last week to ask him to exchange it for a couple of loaves. He declined, for the dress was so dirty and ragged that it was not worth one loaf.

They have a governess who has given notice to leave, and they are trying all they can to drive her to go before her three months are up, so as to forfeit her quarter's salary. They cheated their last governess in like manner out of 14£. *[sic]* Mrs. B makes butter out of her cream when sour; she took it the other day to the little shopkeeper at Mary Tavy and told him he might have it 2d. below market price. He bought, but all his customers who bought Mrs. B's butter have returned it in his hands as too nasty to eat.[1]

May, the eldest daughter is painfully conscious of the state of his house, the poor girl said to Mrs. Russell, the Rector's wife at Mary Tavy, "O, Mrs. R. do advise me what to do. Shall I become a Hospital nurse or a Sister of Mercy. For I must get away from home; and I do not know what else to become. No one would marry me who knows the dirty hole in which I live. But I do not want to be either." The children go to Mary Tavy to entreat to be given biscuits or bread and butter as the food at home is so nasty. When I was there one day they had pork for dinner, burnt outside and really raw within an inch of the skin. The tumblers were so dirty that they looked like bad opal glass. They have a fine old oak table but so high that those who sit at it look like dogs squatted on their tails begging.

One of the unpleasantnesses the governess has to endure now is, that Mr. And Mrs. B. will not speak to her, and at dinner will not pass her food to her. Mr. B. puts it down on the floor behind him and she has to leave her place to pick her plate up. The Bishop gave Mr. B. the living – like all the Bishop's appointments it is a mistake. The squalor and meanness of the Rectory and its Rector are the talk and derision of the village. When Mr B. wants supper, or something to eat, he goes into the larder, cuts off a rasher of bacon, and fries it over his library or the dining room fire on the shovel, and eats it with a hunk of bread. Before the Bishop gave him Peter Tavy, he was at Brent Tor, and in the parsonage there, he had the hens roosing *[Presumably roosting intended]* on the stairs, and old sacks laid on the staircase in place of a stair-cloth. When ever I come away from that house I feel tickling all over, as though I have carried away a colony of fleas.

---

[1] Mr and Mrs R Bryant: See also the entry for 10 June 1882. There are honourable accounts of the adventures of the Rev. Dr. Bryant in *Further Reminiscences* pp 244-5, 271 with no hint of parsimony.

Not more than eight years ago the Revd. Thomas Roberts was rector at Belstone, a man of most repulsive face. He bought the living. One day about nine or ten years ago when my aunt was driving through Okehampton she found an excited crowd about the court, and on asking the reason heard that the rector of Belstone had been summoned before the magistrates for starving and maltreating a boy who lived with him, his wife's son by her first husband. When he came out of the court, the mob hooted and pursued him with curses and jeers to the inn where he took refuge. He had been found guilty and reprimanded and fined by the magistrates.

Rebecca Adams now living at Lew Quarry was born in this rectory house, her father and mother attended to parson Thomas who was curate of Lew. The Rector Mr. Elford resided in Tavistock. Thomas had a pupil, and he, (Thomas) was a misshapen fellow, with long arms and very big hands. He and his pupil had frequent squabbles. One day Rebecca's father was called by the noise into the library, and found Thomas and his pupil rolling on the floor together, fighting. The parson had his pupil by the throat with one of his huge hands, and in the other he held his big knife, closed, and he was jabbing at the young man's head with the closed knife, bruising and cutting it with the end where the blade joints are, and was screaming with rage, whilst the pupil howled with pain. The man dragged the parson off, and locked him into the dining room till he cooled, and sent the young man up to his bedroom. [1]

One would have supposed that such things were altogether of the past, but the Bryant's household and treatment of their governess, if less brutal is equally wicked. The governess is a Miss Fowler, daughter of the Chaplain to the workhouse at Bath, a strong Calvinist, he turned his daughter out of his house when she was eighteen and he has not seen her since, nor given her a penny, because she is a Catholic in her faith. She is now aged 22. Her younger sister who became a Roman Catholic he also turned out of the house.

Mr. Elford who was rector of Lew in old Madam Gould's reign, lived in Tavistock, and when the Bishop asked him why he was non resident, made the excuse that there was no barber in Lew who could curl his wig and shave him. In those days only old madam and the clerk could read so the clerk was wont to give out the psalms thus, "Let madam and I sing to the praise and glory of God." [2]

I have taken these extracts from the Register of Mary Tavy. Bapt. 1756 12 Sept, "Robert Elford child of Susanna Elford by her sister's husband, to whom she was married with the consent of her sister, the wife, who was at the wedding."

---

[1] The Rev. Caddy Thomas, appointed 1820. The story of his fight with a pupil is chronicled in *The Church Revival* p 128, and *Early Reminiscences*, p 164
[2] The Rev. Elford's Wig: *Early Reminiscences,* p 154. *The Church Revival,* p 128

Under the banns I see 1760, William Creedy, sojourner and Susanna Elford were called the last 2 Sundays in Feb. and 24th. Mch., but whether this W.C. was the brother in law and father of the child, the register does not say.[1]

In 1691, on March 12 occurs a humble entry, how one Willm. Warden a currier was whipped by the parson and church wardens of Whitchurch and ordered to be passed on as a wandering rogue from parish to parish by the officers then in 26 days to his native place, Cheshunt in Hertfordshire, and how, as the wardens were conveying him on horseback over Blackdown, he died on the back of the horse, and was buried the same night. [2]

Fig. 15 Shape of Shield from a 16th Century Pedigree.
[Of uncertain significance to the diary]

Another odd entry 1567, 23 Sept "Creature of God, son of Wm. Elford, buried. Six days later his wife Joan was buried, so probably this was some monstrosity. This next entry implied some suspicion of Mrs. Cake's fidelity. Bapt. 1627, 5 Aug "Nicolas filiat *[sic. ?filius]* Mr. Johan Cake jam senio confecti"[3].

The late Mr. Worth of Worth, the parson, and brother of Mrs. Lloyd Jones[4] (Worth) was an unredeemed blackguard. When he was in Jersey — I think —a lady made a dead set at him to get him to marry her daughter, a very sweet good girl; the mother was mainly anxious to secure a man of property and family as a son in law. The son was strongly opposed to his sister marrying such a scoundrel, and remonstrated, but in vain. Then he and some friends one night made Worth drunk, —which he was always ready to become, stripped him as naked as he was born, and brought him in a cab to the door of the house of the lady he was engaged to, the brother opened the door and led the naked reeling fellow into the room where his mother was and then thrust him before her with these words. "There! See the beast you are going to give your daughter to!"
Worth staggered, hiccupped and fell on the carpet. The lady was obliged to obtain assistance to have Mr. Worth removed, for her son went away and left him there,

---

[1] William Creedy: *A Book of Dartmoor*, p.137
[2] William Warden: *A Book of Dartmoor*, p.136
[3] jam senio confecti: Translation: *Now done in by old age*
[4] Mrs. Lloyd Jones. See also the entry for 21 November 1880.

but in spite of this she persisted in making her daughter marry him. The marriage turned out better than might have been expected, for the young wife did manage to control her beast, and bring him to some sort of decency and order, and he was to a great extent reformed by his marriage with her.

Cutting from unnamed newspaper pasted in the middle of entry for 24 June: Speech at Kelly college. 3 Aug. 1882:

The Rev. S Baring-Gould said it was with the greatest pleasure that he found the duty devolved upon him to propose a vote of thanks to Lord Devon for his very great kindness in coming to encourage the school with his presence, and to give away prizes to deserving boys. It was with great pleasure that he did so, and he spoke he believed in the name of all those who were connected with the place – the trustees, the masters, the boys, and all those who were interested in the school, which of course comprised the whole of those now present that day. He did so, however, with some sense of trepidation as well as pleasure, because it was a difficult thing to express the thanks they felt —the gratitude that was in their hearts towards his Lordship, without saying something which might appear anything like flattery, and although he might express the very feelings of their hearts he might say more than it was advisable or pleasant for his Lordship to hear. On the other hand if he said too little he might not fully express their gratitude, and thus in trying to escape Scylla fall into Charybdis.

He felt that immense gratitude was due to Lord Devon that day, because that school was a young school; it was an ambitious school, although at present it was only a small one; and it was to a young and small, but hopeful school that a word of counsel and encouragement and the presence of one who could give it were of great importance. Kelly College was an ambitious school, and it had every right to be an ambitious school. It stood in one of the most beautiful parts of Devon, with magnificent buildings, and a noble endowment, it had excellent masters, the freshest and purest of waters from Heathfield, and the freshest and purest of air. Kelly College, he repeated, had every right to look forward to a great future, and the school had a right to be an ambitious one — (cheers.) Now it was with schools and institutions when they were young as it was with boys and young men.

They started with the most magnificent expectations, and with the most complete confidence that they would prosper and go through the battle of life without difficulty; but after a while a time came when a feeling of depression stole over the heart; when it was found that success did not come so soon as it was expected, and that prosperity was to be wooed and would not come speedily when invoked.

Then it was that young institutions, as with young boys and men there came a feeling of depression and disappointment. And he had no doubt that those present who were old could look back to the past and remember when their early hopes were dashed, and life did not look to them so full of enjoyment as it did a few years before; and then some kind friend — an elder — gave them his advice, and urged them not to lose heart, but to pick up courage; and that was a turning point in their career, and they looked back with a great thankfulness to him who then gave them a word of encouragement.

Now they felt the greatest gratitude to Lord Devon for so kindly giving them a word of encouragement and the cheering of his presence when the college was still young, and when it had not made such rapid progress as was hoped at the outset. They were often impatient because success did not come to them all at once. They forgot that... *[Several lines here obscured by gummed paper]* ....it should look forward to the time when it would take its place among the great schools of the kingdom.

Some of them who may have read Besant and Rice's[1] "Ready Money Mortiboy," would remember that when he came back from America he drew up a table of ten commandments, and when called upon by the vicar of a parish to address the school children, and he came to speak a few words to the boys, the two commandments young Ready Money uttered with stentorian voice, with all the weight of American experience, and with all the eloquence he had at his disposal, were these — in the first place, never be satisfied with what you have got; and in the second place — never lose confidence in yourself — (cheers.) If boys would start in the race of life with these two maxims they were pretty sure to make their way in this world, and it was the same he thought with young institutions — if they would never be satisfied with what they had got, and if they would never lose confidence in themselves, then a bright and prosperous future would be open before them — (applause). But if they remained contented with their present state, and if they had no great ambition, and worst of all, if they lost confidence in themselves, then it was all up with them. Now the Germans had a fable which they told that was very much to the same effect as "Ready Money Mortiboy."

A woman once invited a fairy to be god-mother to her son, and on the fairy asking what gifts she should bestow upon him, the mother replied — give him impudence —(laughter). "What," said the fairy, "will you not ask for wealth, rank, and many friends?" "No," replied the mother, "If he has got impudence he has got everything that the world will give him." —(renewed laughter.) Impudence only came of self-confidence. He was not a fairy god-father of Kelly College he was sorry to say, and all he could do that day was to give it his very best wishes, and the very best wish he could offer Kelly College was plenty of impudence and self-reliance, and that it might never lose confidence in itself, and then let the future take care of itself for a bright and prosperous one was pretty sure to ensue — (laughter and applause.)

The rev. gentleman alluded to the custom among the Norsemen, when they were going upon any long and dangerous expedition, to ask some great man to lend them his presence. Many were the stories of how the young men fought, and thought they were saved from peril by the sudden flashing out of the presence of him whom they had invoked. Kelly College that day had invoked the assistance of the Earl of Devon and his Lordship had shown them his presence —(applause.)

---

[1] *Ready Money Mortiboy, 'A matter of fact story'* by Sir Walter Besant, historian and novelist, 1836-1901, and James Rice, novelist, 1843-1882

They would hope that with that presence came encouragement, and that it was an earnest of a brighter future —(much applause.) He had been asked by the headmaster to address a few words to the boys. He had already said that they were not to lose confidence in themselves; that they were never to be satisfied with present attainments, but to press on to something better. Now the piece of advice he was going to give was of a different sort. It was that they must never expect to enjoy all the advantages without experiencing some of the disadvantages of life. Wherever they went, and whatever they undertook, he knew youth was sanguine, and boys looked forward to a future as to a time full of rosy light, and when they would only have to ask for anything the world would give, and it would be theirs; when they would only have to put up their hand for anything they required, and it would be put in their palm. But he wished them to remember that it would be with them in their life as it was in their school days — there would be advantages and disadvantages largely mixed together.

The rev. gentleman then related in an amusing manner an incident which once came within his own experience. He said when a young man he once visited an auction, and among the articles to be disposed of was a comfortable looking rocking chair. Being at that time a bachelor and a great reader he was anxious to become the possessor of that chair. But with the chair was offered a rusty frying pan full of holes, and the person who purchased the chair had to take the frying pan as well — (laughter.) He purchased the chair and said he did not want the frying pan, but was told that having purchased the easy chair he must take the frying pan also. He offered the frying pan to anyone who would take it, but everyone declined to accept it, saying, "No, you have got the easy chair, and you must carry home the frying pan" — (much laughter.) It was the rule of life that, whenever they had something which was good, there was always something disadvantageous with it —that with the rocking chair there was always a rusty frying pan (laughter.)

The farmers had rejoiced because there was no frost during the winter now they were lamenting that the harvest was bad. He went early in the spring to the nursery of Mr. Yeo who was rejoicing at the mildness of the season, but a month ago the same Mr. Yeo was seen by a visitor to his nursery going along, bent under the weight of a wheelbarrow full of a sort of black mixture. When Mr. Yeo was asked what on earth he had in it, he put the barrow down sadly, and drawing a heavy sigh from the bottom of his loaded heart, and wiping the dew-drops from his brow, he replied "Slugs, sir, slugs" — (much laughter.) There had been no frost through the winter. It was another case of the rocking chair and the frying pan —(laughter.) Some of the boys before him were growing up, and would soon have to go out into life. In the matter of profession they were full of hope. They thought the profession on which they had set their hearts, and the life they had chalked out for themselves was sure to be prosperous. He hoped and trusted that they would be prosperous in whatever profession might be theirs, but they were altogether mistaken if they thought they would not have disadvantages. They would probably remember when they met their first rebuff the story of his frying pan —(laughter.)

In some years to come they would be thinking of settling down and choosing a wife – (laughter.) — who would be the ideal of all perfection — (renewed laughter.)

And then they would think when they had earned enough to support a wife and they had the beautiful creature before their eyes, that they would indeed stick to the rocking chair of life, but they would find even then, that there was a rusty frying pan as well —(much laughter and prolonged applause.)

1882 **3 July:**

In Launceston. Called on Mrs. Smith at Dockacre, the widow of the surgeon on Lew Down,[1] when I was a boy. Dockacre is a very curious house that belonged to the Bedford's. It is one room thick, built of timber and plaster, with a succession of gables in front. The house is let with a bundle of old walking sticks which Mrs. Smith showed me. They are entered in the lease. One of the walking sticks is the backbone of some creature, I suppose a serpent. Another has a handsome copper gilt head, a third is prettily inlaid, and a fourth has a musical instrument in the handle like a child's pan pipe with metal tongues. Also two quite ordinary sticks. The saying is the house is unbearable without the sticks in it. Those who rented the house before Mrs. Smith were there two years and left it unable to endure the discomfort any longer. The noises, the pacing and knocking in the house gave them no rest. They left the bundle of sticks at the lawyers. Mrs. Smith took them to the house, but then, —she slated over all the rat holes, and that probably accounts for the cessation of noises.[2]

A more curious tenancy is that of Tresmarrow near Launceston, where the house goes with a skull. The farmer now there buried the skull, but the noises, —voices — knocks and tramplings heard at night were intolerable, so they dug the skull up again and restored it to the place in the apple chamber, where it now is, —then the sounds ceased.[3]

1882 **4 July:**

Pengelly tells me that a waiter at the Clarendon Inn once informed him that but for him my grandfather would have lost every acre he had. This is probably an exaggeration but still it shows that my grandfather was playing desperately. The story is this. My grandfather was wont, when he went to Exeter to put up at the Clarendon; and there played. He was playing one night with a gentleman and losing terribly, when the waiter observed that there was a mirror behind my grandfather, and that his opponent looked into it and read his hand. He went at once to the landlord who came in and ordered the gentleman to refund and leave the house. After that my grandfather never played in the Clarendon again.[4] He contested Honiton, and that cost him several thousand pounds. The Coryton

---

[1] Dr Thomas W Smith and his wife Maria
[2] **Dockacre walking sticks***:* **Explanatory endnote 42.**
[3] The Tresmarrow Skull: A *Book of Folklore,* Chapter 8
[4] William Baring-Gould's gambling luck: *Early Reminiscences,* p 240

property was then for sale and if he had not tried to stand for Honiton he might have bought it. Pengelly tells me that when he was a boy he remembers helping the old gig up into the hay loft, as my grandfather was in fear of the bailiffs coming, and he did not want the gig to be seized. Pengelly confirms the story I heard at Staverton about Edward Gould having shot a man with whom he had gambled, so far, that he had always heard that Edward Gould had killed a man, but he had not any knowledge of the circumstances.[1]

1882 **1 Aug:**
Mary, Margaret and Edward[2] have returned from Freiburg where they have been at school for ten months. Mary is very white and tall and has had bad irruptions over her face caused by poverty of blood. Edward is thin but very well. Margaret seems to have suffered least. It is well they are home as they might have become seriously out of health by a longer stay. Mary particularly. German food does not suit English growing children. It is clear from their manner that the two girls have been well cared for and that the tone of the school is good, honourable and refined. Dear Mary is as sweet as ever, Margaret as funny and natural. Sabine has lost none of his frankness and has the same honest truthful look in his brown eyes, and his heart is as warm as ever, dear fellow.

1882 **3 Aug:** Went to prize giving at Kelly College and met Lord Devon, and made a speech which I have pasted in elsewhere.[3] Lord Devon hopes that Grace and I will pay him a visit at Powderham somewhat later in the autumn.

1882 **14 Aug:**
Lord Lawrence was invited to Windsor to dine. When he arrived at the castle and was preparing to dress he found he had not packed his dress trousers, and had only a light dove coloured pair on his legs. He rang and asked one of the servants if by any chance he could be provided with a pair, but it was some time before he could be fitted. When he came down the Queen had already gone into dinner. Lord Lawrence went into the dining room and slipped into his place on the left side of the Queen —he was the guest of the evening — and the Queen would not notice him thinking this a gross breach of etiquette. Lord L. told his story to the lady on his left, who was vastly tickled, and told it to her neighbour and the story travelled around the table, and reached the gentleman sitting on the Queen's other side and he told her Majesty, who at once turned to Lord Lawrence all amiability, and ever after when she met him, could not forebear smiling at the recollection of his trouble.[4]

---

[1] Edward Gould's trial for murder: *Devon Characters and Strange Events.* Series 2. pp 218-220
[2] Children's ages: Mary 13, Margaret 12 and Edward 11
[3] Kelly speech: see entry for 24 July 1882
[4] Lord Lawrence and Queen Victoria: *Further Reminiscences*, p 156.

1882 **23 Aug:**
Receipt for Cider cup 1 qt. Cider, 1 glass brandy, 3 glasses sherry, sugar to taste, 1 lemon, ¼ nutmeg and 1 stick cinnamon. More brandy may be added.[1]

1882 **24 Aug:**
School treat winding up with procession of children with banners to the church; we had the mothers and teachers to tea, and these fell in behind the children, and the scene winding down the hill was exceedingly pretty. At church we had chandeliers and altar brilliantly lighted, and as the children came in they gave up their banners which were ranged round the chancel. The children were seated in the chancel and the parents occupied the rest of the church. We had a bright children's service and metrical litany and the children sang out lustily. I catechised them before their parents, and all the service was over in 40 minutes. It was altogether charming and striking; and I hope will have delighted those there. The children answered well and were proud to show what they had learned before their parents. Never before since the Reformation has there been anything like it in the church.

1882 **19 Sep:**
Mr. E. Russell has been staying with we *[sic]*, he is the son of Lord Edward Russell; he is in delicate health, a very charming man.

1882 **25 Sep:**
Went to Staverton to finish the register of Totnes.

1882 **27 Sep:**
Went to Salcombe to preach at Maitland Kelly's harvest festival. Heard a good story of the Bishop He was holding a Confirmation at Modbury and lunched at the parsonage, where several of the neighbours were invited to meet him. Mrs Green, the wife of the Vicar, is a queer sort of woman, not very mannerly. At table she said, "Oh, Bishop!" (She did not call him My Lord) "What do you think happened to my aunt? She was going to America, when she dreamed that the vessel was lost with all hands on board. She thought nothing of this, but next night dreamed it again. Now, Bishop, was not that remarkable? So my aunt thought, and she did not go by the vessel. And the ship was lost and all who sailed in her. Now, don't you consider, Bishop, that this was a remarkable intervention of Providence for the saving of my aunt." "Well, Ma'rm, as I don't know your arnt, I carn't say." This was told me by Maitland Kelly who was there and heard it.[2]

1882 **2 Oct:**
To Crediton. Have been over Fulford House. The carving in the hall simply magnificent, but in awful condition. It was patched up by Nash more than half a

---

[1] Sabine's Cider Cup: Made and consumed by the transcriber and his family at a New Year's party 2005. Recommended.
[2] **Archbishop Frederick Temple and the Aunt:** *Further Reminiscences*, **p 116-7. See also explanatory endnote 21**

century ago and stuff of Grinling Gibbons in lime wood from the Ballroom was put with it, very beautiful but quite out of keeping with the Henry viith. work in oak. Now the lime wood is utterly eaten away by worms and gone past recovery. The oak will go next. Wind and rain blow in at the great staircase window on the parquetteire floors. It is sad.[1]

1882 **4 Oct:**

"Who made your body?" asked a Sunday school teacher of a little girl. "Mother made my body," was the ready reply, "But aunt made my skirt."

6 Oct 1882:

John Bright made a speech the other day, extraparliamentary, on reform. He said that the upper classes, the intellectual, the cultured classes were bitterly opposed to Mr. Gladstone's government, and that for the carrying out of any work of reform or any beneficial change the appeal must be made to the bottom and not to the top of the social body.[2]

> "Begin at the Bottom and not at the Top
> Leave out all the Gentry appeal to the shop
> Bid ignorance, prejudice govern! Why so
> To this doctrine I give an emphatical no.
> But —begin at the bottom of John Bright Esquire
> With a good cat – o' – ninetails of whipcord and wire
> Begin at it lustily, stingingly then
> To this maxim I yield a right cordial Amen"

1882 **10 Oct:**

Have been engaged a whole week at writing a series of Church songs "I'm a little Pilgrim" "The Church is my mother" "The vessel of the Church" "The Church's Salvation Army."

1882 **12 Oct:**

Heard old Mr. Garde tell a story some years ago to show the primitive ways of inns in Cornwall in old times. He was travelling when a young man in Cornwall and he put up at a little inn. It was then not at all uncommon for guests to sleep in one room with only a board partition between them reaching halfway up to the ceiling. Garde was given his bed in this long room, and some man was in the next compartment, who at supper had certainly indulged rather much in apples. During the night Garde heard him groaning and talking to himself, "O dear! Dam these windy apples! I know I shall! I'm sure I shall! I bet a guinea I shall! I cannot hold it in! I bet a guinea I shall explode!" A minute or two after the explosion followed. Garde tapped at the wooden partition with his knuckle and said "Won your bet, Sir!"

---

[1] Little Fulford: (to distinguish it from Fulford House, Dunsford.) later known as Shobrooke Park. Built by Sir William Peryham in the 1580s
[2] **John Bright's Bottom: Explanatory endnote 43**

Some five and twenty or thirty years ago I rode over the moor to Bovey Tracey, and put up there for the Sunday. In the morning I asked the Landlord where the closet was. "Closet Sir!" he answered "lor a mussy! We've no closets here. Folks go out into the backyard, anywhere." Seeing I hesitated, he added, "There's a reverend gentleman staying here, and as he's rather old and shaky on his pins. I hold a pole against the wall and he sits hoover that. I'll do the likes for you if you be fantastic."

1882 **14 Oct:**
Receipt for "Strain oil" oil of Brick, 2 oz. oil of Spike. 2 oz. Oil of Pelis, 2 oz. Mix and rub well into the sprain. This will also heal cuts and bruises, and is good for cattle and horses as well as human beings.[1]

1882 **21 Nov:**
The 110th Court Pengelly has attended. Edward dines with the farmers, this makes the fourth heir Pengelly has seen at the Court.

Went over the other day to Sheepstor. Had not seen it since the "Restoration," the magnificent screen has been destroyed. I received from the builder, Blatchford, a few scraps which I have given to Mr. Cooke the vicar, and he has set them up in his church with an alms box underneath it and a paper stating that the screen was destroyed in 1862, and that contributions are requested for his restoration. Sir Massey Lopez came into the church and saw this, "Dear me," said he, "I did not know that I had destroyed anything worth preserving." Fortunately Mr. Walker, Vicar of Walkhampton has got good drawings of the screen before it was destroyed. But the vicar of Sheepstor is so very poor that he cannot hope to do again what was undone so lately, a new screen would cost about £200.[2]

I saw the old house of the Elfords, Longstone,[3] not much of the ancient house remains, and the principal part has been pulled down I suspect.

//////   modernized in 18th Cent. and adapted for farm

|||||| ancient, date 1633.

Dotted area   ancient, destroyed

[Several indecipherable works struck through followed by] As ground falls away rapidly *(?) [then another indecipherable word struck through followed by]* only a wall. cant therefore form a terrace.

a — b. main gate now walled up and used as barn.

---

[1] **Strain oil: Explanatory endnote 44:**
[2] Sheepstor screen: *A Book of Dartmoor*, pp 228-9
[3] Longstone, Sheepstor and the windstrew: *A Book of Dartmoor*, pp 220-1

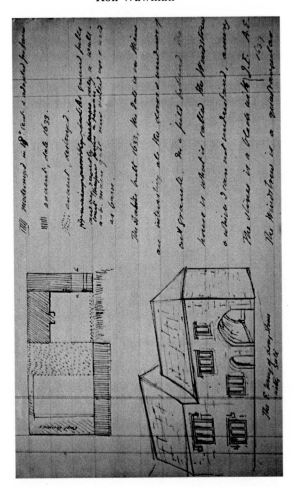

Fig. 16 *Longstone, old house of the Elfords at Sheepstor*

The stables built 1633, the date is on them, are interesting all the doors and windows of cut granite. In a field behind the house is what is called The Windstrew and which I cannot understand, among the stones is a block with 1637 J.E.   A.E. The Windstrew is a quadrangular block of cut granite stones. I did not measure the sides, but I fancy about 15 ft. each way. It rises 3 ft. 6 from the ground, a solid basement of stone, such as might be the basement of a gallows. I suspect that it was a dovecot, square not round like that at Pridhamsleigh. Same day I went to Meavy and saw the "Great House" an interesting and fine specimen of a late mansion of about Charles IInd. time belonging to the Drakes. Half this has been pulled down, but the porch and all the buildings on the left remain. The state rooms and grand staircase were on the right, and those have been destroyed. The panelling was removed when it was pulled down by the late Sir Trayler Drake to Buckland Abbey. [1]

---

[1] Great House, Meavy: *A Book of Dartmoor*, p 236

1882 **Sunday 26 Nov:**
Began to write "John Herring" on All Saints' Day but did not do much to it, and recast the first chapter on the 11th and have since written twelve chapters.

Have been absent for a week doing the Registers of Woolboro'[1] Newton Abbott, *[sic]* Bovey Tracey, Chudleigh and Abbots Kirswell. At the last place saw the old Church house with oak doors.

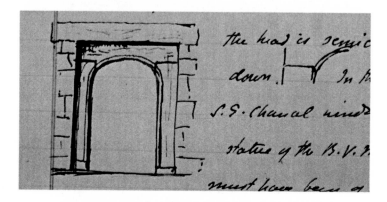

Fig. 17 Abbot's Kirswell Church house

The head is semicircular and cleverly notched down. In the church, at the angle of S.E. chancel window is a life size —or larger statue of the B.V.M. terribly mutilated. It must have been of great beauty. The pose of the body and hair and draping are fine.[2]

1882 **21 Dec:**
I began to write "John Herring" on Novr. 1st. , but was unable to do more than the first chapter for a fortnight. I have now got to the 24th.[3]

1883 20 Jan:
Have been engaged in planting alternate chestnuts and ~~maple~~ limes to form an avenue from the Bridge over the Lew water to the Church park on one side and the fork of the road to Lew Quarry on the other. The putting up of the railing has occupied the men a month.

I have just torn down the following notice stuck up against the linney wall at the crossroads,[4] painted in red.
> "Lord Fokestaff's *[sic]* Stag Hounds will meet, Wednesday Jan 24 at Lew Trenchard at 7 P.M. by invitation; when good sport may be expected as the Hounds will be hunted by that celebrated huntsman Old Tom."

---

[1] Wolborough, nr Newton Abbot, Devon
[2] **Abbotskerswell, statue of the Blessed Virgin Mary: explanatory endnote 45**
[3] *John Herring*: see also the entry for 26 November 1882
[4] Lewdown Crossroads: by Lewtrenchard school

The meaning is this. A young carpenter lives at Crossroads, married not long ago, —
only a few months; and the scandal is about that she has been unfaithful to him. So on
Wednesday night there will be a stag hunt about their cottage. A man dressed in a hide
with cows horns will run, followed by men and boys yelping like a pack of hounds, and
Old Tom as a huntsman with a horn careering them on. I remember a similar affair
many years ago, my father was very angry and interfered, and did his utmost to stop it,
but this only made the matter worse, it went on for weeks. A year or two ago another
case occurred at Coryton, and Mr. Newman had the ringleaders up before the
magistrates, but nothing could be done as no illegal act had been committed, and so
after that the thing was renewed. The best is to take no notice of it, and then they are
content with one night of disturbance. It is an old custom and dies hard.[1]

1883 **29 Jan:**
Gone to Worth[2] to pay a visit to my old friend Lloyd Worth. The house very
interesting but sadly wrecked. It has been pillaged again and again, on the death of
Reginald Worth all the books and furniture were sold by auction and only such
sticks of furniture remain as Lloyd Worth bought in. The great drawing room had a
magnificent plaster ceiling. The dowager Mrs. Worth —still alive had it converted
into bedrooms and a low ceiling placed beneath the other which was broken
through for the stays that held up the modern low ceiling. I went up with a candle
by a ladder between the ceilings and saw how exquisite the old one was.

Old Worth ran off with Mrs. Codrington, and his wife when he wanted to patch up
matters only consented to this on condition of receiving an annuity of £700. There
is also the second dowager on the estate, so that £1,400 goes out in annuities.
Lloyd Worth was Lloyd Jones when I knew him, he married the sister of Reginald
Worth and as R.W. died without issue, Lloyd Jones has taken the name of his wife
and for her, manages the property.[3]

1883 **17 Feb:**
Spent a week at Kingsbridge doing the registers of the churches thereabouts.

1883 **26 Feb:**
Paid a visit to Mr. And Mrs. Woodley of Halshanger near Ashburton. I met the two
Amories there, they are natives of Ashburton and were brought up by their
grandmother. They told me several particulars about Edward Gould which I did not
know. After he had killed the man, and was being tried for it, Dunning saw that the
case was bad against him owing to the evidence of one man who saw him shoot his
adversary. It was full moon, and by the moon light he recognised Edward's horse, and
dress. Dunning got a sheet of almanack printed, i.e. 4 months with the moon altered so
as to make no moonlight on the night of the murder. This he put in his overcoat pocket
bound into his Kalendar. *[sic]* At the trial the witness was cross-questioned as to the
recognition. He swore to it because the full moon shone on Edward Gould. The judge

[1] Lord Folkstaff's staghounds: *Further Reminiscences*, pp 121-2.
[2] Worth, near Northlew, Devon
[3] Lloyd-Worth: See also the entry for 24 June 1882

asked for a Kalendar, to see if the moon then was full. Kalendars were not at that time as common as they are now, and no one in the court had one. Then Dunning said, "My Lord, I believe there is one in my overcoat pocket, at least, there was one yesterday, and if you will send an officer to look, I trust he will find it there." The calendar was found, produced, —and there was no moon on the night of the murder! So Ed. G. was acquitted, and the trick was not discovered till after.[1]

Another story told me by Amory was to this effect. Edward brought his white horse that he had ridden in the battle of Dettingen and captured the enemy's standard, back to England, he had the shoes taken off, and he was turned out on the meadows of Pridhamsleigh, and never allowed to do any further work. One day a man, not knowing the history of the horse and the store set on him went up to Ed. Gould and said, "I'll give you a sovereign a leg for that old white horse yonder." Edward was transported with rage, he rushed into the house and came out with a pistol in each hand and said, "Get off the premises, you scoundrel, or I will blow your brains out with one pistol and send a bullet through your heart with the other," and he chased the man down into the road and over the border. One day the bailiffs were sent into Pridhamslee House. They found E.G. seated on a barrel with a pistol in his hand, "Look here," said he, "I am sitting on a barrel of gunpowder. I don't care a damn for my own life and infinitely less for yours. Unless you take yourselves off this instant, I'll fire my pistol into the barrel, and we shall go together to Kingdom come."[2]

1883 **24 Mch:**
Easter Eve. Finished "John Herring" and the transcript.

1883 **25 Mch:**
Easter Day. Sent "John Herring off to the publishers.

1883 **14 April:**
Offered £100 for copyright. Accepted.

1883 **11 May:**
Baby born.[3]

Heard from Maria Beere some stories of old Madam, she heard them from her grandfather and from old Mary Baker who both had known old Madam. When Madam died all the shutters of the house flew open, and the hind[4] who was in the kitchen, thinking there must be robbers outside ran out, where he saw old Madam standing by the walnut tree at the back of the house near the shippon.

One cold day, old madam was out and nearly frozen, and she saw the workmen engaged on the farm and pitied them. She came in and bade the cook to heat them

---

[1] **Edward Gould, Dunning and the Calendar: Explanatory endnote 46**
[2] Further tales of Edward Gould: *Early Reminiscences*, p 156-7.
[3] Baby: Felicitas (nickname 'Titus') Sabine's 10th child
[4] Hind: farm-servant

jorums[1] of cider. Then she sat down by the fire, and gradually grew warm, then, as she was still in her warm clothes grew very hot, "God bless me," she said, "The weather has changed. Tell the cook not to heat the cyder." I have heard a similar story from old Ball the miller, but he did not tell it of Madam, nor was it of cyder, but an order to take coals round to the poor.

Maria tells me that in old Madam's time the women came to church with folded bright coloured aprons in their hand and these they put on in the porch before entering. Also, she says that my grandmother was very particular about the people kneeling and not sitting, so that the habit of sitting instead of kneeling in church at prayer must have grown up since. I remember when every man bowed towards the altar or parson, and every woman curtsied on entering church. Also at Stowford, — not here — all the people use to bow at the Glorias. [2]

Fig. 18 *Not Elizabeth Gould. Pencil drawing pasted in*

In unknown hand in pencil by whoever drew the picture: Blue satin hat, powdered hair blue eyes, fair complexion – pale blue dress and muslin fichu brown sash — supposed done by Wright of Derby[3]

Undated inscription by Sabine: Elizabeth Gould who m. J. Balguy e.g. picture in possession of Major Balguy

Later undated inscription: Heard 1891 from a sister of Major Balguy to say that this is a mistake. His real portrait of Elizabeth is still with the Halls.[4] It is another Mrs. Balguy.

---

[1] Jorum: large drinking bowl
[2] Maria Beere: *Early Reminiscences,* p 155, Maria Hierne, tales of Old Madam Gould.
[3] **Wright of Derby: explanatory endnote 47.**
[4] Portrait of Elizabeth Gould: See entry for 6 February 1885

1883 29 Sep:

Michaelmas Day. Grace cut the turf and let the water into the Lime Quarry which is now abandoned. I have planted the ramps well with shrubs and pines, at some considerable expense.[1]

Made an excursion this year with Mr. Gatrill, Bamberg, then through the Franconian Switzerland to Baireuth *[sic]*, where I heard the Parzifael of Wagner; thence to Nürnberg, then Cham, Fürth i/w and by the Arber and Osser to Eisenstein,[2] thence to Passau, the Danube to Linz, from Linz to the Traunsee, Hallstatersee, Wolfgangsee, Ischl, Salzburg, Königsee, and home by Munich, just 30 days, cost £15; all included, trains and inns![3]

Received for "John Herring" £100. disposed of "Margery of Quether" to Cornhill for £40

1883 **1 Dec:**

> "Gold maketh not a true Gould
> Loss makes not Gould dross
> Gilded silver makes not gold
> Gould bideth bright however old
> I trust not in gold but in Gould
> For misers Gold get friends Gould"

Sent me by Everard Green, whence he got it I do not know.

It is capable of improvement.

> "Gold makes not Gould nor any loss
> turneth fine Gould to sorry dross
> Silver that's gilded is not gold
> Gold bydeth bright however old
> Trust not in gold, but Gould is true
> Gold is right good but bettered is by U.

1883 **10 Dec:**

> The poet sings the Breath of Morn // His rising sweet
> But I was not in Eden born // So find it no such treat
> Till Sol away the damp hath charm'd // I lie in bed preferring
> And when the world is aired and warmed // 'Tis time enough for stirring.[4]

---

[1] **Quarry Lake: explanatory endnote 48**
[2] Mt. Arber 1457 metres; Mt. Osser 1293 metres; Bayerisch Eisenstein
[3] Map 3: Bavarian tour. Note: The Bohemian part of this excursion appears in *Further Reminiscences*, chapter 13 but the date is incorrectly given there as 1886.
[4] Sabine gave no indication of the source of this verse.

1884 5 Jan:
Attended the funeral of my dear friend Lloyd Worth of Worth. How sad is life, we were the closest of friends at College, like brothers. But I was in Yorkshire and then in Essex, and years passed without our meeting, at last I came here, and then my great delight was that now we were in the same county, we would see much of each other. It was not to be. I visited him last year in January, and when Felicitas was born, I asked him to come down and be her godfather. But then scarlet fever was at Worth and two of his children laid up with it. Then he took them to the seaside, and only the week before Christmas he meditated coming to see me, but at the last moment changed his mind, and went to see his married sister. On Xmas Day he caught cold, inflammation of the lungs set in, and he sank. Life is one series of bitter disappointments.

1884 **18 Jan:**
Received for the Seven Last Words £15, from Tauchnitz for right to reprint "John Herring" £25. from Smith and Elder for "Margery of Quether" £40

1884 **20 Jan:**
Two local Devon sayings just picked up.
"If you scald your backside you must expect to sit on the bladders"[1]
"I don't care to see sheep dressed as lambs" of a woman who dressed young.

1884 26 Jan:
Mrs. Jackman at Broadwood Inn, aged 40, says she perfectly remembers seeing Jack O'Lanterns when she was a child on Bradever Moor between Broadwood and Stowford. She says she always heard they danced over metal underground. Our servant Ellenor *[sic]* Sybella Hawton says that her father has often told her he has seen Jack O'Lanterns between Bratton and Broadwood

William Henry Shopland of Broadwood who is between 40 and 50, has never seen Jack O'Lanterns but he did see this, he says. About 20 years ago a man named William Hicks who was renting some of the glebe, lost his son quite a young man just about harvest time. Shortly after his sister and the nieces were gleaning one evening in this fields, and after they were gone, I (Shopland) and some others who were harvesting near saw a light dancing about just where these girls had been at work, it ran from place to place, the evening was fast closing in, and we saw it perfectly, as a blue candle flame, it moved up and down, and at last settled on a mow. For three or four months after this light continued to be seen in the same field, by myself and others, we used to go and have a look at it, of evenings. The land was dry there and it could not have been a Jack O'Lantern. We thought the young man who had died was troubled in mind about something, and it was his spirit.

---

[1] For 'bladders' possibly read 'blisters' although those knowledgeable in Lewdown Devon dialect are unfamiliar with such usage today.

At Buddle I saw one day a remarkably handsome old woman Mrs. Worden, with a finely cut profile, and a face of a lady. I do not know what her Xtian name is, but her daughter is Joanna a fine girl. Mrs. Worden was engaged when a girl to a young man who gave her a silk kerchief for her neck and bosom, as a keepsake. The young man died, she gave away the kerchief, and married Mr. William Worden the farmer at Buddle. One night the young man stood by her bedside and reproached her having given away the keepsake he had let her have, he did not rebuke her for marrying, but only for this. Then she promised to recover the kerchief and keep it to her dying day, and to be buried with it, tied about her throat and crossed over her bosom. When she said this, he was satisfied, and she in her bewilderment, partly in assurance that she would keep her word, partly as a final farewell, held out her hand to him, —it was her left hand; —he refused it, and then she gave him her right hand. The story is well known in Broadwood, but she does not like to be questioned about it.

The Wulf is a river that flows into the Thrustle, *[Thrushel]* from Broadwood. From time immemorial a ghost has been seen where the road crosses it leading to Portgate. Originally there was no bridge there, but a ford. The ghostly figure used to stand by the water, and when anyone wanted to cross at night, lifted him or her and bore the traveller across. Some say after the bridge was built the ghost disappeared. Others say, not so, it took twelve parsons to lay it. An old person died lately in Broadwood who was the last carried over the water by this spiritual S. Christopher.[1]

Shopland says that he and ~~twelve~~ ten other men resolved to watch over midnight in the tower of Broadwood Church on S. Mark's Eve to see the spirits, but all failed save two, himself and another, and as it drew towards midnight his companion's courage failed and he left. Then Shopland's heart misgave him, and he went away, but he turned and looked before he left the church, and he saw something white drawing itself along, like as a cat might creep, along the roof.[2]

A farmer in Broadwood, by name William Rich, at Town, was very ill ~~this~~ last summer with a complication of disorders, chief of which was, what I suppose was diphtheria but the people said it was thrush. Dr. Budd of N. Tawton was called in and gave the man up, as did the Launceston doctor. Then his relatives sent for a posthumous child to be brought and breath into his mouth, this was done several times in the week – and the man is now well and about, and the child is none the worse.[3]

---

[1] For the stories of Mrs Jackman, Mr Shopland, Mrs Worden and St Christopher see *Further Reminiscences* pp 122-5. For St Christopher, see *A Book of Folklore*, chap. 4
[2] **St Mark's Eve: Explanatory endnote 49**
[3] **Dr Budd of North Tawton, Devon: See explanatory note 50.**

1884 **19 May:**
Grace and I went to Kilkhampton[1] to stay with the Thynnes. Lord and Lady Clinton staying there also. Lovely weather.

1884 **20 May:**
Drove to Wellcombe.[2] *[sic]* Curious old holy well near the Church.

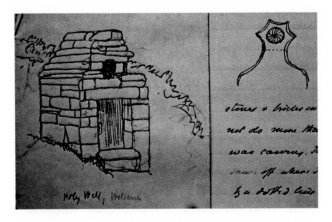

Fig. 19 *Holy Well and bench ends, Wellcombe*

The bench ends have been recently cut away, the tops sawn off and the majority destroyed. Some tracery on the ends, but the few that remained were piled up with stones and bricks on them, and I could not do more than feel that there was carving. The heads had been sawn off where I have indicated by a dotted line.[3]

1884 **14 June:**
A curious story. Julian insists that he was in the vegetable garden a couple of days ago, picking gooseberries when he saw standing among the Gooseberry bushes a little man of his own height 3 ft. 6, with a brown peaked cap, and red jacket and green trousers. He had black hair and whiskers and moustache and short black beard, he looked angrily at Julian, who stood and looked at him, then Julian getting frightened came away and told first Vera, and then Edward. He is very circumstantial in his description which never varies. [4]

I never found Julian tell an untruth and he is perfectly frank about this; Edward tried to put him out by telling me the story with a little difference, but Julian corrected him at once, "No, ~~Edward~~ Sabine, it was not so" then, he told his

---

[1] Kilkhampton, Cornwall, approx. 4 miles northeast of Bude.
[2] Wellcombe, Devon, approx. 4 miles northwest of Kilkhampton.
[3] Wellcombe Church and Holy well: *A Book of Devon*, pp 152-3
[4] Children's ages: Edward 13, Vera 9 and Julian 7

version, and Edward said that it was the same he had told him immediately after leaving the place where he saw the little man.[1]

1884 7 July:
Left for Germany, Freiburg, Bludenz, the Montavun Thal[2], the Patznauner Thal,[3] Finztermunz,[4] Mals.[5] The Ortler[6], Botzen[7] Innsbrück, Munich and home with Gatrill.[8]

1884 22 August:
Returned home.

1884 1 Oct:
Roses climbing in new Greenhouse built this year

S

| E | b   c   d   e   f   g |
| | a   h |

   a.   Charles Lefebvre; b. Rêve d'or; c.? Maréchal Niel d. Marie van Houtte (?);
   e.   Devoniense; f. Belle Lyonaise; g. Cheshunt hybrid; h. Mme Lombarte
[The question marks are by Sabine]

Roses in Spring garden put in autumn 1883

| m   n | a   b   c
d   e   f |
| o | g   h   i
k   l |

---

[1] **Julian's little man: Explanatory endnote 51.**
[2] Montavun Thal: Modern spelling: Montafun Thal
[3] Patznauner Thal: Paznauner Thal
[4] Finztermunz: Hochfinstermunz
[5] Mals: Mals im Vinschgau
[6] The Ortler: The highest mountain in the Eastern Alps
[7] Botzen: Bozen
[8] South Tyrol Tour: See map 4. This excursion is described in *Further Reminiscences*, chapter 12, *The Montafun Thal*, where the date is incorrectly given as 1885.

a. Mme. Charles Trufont; b. (?) c. Mlle. Thérèse Levet[1]
d. Mme. Verlot; e. Mrs. Sophie Fropot; f. David Andry[2]
g. Dupuy Jamain; h. King's Acre; i. Gloire de Dijon;
k. Chas. Rouillard; l. (?); m. (?); n. Antoine Mouton.
[The question marks are by Sabine.]

Filled up this year the blank places in the garden with fruit trees. Rebuilt garden wall and made greenhouses, also brought water from the back of Lew house into the garden. I brought water from the reservoirs below Down House in iron pipes to Lew House in winter 1875-6. This year I built the back rooms to the cottage on the Down now occupied by Seth Perkin on same side of main road as school and near it. Last year I built the additional back kitchen and bedroom to Wooda.[3] This year drained Wooda marsh below the wood, and raised from 6 ft. under the surface a large chestnut tree turned perfectly black, —thought at first it was black oak.

Bought this year at Freiburg the ~~Dresden~~ Ludwigsburg figure of Andromeda on the Dolphin, modelled by Bingler, price £10.

1884 **28 Dec**:
Began to write "Court Royal" about 1 July, finished it (and making clean copy) 13 Dec; began new novel of N. Cornish coast on 22 Dec., name not yet decided. "The Gaverocks" (Jan3/85)[4] Wrote this year "Tommy", "Joseph Barable" "Alex Nesbitt" for Blackwood, already appeared, also "Peter Neilson"[5] and the "Unpardonable Crime," also "Joe Gander" for Longman, also "Fireworks at home and abroad", and "Red windows" for Cornhill; also "In the Lion's Den" "A wax and honey moon" for Illustrated English Magazine,[6] also "Let well alone", "De duobus mortuis" "Wanted: a Bride" not yet disposed of, also for Cornhill, "the Deadleigh Sweep"

Mr. Franks who is cataloguing Sir Josh. Reynolds' works writes that "Mr. Baring sat to Sir Joshua in Feb. 1777, and again in April 1787. Mrs Gould sat in Dec. 1761." In Sir Joshua's account books appears "Lord Ashburton for self and Lady and sketches of the children £231." My impression is that the picture of the beautiful girl we have, which we have called old Madam as a young lady is really

---

[1] Mlle. Thérèse Levet: probably *souvenir de Mlle. Thérèse Levet*, a rose said to have been introduced about 1886.
[2] David Andry: probably Dr Andry, a known rose.
[3] Wooda: a farm on the Lew Trenchard estate
[4] The Gaverocks. This part of the entry presumably made on 3 January when he had decided on a title.
[5] Peter Neilson: This mixture of fact and fiction also appeared as a chapter in *Historic Oddities and Strange Events, 1991, Methuen.*
[6] *A wax and honeymoon*: Although not to be found in the bibliography, this mixture of fact and fiction also appeared as a chapter in *Historic Oddities and Strange Events*.

that of Margaret Gould her daughter, and that Mrs. Gould is put for Miss Gould, as was so often done at that time, when Miss was rather a term of reproach.

Wrote this year both series of "Church Songs"

The back wall of Lew House, dining room was rebuilt 1855, sensation, a silver coin of Edw. II was found.

1885 3 Jan:
Offered £400 by Smith, Elder and Co. for "Court Royal" which I have accepted. For "Thro. Flood and Flame" and for "The Exeter Mail" I received nothing. For "Mehalah" £50; for "John Herring" £100. For "The Silver Store" nothing. For "Germany past and Present" £100. For "Book of Werewolves" nothing, for "Curious Myths" 1st series, if I remember right £25. 2nd series £25. "Post Medieval Preachers" £15. "Mystery of Suffering" £14 "Seven Last Words" £14 "Iceland, its scenes and sagas" nothing, "The Vicar of Morwenstow" I cannot say exactly but about £100, that was a royalty system, and I did not keep an exact account

1885 **5 Jan:**
Went to Plymouth to the funeral of Russell Pasley, poor fellow a sad end to a sad life. He was Sir Thos. Pasley's favourite son spoiled somewhat, would never work, and drank. He died of bronchitis and delirium tremens.[1]

1885 **6 Jan:**
My theory of the picture by Sir Joshua will not hold. In his notebook Sir Joshua distinguishes the Misses from the Mrs. Besides, the style of dress and the character of the picture is too early.

Examination of a Pupil Teacher in Physiology. "What is Reflex action?" Answer with Promptitude, "A rumbling in the bowels"

---

[1] Sir Thomas Sabine Pasley 1804 – 1884, son of Admiral Sir Thomas Pasley, 1st baronet. The Pasleys are related to the Baring-Gould family through Field Marshall Sir Joseph Sabine

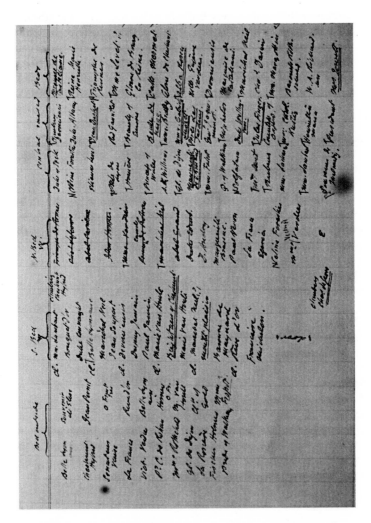

Fig.20 Undated planting of rose beds at Lew Trenchard.[1]

1885 **6 Feb:**
Called on Major Balguy, (Chas. Yelverton) his grandmother was a Miss Gould and
I saw her portrait by Wright of Derby.[2] Major Balguy is now residing at the Priory,
Tavistock. The portraits of the Countess of Sussex and Lady Barbara Yelverton by
Gainsborough are in the Grosvenor gallery lent by Lord Donnington who mar. the
Countess of Loudoun.[3] The Illustrated London News of Jan. 17th 1885 says

---

[1] **Rose bed planting: Explanatory endnote 52**
[2] Miss Gould by Wright of Derby. See also entry for 11 May 1883
[3] The Portraits of the Countess of Sussex and Lady Barbara Yelverton, *Further Reminiscences*, p 82.

The Countess of Sussex and Lady Barbara Yelverton" (35), the mother in white silk and the daughter in white muslin, form a charming group; and one would be glad to know something of two such attractive persons as the one is and the other promises to be — and about whom contemporary history, which at that time was made up of gossip, is singularly silent. Lady Sussex, who had married a great-grandson of Charles II., was a Miss Hall. The second Earl of Sussex's father, a man of retired habits, lived the greater part of his time at Easton Mauduit, in Northamptonshire, and got together a good many portraits of living artists, living and foreign. But there would appear, from comparing this picture with another (72), to be some confusion between the bearers of the title, as there is little in common between the faces.[1]

I shall have it copied. It was painted in 1771 and exhibited at the British Institution 1862, and at Academy 1871; it has been engraved by H. Every in 1871. In 1783 Gainsborough painted Capt Sir Charles Gould, now, I presume in the possession of Lord Tredegar. The size of Countess Sussex and Lady Barbara is 88x 60 inches.[2]

1885 **24 Feb:**
Finished "The Gaverocks"[3]

1885 **11 March:**
Began a new story of Bratton Clovelly. Name undecided whether "Honor Luxmore" or "Broadbury"[4]

1885 **13 March:**
Engaged on Spring garden. Made a pixy well in it. With carved granite over it picked up in the old "mowhay",[5] but whether it came from Orchard or belonged to the old entrance gate to Lew I cannot say. I remember two pillars of the old gateway which were used as entrance to the yard. They remained until about 20 years ago, when my father threw them down and used them (I suppose) for foundations. They were something like those in the Church

---

[1] *Illustrated London News* cutting pasted into the diary
[2] Sabine's copy of the portrait now hangs at Lew House.
[3] Anonymously, *The Gaverocks*, 1887, 1.Cornhill Magazine, 2. London, Smith, Elder and Co.
[4] The novel was eventually titled *Red Spider*. See the entry for 20 August 1885
[5] **Mowhay: See explanatory endnote 53**

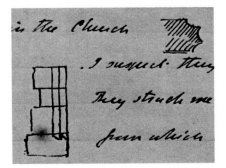

Fig. 21 Old pillars at Lew House

but were not single stones but coursed. I suspect they form the foundations of the pigsty.[1] They struck me, I know as having possibly been those from which the representation of a gateway is taken on one of the church bench ends.[2]

1885 **14 March:**
Went to see Willsworthy, in Peter Tavy, a manor house

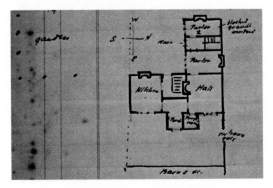

Fig. 22 Willsworthy plan

This is the plan roughly sketched. Parlour No. 2 and back stairs originally one room I imagine, and the door to staircase recently made. To the South magnificent old sycamores planted enclosing a square where were the old gardens. There is only one old granite window remaining blocked; but in the barn is a small window like those in the barns at Wringworthy. To the West a little lower down the hill is an old chapel now completely ruined. Willsworthy was originally a manor house. This is a rough sketch of the face of the house from memory.

---

[1] The pigsty is located in the walled domestic area at the foot of the glen. *The Friends of the Forgotten Garden of Lewtrenchard* hope to confirm Sabine's suspicions.
[2] **Old Gatehouse pillars: see explanatory endnote 54**

Fig. 23 *Willsworthy, barn window*

Fig. 24 *Willsworthy House, front elevation*

I cannot find out to whom the manor belonged, or when the house was built. The place is not mentioned in the Visitation of 1620.[1]

1885 16 March:
Walked with Mary to Coombe-Bow, and examined the remains of the old mansion of the De la Coombes.[2] An avenue of trees leads to the ruins, which occupy a lovely situation. The road is paved. The ruins are now few, most of the buildings have been pulled down within the last few years. It has served as a quarry for the pigstyes and out buildings of Great Close.[3] Only one window of granite, one chimney piece and a chimney stand.

Fig. 25 *De la Coombe Windows*

---

[1] **Willsworthy: See explanatory endnote 55**
[2] **House of the de la Coombes: Explanatory endnote 56**
[3] Great Close House and farm, Combebow, Lewdown

The windows of the usual plain chamfer. The fireplace the same. As the De la
Coombes ceased to live here in Hen. VIth reign this shows that the plain
chamfered granite work must be far older than the date I had attributed to it, Henry
VIIth reign. This is exactly like the older work at Lew House.

Letter pasted in:

22 Grosvenor Sqre, London W
24 March 1885

Dear Sir,
I trust you will forgive me for the length of time it has been in
answering your letter. I am much obliged to you for the photograph
you have sent me of the portrait by Carlo Charatti *[sic]*[1] of Sir Ed.
Gould. I regret to say, that I have not in my possession any of the
Gould portraits, nor can I give you any clue, as to where they may be.
Col. Thornton Gould, as you of course know, married a second time,
a Miss Darmer, but I cannot give you any information beyond this.
His property in Warwickshire passed to his son Henry Lord Grey de
Ruthin *[sic]* and at his death to his granddaughter Barbara Grey de
Ruthyn. After her marriage with George, second Marquis of
Hastings, an act of parliament was passed authorising her to sell the
Gould property and purchase land instead in the neighbourhood of
her husband's estate.
I have never seen any Gould portraits, that were brought from there
and had been there, I think they would have been transferred to Lord
Hastings place, just as the Yelverton's were. The son of this Col.
Thornton Gould by his second marriage, died some 12 years ago in
London not in absolute want but without leaving £20 worth of effects
behind him, I believe his maternal cousin, Countess Darmer saw to
him at the last.

Yrs faithfully
Donnington

1885 **1 July:**
Heard a good story or two. A gentleman, I was told his name, went to town before
Xtmas being bothered by the decorations at which his wife was great, cold dinner,
and that sort of thing. Before leaving she begged him to send her down a text for
the chancel window and gave him text and dimensions. On reaching town he had
forgotten both so telegraphed back for them. The answer arrived "Unto us a child
is born. 6 ft. 9 ins. long by 2 ft. 6 ins. broad."

A bishop came to stay at a parsonage for the night. The lady of the house
instructed the maid to call him "My Lord" always. The Bishop wrote his letters

---

[1] The portrait was by Carlo Maratti. See *Further Reminiscences* p 82.

and rang the bell, "Who will take them to the post?" he asked. The bewildered maid replied, "The Lord, my boy."[1]

A Baptist minister was fond of hot pickles and carried about a bottle with him, at a table d'hote he produced it, and ate some. An American sitting by eyed it enquiringly and desiringly. "Will you have some?" The minister was taken at his word, in went the fork and a capsicum was brought out and put in his mouth. The American swallowed his agony, and when he could gasp asked "You're a minister I redeem?" "I am." "And you believe in Hell fire?" "Of course I do." "Minister — you're the first of your cloth I've come across who carry about a sample bottle with you."

Brooke Lambert, Vicar of Greenwich visited two old men in the workhouse, one an inveterate grumbler was ill and dying, a shivering old fellow. He urged that if the old man were worse he was to be sent for in the night, but next day he found the man was dead. He remonstrated with the others. "Oh, Sir! We couldn't be so bold as to send for a gentleman like you. But, be content, Sir, I said to him all that was necessary, and just what you'd have said." "And pray what did you say?" "Well, Sir, I axed'n where he thought he was going, and when he said he feared he be sent to Hell, 'You cantankerous, unthankful, old vagabond,' said I, 'is that the way you talk, when you ought to be grateful to have such a warm place provided for you to go to.' "

An old Devonshire man with a wooden leg was dying. "Roger" said his wife "I can't help thinking of our boy Bill as died come 5 years. You'll be seeing him I reckon." "Maybe" "Well he'll be rare interested to hear how us hev been a going on. You'll mind and tell he about the new linney, and the pig we killed at Xtmas that weighed some. And you'll tell'n" —"Now do'y leave off, Priscilla. Do'y think I can go stamping about among all the quality to find our Bill and tell'n about the pigs —it's clean onrasonable."

1885 **20 Aug:**
Finished Red Spider. It has gone through several alterations. The original scheme was very different from what I afterwards planned the story to be, indeed little or nothing of the original is kept except the quarrel of the brothers in law and the mise en scène.

Have sold the Gaverocks to Smith, Elder and Co. for £400. Red Spider for £150.[2] Eve £150[3]

---

[1] The Bishop's mail: *Further Reminiscences*, p 117. There it is attributed to Bishop Temple.
[2] Anonymously. *Red Spider,* 1887, 1. Temple Bar. 2. London, Smith, Elder and Co.
[3] Anonymously, Eve. 1. 1887-8, Longman's Magazine, 2. 1888, London, Chatto and Windus

Have had the full length portrait of W. Petty in red coat copied as the original was in so bad a condition. It was put up by my father to block a window from which the glass had been removed and was blown down over a chair and torn. I asked to be allowed to have it restored, and spent £10 on its restoration, but this was imperfectly executed at Exeter and now it is in so bad a condition that I have had it recopied, knowing it was past restoration, the head and shoulders as far as can be preserved shall be cut out and kept.[1]

Baby boy born on 7 Aug. he is to be called Henry[2], as Henry Gould obtained Lew in 1626, and this is my first boy born here.

1885 **29 Sept:**
Michaelmas Day. I married Alexr. Baring to Louise Thorne at the British Embassy, Paris. She is very sweet, young 19 years, has been educated by Miss Sewell. Her mother is married again to Mr. Parish. They are Americans. I could only hurry to Paris spend two nights there and return as on Tuesday *[29 Sept]* we move into Lew House. What struck me as pretty in Louise was this. On the evening of my arrival I dined with the Parishes, and as Mr. Parish looked at me, I said grace. So also at the breakfast. Now this is unusual among Americans, each says grace for himself if any be said.
As Louise was in the train leaving with Alex, for Fontainebleau, she leaned from the window and said to her father and mother, "Do remember this evening at dinner to give Mr. Baring Gould time and opportunity to say grace." Then presently out came the sweet face again, and she said "He has only tonight in Paris, do take him to the theatre francais or to see something he would like." So thoughtful and kindly. Dear Alex is so frank, warm hearted and true that he must make any woman happy, and I do believe that Louise is one to do her best for him. She has much strength of character and is highly cultivated.[3]

---

[1] Mr Petty's portrait: John Petty m. Diana Amelia Sabine; *Early Reminiscences*, pp102-3, 107; DRO letter Sabine to his mother from Hurstpierpoint,1857 November 10, informing her of his intention then to restore the portrait.
[2] Henry: Sabine's 11th child and 4th son.
[3] Marriage of Sabine's cousin, Alexander Baring, *Further Reminiscences*, p 153.

Part 4. Lew House at Last:
October 1885 to November 1899

1885 **1 Oct:**[1]
Arrived home.[1] The last change made till the great one of all. I slipped in without anyone seeing me, left the carriage and came by the garden, that I might on crossing the threshold of my dear house, say a prayer to God to bless me in the home of my ancestors to which I have come at last to make it a home, and to enable me to remain in it; I shall have difficulty as times are so bad, and my income is reduced. Grace is truly marvellous. The way in which she managed the moving, organised everything shows real genius. The Sperlings move today into the Rectory.[2] No hitch, all worked on wheels, thanks to dear Grace. She is a general in the house.[3]

1885 **2 Nov:**
All Souls Day. Had mass in church, the first on All Souls probably since the Reformation; and remembered all my family gone before here and at Staverton.

1885 **9 Nov.**
Hamilton Pasley and his wife have been with us for ten days. He is very warm hearted, delighted to make friends with his relatives on his father's side. Lady Pasley was a very queer woman and kept Sir Thomas and her children away from his relations, and them at a distance. When he was Admiral in command at Devonport my father and mother drove to Plymouth to call on them, and Lady Pasley was almost rude, so that my father would not ask her or any of her daughters to the house. He and Sir Thos. were as brothers together when boys, and he felt it much. The dear old admiral was very warm hearted, and had much to suffer from his wife. Capt. Hamilton Pasley says that he does not care for all of the Mynards, his mother's family; and I see how he clings to ours. The tears were in his eyes today as he said goodbye.[4]

The Bishop of Exeter our guest today and tomorrow.[5]

1885 **11 Nov:**
A confirmation here. Eighteen candidates from this place, all but four young men and boys. The total number confirmed here 50, the confirmation went off very smoothly and well, the singing good, the day fine, the bells ringing, the bishop delighted, the lunch good. The bishop was charmed with Lew and so astonished at

---

[1] Arrived home: Two days after the move from the Rectory to Lew House.
[2] Although eventually the Sperlings purchased and rebuilt the Rectory, at this point it was leased to them. See entry for 23 August 1886
[3] Move of House by Grace: *Further Reminiscences*, p 155
[4] Admiral Sir Thomas Sabine Pasley 1804 – 1884: son of Admiral Sir Thomas Pasley, 1st baronet. Descended through the Sabine branch of the family.
[5] **Bishop of Exeter: Dr Frederick Temple. Explanatory endnote 21.**

the house and the scenery and the order of everything. Pengelly whilst driving him away heard him talking of it to Mr. Grylls his chaplain

1885 **12 Nov:**
Began to remove parapet above the stair case window to the East, as it leaks and is rotting the roof. My father put up the parapet at considerable cost round the house, but it is not a success as it arrests the water from the roof and throws it back. We have made a curious discovery. The original staircase window was eighteen inches higher, and 6 ft. wide. The present window is 4 ft. There is a huge oak lintel 8 ft. 10 above it, and traces which show that beneath it was an oak (?) *[SBG's question mark]* three light window. I do not think it was granite but cannot tell till the plaster is cleared away.

1885 **1 Decr.**
Began upon restoration of drawing room. I find I must remove the whole wall as the heavy parapet leaning on the edge of the wall has split it. No wonder the water has penetrated the wall[1]

Fig. 26 *Decaying parapet at Lew House*

The parapet is much heavier than in my sketch. We have made interesting discoveries. The windows prove to have been three light and of granite, and have been narrowed in Chas. II or Queen Anne's reign. The old fireplace probably of the house of the Trenchards in Henry IIIrd reign has been disclosed. It is very large, and has been badly injured by being chipped away to allow of the panneling *[sic]* added in Chas II reign when a new fireplace was constructed within the other occupying half the space. The carved oak chimney piece I remember was to this smaller fireplace.

---

[1] **Construction of the parapet:** *Early Reminiscences*, **p 248. See also explanatory endnote 62.**

Fig. 27 *Drawing room chimneypiece at Lew House*

The whole of the face and chamfer of the jamb (A) has been cut away to allow of the filling in and the stiles of the panelling making it impossible to restore it. The top stone has been similarly mutilated. One of the window sills was inserted to act as a dowel to the new fireplace. The opening of the lights is 15 ins.

1885 **4 Dec:**
Found a fireplace in the dressing room; chimney opened into that of the drawing room, it was not of granite but of oak. The dowel was beautifully chamfered.

Fig. 28 *Chamfered dowel:*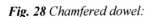

The oak beams of the ceiling had apparently been similarly chamfered , but this had been mutilated when my father reduced them so as not to be so conspicuous in the room.

Fig. 29 *Chamfered beam:*

They were also moulded, he cut this back several inches and as the beams were weakened, he put iron plates on either side. Only indications of mouldings now is where not hacked away.

1886 5 Jan:
Another of the granite windows of the drawing room has been found both top and bottom. One sill has also been found built into the back kitchen wall, and another was laid as a step in the barn. I am using all these in the tower I am about to build, but as the mullions and jambs have been broken I am obliged to use the windows at half their original height.

1886 1 May:
Of the windows put into the façade of the house to the East those of the drawing room and the two above, and four of those in the library and rooms above are old. The four light windows in the S. Gable are not old, with the exception of part of the drip stone. The window, one light in the gable is old, it was found in the wall filling. The arch in the garden wall is old, so are the door and window into the tower. The doorway with M.G. 1682 I have moved from Waddlestone,[1] it was I believe put up by Henry Gould on the birth of his second son Moses, for whom he designed Waddlestone to be the house and manor. Waddlestone is a manor, as well as Lew, but Orchard never was.[2]

1886 **11 June:**
An afternoon performance, the first of "Mehalah" arranged by Messrs. Poel and Palmer. Miss Marie Burke was Mehalah, and rendered the part perfectly, and looked it. Herman Vegin *[?]* was Rebow, but did not know his part. The last scene of the play is miserable and must be recast. I will write a last scene. Theatre Gaiety.[3]

1886 **12 June:**
Whitsun Eve. From London to Brussels

1886 **14 June:**
Aschaffenburg. Heard news of the King of Bavaria's suicide.

1886 **15 June:**
Nürnberg.

1886 **14 July:**
Visited the Pegnitz Thal, Wunsiedel, the Fichtelgebirge, then Prague, the Riesengebirge, with Weckelsdorf, Adersbach rocks, the Schneekoppe. Görlitz, Dresden and so home.[4]

1886 **15 July:**
Found the masons had done nothing during my absence.

For the Boathouse erected 1885
> Thy brea**D** upon the **W**aters **C**ast
> In Certa**I**n Trust to f**I**nd
> S**I**n**C**e **W**ell thou know'st God's eye doth **M**ark
> Where f**I**shes' eyes are blind

---

[1] Waddlestone: A farmhouse then on the Lew Trenchard Estate. Also known as Warson.
[2] Orchard not a manor house: the basis for this claim is not known
[3] Dramatisation of Mehalah by William Poel and W H G Palmer. The play had a brief run.
[4] Bohemia, The Riesengebirge and Dresden: Map 5; *Further Reminiscences* chapters 13 and 14; *Cliff Castles and Cave Dwellings of Europe*

D=500+W=510+C=610+I=611
+C=711+I=712+I=713+I=714
+C=814+VV=824+M=1824
+VV=1834+I=1835+L=<u>1885</u>
This is by Gatrill[1]

1886 **11 Aug:**
Began to open out between the backstairs passage and the drawing room, and found a very similar arrangement to that in the hall. This I restore; but I reduce somewhat the wall at the back of the fireplace which is now quite 6 ft. so as to show a chimney breast in the library.

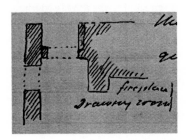

Fig. 30 *Lew House: Drawing Room fireplace plan*

It is possible however that I may find it impossible to do so. Found a curious old grey bottle in the wall or rather under the floor of the upper storey at the passage between the Drawing room and Library. The panelling of the drawing room is being put up. It is with a slight difference a copy of a couple of old arcades[2] that were painted, but the pilasters are new altogether. The two old arcades were shorter and not so wide, and lacked this cusping.

1886 **12 Aug:**
Grace and nearly all the family gone to Bude. Mary, Leila and Daisy have been miniaturised, or rather photographed for miniatures which are to be executed in Nürnberg.

1886 **22 Aug:**
Finished "Richard Cable" all that remains to be done is to polish up a few pages here and there. I have sold the serial issue of it to Messrs. Chambers for £350.[3]

1886 **23 Aug:**
Dined at the Rectory, Mr. A. Grant brother of Mrs. Sperling who lives there, renting it of me, told me that a few nights ago between ten and eleven, he was

---

[1] Boathouse Riddle: *Further Reminiscences,* p 155.
[2] Copied from the arcades in the dining room at Sydenham House, Marystowe.
[3] Anonymously, *Richard Cable, Lightshipman,* 1.1887 Chambers Journal, 2. London, Smith, Elder and Co.

walking along the road from Lew Mill behind the avenue, when he saw a figure walking in the avenue, dressed in a long pale coloured dress. The figure was at the extreme end, nearest the quarry. As our house is locked up, and I go round and see it is, every night at a quarter to ten (prayers at 9.30,) it cannot have been one of our party or servants.[1]

On the night of 11th I was in the hall writing till half past one waiting for Mary and Leila and Daisy who had been to a concert and dance at Broadwood, when, wondering that they were so late I went from the settle where I was seated to the porch, the inner door of which was open. As I turned to come towards the porch door I heard feet coming after me, and I turned on the granite lintel, when I heard a burst of harsh laughter, apparently close to my ear. The tones were too harsh for a human voice. As it was not repeated I was unable to trace it to any natural cause.

1886 **24 Aug:**
Have found and opened out a large granite fireplace in the library, with plain chamfer. 4 ft. 11 in. wide in the clear. As the side stone on one side has been hacked into and mutilated when a marble mantelpiece was put in, I cannot use it. I leave the upper stone in place and put another old fireplace in beneath it. The floor of the room had been lowered after the house was built, and so the fireplace stood too high for use.

A grievous discouragement to me is that I can find no sale for any of my historical and mythological articles. I have written a book on Weird Myths, and have tried three publishers and none will take it. I have sent three separate articles to magazines, and they have been refused. I have written essays on the lives of little known persons, and on special historical events, and cannot get any magazine to accept them. The editors always say 'send us a story'

And here I protest that I write novels with anger and heat because they take me off my proper course of study, history, especially ecclesiastical, and mythology which is my favourite study. I write only because I can not build and restore this house, I can not live on the estate, without supplementing my income from my pen. When I have finished a novel, I regard it with loathing and bitterness against it, as having engaged my time and thought which might have been better employed. If the novel could do any good it would be other, but the novel is now read only to kill time. I have said my say on novel readers in "Richard Cable." I will add that I hate lending any of my novels except to special friends who I believe can appreciate them, and that if I see a young lady reading one of them, I leave the room, the sight irritates me beyond endurance.

1886 **28 Aug:**
An interesting discovery made today. It seems that the earth in front of the library has been lowered at some time, also the floor of the library, whereupon the S.E.

---

[1] Haunting of the Avenue: *Early Reminiscences*, p 160.

angle of the building gave way. Then a granite doorway was taken out from where the present door is, and put in, one stone on another to build up a new angle. As the floor of the library had been lowered, the old granite doorway would no longer do, unless underpinned. Instead of doing this it was removed and used as described. Unfortunately the masons smashed one of the pieces of the arch not knowing what it was, before I came and insisted on an examination of the granite. In the ground outside the drawing room where was a flower bed was discovered a pair of dog-couplers.[1] Under the floor in the library, a brass token 'spiel-mark'[2] for cards, with a locomotive on it, modern, that is probably dropped in my father's time through the chinks of the floor.

Grace and all the children returned from Bude looking very well.

1886 **24 Sept:**
A singular matter. Tonight my wife and Miss Deason[3] and Mary were returning in the carriage from ----------. I was out dining at Rampenstein. When the horses came to the gate they plunged and refused to go into the drive, and Miss Diason saw a tall black figure standing near the gate inside. She thought it was I trying to frighten them, and uttered a cry. Pengelly whipped the horses, and had much ado to get them past. My wife and Mary did not see the figure, as it was on the side of the wagonette[4] on which they sat. Pengelly had some difficulty in returning after having deposited the ladies at the house. Both horses trembled and stood still and positively refused to go past the spot where Miss Deason had seen the figure, and Pengelly was obliged to descend from the box, and lead them past, but even so he could only persuade them with difficulty.

1886 **4 Oct:**
In the bedroom over the library found there had been an open fireplace of granite with the bottom and hearth paved with slates as in the hall. This had been covered over and enclosed with bricks for a small grate.

Received £50 for "Little Tu'penny" from the Graphic.

1886 **16 Oct:**
Received £350 from Chambers for use of "Richd. Cable" in their serial.

1886 **22 Oct:**
Received £400 from Smith and Elder for entire rights in "The Gaverocks" and offer at £350 for "Richd. Cable" after publication in "Chambers Journal"

---

[1] Dog-couplers: For walking two dogs together.
[2] Spiel mark: German term for a game counter.
[3] Miss Deason: Margaret Deason. A friend of Grace whose death on 14 March 1900 is mentioned in a letter to her daughter-in law-Marion in 1900.
[4] Wagonette: A horse drawn vehicle with two back seats running lengthwise and facing inwards.

1888 Sep 7:
After a gap almost 2 years [Oct 86 to Sep 88]:

> The Bellever week is the bravest week
> Of the twenty-five in the year.
> It is one to tweak a teetotaller's beak
> And to make a methody swear.

We leave our troubles and toils behind
Forget if we've got grey hair
A parcel of boys, all frollic *[sic]* and noise
Protesting Be gone dull care.

Our bruises our bills, our imag'nary ills,
We remember them all no more
O'er ~~bramble~~ branches and ~~break~~ brake, o'er the hedge of a take
We gallop in sunshine or pour,

Though sure of a stogg in a Dartmoor bog
Or a turn up of heels at a wall
Yet never a jot of damage was got
By a flounder or by a sprawl.

There's hardly a puss[1] is deserving a cuss
For coursing, beyond the moor
In Bellever week the beagles speak
As they never spoke before.

There's nowhere a run so brimming with fun
Nor a sport that can compare
For man or for horse, over heather and gorse
As coursing a Dartmoor hare.

The Sarracen's *[sic]* head is full as an egg,
And every farm and cott.
The jolliest set together are met
In the out and out jolliest spot.

Nowhere else does a joke such laughter provoke
Or a tale so hearty a roar
Or a song that is sung with stentorian lung
So certain of an encore!

When Bellever week comes round again
My wife! —Let her storm and sneer.

---

[1] Puss: hunting term for a hare.

If not tucked up in bed with a stone at my head
By Gorrah! —But I'll be there!
Sep. 7 1888[1]

      The Lamerton Hunt Song
On a beautiful morning dull morpheus scorning
To the Lamerton hunt we repair.
Both master and varlet, in fustian and scarlet
Alike in the pastime to share.
The bushes all dripping with dew
The heavens are cloudlessly blue.
From the countryside round, gather horseman and hound
To rout Reynard from out of his lair.

Whilst we're drawing the bushes the crafty fox rushes
Away and to Broadbury leads
The pell mell in his rear, with a yelp and a cheer
And the bugle, go rider and steeds.
~~Trara-rah~~ Tantivy! He'~~will~~ famously run
And many be distanced 'ere done.
We start thirty or more, but will hardly be four
At the finish tonight when he bleeds.

He is ancient and cunning, one can see by his running
And has often been hunted before.
By Jove! No mistaking, to the water he's taking
To double on Liddaton Moor
He has gobbled a gander or two
And destruction is justly his due
We as nemesis follow, with horn and with halloo!
And will finally settle his score.

Besplashed without hat on, we gallop thro' Bratton,
Tar-ra –rah! Towards Hallwill he steals.
Through furze break and bracken, without check, without slacken,
Only five of us still at his heels.
Now both Hawkeye and Freckelles *[?]* lag
And Harlequin, Schowell *[?]* fagg,
Some are left in the lurch at the Smithy and Church
Such a mess the best metal reveals.

Then hurrah for the master bemired as with plaster
~~A salute~~ One for sly Reynard who ran till he died

---

[1] **Bellever Day: See explanatory endnote 57**

A cheer shall not be lacking, the Lamerton backing
Also one for the cobs that we ride.
They have all done their duty today
From morning till evening grew grey
Tra-ra-rah! Out of breath, now we're in at the death
Here is one for the Huntsman beside.[1]

1889 Jan:
Laid up with bad bronchitis attack from Xtmas.

1889 **4 Feb:**
Left Lew for Italy.[2]

1889 **8 Feb:**
Arrived in Milan, got another bronchitis attack

1889 **11 Feb:**
Went on to Genoa

1889 **25 Feb:** Left Genoa

1889 **26 Feb:**
Arrived in Rome, where remained till March 13 when I went to Florence. At
Florence I remained till March 20

1889 **30 March:**
Reached home.

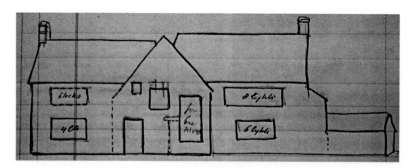

Fig. 31 *Lew Mill Dower House front elevation*

Lew Mill[1] I have been redoing up; on picking off the plaster the house proves to
have been much altered at different times. My grandfather altered the roof in the
clumsy way now over the gable. Originally the face seems to have been:

---

[1] **The Lamerton Hunt Song: See explanatory endnote 57**
[2] 1889 Visit to Italy: See map 6. *Further Reminiscences,* chapter 16.

Fig. 32 Plan of gable alterations Lew Mill

The recess was a doorway up steps leading to the upstairs drawing room. This must have been done when the house was rearranged. Originally what is now panelled sitting room and bedroom over was hall. There is ornamentation in roof above the plaster. Then it was floored across and a best parlour made upstairs with 8 lights, now reduced, below 6 lights, at some time the wall on the left of porch was removed and brought out to level of porch. Traces of roof having come down level with the other side are observable under plaster. The wall or buttress on rt. of recess is not keyed into the main wall of house and is an addition. The original right porch wall must have been destroyed when the staircase was made.

1889 **17 July:**
Have written to Bligh relative to Daisy, and spoken to her. My letter to him is this:
"I do not wish to be hard on you, for I have very great and affectionate regard for you, but I must consider what is due to me as father, and to Daisy as my child. I do not think it wise I have had a talk with Daisy, and told her what I had written to you, that I wished that three years should elapse before anything like an engagement should take place, leaving her free, that I objected to letters passing between you, and anything that was not above board, and I told her what were the circumstance under which the property is tied, so that I cannot leave anything out of it to a daughter, except she be unmarried or a widow; that I thought you must be able to show you have an established business and a sufficient income, before you thought of marrying, and I asked her whether she objected to my arrangement and to what I proposed. She agreed to it at once. It may happen, of course, that you meet, but the writing must stop. Three years is not such a great time to wait. I am very sorry if I seem to be hard on you, but it is not that I do not warmly regard you, but on the contrary, rather because my regard for you is so great that I wish you not to be precipitate, and also for my child's sake, I do not wish her to be hurried to a step which she might regret.
I remain etc."
I read this over to Daisy, and she said "I like it."[2]

---

[1] Lew Mill: Sabine was referring to Lew Mill Dower House, not Lew Mill farm and mill
[2] Letter to Bligh: It seems likely this was to Sabine's cousin, Bligh Bond, then aged 25. See 27 July 1891 for a similar letter to a Mr Tripp concerning Daisy.

1889 **28 Aug:**
Finished "Urith," don't think anything of it myself. Poor stuff.

1889 **29 Aug:**
Sent "Urith" off on approval to Ed. "Cornhill", (refused)

Have begun to build an addition to "Brent Tor View" on Lew Down

1889 **17 Sept:**
Commenced at Plymouth to lecture on the Songs and Ballads of the West.[1]

1889 **15 Oct**:
Dear Edward left us; a rainy day. We all met in church when I had the office for those about to travel, and gave him my blessing. He went to Guildford,[2] and sails on S. Luke's day.[3] Edward is a very dear boy, everyone loves him, so perfectly gentlemanly in his manner, so upright in mind, and with such a true sense of honour, I doubt not also with deep true love and fear of God in his heart. It is time he should go, as Alex Baring is about to leave the firm of financiers into which Edward goes, and also because he has learned all he can at the school at Tavistock, and is liable to be spoiled by his sisters and others who make a great deal of him. He has no small opinion of himself, and cannot endure contradiction.

1889 **5 Nov:**
Mary thrown whilst out hunting. The horse suddenly swerved down a side lane following some of the hunters, when she purposed to hold to the main road. Her foot and skirt caught and she was dragged a long way, providentially in the gutter and not on the road, where her face would have been cut to pieces. Coming along the side road was a trap. It was feared by the hunters that Mary's horse would make a dash and in passing the trap sling her against it. The horse, however turned sharply round and dashed against a gate which it shivered to atoms. This disengaged Mary's foot, her habit was torn off and she was released. She was taken to a cottage, her face washed, she borrowed a skirt from the woman of the cottage and she managed to ride home; she was much shaken and hysterical on her arrival, but went to bed and in two days was quite well.

1889 **19 Nov:**
Lectured on "Songs of the West" at the Guildhall, Plymouth, quite full, enthusiastic audience.

1889 **20 Nov:**
Lectured at Launceston. Very successful also.

---

[1] **The First Songs of the West Lecture, Plymouth or Tavistock? See explanatory endnote 58**
[2] Presumably Edward was to stay with Sabine's cousin, Francis Baring-Gould at Merrow Grange, Guildford.
[3] St Luke's Day: 18 October

1889 **5 Dec:**
Lectured at Bristol. Lesser Colston Hall well filled.

1889 **7 Dec:**
Had bronchitis attack.

Newspaper cutting pasted in: The Globe Dec. 27 1889:

SONGS OF THE WEST
AN INTERVIEW WITH THE REV S. BARING-GOULD

Mr. Baring-Gould, fresh from his Dartmoor home, has been lately busily engaged at the British Museum in tracing to other countries some of the songs and ballads of Devon and Cornwall. In a cosy room in Keppel-Street he extended to me at the close of one of his laborious days of research, the genial welcome which visitors to Lew Trenchard where he discharges the duties of parson and enjoys the privileges of squire, delight to remember. One of the most accomplished scholars and versatile writers of our day, his learning sits lightly upon him; and it was with a meek and unaffected grace that he expressed his willingness to talk to me about the work which is now occupying his time. The tall figure and finely carved features bear some traces of the energy which has enabled the author of "Mehalah" to acquire an equal ease in dealing with comparative mythology and preaching village sermons, in discussing Icelandic sagas, and writing popular fiction; but to the ordinary observer they display no sign of the delicate health which compels him to spend the greater part of the winter abroad.

IGNORANCE THE BULWARK OF BALLADS

"How long" I asked, "have you been making your collection of West-country songs?" — "I started about two years ago. At present I have collected two hundred, but there are heaps more. Next summer —I can't get about in the winter —I shall go through Cornwall, where I have been very little as yet. How came I to think of collecting the ballads of the West? Well, I was at a hunting dinner party where several old hunting songs were sung. What a pity it is, I said, that our old songs, which have been the poetry of our villages, should be dying out. That started me thinking what a very good thing it would be if a collection were made of them. Many of my hunting friends promised to give me all the songs they knew, and I undertook the task, which has really proved an interesting one. My first effort, however, was a failure. I went round the farmers in the neighbourhood, but they knew scarcely any old songs. I found that the songs which they called old were written by such men as Dibdin.[1] It then occurred to me that when I was a boy I used to ride out across Dartmoor, and staying at the wayside inns, to hear old labourers sing quaint ballads in tap-rooms. To the labourers, therefore I went. In fact, the old farm men seem to be the only people who know anything about our old ballads.

---

[1] Charles Dibdin: 1745-1815. Popular song writer. His nautical songs include Tom Bowling.

Being able to read the farmers had learned modern songs. The ignorance of the labourers has preserved their acquaintence with our traditional melodies."

SETTING TO WORK

"what was your *modus operandi*?" —"All the old 'song men', as they are called, living in the neighbourhood of Lew Trenchard were invited one by one to my house. I invited them separately, because shyness would probably have sealed their lips if they had come in batches. All of them were old men between seventy and eighty. The ice broken with a glass of grog —no! I don't believe in teetotalism, not a bit of it —they were ready to pour forth every quaint old song they knew. The dear old fellows were delighted. Many of them had not sung for thirty years. They had been pooh-poohed by the younger generation, which knows nothing of the old ballads, and delights in the music-hall melodies come down from London. They began to think that their worth was just being discovered. Our method of procedure was a very simple one. They sang all the songs they knew. After each song they slowly and gravely dictated the words to me. While they were singing my co-editor, the Rev, H F Sheppard, took down the airs. If he was unable to be present another distinguished musician, Mr. F W Bussell, a fellow of Brasenose College, Oxford, filled his place. Sometimes, however, neither was able to attend, and then I had to learn the airs, play them upon the piano, and afterwards note them."

IN SEARCH OF SONGS

"But, of course, I did not confine my efforts to my own neighbourhood," continued Mr. Baring-Gould, talking in his earnest, energetic way, which reaches its height when he explains his broad views concerning the origin and development of religious belief, but remains when he speaks even of the humblest duty he discharges in his parish. "Last summer I made very many excursions to out-of-the-way villages in all parts of Devon. When I heard where a 'song man' was to be found, I went to the village, put up at the inn, and invited him to come and see me. At first most of the old fellows were somewhat shy. It took them some little time to quite understand my mission, but under the influence of a little genial hospitality they gradually thawed into melody. They saw that I knew them and understood all their ways, and eventually their enthusiasm knew no bounds. I think I never saw such a mixture of pathos and humour as the sight of these old fellows singing their songs. Toothless and tottering, with voices so thin that many of them were scarcely audible, they went through all the ballads with which they charmed their sweethearts in their youth, delighted with the thought that they were doing in their closing days a most important work in preserving the literature of their county. I am very fond of the dear old men. Ah, yes, I dare say some of them will find their way into my novels.

WEST COUNTRY SONG-MEN

"The old man from whom I obtained most songs worked in my parish as a hedger.[1] He is nearly eighty years old, and hasn't a tooth in his head, but he has a wonderful store of old ballads. Like most of the 'song-men' he comes from a musical family.

---

[1] James Parsons: Lewdown singing man

His father was known as the 'singing machine'! When once he started singing no power on earth could stop him from singing every song he knew. A perfect mine of ballads was a fine, white-haired old man, living in Launceston.[1] One of the most valuable of my old friends was a poor old cripple, who crawls along on two sticks. He earns a little money by breaking stones, and the parish gives him half a crown a week for himself and his wife.[2] You know that we have been giving concerts in Devon, at which the songs and ballads I have collected have been sung.

Well, all the proceeds of the concerts have been given to the old men who supplied me with the ballads, each receiving five pounds. Since I gave the poor old man of whom I am telling you his share of the profits the guardians of his parish have talked, I regret to say, of stopping his allowance."

"NOW THE LABOURER'S TASK IS O'ER"
"Quite a sad little story," Mr. Baring-Gould went on, "belongs to another of my melodious friends. His name was Will Huggins. Before I started for Italy last year he promised that he would try hard to collect some songs for me. He hobbled about all over the neighbourhood, asking all his old friends to sing, but before I returned he died, and all the songs he had learned by heart with him. Drink had a little to do with his end, but he was a dear old soul. As you may suppose some of the words of the ballads I have collected are not exactly suited to these days of greater refinement. In one or two instances slight alterations have been necessary. The words belonging to one Elizabethan air are such that I have felt bound to leave out the whole of them, and in their place I have put some lines of my own written in honour of old Will Huggins."

Opening a well bound volume which lay by his side, and turning to a song called "The Old Singing-Man," Mr. Baring-Gould showed me what he told me was his sole poetic effort. The first verse runs:-
> "I reckon the days is departed,
> When folks ud a listened to me,
> And I feels like as one broken-hearted,
> A-thinking o' what used to be.
> And I don't know as much be a-mended,
> Than was in them merry old times
> When wi' pipes and good ale, folks attended
> To me and my purty old rhymes."

THE OLDEST BALLAD
"Have you been able to trace any of the songs in your collection?" "Very few indeed. You see I discard all the ballads which have been published, and many have been thrown overboard in that way. Strange to say most of the words and airs I have succeeded in tracing go back as far as the reign of Henry VII. I found out today that forms of one of our ballads exist in Scotland and in Sweden. Passages which are not

---

[1] James Olver: Launceston singing man
[2] John Woodrich: Lewdown singing man

in the Devon version are in the Scotch, and some which are not in the Swedish are to be found in ours, but they all unmistakably belong to the same Devonian origin. Four verses missing from one of our oldest ballads, 'The trees they are so high,' I also found in a Scotch version. One of the most popular of our old songs, 'By chance it was.' I have discovered word for word in a collection of ballads made in the time of Queen Elizabeth. I have been unable to trace anywhere, however, the oldest ballad in our collection. It is a very weird one as I think you will say." And Mr. Baring-Gould again placed in my hands the precious volume wherein I read:-

> "Cold blows the wind of night, sweetheart,
> Cold are the drops of rain.
> The very first love that ever I had
> In greenwood he was slain."

These are the opening lines of a charming old ballad, full of the weird pathos so dear to our early song-writers. It tells me in a charming style the sad story of a girl who sits upon the grave of her dead lover, weeping and asking for a kiss.
From beneath the ground the voice of the dead man answers that a kiss from his cold clay lips will mean her instant death, but she lovingly persists in her request. Slowly the head of the departed lover rises through the earth. As they kiss a bramble leaf falls between their lips.

EASTWARD HO!

As I was about to take my leave I asked Mr. Baring-Gould whether he had decided to lecture in London on the Songs of the West. "I shall be in town again in January, on my way to Italy," he said; "and if the ladies and gentlemen who have been singing the Songs of the West in Devon decide to visit London at that time, I shall lecture, but they have not yet made up their minds to come to town. I have been asked, however, to deliver three lectures on the songs and ballads of Devon and Cornwall at the Royal Institution, and I have arranged to give them on my return from the continent at the end of May or the beginning of June."
A genial goodbye, a hearty grip of the hand, and I was out in the cold night, which a small errand boy, pursuing his way through Keppel Street, was making hideous by shouting out at the top of his small voice a popular ditty, with the monotonous refrain, "She's my honey, I'm her joy." As this melody of modern cockneydom died away and I passed through the great central squares, round which the wind was running its fierce race, there came ringing in my ears the better words of noble ballads which have been sung by the sturdy men of Dartmoor for hundreds of years.

1890 18 Jan:
Lost my voice again and bad with bronchitis.

1890 **21 Jan:**
Leave for Italy. No building done to Lew House in 1889. In 1888 I built the gallery to E. and used old windows, two from Lew Mill, one with angle light was given me by Miss Buller of Pound[1] from an old farm house that was being repaired.

---

[1] Pound: Seat of the Buller family at Buckland Monochorum.

I have been unable to complete more than the walls of this gallery, as my funds were very low. I had in Jan 1889 to borrow £500 from the City bank Exeter, and deposited there as security, the Deed of resettlement of estate and my affidavit relative to the policies on my own and my wife's lives. Should I not return from abroad, having succumbed to my bronchitis, then I should like Edward when able to complete Lew House according to my plan, or as near as he can at his convenience.

1890 **27 Jan:**
Got as far as Guildford on 23rd when I began to sicken. I went on to London and was laid up there with bad influenza till Feb 10. In the meantime Felicitas fell ill at Lew and nearly died, of congestion of lungs following influenza.

1890 **12 Feb:**
Arrived at Freiburg

1890 **14 Feb:**
Began to be unwell again

1890 **20 Feb:**
Left Freiburg and reached Rome on Sat Feb 22. Lodged at Signora Sopranze, Campa Marzio, paying 7 francs a day.[1] At Rome I worked hard at the Identification of the portraits of the Emperors. I suffered much from rheumatism and gatherings in my ears and glands of throat and mouth, due to the remains of influenza.

1890 **29 March:**
Left Rome for Florence. Was unwell again at Florence.

1890 **8 April:**
Left for Nice and Provence, to write a book on Provence for Messrs. Allen.[2]

11th at Fréjus on way to -.

1890 **11 April:**
Marseilles and then Arles

1890 **12 April:**
Visited Les Baux

1890 **15 April:**
To Carcassonne

---

[1] 1890 Visit to Italy: *Further Reminiscences*, chapter 17. The Provence part of the tour is not mentioned here.
[2] 1890 Visit to Provence: Map 7. See *In Troubadour Land. A Ramble in Provence and Languedoc.* W H Allen, London. 1891

1890 **16 April**:
To Narbonne, Beziers and Montpellier

1890 **17 April**:
Visited Maguellone[1]

1890 **18 April**:
Back to Arles

1890 **19 April**:
Nimes

1890 **21 April**:
Aix

1890 **22 April**:
Battlefields of Méounes and Pourrierès

1890 **23 April**:
Avignon

1890 **24 April**:
Valence and Vienne

1890 **25 April**:
To Paris

1890 **28 April**:
Left for London

1890 **30 April**:
Reached home, well, thanks to God.

1890 **31 May**:
Lectured before R. Institution, London on W. of England Ballad and Music. Mary had left London on 29 April for Freiburg.

1890 **7 June**:
Lectured again

1890 **14 June**:
Lectured again

---

[1] Maguellone: The Cathedral of Maguelone

1890 **16 June**:
Returned to Lew. Before leaving Lew I had finished and sent off my book on Provence.

1890 **2 July**:
visit… BVM.[1] Began my novel "In the Roar of the Sea"

1890 **21 July**:
Began to redo dining room, alter fireplace. In making the fireplace we found granite doorway and three light window in the wall built in. My father had rebuilt the chimney, and he must have pulled them out of the old wall and used them for the chimney he built. Apparently the door had been that opposite the porch door and window had looked from drawing room into courtyard behind the house now part built over by the dining room

1890 **7 Aug**:
Grace went to Bude.

1890 **11 Aug**:
Vera fell ill at Bude with Scarlet fever.

1890 **12 Aug**:
Left Bude. Miss Biggs telegraphed for to receive Vera.

1890 **13 Aug**:
Returned home, all disinfected in the house.

1890 **21 Aug**:
Kitchen maid attacked.

1890 **22 Aug**:
Harry attacked.

1890 **23 Aug**:
Julian attacked. Nurse arrived from S. Lucy's home Gloucester.

1890 **24 Aug**:
Housemaid and under nurse sent to empty cottage, the latter attacked. Dining room converted into hospital. Butler's children attacked and he sent away to be with them at Down House

1890 **25 Aug**:
All rooms in which fever had been disinfected.

---

[1] Visitation of the Blessed Virgin Mary, 2 July. Luke1, 39-50

1890 **26 Aug**:
Reorganisation of drainage of Lew House begun

1890 **5 Sep**:
Julian discharged

1890 **10 Sep**:
Harry discharged.

1890 **20 Sep**:
Miss Biggs and Vera return from Bude

1890 **11 Oct**:
Kitchen maid discharged[1]

1890 **14 Nov**:
Went to Oxford and delivered a lecture on Songs of the West

1890 **15 Nov**:
Did same in afternoon

Undated:
Have found the following copies of verses, made at the time of the Bulgarian atrocity excitement. They have been lying in an old box or drawer for years.[2]

The Turk and the Tory

> By Allah! The Turk with his blade and brand
> Is ruthlessly thinning a nation down!
> Red murder and rapine race hand in hand,
> Through hamlet and village and smoking town.
> And the fleet of old England is keeping the ring
> For the Turk unmolested to have his fling.
>
> Wild women are leaping and shriek in flame,
> Their infants beheaded and spiked, the same
> Weak maidens are outraged and dead in shame
> The ravening Turk is yelling for more
> But the premier of England has ~~laughter~~ jests and sneers
> For women's dishonour and widow's tears

---

[1] **Scarlet Fever Outbreak: Explanatory endnote 59**
[2] The Bulgarian Excitement Verses: Pasted into the diary and undoubtedly in Sabine's handwriting. Presumably the verses had been in a drawer since 1876.

The heart of the Tory is hard as stone
The lives of the harmless are winnowed chaff
The rest of his gold must have gnawed to the bone
When human misery wakes a laugh
And quivering zeal to rerivet the chain
On the victim who's writhing in ~~blood~~ wrath and pain

The blood that has splashed from the wild beast's paw
On the scutcheon of England has left a smear
The panther red spattered is dubbed Bashaw
The laughing hyena is made a peer
The blood of our brothers calls out to God
- For the Turk a gallows. The Tory a rod.

O Lion of Britain! Awake, arise,
With bristling mane and a wrathful roar.
Bid Liberty dawn on those Eastern skies
And tyranny trample and blight no more.
To the bats and the owls with the Tory and Turk
The jabbered excuse and the fiendish work.

The Tory War Cry

Draw the sword, strike the drum for the Turk!
For tyranny, licence, and wrong!
Though the sentence of God is gone forth
And Dagon is fall'n all along!

Though the crescent be waning to night
Oil, varnish and scrub till it shine!
Though the idol be crumbled to dust!
We'll patch it with fish glue and twine!

Draw the sword for old rotten misrule!
For the holders of Musselman stock!
Be to comrades, the brothers in arms
Of the heroes who ravage Batok!

That the garden of God be a waste,
The cross may be trampled in mire,
That to earth reek with innocent blood,
And civilization expire.

That weak woman may drain to the dregs
The cup of dishonour and pain,
That the life that is dawning may die
—Ho! To arms against Abel for Cain. [1]

Undated:
In "Church Songs" my tunes are those to which are no indication as to origin.
"Sunday Evening" is adapted from "Trovatore" and "Ladder of Gold" adapted
from Schubert's "Am Linden vor der Thore" [2]

1891 undated:
Have been greatly delayed over drainage to house by having to do up cottage at
Lew Mill for gamekeeper, cottage at Lime quarry for gardener, cottage at Lew
Down for schoolmaster, and building and roofing new linneys and cartsheds at
Wooda, also enlarging back kitchen at Down House.

1891 5 March:
Finished "The Tragedy of the Caesars" [3] on which I have been engaged more or
less since my return last year from Rome.

Have planted 50 Scotch pines in Rookery behind Lew House: I am engaged in
walling in vegetable garden. Have planted in upper garden about 50 apple trees and
filled completely with currants and gooseberries. Laid out ground today at the Y
for pair of cottages. [4]

1891 30 March:
Easter Monday. Began "Curgenven"

1891 14 April:
Foundation stone of the cottages at the **Y** laid by Harry. [5]

1891 20 Aug:
Edward came to Lew. Gave him a peal of bells.

Have been on the Cornish moors planning prehistoric? *[SBG's question mark]*
village at Trewartha [6] marsh, stayed at Trebartha Hall where I saw the old Spoure

---

[1] **The Turk and the Tory: See explanatory endnote 60.** This poem, expressing
fury at the then Prime Minister, Benjamin Disraeli, was sent to William Gladstone,
with slight changes and a covering letter 23 Sep 1876.
[2] **Am Linden vor der Thore: Der Lindenbaum. Explanatory endnote 61**
[3] S Baring-Gould, *The Tragedy of the Caesars*, 1892, London, Methuen and Co.
[4] The Y: These cottages known as 'The Wye' were built at a Y-junction in
Lewtrenchard.
[5] Henry or Harry: Then aged 6 years
[6] Trewartha: See Trewortha in *A Book of Cornwall,* pp 83-5

MS date 1694 drawn up by Edmond Spour *[sic]* It contains pedigrees also portraits, (Note some Bonds of Holwood[1] in *[sic]*

In some verses on Trebartha in the book occur

> "Of neighbourly Gentry there can be no want
> Cornwall was never of that honour scant
> Although it be so far distant from Court"

Not so now. In the same poem:-

> "And to fine Fowling he that is and loves
> Of that delightful sport
> Let him streight *[sic]* here resort
> He cannot miss of Duck, Cock, Tail and Plover
> Widgeon, nor wild Goose, Hearn or Snite,
> Nor Dove nor Thrush nor Hattes[2] flight
> Heath poult nor Partridge, nay nor Pheasant,
> If this don't please I know not what is Pleasant

It records among the outbuildings "a windstone as the servants call"

Fig.33 Quern stone, Trebartha

Stone ~~hammer~~ crusher for quern found at Trebartha. The round hole is for the finger to pass through. It fits the hand excellently.

1891 **27 Aug**:
Children and Miss Biggs went to Port Isaac

1891 **27 Aug**:

> Dear Mr. Tripp
> I have been turning over the matter in my mind about which we spoke. It appears to me: $\alpha.$ That you and Daisy have not seen much of each other: - $\beta.$ That you have at present nothing on which to marry, and only prospects as to the future more or less likely to be

---

[1] Holwood: Nr Saltash, Cornwall
[2] Hattes: It has not been possible to identify what sort of birds are or were 'hattes.'

realised: **γ.** That you do not propose to marry till these prospects are realised.

Thus I cannot say that this is satisfactory to myself or to Daisy's mother, and I think I must ask you to let the matter remain in abeyance till you have something definite and certain as to the means of supporting a wife; for as I told you I am precluded by the act of settlement from doing anything but what is infinitesimally small for my daughters, the property being heavily encumbered already. I do not think it would be fair on these prospects to hold Daisy to an engagement that may have been hastily entered into on passing liking and which might stand in her way of something more satisfactory to her family. I must say that I have heard only well of yourself, personally from Mr. Hussey Gould, nevertheless the engagement would not be one her mother and I would care to encourage, and though, should she persist in her liking, we might eventually have to submit, it would be merely submission without cheerfulness.

I remain etc[1]

1891 Aug 29:
Letter from Julian on holiday in Port Isaac to his elder brother Edward, pasted in:

August 29th 1891

Dear Edward

It is very jolly here, the Doctor and his wife are very nice also. When we arrived here on Thursday it was very wet we could not go out at all, but today it has been very fine, we got up at half past five and were on the rocks by six we just scrambled about the rocks till about half past seven then we came back and read till about eight then we saw the fishing boats going out to sea So we rushed down and looked on at them getting ready for putting out but then we had to go back to half past eight breakfast directly after we went down and had a bathe which we enjoyed very much.

Then we watched the boats coming in. Very few had any at all because they ---- *[words obscured by gummed paper]* there was too big a swell on. One bigish boat came in and brought about 50 mackrels which was the bigest catch they got another came in with about 40 mackrel which was the next bigest catch they had then we went home to dinner at one. The kids and Miss Biggs went down to the beach at Port Gavern this morning directly after dinner we went to Port Gavern, all of us and saw them loading one ketch called the Telegraph, and unloading the other one called the Sylph, wimen were used in loading the the Telegraph one had brought coal and the other had brought siment. The Telegraph was going to take back slates.

---

[1] Letter to Mr Tripp: The identity of Mr Tripp is not known. It is not clear whether this is a draft or a copy of a letter. Daisy (Margaret) was aged 21 in 1991. See also a similar letter 17 July 1889 to 'Bligh.'

I expect she will start again tomorrow morning, we stayed at Port Gavern till six and came back to half past six tea and supper combined. they do have a ripping Yorkshire ham here directly after dinner today we went to see if we could go out in a boat but the man said we had better come tomorrow or next week because there was a big swell on that is why they did not catch very many fish, there are a few visitors staying here there is only one more lodging place in the village, There are some very musichal people staying here who are called Bower two of them are profeshinols who come from London they are going to give a concert here in ade of something to do with the church. all the kids are very well so far and also Miss Biggs. I expect we are going to pick mushrums tomorrow before breakfast there are a great many around here. When we were coming here we came to Plymouth we had to wait some time and then it was a quater of an our later and when we did get in it was lovely we passed over Saltash bridge and saw thousands of steamers and men o war and small rowing boats and then we came after a long time to Bodmin road and changed there and we did not have to change at Bodmin. I left my waterproof cape in train at Bodmin road and just as the train started a boy that was in carriadge put his head out of the window and held up my waterproof cape I yelled at him to throw it and it pitched on the track just by my side, I was right over on the other side of the railway, it was raining most of the time we were in the train and just after we got out of the train it stopped (on purpose for _me_) and we had a dry drive all the way to Port Isaac and we tried to see who could see the sea first I did of course Port Isaac is such a rummy little place it has a very narrow bay of its own and about thirty boats drawn up on the sand and about 40 cotages behind all jumbled up in a mass the Doctors house is on the top of the hill. If you see Allan tell him I will kick him next hollidays but nethertheless I send him one whole hiss all for himself half one for Tommy. Give my love to every one

I remain   Your most loving brother J B Gould[1]

1891 **4 Sep:**
Finished "Curgenven"

---

[1] Julian: aged 14 when this letter was written

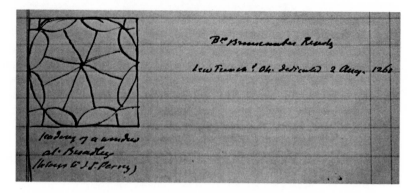

Fig. 34 Leading of a window at Broadley
(Belongs to J.S. Perry)

Bp. Bronscombe Register
Lew Trenchd. Ch. Dedicated 2 Aug. 1261[1]

1891 **24 Dec:**

Put in, in the old orchard opposite the yard where is furnace,[2] and below Cott's Lane,[3] and also in the field above the highway to Lew Down and the short steep way "the old road"[4] – 600 apple trees.

The cottages at the Y approaching completion.

A small tower with room below and room above begun at Rampenstein to increase accommodation.

The past year has been one of storms of winds and rain. I have disposed of serial rights in "Mrs Curgenven of Curgenven" to the Cornhill magazine for £300.[5]

On the evening of 5 Novr, returning from Trewartha with Mr. Thomas (Ordnance Survey) was nearly lost in Redmoor Bog. *[sic]* I sank to the shoulders and had the utmost difficulty in keeping myself above water, the bog sucked off one of my

---

[1] Lew Trenchard Church was dedicated to St Peter by Bishop Bronscombe. There does not seem to be any connection with either the Broadley window or the adjacent text.

[2] **Furnace field: See explanatory endnote 62**

[3] Cott's Lane. Location uncertain but possibly the lane from Lewtrenchard church to Middle Raddon.

[4] "The Old Road": From west of the Furnace field to Lewdown, described as Lew Hill by Sabine in *Early Reminiscences*, p 154, and now known by locals as Ragged Lane

[5] Baring-Gould S. *Mrs Curgenven of Curgenven*, 1. 1892-3 Cornhill Magazine, 2. 1893, Methuen and Co.

gaiters. Mr. Thomas was unable to come near me. I only got out by raking the moss with outstretched arms holding the stick level (horizontally) between my hands.[1]

1891 **26 Dec:**
Started for Teck to do articles for 'Graphic' in relation to approaching marriage of Duke of Clarence and Princess May of Teck. reached Stuttgart 10 p.m. on 27[th.] spent morning of 28th over collecting photos and books then went on to Kirchheim.[2] 28[th.] went to Teck. wrote articles and posted them 29th. Started on return 30[th.] reached London evening of 1st Jan.

On Jan 4th went to the Ely fens to work them up for scenes of a novel "Cheap Jack Zitta"

Returned with heavy cold to London 6th. too unwell to travel on 7th Returned home 8th. Laid up with bronchitis attack.[3]

Find the Cornhill accepts Curgenven and gives £300 for it.

Edward writes his salary again advanced now has £180 per ann.

1892 11 Jan:
The Sprig of May

[In 1468, Count Eberhart of Würtemberg, Lord of Teck, went to the Holy land. He plucked a twig of white thorn at Bethlehem, and brought it home. He was but 6 months on his pilgrimage. He planted it in his garden and it grew and throve, and he held it to be a pledge from heaven that God would be with him, his family and land. He was the first Duke of Würtemberg and Teck created 1495]

> The Gallant Count Eberhart forth did ride
> From Teck with a knightly band.
> His good sword girded at his left side
> But a pilgrim staff in hand
> And he said, I will seek
> Where the day doth break
> God's benison on my land.
>
> To Bethlehem city Count Eberhart came
> Where the seraphs once did sing

---

[1] *Lost in Redmire Marsh with Mr. Thomas of the Ordinance Survey: Further Reminiscences* p 246-252; *A Book of Cornwall* page 86.
[2] Kirchheim: The ancient capital of Teck
[3] Visits to Teck and the Fens of Ely: Briefly mentioned in *Further Reminiscences*, p 252.

From out of a welkin in lambent flame,
Noel to the new born king.
There he stood by a thorn
Dew spangled at morn
And white as an angel's wing

Then a twig from the tree Count Eberhart brake
A twig from the thorn brake he
As he said 'Pray God for sweet Jesus' sake
He'll be with my own land and me
And may this be the sign
Of the favour divine
If the twig grow into a tree'

Six months and a day are over passed
Then Eberhart did return
On the deep blue sea, he sailed as fast
As a bird on pinions borne
And ever in hand
On water and land
He carried the flow'ring thorn

Then he planted the May from Bethlehem
Still wet with the Angel dew
In his Swabian garden — from twig to stem
From stem into trunk it grew
And the sun they say
Dancéd that day
It was planted —the wan moon too.

The rainbow dipped her foot in gold
And lightly the tree trod round
The thundercloud passed —and Southward rolled
Unscathing the holy ground
And all the night long
there was heard —as a song
without words —a wondrous sound

 In the Swabian land still groweth the May
So sturdy, with blossoms pale
And Count Eberhart's line is strong today
And knoweth not fault or fail
Through centuries three
And forever —race and tree
Are lusty and young and hale

To the Swabian tree comes a princely hand
To gather a sprig of May
In the garden of roses of Angle-land
To root it for ever and aye
And the bells will ring
And the maidens sing
With the lads, as in time of hay

O flow'ret watchéd by angel eyes
And white as the whitest bloom
And sweet as the breath of Paradise
Is the May our prince brings home
In gladsome rout
We will all turn out
For our hearts are full today
In a merry throng
To welcome with song
Our prince with his sweet white May.

1892.
The death of the Duke of Clarence has made the above of no use. [1] Laid up with
bronchitis attack. Willy, Barbara, John down with scarlatina.

1892 **29 Jan:**
Began "Cheap Jack Zitta"[2] *[sic.]* Laid up with bronchitis

1892 **29 Feb:**
Left Lew for Sth. Of France[3]

1892 **1 Mar:**
Shrove Tuesday arrived at Limoges

1892 **3 Mar:**
Arrived at Brive

1892 **9 Mar:**
Visited prehistoric structures Les Eyzies – on to Perigueux

1892 **11 Mar:**
Arrived at Cahors

---

[1] **Teck, the Duke of Clarence and Queen Mary: Explanatory endnote 63**
[2] **Cheap Jack Zitta not Zita: Explanatory endnote 37**
[3] **Visit to the South of France: See explanatory endnote 64.** Tour of the
Dordogne map 8

1892 **19 Mar:**
Left Cahors

1892 **21 Mar:**
Gramat

1892 **25 Mar:**
Brive.

1892 **26 Mar:**
Paris

1892 **30 Mar:**
London

1892 **4 Apr:**
Home

1892 **16 Apr:**
Easter Day. Finished "Zita" *[sic]*

Dickinson staying with us.[1]

1892 May 24
Newspaper cutting pasted in:
Dev. And Ex. Gazette May 24th 1892:

LEW DOWN

The half-yearly rent audit of the Rev. S.B. Gould was held at the Lew Down
Inn on Tuesday. Mr. Chowen (of the firm of Ward and Chowen) received
the rent from the tenantry. A dinner was provided by Mr. And Mrs.
Hutchings. Mr. Chowen presided. After dinner the health of the Rev. Baring
Gould, coupled with the name of Mrs Baring Gould and family, was drunk
with great enthusiasm.
Some amusement was caused among a large number in the parish by the
announcement of the banns of an old man named George Ball, of Lobb-Hill,
about 70years old, and Joannah Kellaway, about 45 years. A good many
people having made known their intention of being at the wedding if
possible, the old gentleman decided to "nick 'em" if he could. He therefore
made arrangements with the rector for the wedding to be on Monday
morning last at 8 o'clock. In his best clothes he went alone across the fields
to the church, and Joannah came from her house to the church alone. A
grocer living near by acted as witness. After the service they proceeded

---

[1] Dickinson: Presumably this was A W Harvey Dickinson, the future husband of
Sabine's daughter, Mary.

separately to their homes. In the evening a number of young men met to
give the "happy pair" what they call "a good kettle band." Two young men
in disguise rode on horses carrying flags at the head of the procession.
George, being annoyed at the proceedings, tried to drench them with water,
but finding he could not stop the fun, he said, "Thee might as well have let
my old doman *[sic. Presumably a typo and should read 'woman]* come up
first before you made this noise." The band, it is said, intend to do honour to
the lady after she has reached her husband's home. They will meet next
week, and after music will have a coffee supper provided by friends near by.

Undated:
Mary engaged to Mr A W H Dickinson

1892 **15 Aug:**
Began "The Queen of Love" finished it Oct 30, and was in London 10 Oct. – 21st
and in N. Devon week 22 –27 Aug. The book was written in 47 days

Undated[1] —

To my distress I learned that Dunsland was advertised for sale.
I wrote at once a very strong and earnest letter to AWH Dickinson entreating him
not to sell it. My belief is that Cecil Bray, the solicitor at Holsworthy is at the
bottom of this. I suspect that the Coham-Flemings want to get Dunsland and they
are pulling strings behind Cecil Bray's back. He has urged it on Mrs. Dickinson,
who has no love for the place as it does not agree with her, and is associated with
rather unpleasant recollections —the difference with the Cohams who wanted to
secure it and expected to have been left the house and estate. They have the
moveables and carried away all the family portraits, and sold the books and
furniture. Since Mary's engagement they have taken no notice of it, though we
know Mrs. Coham and Mrs. Coham-Fleming her daughter. They are evidently
angry and annoyed at not getting the place.

On Sep 26th I heard from AWH Dickinson. "I write to thank you for your letter,
and to say that we have taken your advice, and put a stop to the sale. I am certainly
glad at the step we have taken, as I quite sympathize with a good deal you said. I
hope you got my wire I sent off this afternoon."

After a month or two Bray was again at Mrs. Dickinson but happily without
success. When it came to the drawing up of the marriage settlement, Harvey
Dickinson wrote me that the instructions given to Bray were that in it, it was to be
settled that the property should not be sold without the consent of Mrs. Dickinson,

---

[1] Mary's wedding: Presumably this entry was written after 11 Jan 1893, the date of
Mary's marriage. Sabine wrote of events related to the marriage between Sept 92
and 11 Jan 1893 in style and ink suggesting entries had all been entered on the
same day.

Harvey Dickinson and Mary. When, however, the draft settlement reached me, I found that Bray had omitted the proviso related to Mary's consent. I produced Harvey's letter and insisted on its restoration.

On the marriage day by the time service should be said, no settlement and no Cecil Bray had arrived. I was very uneasy and called the bridegroom out of church and asked him if his mother had signed it. He answered me that she had; and after the service was over Bray arrived and the settlement was completed. Mary is secured in event of widowhood £200 per ann. out of the estate and I undertake that she should receive from me annually £50 for her separate use; in the event of her death this sum will be paid to Harvey for the use of any children there may be.

The wedding day was lovely and all the neighbourhood was present. The village kept fête. The church was very prettily decorated. Screen of evergreens, altar candles lighted, and service choral. Mary looked lovely —so did the bridesmaids, they were in white touched with green, animated snow-drops. An amusing incident occurred. When the carriage was at the door to take away bride and bridegroom, Mary came down first and was told that Harvey was in the carriage awaiting her. So she stepped in. The driver, concluding that all was right, started, rice and slippers were thrown, and prolonged cheers given. Then Harvey who was dressing upstairs popped his head out of the window, and saw his bride driving away. This upset him completely and his best man had to complete his dressing for him. Meanwhile Mary had stopped the carriage, and drove back amid tremendous cheers and laughter, and she had to wait and receive chaff for over 20 minutes, till the bridegroom was ready. In fact he had lost both his hats. The top hat was somewhere in the house unrecognizable, and that in which he was to travel had been left at the Rectory. So the best man jumped into the first trap he could lay hold of, drove up to the parsonage and returned with the hat.

Pasted in: Two newspaper cuttings.[1]

---

[1] *Two newspaper cuttings:* One of Mary's wedding on 11 Jan 1893 but with the name and the date of the newspaper not given. The other a report of the wedding of Sabine's half-sister Leila's in April as reported in the *Tavistock Gazette* on April 21 1893and in undated report in the *Launceston Weekly News.* These have not been transcribed.

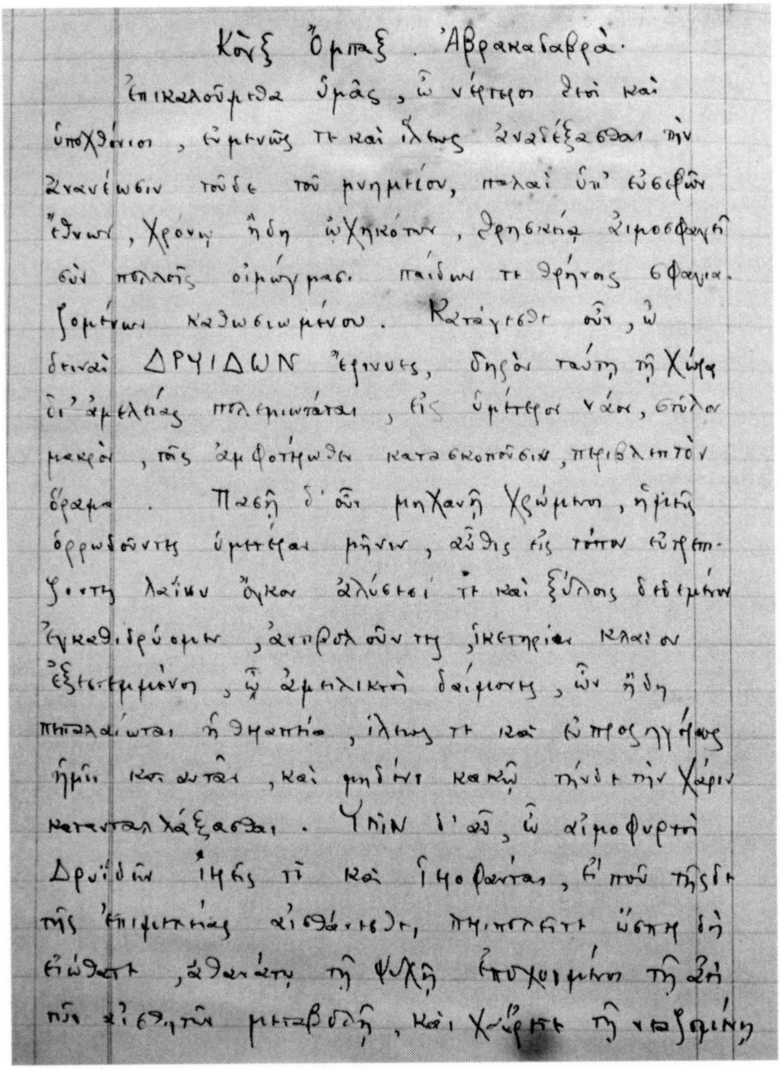

Fig.35 Undated page of Greek handwriting

Translation by Pamela Hunwicke:

Konx Ompax Abracadabra[1]

---

[1] **Konx Ompax Abracadabra: See explanatory endnote 65.**

We call upon you, O lower gods and under the ground, both kindly and mercifully to receive the renewal of this monument, long ago consecrated by devout peoples, already departed in time, with blood shedding worship accompanied by many wailing and lamentations of sacrificed children.

Come down therefore, O dread furies of the DRUIDS, most hostile too long to this place because of neglect, to your temple, a great pillar, a conspicuous spectacle to those looking at it from both sides.

Therefore using every device, we, shuddering at your wrath, again preparing for its place, set up a stone mass, bound with chains and pieces of wood, beseeching *[you]* wreathing a suppliant bough, O implacable deities, whose worship is already ancient, graciously and affably to come down to us, and *[?]* grant this favour to no evil person. To YOU again, O blood-stained priests and hierophants, if perchance you perceive this act of diligence, wander around just as you were accustomed, angered[1] in your undying spirit at the eternal change of things that are perceived, and rejoice at the renewal.......[2]

Pasted in letter from the Rev. H F Sheppard[3]:

Thurnscoe Rectory
Rotherham
Dec. 3 1897

My Dear Baring Gould

I quite feel with you about S of W.[4] whether the world will endorse your opinion that it is your magnum opus I cannot say, —you have done so much in so many ways. But it certainly has a special value beyond your other writings in that its interest cannot be ephemeral whatever theirs may be. S of W is a record, and a valuable and reliable one, of what is passing and soon will have passed away. At present it is I suppose to many persons, but one aspirant to popularity amongst many others —a collection of pretty songs: and if that were all, it would hardly hold its run against the productions of enterprising publishers who can command the voice of songsters, the ear of the public and the support of the newspapers. But when the time shall come for the whole question of English folksong to be scientifically, comparatively and critically examined —one may almost say phraseologically examined —then the worth of S of W will be felt. They are not national so much as racial.

---

[1] Reading επιχωομενοι
[2] **Abrupt ending: Explanatory note 65.**
[3] **Letter from the Rev. H F Sheppard: See explanatory endnote 66**
[4] S. of W: (and similar abbreviations elsewhere in the letter) Sheppard was referring to *Songs of the West*. S Baring-Gould, H F Sheppard and F W Bussell, 1895, London, Methuen

Some of them no doubt, but I think by far the small minority, have features in common with songs collected in other parts of the kingdom, in which case the filtration will have been inward, from without. But the great bulk of them fairly represent, I believe, the Celtic element in English Song —as it is nowhere else represented.

The part which you assigned to me in the work, whatever may be its demerits, I shall always have a pride in, and look back with pleasure to the days when we "went a gypsying" and collecting material; and when from time to time you led my weary old limbs long tramps of 6 or 8 miles, so beguiling the way with springy Dartmoor turf and springy Dartmoor air, and your own springy companionship that I knew neither fatigue nor satiety. For they were pleasant days and it is pleasant to look back upon them: but they are past. Dartmoor is too far away now. Not but what that region and I <u>may</u> see each other again one day. This place is getting quite beyond me. The curate I had did at least as much harm as good: and I don't seem likely to find the right man. If I was sure that <u>they</u> would grant me my <u>third</u> as pension (and they ought to do it after 40 years work in the diocese) I think Devonshire a not unlikely place to which to retire, unless somewhere abroad offered special pecuniary advantages.

But this is mere speculation. —I rather incline to prefer the Garland[1] to S of West. I almost think that the level of the ~~songs~~ melodies is higher, and that there is less doubtful material (not that I am prepared to maintain it) But this I do think, that two books taken together, are a really worthy contribution to the national folkmusic.

Of course they are more to you than other things you have done, they are part of your life, they are mixed up with your home, your tenants, your property, your surroundings, your place in the world, your individuality. They belong to Lew Trenchard. Other people have their gardeners, grooms, cooks and pages, <u>you</u> have your bards. They are part of your appanages. Your retinue is unique, mediaeval, feudalesque. You might hold an eisteddfod at L. T. by merely summoning your minstrels. The situation is Ossianic.[2]

"On the grassy hill of Larmon, comes forth Fingal Baring Gould; majestic; like a watery mist, he summons his minstrels: behold the bards

---

[1] The Garland: Sheppard was referring to *A Garland of Country Song* by S. Baring-Gould and H F Sheppard, 1894/5, London, Methuen

[2] *The Works of Ossian* were published in 1765 by James McPherson who claimed they were based on manuscripts he had found. Despite doubts about their authenticity, these poems became a strong influence on romantic and folklore literature over the next 100 years.

of song—Greyhaired Helmore! Stately Fone! Parsons with the tuneful voice! The soft complaint of Woodrich![1] Silvering the wild hill summit slowly rose the moon but the Lords of the bards were sad till the wine cup gleamed around. Fingal Baring Gould stood apart. He leaned upon his staff. The night wind gently lifted his shaggy hair."—Then follows the address of the chief: the episode of the unexpected entrance of the bard of the stormy north, an ancient Sheppard; his head white with the snows of ages; his harp in his hand; the whole concluding with considerable distribution of largesse, and the probable inebriation of the bards. —

So glad to hear that the Red Spider is once more spinning her web:[2] may no rash hand of chambermaid —I mean of chamber<u>lain</u> interfere with its due completion and production. If he finds evil suggestion in <u>that</u> drama he must be a nice man of eminently nasty ideas,

I am glad to hear that Vera is better but my dear man you have let slip a grand opportunity. Nothing helps people to understand, appreciate, and thoroughly like Gregorians, as singing them without music. O if we parsons would repose less upon organs and choirs and throw ourselves more upon the bosoms of our congregations, how very much better and heartier our psalms and hymns would be![3] But no. As soon as we discover a youth with a mellifluous voice, we pluck him out of the body of the ch. where he may be *[?]* set good example to others, and plant him where he is led to think that like "the blessed Glendower" 'tis his to sing and theirs to hear.[4]

Mary[5] has come back in good fettle and has —as usual —a round of visits to pay, but for the present I believe Devon is beyond the range. Later on should she go that way I am sure it would be a great pleasure to her to see Mrs Baring Gould and all of you again
Vale
Yrs. faithfully
H F Sheppard

Look at my humble muse! and be lenient.

---

[1] John Helmore, Samuel Fone, James Parsons and John Woodrich could be considered the finest of Sabine's 'Singing Men.'

[2] The light opera *Red Spider* with music by Learmont Drysdale and libretto by Sabine. Brief and reasonably successful provincial tour in 1898.

[3] Vera: Sabine's daughter, Veronica, was an organist at St. Peter's Church.

[4] The blessed Glendower: This quote has not been identified but refers to Owen Glendower. Another Victorian letter by John L. Motley quotes ".... You are a blessed Glendower, *'Tis yours to speak and mine to hear* "'

[5] Mary: Sheppard's daughter.

1894 15 Aug:

W. Pengelly died, aged 78. He had been 71 years in the service of the family. He entered my grandfather's service when 7 years old, he was permitted to clean the boots at 10. He served as horseman with carts, but my father promoted him to be coachman and he went with us to Pau and Bayonne. Last year he ran a black thorn needle into the palm of his hand. It was not properly extracted and he suffered terribly in his hand and arm for months. This broke him down and strokes followed. I communicated the old man the day before his death. For some time he has been childish, but very happy, and laughing at trifles, and always protesting that he was very well, never felt better. He did not always know his own daughter, but never failed to recognise me, and was always pleased to see me.

1894 **20 Aug:**

Our housemaid Elizabeth Collins has been for a month in the hospital with white swelling in her knee. When she returned on Friday last Baby[1] said "Lizzy I hab *[?]* prayed God every day for your bad leg." Last winter John[2] had hurt his knee. When he said his prayers he said "Dear God. I cannot kneel because I have cracken my knee" Nurse would not give him pudding the other day because he was naughty. So he said "Nan! When I am a parson I shan't let you come to my church."

Pengelly remembered whenever the carriage went out with any on a journey to Exeter or Teignmouth or to a dinner party, a brace of pistols was always part of the ladery[3] and it was his duty to put a cudgel under the seat of the coachman.

1894 **1 Oct:**

Began the alteration and extension of the back wing (E) of Lew House

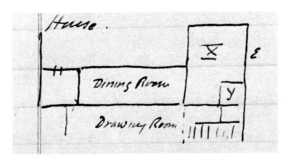

Fig. 36 *Plan of back and rear east wing Lew House*

Originally there was no Dining Room but a passage, which passage was itself an addition of uncertain date. The original house was but a single room thick at

---

[1] Grace: Sabine's youngest child, then aged 3.

[2] John: Sabine's 14th child, then aged 4.

[3] Ladery: presumably Sabine was referring to the lading or load of the carriage.

Hall and Drawing room , and the window from Drawing room looked into
Courtyard at the back. The Dining room was built by my father so as to occupy
a portion of the back court. The room in the wing X used to be my grandfather's
office, and there was a W.C. at Y.

1894 **18 Oct:**
In pulling down the E and W walls of X we have found the remains of granite
windows 2 ft. 11 in. high. The window to W. was of granite but removed when my
grandfather put in a French window for admission of such as desired to consult
him in his office. As the N. wall of the wing was falling my father rebuilt it.
Among other finds is the sides *[sic]* of a large granite fireplace and a chamfered
granite door. Several of the window jambs recovered have been broken and used
up in the wall built by my father.

Dear little Harry went to school at Cordwallis at the ~~beginning~~ end of September.[1]

1894 **18 Dec:**
Finished "The Broom Squire". Interrupted in the middle of the story and begun
"Guavas" wrote half of that and then finished the "Broom Squire". I did a chapter a
day but was interrupted by having to go to Thursley to make sure of dialect etc. in
November.

1894 **25 Dec:**
Xtmas Day. At early celebration. Daisy, Julian, Vera, Willy, Edward
communicated. Mary could not come till the morrow.

1895: 1 Jan:
All the children from Edward to baby Grace dined with us. The first and probably
the last time together. John sat by his mother at the head, baby at the bottom by
me. [2]

The house building at Ardoch *[lodge]*[3] for my stepmother is not my design. It
ought not to have been so hideous. I had made a design but she was not prepared to
give so much as it was estimated to cost. So Mr. Ward[4] taking my design as basis
vulgarised the whole —and the result will cost her as much as if she had had my
design carried out.

---

[1] Harry (Henry): Then aged 9 years. It has not been possible to identify this school.
[2] Ages of children at this gathering of the whole family: Mary (25), Daisy (24),
Edward (23), Vera (19), Julian (17), Willy (16), Barbara (14), Diana (13), Felicitas
(11), Henry (9), Joan (7) Cicely (5), John (4), Grace (3)
[3] **Lavinia and the cost of Ardoch Lodge. See explanatory endnote 67**
[4] Frank Ward of Ward and Chowen, then agents to the estate

1895 **1 Mch:**
A winter of unusual severity. From Jan 1 nothing but frost with the exception of a slight break of a few days. The roof was off the E wing of the house, and we could not keep the house warm. Nine of the children, all but Vera, and Harry who was at school, and Daisy in London were down with measles. But have recovered. The weather changed on the last day of February.

Today the building which has been interrupted for two months, and before that by rain for over a month has been recommenced.

1895 **16 June:**
1st S after Trinity, Arthur came to be my Curate, preached his first sermon, on the love of God. I can not be too thankful to God to have him here, and that thus he started having struck the keystone of his Ministry here. He is thoroughly in earnest, and the love of God is shed abroad in his heart, therefore I am confident; all is well.[1]

1895 **18 June:**
Heard of Edward's engagement to Marion Linton; an American hope and trust it will be to his happiness and that of dear Lew. He says nothing whether she is a churchwoman. To me that is the first consideration – the kingdom of God first.

1895 **20 Sept:**
Julian has been told two stories by r Symons of Coryton *[sic]*
1. When Edward Gould had killed the man who recognised him when robbing him, he had his horse shod with shoes reversed and galloped to Lew, over East Cott Beacon.
2. Old madam is said to walk at night from Morson to Lew over Galford Down, and Symons says he has heard the rustling of her silk dress as she passed him, but had never seen her.[2]

1896 8 Feb:
Hussey Gould died. Cremated Feb 11, to be buried at Beaconsfield, in vault where his father and mother lie

In 1879 Jonas Squire of Callisham Farm, Meavy (coming originally from Highampton) when there was a sickness among his cattle, sacrificed a sheep and burnt it; to the Good Folk on the moor above his house. He told the vicar Rev. G V Gray without any idea that what he had done was superstition. – The cattle did well after.[3]

---

[1] **Arthur Baring-Gould: Explanatory endnote 68**
[2] Haunting: For this and other stories of haunting by Old Madam see *Early Reminiscences* pp 162-163.
[3] A sacrificial sheep: *Further reminiscences*, p 127

1896 **27 May, Whitsun Tuesday**:
Vera laid the foundation stone of the new ballroom.[1]

Some of Vera's malaprops: "Mamma, I am so hot, the prepositions are running down my face"
"Do you like Meddlesome's Songs without Words?" (Mendelssohn)
"Mamma has just put on a cremation garment" (Combination)
These —some years ago.

I began "Perpetua" on 21 Apr., and finished it 14 May. I began copying it 18 May and finished copying 30 May.

1896 **31 May**:
Last night a curious instance occurred of the persistence of superstition here. At Portgate lives a cattle dealer. Two years ago his daughter had influenza and has been queer in the head since. He consulted a white witch in Exeter who said the girl had been ill wished by a light haired stout woman. He concluded it was Mrs. Tubb who keeps a shop (grocery) at Pt.gate. Resolving to be revenged he set fire to the thatched roof at night under which 6 persons slept. By mere chance Mr. Tubb woke in the night, heard a strange sound and went outside to look. Saw his roof in flames. He had but just time to get his family out before the roof fell in. The man in setting fire to the thatch used 3 matches, his footprints could be distinguished where he had climbed, he had also dropped 3 (three) ½d stamps from his pocket. No sufficient evidence can be got to bring the matter home. Tancock, the man, said that when he went to Exeter the white witch showed him the face of Mrs. Tubb in a glass of water. She told him that the person who had bewitched his daughter passed his home every day but never entered it but that on the following Saturday she would do so, and ask him to buy a little meat. And he further says that on the ensuing Saturday for the first and only time Mrs. Tubbs did come into his house and ask if he would take some meat.[2]

---

[1] Vera: Aged 21 in 1896.
[2] **Arson at Portgate: See explanatory endnote 69.**

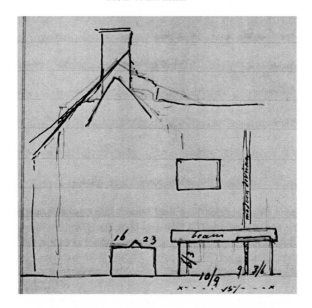

Fig. 37 North wall of ballroom, Lew House

In pulling down for ballroom the indication of the early roof has been found at a sharp angle. There are marks of a window that has been blocked up. The present Hall door is across the old doorway that was 4/3 wide and there was a window at the side, of oak mullions etc.

A great quantity of remains of granite windows, and of an arched door have been found, when the room was converted into a kitchen it must have gone through great alterations. I believe this to be the earliest part of the house and to date from Henry IIIrd's reign. The fireplace has the date 1623 painted on the granite, but did not belong to this place. The window that was blocked, lighting a room above was also of oak not granite. There seem to have been two alterations of this part of the house, and probably of the other part as well.

The original house was nearly as large, but had not the present library, and it extended back in two wings. The windows and doorways were of oak and Roborough stone; then in the beginning of the 17th cent. some of the windows were taken out and granite windows and doorways inserted, but not throughout. In or about 1720 a further alteration was made, the library was added on and the whole house plastered, and set out to instate stone with V joints at the angles

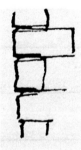

Fig. 38 Quoin stones, Lew House

Then the drawing room was panelled, there was a large painting on panel in the centre of a lady lying asleep under a tree and cherubs flying in the sky and strewing roses. I remember this picture, it was enclosed in a chimney piece rather handsome of the beginning of the 18th cent. About 1810 my grandfather came to Lew and he replastered the whole house, and washed it <u>yellow</u>.

He first removed the panelling of the ~~dining~~ drawing room except the chimneypiece which was not taken down until about 1843. The picture was then hung in the W.C., and there remained till my father made a new closet when the picture was thrown away and I have in vain hunted for it. The lady was almost nude, with blue dress about the lower limbs, but stomach exposed, and she had a babe of about 3 years old lying in her right arm.

*Fig. 39 Painted panelling at Lew House as
remembered by Sabine from his childhood*

I think she had a wreath of red and white roses on her head

My father undertook the entire redoing of the house in or about 1850. He added the dining room. Formerly there had been a passage room there, not wider than 8 ft. and the house was all under one roof. Moreover that passage was an addition of 1720.

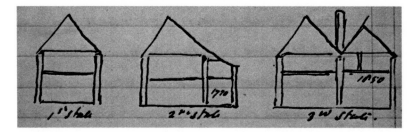

Fig. 40 *Creation of dining room extension, Lew House*

Above the passage of 1720 was a set of bedrooms, and access to the bedrooms over the drawing room, the ~~present~~ then best bedroom was either by the front or by the back stairs. As there was no passage from one part of the house to the other upstairs except through the best bedroom, my father threw the bedrooms over the passage together and made an upper corridor. But in 1850 by widening the back he was able to obtain passage and bedrooms.

I have not altered this part of his arrangement. He removed the gables and hipped where he could not get 2nd. of them together, and carried a handsome cornice of ciment *[sic]* round three sides of the house. In order to do this the gables had to be hipped and lead gutters to be made. Over the front door he put a pediment in the Italian style; and the whole house he cimented *[sic]* and lined out in imitation of stone; and this was painted with stone coloured oil paint every six years.[1]

All he executed was well done but in the taste of the period. My dear Aunt Emily never relished my alterations, she said I was undoing all her father had done and putting back all he cast out, and she regards it in the light of a slight on his taste.

1896 **15 Oct:**
Began "Domitia Longina"[2], have finished "A Study of S Paul"[3] This practically finished on Thurs. Sept 29

1897 1 Feb:
Edward and his wife Marion arrived.[4] The workmen took out the horses and drew the carriage to the door. Triumphal arch up. Bells ringing

1897 **2 Feb:**
Small dinner

---

[1] **Construction of the parapet:** *Early Reminiscences*, **p 248. See also explanatory endnote 62**
[2] Baring-Gould S. *Domitia,* 1898, London, Methuen
[3] Baring-Gould s. *A study of St. Paul, his character and opinions,* 1897, London, Isbister and Co.
[4] Edward and Marion came to Lew following their marriage 17 November 1896.

1897 **3 Feb:**
Large Dinner party

1897 **11 Feb:**
Dinner party

1897 **17 Feb:**
Ball

1897 **18 Feb:**
Edward and Marion left, also Julian

1897 **20 Feb:**
Julian sailed[1]

1897 **23-24, 25**
Terrible storms, most of houses in Lew Down had roofs ripped.

1897 **25 July:**
Bad cold that lasted with me voiceless till Aug 1.

1897 **2 Aug:**
Went to Post Bridge and began to get better.

1897 **12 Aug:**
Telegraphed for John[2] dangerously ill; all night expected his death. Watched and prayed. He rallied at 3.15, but from 10.30 he had the rattle in his throat; was unconscious, face drawn and he could hardly breath.

1897 **18 Aug:**
Again John in a state when we expected his death every minute. All morning of 19th in much the same condition

1897 **19 Aug:**
Rallied slightly at noon. If ever a life was granted in answer to prayer his was. Yet I never asked that it should be given unless God saw that he would grow up to be a good man fearing and loving Him, and working for the church and the benefit his fellow men.[3]

1899 4 Nov:
Laurence Burnard asked me for Barbara. [4]
There follows an unfinished draft or copy of his reply:

---

[1] Julian sailed to Sarawak where he worked for Rajah Brook
[2] John was aged 7 at the time of this serious illness.
[3] It is likely that many, if not all, the entries between 1 February and 19 August 1997 were written on 2 dates, ie 25 February and 19 August.
[4] **Laurence Burnard and Barbara: Explanatory endnote 70**

1899 **10 Nov:** My answer.

> I have delayed writing to you till my return from the Potteries that I might well think over what you said to me on Saturday.
>
> It seems to me from what Barbara tells me, that you would not be in a position to marry for some 18 months. Now B. is really in her ways and mind so much of a child still that I think it very advisable, in so important a matter, that she should not engage herself, till she has had time to decide whether she is in earnest or not. She is such a butterfly that is thoughtless when to alight, that I think for the happiness and security of all, it is………..[1]

---

[1] At this point Sabine had reached the bottom of a page and the reader will avidly turn over and expect to find the rest of this letter but will find — nothing. The copy or draft of a letter was never completed.

As a record of events the diary stops at this point. What little does follow suggests relegation of the diary to minimal use of the remaining pages as a notebook. On one page are what appear to be the pencilled memorial inscriptions of Sabine's ancestors. These may have been used by Sabine as the basis for the inscription on the brass plate to the memory of some of his ancestors on the south wall of the chancel and next to the screen at St Peter's Church. Elizabeth, wife of Edward Gould, appears on the brass plate, with an improbable date of death, but not in the inscriptions in the diary.

Following the memorial inscriptions there are 56 blank pages and finally on the very last page of the ledger an undated incantation on how to stop bleeding.

Why does the record stop here and why so abruptly? Was there an interruption? If so why did Sabine not return and finish entering what he clearly regarded as an important letter? It is only possible to speculate. There had been previous long breaks in the narrative but never in mid-flow. Time for, and interest in, the diary seemed to have waxed and waned over the years but Sabine never lost sight of the fact that within the covers was an invaluable store of anecdotes, gossip, feelings, family and personal history.

Here under lie interred the Mortal
Remains of
Edward Gould of Lew Trenchard Esq
Who died ye 14 Nov. 1667
also of
Henry Gould of Lew Trenchard G.
Son of ye above, who died ....
also of
Sarah Gould daughter of ye above Edward Gould
buried 13 March1728
also of
Susanna daughter of ye above Edward Gould and wife of Peter Truscott Gent.,
who was married 19 Mch
and was buried 23 March 1729
also of
William Gould of Lew Trenchard Esq. son of ye above Henry Gould
buried 24 June 1735
also of
Mrs. Elizabeth his wife, daughter of Philip Drake of Littleham Esq.
buried 6 Aug 1727
also of
Mrs Elizabeth Ellis, wife of the above Henry Gould
and afterwards of ye Revd John Ellis
buried 17 Jan. 1748[1]

After 59 blank pages the following incantation appears on the last page in the ledger:

Charm for staunching Blood given by Jas. Stevens (honest Jimmy) an old miner. Mary Tavy. Oct. 4 1897[2]

> "Jesus was born at Bethlehem
> Baptized on the river of Jordan
> The water was wide and rude against the child
> And he smote the water with a rod
> Then it stood still and so shall your blood
> (name of person) stand in the name of the F and the S and of the H G
> (Repeat 3 times)

Cure for rheumatism, wear a hare's foot.

---

[1] **Memorial Inscriptions: Explanatory endnote 71**
[2] **Charm for Staunching blood: Explanatory endnote 72**

Entries in The 1862 Family Bible

The Family Bible of Sabine Baring-Gould

Transcription and Commentary by R J Wawman

The Holy Bible
Oxford: Printed at the University Press.
Sold by E. Gardner and Son, Oxford Bible Warehouse, Paternoster Row, London.
MDCCCLXII

Commentary

The following transcriptions of manuscript entries by Sabine Baring –Gould in this family bible are made from a photocopy of 5 pages of entries held in a *Gould Family History File* at the *South West Studies Library*, Exeter. The original bible is held at *Plymouth Central Library* but the exact whereabouts are currently unknown. One reason for the existence of this family bible and the entries in it can be gleaned from this excerpt of a letter written by Sabine to his father on 20 October 1871:

> *"I want to know how old I am. I have lost all count of my life, and had to put in all by guesswork in the census. Now I have determined to put down dates in a big Bible, so I should like your birthday, and year, mamma's and mine, also, if you can remember, in what year I went to school at Vevey, at Manheim [sic], London, Warwick, and at College."* [1]

Sabine's difficult handwriting and the poor quality of the photocopy lead to a situation in which whilst most entries in this bible can be accurately transcribed, others depend partly on context, some can only be verified by information from other sources and a few are uncertain.

The date when the entries were first made is uncertain but the structure and content of the list of births, marriages and deaths on the first page would suggest that entries were first made after the birth of Sabine's son, William Drake, in 1878 and before the birth of Barbara in 1880. Perhaps it is not a coincidence that Sabine began the *Diary of Sabine Baring-Gould* in 1880. With the exception of John, the births of the seven youngest children including Barbara are not recorded in the list. The entry for John is incomplete and the handwriting not so bold and less precise, indicating it was probably added at a later date, perhaps in 1897 when John was desperately ill and, for several days, not expected to survive. The list of births, marriages and deaths remained otherwise incomplete apart from the addition of the death of his sister, Margaret, in 1903.

---

[1] Family letter Sabine to Edward Baring-Gould, 1871 October 20. Devon Record office. Deposit Box 5203. Box 25.

Entry of events occurring before the opening of the record will have depended either on memory or on other sources, including his father. Sabine did not enter events as they occurred. It is possible he intended to bring the entries up to date at the end of each year, but variations in his handwriting and quite serious errors in the entries for the years 1884 and 1885 suggest that he sometimes wrote up entries for several years at a time. There are indications that all the years up to1879 were written on the same date; this may also be true of the years 1881 to 1887, 1888 to 1890 and 1891 to 1898. Despite these drawbacks this is an invaluable record providing researchers with a reasonably accurate guide to very many events in Sabine's long life.

The last entry in the bible is for 1921 by which time SBG's horizons had shrunk, and his health had deteriorated to the extent that, two years previously, management of the household had passed to his son Edward and his daughter-in-law Marion. Sabine did not take easily to this loss of control and the 1921 entry gives a hint of resentments that are echoed in letters written to Evelyn Healey during his last years.[1]

---

[1] Letters to Evelyn Healey, 1917-1923, Merriol Almond.

Entries in the Family Bible

{William Baring–Gould   b. May 30 1770   d. 1846
{Diana Amelia Sabine   b. May 4 1775 mar.   d. Aug 7, 1868

{Edward Baring-Gould   b. July 21 1804 mar. S Sidwell's Exeter 10 May 1832
                                        d. May 2 1872
{1.Sophia Charlotte Bond b. Nov 12   1808   d. Dec 6 1863
{2.Lavinia Maitland Marshall nee Snow   b. Dec 8 1828
1.{Sabine Baring-Gould   b. Jan 28   1834. at Exeter. bapt. S Sidwell's
                                     conf. B of Ely   1853
  {Grace Taylor   b. Mar 27   1850 at Ripponden, bapt.
                                   conf. B of Ripon 1866
                                 mar.   May 25 1868

1. Mary Baring-Gould   b. April 20 1869 at Dalton bapt. April 28
2. Margaret   "   b. Aug 9   1870 at Dalton bapt. Aug 17
3. Edward Sabine   "   b. Nov 17 1871   "   "   Dec
4.Beatrice Gracieuse   "   b. Jan 7   1874 at E Mersea bapt. Feb 2 F.
                                       Purification
          F. Annunciation 1876. [1] buried at Lew Trenchard.
5. Veronica   "   b. Aug 14 1875 at E Mersea bapt. Sept 23
6. Julian   "   b. Sept 5 1877 at E Mersea bapt. Michaelmas Day
7. William Drake   "   b. Dec 21   1878 at E Mersea bap. Jan 21 d. 17 Aug
                                           1921

8. John Hilary   "   b.[2]
3. William Baring-Gould   b. Oct 25   1837 d. Feb 21 bur Feb 26 1880 at
                        E Mersea, born at Bratton Clovelly
2. Margaret Ellen Baring-Gould   b. March 23 1835 at Belmont Exeter, m. May 28
                        1857 to Rev Theo Marsh MA b. May 10/25
                        d. Dec 1913
4. Edward Drake Baring-Gould   b. May 11 1851
5. Arthur Baring-Gould   b. Dec 15 1865
6. Leila Baring-Gould[3]   b. Feb 17   1869
Mary was born at 12.15 P.M.
Margaret "   "   "

---

[1] The Feast of Purification of BVM is 2 February. The Feast of the annunciation is 24 March. Beatrice died 25 March 1876 and was buried 29 March. See entry for 1876.
[2] John should be number14! This entry was probably made in August 1897 when John was expected to die. Sabine's other children, i.e. Barbara, Diana, Felicitas, Henry, Joan, Cicely and Grace are all missing from this list!
[3] 3, William; 2 Margaret and 4 Edward Drake are Sabine's 3 siblings. 5 and 6 Arthur and Leila are half-siblings

Sabine Baring-Gould

1834: Jan 28, born at Dix's Field Exeter and baptized at S. Sidwell's Church

1836: Went to live at Culm Court, now Eversfield Lodge, Bratton, where Willy was born.

1837; July 5, went to Pau

1839: July. Returned to England. Lodged in Dix's Field

1840: Sept. Went to Germany and Switzerland. Wintered 1841/2 at Vevay, put to day school there

1842: In Spring went to Salzburg, thence to Vienna, and Prag. *[sic]* Wintered at Dresden 1842/3

1843: In summer went to Schandau in the Saxon Switzerland.[1] Wintered at Mannheim 1843/4 where I went to school.

1844: Summer at Muggendorf[2] in the Franconian Switzerland. Returned to England in August.

1845: In London top of Albemarle St., went to King's College School. My father went to Warwick and I was left behind with Rev. Hayes in Queen's Square

1846: Was taken away in spring, ill and went to Warwick. My grandfather died, and my father went to Lew Trenchard. I was left with William at school.

1847: Had whooping cough, lungs affected and in Sept went to Pau with my father and family and Mrs Bond[3] and family

1848: Returned to England

1849: Oct 11. Went again to Pau

1850: May 11. Drake born. Went the summer at Argelès,[4] Went for the winter to Bayonne.

1851: July 11, returned to England, as Lew House was let, went into lodgings at Tavistock

---

[1] Saxon Switzerland is now a National Park N E of Dresden. The town is Bad Schandau.
[2] Muggendorf is N. of Nürnberg
[3] Mrs Bond: Sabine's maternal grandmother
[4] Drake was born at Pau. Argelès is on the Mediterranean S of the Hautes Pyrenees

1852: May, came to Lew; I went as boarder to the Rev Harvey Goodwin at Cambridge.[1]

1854: Entered at Clare Hall[2]

1857: Took my degree of B.A. Went to Hurstpierpoint. Wrote "Path of the Just"[3] MA 1860

1861: Travelled in Iceland.

1863: My mother died

1864: Went to Horbury. Ordained deacon.

1865: Was ordained priest, founded the Horbury Bridge Mission.

1866: Appointed to Dalton, Advent.

1867: Wrote "Through Flood and Flame" begun Aug 31, vol 1 finished Sept 14; whole finished Dec 14[4]

1868: Wrote "Silver Store" pub.[5] Married May 28. Went to Switzerland. Began "Origins and Development of Relig. Belief"

1869: *No entry*

1870: *No entry*

1871: Jan 11 received offer of E Mersea, accepted Jan 14, came to E Mersea, March 21, inducted March 27, visited Belgium May 31 returned June 14. Sabine[6] born Nov 17, at 12.45 PM. Began "Lives of the Saints"

1872: Went to Belgium, heard there of my father's death, returned to Lew and remained there until July 20. Attended Alt Kirche congress at Cologne.[7]

1873: Went with Grace to the Dolomites and Franconian Switzerland[1]

---

[1] Sabine was sent to the Rev Harvey Goodwin by his father to prepare, unsuccessfully, for a degree course in mathematics.
[2] Entered Clare Hall to read classics.
[3] *Path of the Just* was first published by Masters in 1854, reprinted 1857.
[4] Anonymously, *Through Flood and Flame*, 1868, London, Bentley.
[5] Baring-Gould S. *Silver Store, collected from Medieval , Christian and Jewish Mines*, 1868, London, Longmans and Co
[6] Eldest son: Edward Sabine
[7] **Alt Kirche Congress: Explanatory endnote 73**

1874: Went to Moselle and Eiffel with Gat'[2]

1875: Wrote "Village Sermons." began Jan 15, finished Apr 11[3] Began "Crescentia" Apr 26.[4] Went to the Allgau Alps May 31. ret. June 19 Veronica born Aug 14. bap Sep 23 Went to Belgium Oct 18 ret. Oct 29. Wrote memoirs of R Hawker[5]

1876: At Lew with family. Church rest. there begun Jan 12, began on House Jan 19. Beatrice died March 25. bur. 29th. Returned E. Mersea Apr. 8. Wrote "Wafted Away"[6] Apr 15, Returned to Lew Apr. 24. Back at Mersea May 6th. Willy went out of his mind.[7] Planted cedars about gardens and lawns also Orchard wood, also S side of lime quarry.

1877: Went to Partenkirchen and Oezthal.   Returned   . Left for Freiburg Oct 11, arrived   , Julian born Sept 5. In autumn planted some bird cherries in wood opps. Lew House, also the Lime quarry ramps, and Raddon wood.[8]

1878: Returned to Mersea after winter at Freiburg,}11 . 11. 79[9] In autumn planted 800 maples in Lew wood, also yew walk and trees under slate quarry ramps. Put up in Lew church monuments moved from Staverton Oct 1877. Wrote "Germany, Present and Past."[10] Visited Montunthal Inn 1878[11]

---

[1] 1873 Tour: A description of this visit appears in *Further Reminiscences*, chap 5. This refers to Wurzburg and Northern Bavaria but only briefly mentions the Dolomites

[2] This visit to the Moselle and Eiffel with Sabine's friend, the Rev. J M Gatrill, is described in *Further Reminiscences*, chapter 6

[3] 11 April 1875: The date 11 April has been altered and cannot be verified for certain

[4] *Crescentia*: The transcriber is reasonably confident of the transcription but there is no publication in the bibliography with a title remotely resembling this.

[5] Baring-Gould S. *The Vicar of Morwenstow, being the life of Robert Stephen Hawker, MA*. 1876, London, Henry s King and Co.

[6] *Wafted Away:* Pamphlet 1876. London J G Palmer

[7] **Willy went out of his mind: This date is incorrect. See explanatory endnote 26.**

[8] 1877: Sabine never returned to this entry to add the missing dates

[9] 11 . 11. 79: This date was written faintly, probably at a later date, and is of uncertain significance

[10] Baring-Gould S. *Germany, Past and Present*, 1879, London, C Kegan Paul and Co.

[11] Montunthal Inn 1878: This entry appears to have been scrawled hurriedly at a later date. 'Montunthal' does not exist. Most probably Sabine meant 'Montafun Thal' which he visited on other occasions. Montafun is close to Bludenz and the R. Inn. The year 1878 does not appear in *Further Reminiscences*

1879: At Mersea. Wrote "Sermons for Children," translated "Ernestine"[1] wrote "Glory: A Romance of the Essex Marshes"[2] Lectured on "Woman's Place and Duties" at S. Augustine's, Queen's Gate. Made acquaintence of Edward Gould at Colneford House. *[Essex]*
1880: Went again to Freiburg.[3]

1881: My uncle died, nominated myself to Lew Trenchard. Returned from Freiburg
Summer at Laufenburg[4]

1882: *No entry*

1883: *No entry*

1884: ~~with Gat~~ did not go abroad.[5]

1885: With Gatrill to the Montafun *[sic]* and the Ortler, back by Innsbrück and München.[6] Wrote "The Gaverocks."[7] Michaelmas came into Lew House. Nov 1 began alteration of drawing room and library[8]

1886: With Gatrill to Prag *[Prague]* Riesengebirge and Dresden. Wrote "Richard Cable."[1] Began the tower and terrace.

---

[1] *Ernestine*: English translation of *'Arzt der Seele'* by Frau von Hillern. Published 1879 London De la Rue.

[2] Glory: written above the word 'Glory' is *'Mehalah'* in a fainter hand and probably written at a later date.

[3] Freiburg 1880: The family's residence here is recorded in the Diary part II.

[4] Summer at Laufenburg: This part of the entry was scrawled in probably at a later date. 'Laufenburg on the Rhine, Baden side.' Sabine stayed with his family at a favourite haunt 'Der Krone'

[5] Sabine wrote *'with Gat'* then crossed this out and wrote the simple entry: *'did not go abroad.'* This entry confirms the suspicion that throughout the bible the entries for several years were written at the same time, and often long after the events recorded. In this instance Sabine was right first time. It is manifestly clear from his diary that he and Gatrill did go abroad in 1884. Similarly the travels recorded for 1885 actually occurred in 1884. His only trip abroad in 1885 was to Paris to officiate at the wedding of his cousin Alex Baring who was married on the same day that the Baring-Gould household moved into Lew House. He was away a mere 4 days.

[6] Montafun and the Ortler: This journey was in 1884 not 1885. See *'The Diary of SBG'*

[7] Anonymously, *The Gaverocks*, 1887, 1.Cornhill Magazine, 2. London, Smith, Elder and Co

[8] Drawing Room and Library: According to the diary, work started here 1 Dec. not 1 Nov

1887: With Gatrill to Italian Lakes and Milan. Wrote "Arminell."[2] Planted much larch and scotch. The drawing room opened complete at Easter.

1888: Began collecting folk songs and music of Devon and Cornwall. Began in May

1889: Repaired Lew Mill house. Spent Feb and March in Rome. Edward left for N York Oct 15. Built on an addition to 'Brentor Blick'[3]

1890: Laid up in winter again. Left for Italy 21 Jan. Remained abroad to the end of April. Wrote "In the Roar of the Sea."[4] Attack of Scarlet Fever in the house. Aug 11 – Sep 20.[5]

1891: Drainage of Lew House redone: began in Oct.1890. Wrote "The Tragedy of the Caesars."[6] Began "Curgenven"[7] Easter Monday. Planted scotch pines in the Rookery. Built two cottages at the Y. Planted some scarlet oaks and liquid amber about the gardens. Edward returned to England May 15. Harry broke his arm July 5

1892: Went to Brive and Cahors. About 2 months. Enlarged Rampenstein. Wrote "Queen of Love"[8] and "Zita"[9]

1893: Mary married Jan 11th. Leila married April 19th. Went with Geo. Young[10] to Brive and Courses of *[River]* Vezère in Spring. Reorganised water supply of Lew House with reservoir. Wrote "Kitty Alone"[11]

1894: In the autumn began the E. wing of the house at the back, but little progress owing to bitter winter. Wrote "The Broom Squire"[1] and "Noemi."[2] Influenza epidemic. 14 ill in the house, Rather a trial.[3]

---

[1] Anonymously, *Richard Cable, Lightshipman*, 1.1887 Chambers Journal, 2. London, Smith, Elder and Co.
[2] Anonymously, *Arminell, A Social Romance*, 1889, Temple Bar
[3] Brentor Blick: 'Blick' is German for 'view'. The entry in the diary for 29 Aug 1889 confirms that Sabine was engaged in building an addition to 'Brentor View' in Lewdown
[4] Baring-Gould S. *In the Roar of the Sea: A Tale of the Cornish Coast*, 1892, London, Methuen and Co.
[5] **Our Scarlet Fever Attack: See explanatory endnote 59.**
[6] S Baring-Gould, *The Tragedy of the Caesars*, 1892, London, Methuen and Co
[7] Baring-Gould S. *Mrs Curgenven of Curgenven*, 1. 1892-3 Cornhill Magazine, 2. 1893, Methuen and Co.
[8] Baring-Gould S. *The Queen of Love*. 1894, London, Methuen & Co.
[9] Baring-Gould S. *Cheap Jack Zita: A Story of the Ely Fens*. Serialised in *The Queen*
[10] Sir George Young, Bt: Sabine's cousin.
[11] Baring-Gould S. *Kitty Alone: a story of three fires*. 1894, Good Words.

1895: Continued library wing and new dairy, larder, coalhouses and cloister at back, the latter copied from one at the Poor House, Moreton Hampstead.[4] Went in Nov. with R *[Robert]* Burnard to Saumur. Loudon, Poitiers, Cirroi, Confolens. Home by Tours. Wrote Nap. Bon![5] and "Guavas"[6]

1896: Kitchen completed. Altered and raised drive and set up new gates and piers.[7] Wrote "Bladys."[8] Rebuilt W. wing of the house.

1897: Edward and Marion arrived 1 Feb. Vera engaged to be Fred Winter. *[?]* Wrote "Domitia,"[9] and "An Old English Home,"[10] also "Study of St. Paul,"[11] this partly in /96. Completed Ballroom and the whole West wing, except panelling of the room at the back. The ornamental chimney piece of the ballroom was bought from a carpenter's yard at Colmar in 1881. It had formed part of a rescued altar piece from a destroyed chapel. Most of it had been used up for balcony in the marketplace Colmar. The rest adapted and the 3 pannels *[sic]* new carved. Among this the coat of arms reproduced from a cornelian seal found many years ago in Whittlesea and offered to my father and uncle for 30/- and refused by them. Happily I found letter and impress of seal.[12] John dangerously ill in autumn.[13] Vera injured her knee by fall from bicycle.

1898: Production of Red Spider.[14]

1900: In Sept excavated prehistoric cemetery at Harlyn Bay.[15] Oct 20 arrived in Dinan

---

[1] Baring-Gould S. *The Broom Squire*, 1895, Graphic.
[2] Baring-Gould S. *Noémi. A story of rock-dwellers.* 1894, Illustrated London News,
[3] This influenza epidemic is recorded in several letters to his daughter Mary that year. It is evident from these that the outbreak was serious. *rather a trial* was an understatement
[4] Alms Houses, Moreton Hampstead: *A Book of Devon*, p 226
[5] Baring-Gould S. *The Life of Napoleon Bonaparte.* 1897, London, Methuen & Co
[6] Baring-Gould S. *Guavas the Tinner.* 1896, Serialised in *The Queen*
[7] Piers: Gate pillars
[8] Baring-Gould S. *Bladys of the Stewponey,* 1897, London, Methuen & Co
[9] Baring-Gould S. *Domitia*, 1898, London: Methuen & Co
[10] Baring-Gould S. *An Old English Home and its Dependencies*, 1898, London, Methuen & Co
[11] Baring-Gould S. *A study of St. Paul, his character and opinions,* 1897, London, Isbister and Co.
[12] **Wax impress of a Cornelian seal: See explanatory endnote 74**
[13] John's illness: It is evident from the diary that John was expected to die. Did this prompt the start of an entry for John on the first page of bible entries?
[14] The Light Opera *Red Spider* with music by Learmont Drysdale and libretto by S. Baring-Gould. Moderately successful provincial run in 1898.
[15] Harlyn Bay: Near Padstow, Cornwall.

1901: Barbara married 8 April Easter Monday[1] 17 Dec returned to Lew from Dinan

1903:[2] Left Lew 5 Oct for Wiesbaden. Returned to Lew 25 Nov. Margaret[3] died 13 Dec.

1903: Edward Bond died

1904: Went to Pau[4] in early part of year. In the fall went to Rhine[5] with Mamma and Grace[6]

1905: Went to Riviera in early part of the year

1906: Partly rebuilt the inn Lewdown.

1907: Julian returned from Borneo, and Willy from Minneapolis. Diana and Joan married Oct 3

1908: Went end of Sep Michaelmas Day from Lew to Munich, [7] where Felicitas got engaged to F. Fiske.

1909: Returned in March to Lew.

1910: Left Lew on 27 January and was taken ill in London where I remained ill for a month but left on March 1 and went to Vendôme, Tours, Poitiers, Perigueux, Cahors and was home for Good Friday. In June went for a fortnight to Stuttgart on to Teck[8] and the Alb.[9] William Drake was married at Minneapolis to Harriet Stuart on 12 Oct. Julian married Joan Ramsden at Bridestowe. This summer Joan *[nee B-G]* and her husband and child, Mr Priestley was home from Bombay. The vestry added to Lew Church, the gift of Sophie H.[10] and Willie B-G.[1] Began the restructure of Lew Mill House.[2] Went for winter months to Munich:

---

[1] Verified by almanack

[2] There is no entry for 1902. It might be assumed that the first of two entries for 1903 should be for 1902 but it is known that Sabine's sister Margaret did die in 1903.

[3] **Margaret: Sabine's sister. See explanatory endnote 30**

[4] Pau: It is clear from a letter to his daughter, Mary, on 4 February 1904, that Grace also accompanied Sabine on this visit. It is likely the visit was also used as part of his research for *A Book of the Pyrenees*, London, Methuen, 1906

[5] The Rhine: Presumably this visit was also used to research *A Book of the Rhine from Cleve to Mainz,* London, Methuen, 1906

[6] Mamma and Grace: Sabine was referring to his wife, Grace (Mamma) and his youngest daughter, Grace.

[7] Munich: It is evident from a letter to his daughter Mary that his wife, Grace and two of his daughters, Felicitas and Grace, accompanied Sabine on this visit.

[8] **Teck and Queen Mary: See explanatory endnote 63**

[9] The Alb: Swabian Alb, mountain range in Baden-Württenburg near Stuttgart

[10] Sophie Harriet: daughter of the Rev. Charles Baring-Gould

1911-12: Winter the gallery of Lew House completed. Enlarged S window of chancel and stained glass added. Painting by Deschwanden put up over the altar.

1913: heating apparatus put into house. Built holy well in glen[3] and made rose garden.
Julian and his wife returned from Borneo, and left Feb. 1914. Spent part of winter in the South of France, at Bordeaux, Bayonne and Pau. Returned after Christmas by way of Toulouse to England. Grace[4] m. C. Calmady Hamlyn 16 July.

1914: Willy and Harriet arrived. On declaration of war they were compelled in all haste to return to the States

1905 *[1915 intended]*: Felicitas md. Capt. Sydney Eyre,[5] 5 May.

1916: Cicely[6] md. Capt. Frank Newport Tinley 5 Decr. My dear wife d. 6 April.

1917: *No entry*

1918: *No entry*

1919: Change of household. Edward and Marion came to reside in Lew House July 1

1920: Gave Deschwanden painting of our lady and children to Tavistock church and paintings of S. Benedict and S. Gregory to the Monastery of Buckfast.

1921: Gave the painting of the Crucifixion and of Ecce Homo for Lew Church, as Marion wants to turn all religious pictures out of Lew House.[7] A year of unusual fair weather and drought. During this and last year have been engaged in repairing cottages and farms, settling the farmers and 3 farms Orchard, Wooda and Holdstrong. Henceforth the farmers will do their own repairs, so that Edward will come into the estate unencumbered. It seems to me that since my father's death in 1872, forty-nine years ago I have been employed incessantly in executing repairs. Edward will reap the advantage.

---

[1] Willie B-G: Sabine's son
[2] Restructuring of Lew Mill Dower House took place prior to leasing to Julian's in-laws, the Ramsdens.
[3] **Holy Well: See explanatory note 75**
[4] Young Grace, then aged 22.
[5] Felicitas married Sydney Ayre not Eyre. What happened to F Fiske? See entry for 1908
[6] Cicely aged 27
[7] Marion and Religious paintings: Evelyn Healey letters, Merriol Almond. When considered alongside letters LVII, 31 May and LXXIII, 14 Nov 23 this entry is evidence of tensions in Sabine's relationship with Marion, his daughter-in-law.

The Man Behind the Diary
By Ron Wawman © May 2009

The Man Behind the Diary

1. A Brief Biography of Sabine Baring-Gould

Sabine was born on 28 January 1834, the eldest son of Edward Baring-Gould, squire of Lew Trenchard, Devon, and his first wife, Sophia. He received little formal schooling during his formative years, many of which were spent accompanying his parents on their tours of the continent. As a child, Sabine was a daydreamer and often to be found with his head in a storybook. For this he incurred the disapproval of his overly strict father who was determined to mould his son into a mathematician and engineer despite Sabine never showing the slightest aptitude or enthusiasm for these subjects. As Sabine grew up Edward would have been unimpressed by a son much of whose time was spent on such activities as rambling across Dartmoor, drawing sketches of fragments of stained glass in churches and writing poetry. His long term plan for his two eldest sons was simple and predictable—Sabine, the elder, would enter the army and eventually succeed to the estate while his younger brother, William, invariably referred to as Willy, would be groomed to succeed to the living at St Peter's Church, Lew Trenchard. It never occurred to Edward that either son might have other ideas, or, if it did, he was confident that children could be disciplined and moulded to whatever their father decided.[54]

In 1850, at the age of 16, Sabine achieved some distinction by carrying out the excavation of a Roman villa whilst the family was resident in Pau, France. His findings, meticulously recorded after the standards of the day, were briefly reported in *The Illustrated London News*[55]

Following the family's return to England In 1853 and in a last attempt to prepare his son for a degree course in mathematics, Sabine was sent by his father to the house of the Rev. Harvey Goodwin, a Cambridge don and senior wrangler who eventually became the Bishop of Carlyle. He was to be tutored by Goodwin in mathematics. When this proved unsuccessful, Edward finally accepted the inevitable and later that year Sabine entered Clare College to read Classics. In 1857 he was awarded a 3rd class degree and, by doing so, again incurred the displeasure of his parents. At this distance in time it is easy to see how the breadth of Sabine's intellectual curiosity was bound to clash with the need for a disciplined application to degree course work. Whilst at Cambridge Sabine was involved in the formation of a Society of the Holy Cross, a manifestation of Sabine's deep and lasting commitment to the Catholic Revival in the Church of England for which his father had no sympathy. Edward *would have shared this attitude with most Victorian upper and middle class fathers who commonly regarded Puseyism as fit only for women and the weak-minded.*[56]

Soon after coming down from Cambridge Sabine left home following a serious disagreement with his father over his intention to take Holy orders. He also refused to accept the teaching post his father had arranged for him at Marlborough

Grammar School because his uncle, Frederick Bond, who was headmaster, also had no sympathy with the Anglo-catholic cause. Without telling his parents where he was going, he headed for the flagship Anglo-catholic church of St Barnabas, Pimlico, London and the Rev. Charles Lowder. Lowder was a leading member of the Catholic Revival in the Church of England, the greatest of the slum priests and founder of the *Society of the Holy Cross. (SSC)* Lowder was an important influence on Sabine's early years. Not for the first time he stayed at St Barnabas for two or three months and undertook unpaid lay work both in the choir school and in the surrounding community until what little money he had ran out. At this point contact with his parents was re-established and he reluctantly bowed to his father's insistence that he leave London. Although a level of reconciliation was achieved, Sabine did not return home and persisted in his refusal to take the post at Marlborough, preferring instead to take the paid teaching appointment found for him by Lowder at St John's Middle School, (now known as Hurstpierpoint College) Sussex.

There I was satisfied I had found the place and work I wanted[57]

This was one of the schools founded by the Rev. Nathaniel Woodard to ensure that the 'middle classes' received a 'church education' with frequent access to the sacraments of Confession and the Eucharist. It was no co-incidence that Woodard was also a leading member of the Anglo-catholic Revival although, unlike other members of that revival with whom Sabine was associated, such as Lowder, Nathaniel Woodard was not 'advanced' in ritual terms and so did not invite open hostility and accusations of 'popery'. Sabine, likewise, achieved no notoriety for extravagant ritual during the course of his life. Sabine taught at St John's for eight years before at the age of 30, a year after his mother's death, once more seeking his father's permission to take Holy Orders. This time, his father gave his consent but made it clear that if Sabine did take Holy Orders he would never inherit the estate, which would pass instead to his younger brother, Willy.[58]

During Sabine's three years as a curate at Horbury in Yorkshire, he successfully established a thriving church mission at Horbury Bridge under the fatherly eye of the vicar, the Rev. John Sharp. Sharp was another leading member of the Catholic Revival. At Horbury two other significant events occurred. One was the first performance of his famous hymn *Onward Christian Soldiers* at a Whit Sunday school march. The other was his engagement to Grace, a Yorkshire mill girl half his age. They married in 1868 soon after Sabine had left Horbury, but only after Grace had been sent away for 2 years to learn how to conduct herself as 'a lady.' Neither family approved of the marriage and no member of his family attended the wedding. There are some who suggest[59] that Grace, with her eventual transformation from Yorkshire mill girl to member of the gentry and no trace of a Yorkshire accent, was a model for Bernard Shaw's Eliza Doolittle in *Pygmalion*, but, although Shaw may have visited Lew, there is no firm evidence that Eliza was modelled on any one person.

At the end of 1866 Sabine was appointed to a perpetual curacy in the small village of Dalton near Thirsk. He was unhappy in this sleepy and isolated rural parish, a sharp contrast with the busy industrial town of Horbury. In 1871 Sabine sent a copy of his recently published book *The Origin and Development of Religious Belief,* [60] to the Prime Minister, William Gladstone. Gladstone was impressed by the book and, recognising in its author a kindred theological spirit, offered Sabine the crown living of East Mersea, Essex. Sabine accepted the offer with alacrity, partly because his rapidly expanding family was outgrowing the limitations of the vicarage at Dalton and partly because of the constraints imposed on him by Lady Downe, the domineering church patron. In many ways the isolation of the desolate Essex salt marshes provided its own frustrations for a man who craved intellectual stimulation. However, from East Mersea, he could, and often did, travel by rail to London[61] and the library of the British Museum where he is still recognised as a frequent user.

At the time of his marriage in 1868, Sabine probably remained convinced that he would never inherit the Lew Trenchard estates, but by this time, unknown to him, his younger brother, Willy had become seriously ill, both mentally and physically. This no doubt influenced his father's decision, not long after Sabine's marriage, to make Sabine, rather than Willy, the principal beneficiary of his father's will. Sabine was probably unaware of his father's change of heart before being informed in a letter written by his father in 1871.[62] After his father's sudden and unexpected death in 1872,[63] a mere eleven days after the completion of the settlement of the estate, it became clear to Sabine that the finances of the estate were in a parlous state and that, despite inheriting, he could not afford to move into Lew House but must instead rent it out and use the income to meet every day expenses. Ten long years were to pass as rector of East Mersea before he finally took up residence as the 'squarson' (squire and parson) of Lew Trenchard. By then he was establishing himself as an industrious author and scholar in many different fields. Later he was to add the collection of West Country folk songs to a remarkable list of achievements. Indeed, he regarded the collection of folk songs to be his greatest achievement.[64]

All his life Sabine was fascinated by his family pedigree and, from the age of 17, when he formed his three purposes in life, had resolved that, one day, he would renovate Lew Trenchard Church and restore the Gould estates to their former glory.[65] In particular he dreamed of converting Lew House into a splendid 'Elizabethan' manor house that he could pass on to his successors, but when, on inheriting, the opportunity to fulfil his dreams seemed within his grasp, the money to pay for such an ambitious project was not to be found. Undaunted he turned his skills as a writer and consummate storyteller to the serious business of writing novels. The money he earned from this industry was poured into rebuilding and furnishing the house. He had no time for architects[66] and the splendid, if somewhat idiosyncratic, manor house we see today results from work carried out to his own designs and under his own supervision.

Fig. 41 *Lew House. (Now Lewtrenchard Manor Hotel) Present day.*

More than 40 novels were written by Sabine in all, together with a vast number of short stories. Astonishingly, although novel writing came to take up a large part of his time, he actively disliked writing them and, in his diary, lamented that it took him away from all his other interests.[67] Sabine was remarkably good at painting pen pictures and vividly describing characters. He was particularly effective when writing humorously, but his plots were often improbable and his treatment of characters sometimes appeared, to Victorian tastes, unnecessarily harsh. *Mehalah*[68] was regarded as his best novel and has been compared with Emily Brontë's *Wuthering Heights,*[69] although some critics found the characters in *Mehalah* unpleasant and the harshness of the story uncomfortable.

In the 1890s Sabine was ranked among the top 10 authors and was possibly the most prolific author of his day. His bibliography[70] runs to 70 pages in a size 10 font! He first published at the age of 17 and his last work appeared in print after his death at the age of 89. Those 72 years saw in excess of 62,000 pages in print.[71] Until his very old age he habitually wrote standing at the desk that still stands near the great windows of the library he built and loved. He no doubt earned a great deal of money from his pen, but, as the house and its furnishing swallowed up most of it, he and his family—he had 15 children, 14 of whom survived into adult life—were always hard up and he was, at least once, close to bankruptcy.[72] [73]

Sabine was frequently absent from home, whether on the continent, involved in archaeological explorations on Dartmoor or researching in the Library of the British Museum. These absences, the size of his family, and the almost incessant and at times intrusive building work on Lew House have led some commentators[74] to suggest that Sabine's wife, Grace, was long suffering and even unhappy. There is however much to suggest[75] that the marriage was soundly based and that Grace was a lively and able woman. Before becoming ill with rheumatoid arthritis she was more than capable of holding her own with her husband. She managed the household and large staff of Lew House with quiet efficiency.[76]

Grace died in 1916, during the First World War. Sabine was devastated by this loss and never fully recovered from it. The gravestone he set upon her grave had none of the traditional implausibilities that are commonly seen on the graves of dead wives; instead just three words, moving even today, *Dimidium Animae Meae*—half of my own very soul. The war brought about many changes including different tastes and fashions in literature, and his writing began to lose its popularity. So it was that, writing to the very last, he gradually faded from the public eye before dying on 2nd January 1924, a few weeks short of his 90th birthday.

As we have seen, during his last years Sabine wrote 2 volumes of memoirs under the titles *Early Reminiscences* and *Further Reminiscences,* but the reminiscences are of his ancestors, his travels and the people he met or heard about; very little is about himself or his wife and children. He was probably working on a third volume of reminiscences when he died and there is reason to believe that these were to include more about family life. After his death no trace was found of this manuscript or that of a chapter about the family[77] known, from a letter to his daughter, Mary, to have been written for, but omitted from his posthumously published *Further Reminiscences.*

> *I send you the chapter on dear Mama, that I have reluctantly been obliged to write for the second series of my Reminiscences. When you have read it please send it on to Vera, and ask her to forward it on to Grace at Leawood. I should also wish to hear your and their strictures upon the chapter.*

His eldest son, Edward, suggested that Sabine probably burnt this material,[78] but a personal communication from a descendant[79] confirms that at least one of Edward's children witnessed the burning of the manuscript by Edward himself.

The Man Behind the Diary

2. Getting Under Sabine's Skin

Ron Wawman writes: As a result of working on this diary I have become better acquainted with Sabine Baring-Gould, the man. The process of transcription and analysis has led me into several unexpected but illuminating by-ways, and stimulated the acquisition of collateral information from other sources, particularly family letters. New light has been thrown on Sabine's relationships with his parents, siblings and others and it has been possible to form a more coherent perception of the conflicts and aspirations that drove the renovation of Lew House and the publication of so many novels and short stories.

It was never my intention or expectation that on completion of this work I would be in a position to give a full exposition of the life of Sabine Baring-Gould. There is much more to uncover about the man before the definitive biography can be written. My main aim has been the construction of a working hypothesis identifying some of the principal influences on the development of Sabine's personality, his relationships with others and what drove him to do what he did. It is for the reader to judge my conclusions.

Sabine wrote about his parents and his relationship with them in his two volumes of Reminiscences but the accounts given there are not as full and revealing as those in the diary. What was written in the diary about family interactions impresses as an essentially personal attempt to reach some understanding of why his relationship with his parents was, in many ways, unsatisfactory. It has been useful to consider these reflections on past events alongside letters written at the time they occurred. Thus, as we have seen, it is known from 1857 correspondence with his mother[80] that, at the age of 23 years, Sabine was distressed by his father's harsh disapproval of his choice of career and angry at the unrelenting determination to force his son into a mould of his father's making.

In *Early Reminiscences*[81] Sabine wrote:

> *when I was a boy of seventeen I formed my purposes, and from their accomplishment I have never deviated.*

In *Further Reminiscences*[82], writing about his induction as Rector of Lew Trenchard in 1881, he added:

> *In a very wonderful manner the way had been opened to me for undertaking the three tasks I had aspired to execute when I was a boy of seventeen, although at that time, and for many years after, the prospect*

*was obscure, and I could see no means whereby these objects might be
attained.*

His tasks were to restore the church of St Peter's, Lew Trenchard; to restore and
reconstruct Lew House; to improve the moral and spiritual life of the parishioners
of Lew Trenchard. Sabine gave no inkling of the mental process by which he came
to these decisions at the age of 17 although it can be inferred that this was a very
significant event in Sabine's life. However entries in a recently uncovered and as
yet unpublished notebook probably dating from 1851[83] suggest that these resolves
from which he *never deviated* may have been made at a time of adolescent turmoil
leading to religious commitment.

The notebook includes three pages of biblical texts and references referring to sin,
departing from faith and forgiveness through the blood of Christ. Furthermore
these texts are immediately followed by two short poems written on a single page.
The first poem, one of several love poems, includes the lines:

> *I never have told her how I love,*
> *For what can that avail me....*
>
> *....For tho' we are separated*
> *By no laws which are divine;*
> *Yet 'tis man, stern man prevents it*
> *And she never can be mine*

It is tempting to speculate that that the *man, stern man* of the poem was Sabine's
father and that the subject of his affections was a certain Constance Frazer he met
in Pau and about whom, in *Early Reminiscences*[84], he wrote:

> *There lived on the farther side of the river, a Scottish family named
> Frazer....The three youngest were not even engaged, and vastly pretty
> girls they were – Margaret, Ellen and Constance*

and

> *....the faces of the Frazers have passed completely out of my recollection,
> so that I think my brother has exaggerated my devotion to Constance.
> Indeed, but for my brother's diary, I should not have recalled their
> existence.*

The other poem entitled '*Night Thoughts*'[85] begins:

> *Oh, How I love a night walk. All my thoughts*
> *Come trooping clust'ring round in wild dismay*
> *And some cry shame and others whisper sin*

and concludes:

These warring powers will burst the mansion doors
Of my tortured mind – But oh, I must despair.

It is possible that Sabine's tortured pre-occupation with unspoken love, sin, feelings of guilt and shame together with biblical texts dealing with sin and absolution, prompted a religious conversion and a desire for penitence and absolution. [86] If so this could also explain the formation of his *three purposes.*

Two of the three purposes in his life fit well in the context of penance. These are his determination to restore Lew Trenchard Church and his intention to improve the spiritual welfare of the parishioners. At first sight the third aim, to restore Lew House, sits incongruously beside them. But, taking into account Sabine's difficult and resentful relationship with his father, it is possible that his penance also included reparation towards his temporal father through loyalty to the role of squire and to the family house and estate. This would also help to explain why, in later years, Sabine put the restoration of Lew House before much else — including, at times, the needs of his wife and family.

It is ironic that, in order to preserve the hard won integrity of his own personality, Sabine was later forced to defy his father's demand for unquestioning subservience to the extent that he put himself at serious risk of being denied the opportunity to fulfil his three purposes. This determination to forego a destiny that had become crucial to him rather than *follow the line he had chalked out for me*[87] is a measure of the strength of Sabine's character. Sabine's relationship with his mother is more enigmatic. As a child he adored her, but, as he grew older, and despite evidence from correspondence that he continued to confide in her and to share at least some of his aspirations with her, he was disappointed by her intellectual limitations, the lack of doctrine behind her piety, her readiness to betray confidences and her failure to support him in his struggles with his father.

Fortunately the worst manifestations of his conflicts with his parents had been resolved before their deaths and certainly by the time he began his diary. With the fulfilment of his three purposes within sight Sabine was able, through the pen pictures in his diary, to put the conflicts into context and to understand that his rigid, opinionated father, whilst misguided in his attempts to mould and control his children, was honest and well intentioned. It should be noted however that the visit Sabine and Grace made to Lew shortly before his father's death was almost certainly for the purpose of signing the entail to the deed of settlement by which Sabine inherited. This may, to some extent have contributed to the warmth shown by both Sabine and Grace towards Edward on that occasion.[88]

It was probably inevitable that a rigid and opinionated father would clash with the vigorous, questioning and determined personality of his eldest son. Caught between these two strong-minded men, life must have been difficult for Sophia, but in the mid-nineteenth century it was unlikely that she would be anything other than loyal to her husband.

Although others[89] [90] have commented briefly on the personality and the mental breakdown of Sabine's brother, Willy, they have tended to write disparagingly about him and were patently unaware of the severity of his illness. There is no evidence that the true and tragic extent of Willy's ill health is recorded anywhere other than in this diary. Here Sabine gave a detailed and graphic account of Willy's deterioration from the first manifestations of 'brain fever' in the 1860s, to his incarceration in a private lunatic asylum in 1875 following a violent assault on Sabine, and his death, five years later in 1880. It is evident both from the diary and from comments in Sabine's correspondence with his parents that his father never shared his knowledge of the seriousness of this illness with Sabine and it seems that Sabine, in his turn, also kept his own counsel. Like sexual impropriety, mental instability was an object of Victorian unease. The cause of death given on Willy's death certificate is *general paralysis of the insane*. Sabine's description of Willy's mental and physical symptoms is entirely consistent with this diagnosis. Since the 1920s it has been known that this condition is caused by *syphilis*.

It is difficult to avoid the conclusion that Willy's health was a major factor persuading Sabine's father to relent, amend his will and, in 1871, inform Sabine that he would inherit rather than Willy.[91] His father could, had he been so minded, have held to his original course, continued to deny Sabine and instead left the estate to his youngest son, Drake, who was then aged 20. By this time, however, Sabine was establishing himself as a writer, leading an independent life as a parson in a Crown living, happily married to a personable young wife, and had children with the promise of more. It is likely that this evidence of professional and domestic stability, coupled with the promise of an heir, all combined to persuade his father to do what he had always found difficult — change his mind.

Knowledge of the apparent wilfulness with which Sabine dealt with the conflicting relationship with his father, coupled with a casual awareness of his published work could lead the reader to form the view that Sabine was an opinionated, self-assured and self-interested man who sailed serenely through the adversities of life while at the same time being intolerant and judgemental of others. Furthermore some who have written about him have accused him of being insensitive to the needs of others. They have claimed that he either expected rigid obedience from his own children or simply ignored and indeed hardly knew them.[92] [93] By contrast it is evident from some accounts that Sabine was generous and helpful to others. He is also described as emotional and easily moved to laughter or tears. Others have given examples of the patience and thoughtfulness he showed towards children in general.[94]

It is probable that much of the apparent harshness of Sabine's attitudes towards his own children simply reflects an assiduous adoption by him of the duties associated with the autocratic paternal role that was the accepted norm in Victorian society. The view of Sabine as an essentially caring father is supported by references to the great affection generally shown to Sabine by his children[95] and by the frequent warm and concerned references to his children and grandchildren in letters by him. In an undated manuscript written by his daughter Joan probably in the late 1960s[96] she described an incident in which she and other children, waited until after their father had made his regular night round of the house, had seen that lights were out in their bedroom and had settled them in bed for the night. They then rose, went into the next door bedroom where there was an open fire and proceeded to attempt to light an oil lamp from the fire so that they could continue reading in bed. The lamp caught fire and, in a panic, was thrown down thereby causing a minor conflagration. Sabine was rapidly summoned and, having quickly extinguished the fire, did not then proceed to punish his daughters.

Among several ill-considered criticisms of Sabine has been criticism of the thoughtlessness towards Grace evident in his apparent long absence from Lew at the time of the family's move into Lew House in 1885.[97] However the diary provides convincing evidence that Sabine was only absent from Lew for four days at this time.[98]

When asked by her daughter Cicely why she had so many children, Sabine's wife, Grace, apparently said that children were *the natural fruiting of marriage*.[99] This statement was used by his granddaughter, Cicely Briggs to infer that Grace was ignorant of the facts of life and, by implication, that Sabine was thoughtless in not enlightening her and selfish in taking no steps himself to limit the size of the family. Grace was an intelligent and capable woman brought up in a harsh working class environment during which she would have been made very aware of the realities of life. It is highly unlikely that she was unaware of how babies were made. However, as an adult female member of a respectable middle class Victorian family she would not have contemplated discussing sexual matters even with her daughters other than with the broadest circumlocution. Moreover mid-Victorian moral attitudes towards the limitation of the size of a family by any means other than abstinence were strict. Such attitudes were shared by both the medical profession and by the established church. The phrase *the natural fruiting of marriage* fitted naturally within that moral context and did not imply ignorance.

Another criticism sometimes levelled against Sabine was that he frequently travelled abroad leaving Grace at home to bear children and look after the house. There is some justice in this claim although, again, such behaviour on Sabine's part reflected Victorian attitudes to marital roles. In Sabine's favour it is necessary to remember his almost obsessive pre-occupation with escaping annually to the continent in an, often vain, attempt to avoid chest infections. It is also evident from letters by Sabine to his daughter, Mary, that in the 1900s and early 1910s, Grace frequently accompanied Sabine abroad once her childbearing years were behind her. Moreover it is also evident from other letters that she was often away from Lew, visiting family and friends, when Sabine was in residence. By the early 1900s Grace was suffering from rheumatoid arthritis and it is evident from letters that Sabine was well aware that Grace's health and mobility improved when she was abroad. A letter to Mary from Munich on 8 October 1908[100] described how:

> *Mamma has also developed walking powers and does her two hours easily.*
>
> *She is looking much better*

while in a letter written on 8 March 1906 from Montpelier in the South of France to a parishioner, Polly Davey,[101] he wrote:

> *You should see how Mrs. Baring-Gould walks here – why she would think nothing of walking two or three miles – and when at home there is no stirring her out even as far as the greenhouses.*

The climate alone could not have produced such a dramatic improvement. It is probable that when at Lew, Sabine was often so busy with other activities that he gave himself insufficient time to motivate Grace to keep mobile. It is evident from a letter written to Mary on 13 December 1913 that Grace did not accompany Sabine on a visit he made to Pau that year. It is likely that this was because she was no longer fit to travel such distances. Then in 1914 after an unsuccessful search for the curative effects of a stay in Bath, on 24 July[102] he wrote to Mary asking her to undertake a sick visit to the retired governess to the children, Miss Biggs, on his behalf, because

> *I cannot leave with Mamma so crippled.*

This was written a month or so after the outbreak of World War I. Grace died on 8 April 1916. Sabine never again travelled aboard.

Some of the contradictory comments made by those who have written about Sabine can be explained when Sabine's personal circumstances in the late 19th and early 20th centuries are taken into account. When, as was frequently the case, he was pre-occupied with writing or with the restoration of Lew House, he had less time for others, including children and grandchildren. Grace, in a rare letter to her daughter Mary,[103] felt compelled to apologise for Sabine's reluctance to have his grandsons to stay at Lew at such times. Grace evidently reconciled herself with difficulty to a situation in which she and members of her family were able to see less of each other than they would have wished.

As part of the resolution of the conflicts with his father, it can be postulated that Sabine strove for achievement and approval. He was probably ill at ease when idle and it is unsurprising therefore that he would project these attitudes onto his children and expect all of them to be industrious. He has been criticised for the *"hard time"* he gave his sons who, it has been said, were driven out to work at an early age and given little support by Sabine.[104] Certainly Harry, who died in Malaya in 1913 at the age of 28, does appear to have been firmly dealt with by his father, but before judging Sabine's attitudes towards his children it is prudent to try to understand what lay behind his motives and actions. In his *Sermons to Children,*[105] Sermon IV on *Idleness* includes the following statement:

> *My children! now in the time of youth you form the habits for life. If now you grow up in idleness, you will idle through life, and saunter out of it without having fulfilled the vocation set you when you entered into it. If you grow up diligent, methodical, loving work, then when you are men or women, you will prove yourselves useful members of society, you will hate idleness, and your busy hands or brains will be employed through life, turning the talents entrusted to you to good account.*

The next clue is to be found in a letter from Sabine to his son Edward written on 16 January 1902.[106] This letter, primarily written to congratulate Edward on the birth of his son and heir, is noteworthy for the insightful comments included on the progress of several of his children including Harry:

> *I am taking Harry away from Winchester at Easter, he is doing nothing there, and I shall apprentice him at a foundry in Plymouth I think to make him work with his hands as he will not with his head, but he must also attend to technical education classes in the evening if he is to get on. He is so inert, and shows so little disposition for any particular line of work, that it is disheartening.*

Sabine's diary and letters to family members frequently include references to the activities and problems of his children and often reveal an affectionate concern for their welfare, including that of Harry.[107]

> *....Harry who has gone through hard times. He has to sit in the kitchen and has no room to himself. Even his bedroom is not his own for the man and his boy also sleep in it. I have told him to shift to Erith where he can have lodgings to himself. It will cost me about 15/- a week but I cannot let him be so uncomfortable. He has borne it gallantly, and without complaint – devoured by fleas and it has done him good. He has learned to know and to be able to be on a footing with the British working man, and that is an asset for life. And he has admitted to Alex Baring that he had thrown away his chances and must do his best to revive them. He comes home for a week at Easter.*

Sabine clearly had similar aspirations concerning his daughters as is emphasised in the following proud reference in a 1902 letter to Mary[108] concerning his daughter Felicitas who was in London training to be a nurse:

> *A nice letter from Felicitas*
> *"I love it here, if only my feet did not get so frightfully sore and swollen, the first day I could not put on my shoes. I am in the men's ward, some of them are awfully nice and others are sulky beasts, grumbling horribly, and whatever you do for them it is not right. We have to be up at 6 and*

*breakfast at 7. Then we go on till 10.30 and then lunch; then go on again
until 1.30 then lunch then on again until 4.30 tea, and then on until 8.30
supper, and then to bed. I have 50 spittoons to wash out twice a day.
Some of the men are fearfully ill, one man in the ward with typhoid fever.
Early in the morning I make beds, after that sweep out the ward and wash
the spit-pots and oil the fireplaces, give medicine, take temperatures, then
wash the men and give them breakfast and one's mornings or any part of
the day is not long enough to get the work in. My Sister is an awful dear,
she told me not to make friends in the place, as they are not all nice. We
have 3 days in the week from 3-5, one day from 1 pm to 10 am, and
Sunday afternoons off. So we do not do at all badly."*
*I am so thankful that Felicitas has taken up useful work, it will do her all
the good in the world.*

However in 1909 Sabine wrote along somewhat different lines to Mary.[109] By this
time Felicitas was probably working privately as a nurse:

*I am not a little worried that Felicitas has had notice to quit her situation
on 27. January. She has been having words with Miss Grieg the
housekeeper who doubtless has found fault with her gadding about going
to dances and neglecting her duty. Of course F. can not see that she is at
fault*

In a similar vein Sabine's judgement on his daughter Barbara in the draft letter
written in the diary on 10 November 1899 to her future husband Laurence was:

*Now B. is really in her ways and mind so much of a child still that I think
it very advisable, in so important a matter, that she should not engage
herself, till she has had time to decide whether she is in earnest or not.
She is such a butterfly that is thoughtless when to alight, ...*

However in 1902 he was able to write to Edward[110] along quite different lines:

*Barbara has been however greatly improved by her marriage. Her
expression from being supercilious is changed, and she looks sweet. She
has turned into an exemplary house-keeper as particular as her mother
about all being kept nice and orderly, and keeps accounts in a most
praiseworthy manner and is very particular about balancing them.*

These descriptions show that Sabine disapproved of frivolity and idleness in his
children, while industry and a sense of responsibility were major factors
favourably influencing his attitude towards them.

It is evident from several entries in the diary that Sabine was particularly
concerned for his children at times of illness. The commentary there on the serious
illness of his son, John, in August 1897 provides a good example of this concern.

Rallied slightly at noon. If ever a life was granted in answer to prayer his was. Yet I never asked that it should be given unless God saw that he would grow up to be a good man fearing and loving Him, and working for the church and to benefit his fellow men.

Advice to, enquiries about and anxieties for the welfare of two sons, two grandsons and a son-in-law on active service during World War I are evident in ten out of twelve surviving wartime letters written to his daughter Mary between March 1914 and March 1917. On 1 January 1918 he wrote in a letter to Evelyn Healey.[111]

My youngest son [John] who was wounded in the Flying Corps bullets passing thro the stomach tearing thro' the bowels and thro' the stomach as well and injuring the liver, after five months in hospital came to us for Xmas. He has just gone up to the medical exam and I am thankful to say is not to be sent abroad again but given a home job, and not for some time to do any more flying. I am glad of that, as his nerve has been much shaken.

Sabine's grandson, Edward was also injured in the war and several letters to Edward's mother, Mary reveal his deep concerns on Edward's behalf.

Some references suggest that Sabine was not only fully involved with his children but that this involvement was at times seen by them as intrusive.[112]

Far from sailing serenely through life's adversities, his comment in the diary during the legal conflict with Frau von Hillern suggests that life was by no means experienced as stress free:

I am very much like a buoy. Every wave goes over me, and yet I am never completely submerged. The condition is not a happy one, but there are others that are worse.

Similarly the entry in his diary on 5 January 1884 in response to the death of his *dear friend Lloyd Worth* that *life is one series of bitter disappointments* does not support the view that he was indifferent to the misfortunes of others.

Another stressful event was the influenza epidemic of early 1894 in which, according to the family bible entry and letters written at the time to his daughter Mary, 14 members of the household were ill, some seriously. One member of staff died and Sabine and Grace were faced with a sick family, at the same time as they struggled to maintain a large estate and house despite significant staff shortages and problems. In a letter to Mary[113] Sabine wrote:

Harry seems no better today, and we have now in addition Cicely, Joan and John down, so it is, indeed, a sick house. I am troubled also for Mamma who is beginning to feel that pain in the side from which she was so ill 3 years ago. All this makes me very low and sad

Sabine's comment in the bible entry for 1894 concerning this torrid time, but written at least 10 months after the event, was the typically laconic understatement:

Influenza epidemic. 14 ill in the house, Rather a trial.

From this example it is not difficult to understand how, quite unintentionally, Sabine made his own contribution to the myths that emerged about his insensitivity to the plight of others.

The diary includes several retrospective and reflective accounts of the deaths of family members, but it is Sabine's reaction to the death of his daughter, Beatrice, in 1876 that is most thought provoking. The death of Beatrice features in the diary in July and September 1880, once in *Early Reminiscences*[114] and is mentioned briefly in *Further Reminiscences*.[115] These accounts emphasise the sweetness of the child and suggest an enduring concern that neither Sabine nor Grace had recognised the seriousness of Beatrice's illness or anticipated her death.

Although probably written in 1879 along with many other early entries in the family bible, the entries for 1876 chronicled the dates of significant events with unusual precision. One such entry was the brief statement *Wrote "Wafted Away" Apr. 15th.*

Wafted Away, a short story published as a pamphlet,[116] was one of six publications of work by Sabine in 1876. If the bible entry is accurate, *Wafted Away* was written just twenty-one days after the death of Beatrice on 25 March. However, *Wafted Away* does not give the moving account of the death of a little child that might be supposed from the title. What flowed from Sabine's pen at this time of grief was an exceptionally vicious and fantastical satire that seems to target the whole of humanity apart from the poor and the helpless. Above all else, *Wafted Away* was a withering attack on the Established Church in England. In 1876, the Church was in great turmoil over the Public Worship Regulation Act of 1874, which forbade the use of ritual and the Cross in worship. Sabine was greatly troubled by the impending prosecution, under the act, of individual members of the clergy by such as Bishop Claughton of Rochester. Claughton, whose diocese included Sabine's own parish, East Mersea, was probably the model for the caricature of a bishop in *Wafted Away*, but the intensity of feeling invested in the story is so great that it is necessary to look elsewhere for the prime source of Sabine's bitterness.

The loss of a loved one commonly involves a bewildering mixture of emotions including fear, anger and guilt. Often the anger is projected onto others such as a spouse, or even God, as Sabine acknowledged in *The Mystery of Suffering*.[117] The emotional reaction to bereavement can be so great that the literary output of a writer can be affected by it. The most likely manifestation is the loss of motivation, ideation and confidence associated with a depressive reaction. Loss of output can also result from the difficulty of concentration associated with anxiety or depression. However, it is necessary to bear in mind that pre-occupation with other matters, e.g. having to give attention to grieving family members or attend to an estate, will also affect literary output. Indeed, the need to deal with his father's estate in 1872, and Willy's mental state in 1875 may have contributed to some of the reduction in Sabine's literary output in the 1870s.

The abnormal mood states associated with bereavement can also have a direct influence on the *content* of what is written. Thus it can be postulated that Sabine found great difficulty coping with the intensity of his emotions and thoughts following Beatrice's death and that he projected his barely controlled feelings over her death into *Wafted Away.*

Roger Bristow[118] has pointed out that in the years 1877-8 there was a particularly marked reduction in Sabine's usual pattern of publication. There is no evidence of other life events likely to have affected his literary output to such an extent at this time. According to the entries in the family bible he made two trips to Germany in 1877 and one in 1878. The only entry in *Further Reminiscences* for these years is for the winter family sojourn in Freiburg in 1877-8, but it is obvious from diary entries that the published reminiscences of that visit are often confused with the visit to Freiburg in 1880-1 and are therefore unreliable as indicators of the state of his mind during the earlier visit. Allowing for items already written and sent to publishers prior to Beatrice's death being published in the months immediately following her death in 1876, the sharp dip in 1877-8 suggests the possibility of a direct relationship between the death and the hiatus in publication.

An examination of what few other items were published by Sabine around this time lends further support. *The Mystery of Suffering,* was based on a series of lectures given by Sabine some years previously, but it seems likely that the appearance of this book as one of only two publications in 1877 was prompted by Sabine's personal need to turn again to these lectures for comfort at a time of grief. *The Mystery of Suffering* includes the insightful comment:

> *Every great pain and sorrow produces a marked effect on him who has endured it. It either hardens or it melts. It sweetens or it embitters. It opens or it closes the heart. It sometimes produces a cold, cynical spirit, which disbelieves in love, in hope, and doubts everybody, even God; an effect which even the heathen seem to have observed when they fabled that Niobe, on the loss of her seven sons and seven daughters, was turned, in the excess of her sorrow, into stone. But on the other hand, it sometimes deepens the spiritual life, softens the feelings towards others, opens fresh springs in a formerly barren land, and produces flowers from what was a dry waste.*

What Sabine appears not to have appreciated at the time was that, not uncommonly, sweetness accompanies the bitterness, but is often not appreciated until the bitterness abates with the resolution of the grief.

Out of all the years from 1850 until after his death in 1924, 1878 is the only year in which Sabine published nothing at all. In the following year, 1879, there were three publications of which *Sermons to Children*[119] was one. Sermon X in this collection confronts bereavement in the context of the Resurrection. By 1880 Sabine had returned to a pre-morbid, but by his standards still modest, level of seven publications, amongst which was his novel *Mehalah*.[120] *Mehalah* is especially noted for the unpleasantness of its characters and the bitterness of the story, so much so that whilst the novel has generally been acclaimed as his best, many contemporary critics were troubled by the unpleasantness, which some regarded as gratuitous. In response to these criticisms, Sabine wrote in his diary on 12 December 1880

> *I wrote it when greatly depressed.*

He then proceeded to attribute this 'depression' onto the unfavourable reviews of his book *Germany, Past And Present*[121] that had been published in 1879 at the time he was writing *Mehalah*. This is an unconvincing explanation for such a profoundly disturbing novel. He continued:

> *In the bitterness of my spirit I wrote Mehalah very quickly in a month, without a pause, and poured out in it my wrath and bile. Then I was better*

It is much more likely that, although the *wrath and bile* that marked *Mehalah* out as a novel of some renown, akin to *Wuthering Heights*,[122] may have been **triggered** by the criticisms of his *Germany,* these emotions had their true origins in the last throes of the morbid reaction to the death of Beatrice that had led directly to *Wafted Away.* The description of feeling 'better' after the cathartic experience of writing Mehalah is very suggestive of the resolution of a depressive reaction. Sabine's acknowledgement of the failure on the part of himself or Grace to recognise the seriousness of Beatrice's illness[123] could imply feelings of guilt and it is possible that these feelings exacerbated both the length and severity of the bereavement reaction. Beatrice would have been too young to need the sacrament for the dying, but it could be that Sabine regretted that she did not receive the sacrament of extreme unction to give her both spiritual assistance and strength in her last agony. The erection of the monument to Beatrice in St Peter's Church, Lewtrenchard can be seen as part of the process of grief, as can the commissioning of the painting of *The Viaticum to the Dying* by Edouard Tyck of Antwerp.

The death in 1916 of Sabine's wife, Grace, was also followed by a reduction in the volume of published work, with a fall from ten publications in 1914 to eight in both 1915 and 1916, one in 1917, two in 1918, four in 1919 and six in 1920. All three publications of 1917 and 1918 were on archaeological subjects and in each case Sabine was one of four authors. It is unlikely that the content of these articles would have been affected by the mood of one author. It is widely accepted that the death of Grace was followed by a prolonged depressive reaction, but World War I and Sabine's preoccupation with the welfare of serving family members probably also contributed to variations in publication around this time.

One important area on which the diary throws particular light is the restoration of Lew House. It is evident, especially from the last 14 years of the diary, that rebuilding Lew House had become a major preoccupation for Sabine. It is also evident from the diary that work on the house absorbed a huge amount of money and that the income from the estate could never have met the demand.

That Sabine, a consummate story teller, should have seen selling himself as a novelist as the means to obtain the wherewithal to carry out the restoration is not surprising. Sadly, however, it seems that his unwavering determination to fulfil his destiny through a major rebuild of Lew House led him to put this restoration before everything else. Novel writing and building intruded on his other interests and left him less time and money for family as well as less time for his preferred activities. The frustration generated by the difficulties involved in seeing through the rebuild of Lew House is evident in the diary where, on 24 August 1886, he recorded the loathing he had developed for novel writing. Despite the steady income derived from his novels, money was always in short supply, day to day living was often hand to mouth and inevitably the family suffered. Sabine's relief at the cancellation of a family holiday at Bude for health reasons, when he was busy building the Cloister wing of Lew House, is evident in a letter written in 1895 to his daughter Mary who was living in Bude.[124] This gives some insight into the fine financial line he was endeavouring to follow:

> *Mamma thinks that as whooping cough is about and the little ones have not had it —it will after all be safest* <u>*not*</u> *to go to Bude with them. I also have advised not, as with the building I am behind hand at the back and want to keep down expenses.*

Sabine probably rationalised the problems created for the family by telling himself that the fulfilment of his purposes, the origins for which lay, at least in part, in a personal conflict with his father, was not just for himself but also for his successors and thus the family as a whole. It was therefore appropriate that they should suffer with him.

Sabine laboured on this treadmill, and suffered the resultant reduction in social involvement and sharp conflicts of interest, for some thirty years. This affected personal relationships and probably exacerbated his underlying quick temper and impatience. Hence the views of some observers on his irascibility and distaste for social contact. Sadly, by the early 20th century when his labours were done and he might have expected that he could relax and enjoy his twilight years it was not to be. By then Grace had become gravely ill and she died in 1916, eight years before his own death in 1924.

There is much to suggest from biographies and elsewhere that Sabine never fully recovered from this loss[125 126 127] and that this, together with the infirmities of old age, led to further withdrawal from social contact. The final indignity occurred in 1919, when his eldest son, Edward, with his wife, Marion, having concluded that

Sabine was no longer capable of looking after himself and was possibly drinking heavily,[128] moved into Lew House and took over the management of the household. Sabine did not take kindly to this loss of his hard won independence. He did not conceal his resentment of what he perceived as Marion's autocratic management style and the extent of his bitterness is revealed in a letter to Evelyn Healey written on the 31 May 1923.[129] At Sabine's prompting Miss Healey had arranged a holiday at Lew. Sabine had arranged for her to stay at the Blue Lion and was looking forward to entertaining her and showing her the sights. Marion had her own plans.

> *My dear Evelyn*
> *I shall be away in Exeter till June 18th, but I have told my groom that he and my little carriage are to be entirely at the disposal of your mother and yourself till my return. It is no pleasure of mine that takes me away. I am turned out of my own house by my American daughter-in-law, who is giving the servants their holiday en bloc, with the exception of two who could have managed for one quite well. But it was not to be. King Lear went through somewhat similar circumstances. Charlie Dustan my groom will advise you where to visit and make excursions. I really do think that you will have fine weather. Summer seems at last to have set in.*

There are two other letters in a similar vein

For her part, Marion, by family accounts a gentle but timid woman, viewed Sabine as a menacing figure and is said to have been so fearful of him that she placed a crucifix in the bedroom of at least one of her children at Lew House to protect him from the threat of her father-in-law.[130] Perhaps it was Marion's desperate need to achieve some control over what was, for her, a threatening situation that led her into the conflict with Sabine that further alienated them from each other.

What would have happened if Sabine's brother, Willy, had remained in good health and inherited the Lew Trenchard estates? Presumably this would have removed the monetary pressure on Sabine that arose from the restoration of Lew House. His future would most probably have been other than at Lew Trenchard. He may well have sought advancement within the church rather than retreat to a small rural parish, although the intemperance of much of his published writing about the Church hierarchy would probably rule that out. Perhaps there would have been no pressure to churn out a stream of novels and short stories and perhaps he would have had more time for his family and his real interests. Perhaps he would have been driven by some other 'purpose' and ended up with some other colossal project to blight his later years.

Sabine was certainly a man who stood out from the crowd but there is little or nothing in his actions to justify the epithet 'eccentric.' It is possible, through diligent recourse to primary source material, to find rational explanations for all he did, wrote and said.

The term 'eccentricity' is sometimes used to explain behaviour for which a rational explanation eludes the observer. Bickford Dickinson gave examples of tales of Sabine's 'eccentricity' that originated in irresponsible gossip[131] Sometimes, by giving undue emphasis to certain aspects of behaviour, it is possible to make a biographical account more entertaining and thus more saleable—a common feature of biographical newspaper articles about Sabine in recent years. Perhaps the most extraordinary example of the deliberate use of misinformation for its effect can be attributed to John Betjeman. Betjeman, in a series of broadcast in the 1970s about various hymn writers[132] spoke of Sabine, *as a bachelor curate, lining up a selection of eligible virgins from the village mill and choosing the most fertile-looking to marry.* When challenged by a member of the Baring-Gould family for making a malicious statement, Betjeman's response was along the lines of *well I'm sure I heard it somewhere. And anyway it was not malicious. Surely it was rather charming.* Sometimes authors will themselves refrain from discouraging tales of their own eccentricity in the belief that 'any publicity is good publicity' and will bolster income, but Sabine would have regarded Betjeman's absurd story as offensive to himself, his wife and the people of Horbury.

Similarly, much has been made of apocryphal accounts of Sabine's failure to recognise his own children; these imply he barely knew them. At a children's party in Lew House Sabine, on meeting a small child descending the stairs, said

> *and whose little girl are you?*

whereupon the child burst into tears and said

> *I'm yours Papa!*

Sabine's daughter Joan, who was the subject of this story, offered her own charming explanation for Sabine's difficulties:

> *Having so many children and being so short sighted, as we passed in the passages, he would put his dear hand on one's head and say "Which one are you, dear?"*[133]

Sabine's reluctance to reveal his innermost thoughts and motives left a vacuum for others to fill. Illustrations of eccentricity make saleable fillers

It is evident from several diary entries that Sabine had expected his eldest son, Edward, to follow in his squirearchical footsteps at Lew. No doubt he envisaged that Edward, once he became a successful businessman, would, like his father, plough his earnings into the house and estate. It seems more likely that, in the 1920s, Edward, an astute businessman, knew only too well that small country estates could no longer be self-supporting and would simply swallow up ever-larger sums of money. However one enigmatic passage in a letter written by

Sabine to his daughter Mary in 1911[134] does suggest that Edward might have contributed financially to the completion of the Gallery of Lew House in 1911:

> *Edward is altering the back of the house and going to turn bedrooms over into a gallery.*

If so the enthusiasm would seem to have been fleeting for, after World War I, not only were Edward's interests elsewhere, but also his heart, and he spent little time at Lew. It seems likely that Edward's absence and Sabine's disillusionment aggravated an already difficult domestic situation, with father and daughter-in-law projecting their negative feelings onto each other. It is not difficult to see how, under these circumstances, popular perceptions of an irascible, unsociable, eccentric loner were intensified, although perusal of his diary or, indeed, a perceptive acquaintance with his *Reminiscences* must dispel the view that Sabine was, by nature, unsociable. On the contrary, when he was well, had the time and it was open to him, he revelled in conversation as well as meeting, observing and helping people.

As for Edward, following the death of his first wife, Marion in 1931, he almost completely neglected Lew House and, although he did not die until 1957 at the age of 85, he never lived there again.

It can be said that Sabine was the last true squire of Lew.

"The Man Behind the Diary" References

[54] Baring-Gould S. *Early Reminiscences*, 1923, London, Bodley Head, pp 104–108

[55] Anon. *Discovery of a Roman Villa, Illustrated London News*, 1850 June 15. pp 430, 432

[56] Hunwicke, the Rev. John, personal communication.

[57] Baring-Gould S. *The Diary of Sabine Baring-Gould.* 1880 Sept 12

[58] Baring-Gould S. *Diary.* 1880 Sept 12

[59] Briggs C. *The Mana of Lew*, 1993, Praxis, p31

[60] Baring-Gould S. *Origins and Development of Religious Belief.*1869/70, London, Rivingtons

[61] Baring-Gould S. *Diary.* 1880 Dec 01

[62] Family letter. Edward B-G to Sabine B-G. 1870 Jul 07, Devon RO. Dep. box 5203

[63] Baring-Gould S. *Diary.* 1880 Dec 10

[64] Baring-Gould S. *Further Reminiscences*, Chap.15

[65] Baring-Gould S. *Early Reminiscences*, p vii

[66] Baring-Gould S. *Diary.* 1880 Sep 05

[67] Baring-Gould S. *Diary.* 1886 Aug 24

[68] Baring-Gould S. *Mehalah*, 1880, London, Smith, Elder and Co

[69] Baring-Gould S. *Diary*. 1880 Dec 12

[70] Bristow C R. *A Bibliography of the Works of S. Baring-Gould*, 2005. Available from the author

[71] Bristow C. R. *SBGAS Newsletter* 50. Feb 2006 pp 4—10

[72] Dickinson B H C. *Sabine Baring-Gould*, 1970, Newton Abbot, David and Charles p155

[73] Priestley, Joan. Unpublished notebook.c.1957. Dickinson E.

[74] Briggs C. *The Mana of Lew*, p30, 31

[75] Widdicombe I. *SBGAS Newsletter* 7. 1991 pp 3—5

[76] Dickinson B H C. *Sabine Baring-Gould*, p. 162

[77] Baring-Gould S. Letter to Mary Dickinson, 1923 Sep 10. Elizabeth Dickinson

[78] Lister K. *Half My Life*, 2002, Charnwood, Wakefield, p.125

[79] Almond Merriol, personal communication

[80] **Baring-Gould S. Letter to his mother. Spring 1857: Explanatory endnote 17**

[81] Baring-Gould S. *Early Reminiscences*, p vii

[82] Baring-Gould S. *Further Reminiscences*, p 102

[83] Baring-Gould S. *Notebook*. 1849—51, Devon RO. Dep. Box 5203

[84] Baring-Gould S. *Early Reminiscences*, pp 195-7, 202.

[85] It is likely that the 17-year-old Sabine was familiar with Edward Young's series of poems, *Night Thoughts,* written between 1742 and 1744 and later famously illustrated by William Blake. However Sabine's poem bears no resemblance to Young's monumental work.

[86] Wawman R. *Sabine and the Ministry of the Keys.*

[87] Baring-Gould S. *Diary* 1881 Jan 03

[88] Baring-Gould S. *Diary* 1880 Dec 08

[89] Dickinson B H C. *Sabine Baring-Gould*, p.62

[90] Briggs C. *The Mana of Lew*, p15.

[91] Edward Baring-Gould. Letter to Sabine 1871 July 07, Devon RO. Dep. Box 5203

[92] Briggs C. *The Mana of Lew*, pp. 19,20

[93] Hutton Patrick. *I would not be forgotten. The Life and Work of Robert Stephen Hawker* 2004 Tabb House.

[94] Briggs C. *The Mana of Lew*, p 18

[95] Briggs C. *The Mana of Lew*, p 20

[96] Priestley J. *Mother Mamma*, c.1960s. Dickinson E

[97] Baring-Gould S. Further Reminiscences, chapter 12

[98] Wawman R. *Never Completely Submerged, Introduction*, p xxiii

[99] Briggs C, The Mana of Lew, p 31

[100] Baring-Gould S. Letter to Mary 1908 Oct. 8. Dickinson E.

[101] Baring-Gould S. Letter to Polly Davey 1906 Mar 8. Matthews C

[102] Baring-Gould S. Letter to Mary 1914 July 24. Dickinson E.

[103] **Grace Baring-Gould to Mary. June, year unknown, probably early 1900s, Elizabeth Dickinson: Explanatory endnote 76**

[104] Briggs C. *The Mana of Lew*, p 20

[105] Baring-Gould S. *Sermons to Children, 1ˢᵗ Series*, 1879, London, Skeffington p 28

[106] Baring-Gould S. Letter to son Edward, 1902 January 16, Almond M.

[107] Baring-Gould S. Letter to Mary 1903 March 31, Elizabeth Dickinson.

[108] Baring-Gould S. Letter to Mary. 1902 Dec 2. Dickinson E.

[109] Baring-Gould S. Letter to Mary. 1909 Dec 30. Dickinson E.

[110] Baring-Gould S. Letter to son Edward. 1902 Jan 16. Almond M.

[111] Baring-Gould S. Letter to Evelyn Healey, 1918 January 01, Almond M.

[112] Dickinson B H C. *Sabine Baring-Gould*, p 86

[113] Baring-Gould S. Letter to Mary, c 1893 late February. Dickinson E.

[114] Baring-Gould. S. *Early Reminiscences*, p 159

[115] Baring-Gould S. *Further Reminiscences*, p 145

[116] Baring-Gould S, 1876. *Wafted Away* London, C. J. Palmer, Lincolns Inn Field.

[117] Baring-Gould S. *The Mystery of Suffering*, 1877, London, Skeffington

[118] Bristow C. R. *SBGAS Newsletter 50*. Feb 2006 pp 4—10

[119] Baring-Gould S. *Sermons to Children, 1ˢᵗ Series*, 1879, Sermon X suggests Sabine may have been in the process of resolving his despair

[120] Baring-Gould S. *Mehalah.*

[121] Baring-Gould S. *Germany, Past and Present* (2 vols.) 1879, London: C. Kegan Paul & Co

[122] Brontë E, *Wuthering Heights*, 1847, London, Thomas Cautley Newby

[123] Baring-Gould. S. *Early Reminiscences*, p 159; Baring-Gould S. Diary 1880 July 19

[124] Baring-Gould S Letter to Mary 1895 May 12

[125] Dickinson B H C. *Sabine Baring-Gould*, p 171

[126] Briggs C. *The Mana of Lew*, p 21

[127] Priestley, Joan. c.1957. Unpublished notebook. Elizabeth Dickinson.

[128] Almond Merriol, personal communication

[129] Baring-Gould S. Letter to Evelyn Healey 1923 May 31. Merriol Almond

[130] Personal communication. Merriol Almond.

[131] Dickinson B H C. *Sabine Baring-Gould*, p 82,83

[132] Games S. Ed. *Sweet Songs of Zion. John Betjeman.* 2007, Hodder. pp13,17

[133] Priestley, Joan. c.1957. Unpublished notebook. Elizabeth Dickinson.

[134] Baring-Gould S. Letter to Mary. 1911 0ctober 06. Merriol Almond.

Appendices

Appendix A: Explanatory Endnotes

1. **Ann Clarges, 1880 July 4**: 1666-1670. Daughter of John Clarges, a farrier on the Strand. The lowborn Duchess was regarded with disdain by society. Samuel Pepys described her as *'plain, homely, dowdy'* and *'a damn ill-looking woman.'* Sir Walter Clarges was her nephew, son of Sir Thomas Clarges. See note 6 on the Duke of Albemarle.

2. **Philip Astley, 1880 July 4**: 1741—1814. An ex-cavalryman with a genius for trick riding who has been described as *the father of the modern circus.* See also *Early Reminiscences*, p 157 where he is described as the proprietor of the Royal Amphitheatre, London.

3. **Orchard Barton, 1880 July 4:** old manor house and farm, former seat of the Woods family, Thrushelton. In *Early Reminiscences*, p 153, Sabine claimed that Old Madam said
   Now I can die happy, I have got the Woods out of the parish.

4. **Levite, 1880 July 4:** Sabine was not referring to a priest of an Hebraic-Christian sect. In *Early Reminiscences* p. 101, he refers to the service being *in a meeting house,* but he also wrote that Charles Baring followed Socinian Principles. The Socinians were initially antitrinitarian and eventually became Unitarian. *Young Levite:* (Macaulay TB, *History of England*, 1849, Chap. 3, *State of England in 1685: Clergy) a term often used for a dependant type of clergyman whom the writer held in contempt.* This was probably Sabine's usage of the word.

5. **Portrait of General Monk, 1880 July 18:** Sabine's purchase of this portrait in London is mentioned in a letter to his mother from St John's College, Hurstpierpoint dated 8 Nov 1857. A Col. Spencer who cleaned the portrait, probably c. 1993, wrote that it was
   > *almost certainly painted by Robert Walker, a popular artist of his day, a follower of van Dyke, painting in his style....probably around 1650...before he was created Duke of Albemarle. The inscription was probably painted at a later date which is borne out by the fact that the baton carried by him was originally a spear which has been painted out and the inscription painted over it.......it has suffered a good deal of paint deterioration, and has further suffered from an unsatisfactory restoration in the past.*

6. **Daniel Radford, 1880 July 22**: Daniel Radford eventually became a very close friend who inspired Sabine to commence his collection of Folk Songs. These very uncomplimentary comments were written before he got to know Radford well. It is likely that at a later date Sabine deemed it

prudent to remove them, possibly when writing *Further Reminiscences*.
Here he wrote

> *Further acquaintance caused me to value him ever more and*
> *more, and to love him. In fact I do not know any man who, in my*
> *middle life, exercised a stronger influence over me.*

Although the comments smack of snobbishness it must be said that
Sabine was simply recording the snobbish gossip of others. An excessive
reliance by Sabine on gossip was not infrequently associated with
inaccurate judgements. For more on Daniel Radford: *A Book of
Dartmoor*, p 132; *Further Reminiscences*, pp 250, 184, 268—9.

7. **Council of Nantes AD 658, 1880 August 8**: In A.D. 658 the Second
    Council of Nantes decreed:

    > *As in remote places and in woodlands there stand certain stones*
    > *which the people often worship, and at which vows are made,*
    > *and to which oblations are presented—we decree that they be all*
    > *cast down and concealed in such a place that their worshippers*
    > *may not be able to find them.*

    Sabine's comment in *The Book of Brittany*, p 20 was

    > *Now the carrying out of their order was left to the country*
    > *parsons, and partly because they had themselves been brought*
    > *up to respect those stones, and partly because the execution of*
    > *the decree would have brought down a storm upon their heads,*
    > *they contented themselves with putting a cross on top of the*
    > *stones.*

8. **Russell, Radford and Froude, 1880 August 14**: *In Old Country Life*, on
    Hunting Parsons, pp 146-173, Sabine wrote at length about John Froude
    and Jack Radford giving them the names Chowne and Hannaford
    respectively. They are mentioned in the *Book of Devon*, p 99; Froude
    appears in *Further Reminiscences* p 140; John Russell in *Early
    Reminiscences* p 238; Froude and Russell, at length in *Devon Characters
    and Strange Events series 2*, pp 125-159 as *'Two Hunting Parsons.'* Jack
    Russell was a renowned hunting parson. He was closely associated with
    Arthur Harris of Hayne who in 1830 built St Hubert's Hall in the grounds
    of Hayne Manor in honour of Russell and on the spot where Jack Russell
    ran a fox to ground. Russell is also associated with the terrier named after
    him. St Hubert is the patron saint of hunting.

9. **The Primitive Methodists, 1880 August 15,** were not then members of
    the Methodist connexion by who they had been disowned in 1810. They
    introduced 'Primitive' in the title as meaning 'Original.' Unlike the
    Wesleyan Methodists, they were drawn largely from the working classes
    and relied on charismatic, untrained preachers. They adhered to no central
    doctrinal control and could be described as having a rebellious militant
    streak with left wing political leanings. They lacked 'respectability' and

were viewed with hostility by the 'establishment' including the established church. They were often referred to by the derogatory name 'Ranter' presumably in recognition of a similarity to a 17th century group of puritans also known as Ranters. Over the years they mellowed and moved close to the Wesleyans Methodists with whom they were finally reconciled in 1932

10. **The Rev. John Wollocombe, 1880 September 5**: Rector of Stowford. Author of the autobiographical *From Morn till Eve* 1898 London, Skeffington. Wollocombe gives a fine account of the origins of St Hubert's Hall and activities in it.

11. **Architects, 1880 September 5:** In the Baring-Gould Archive, Box 5103 at the Devon Record Office, are two recently discovered plans of Lew House drawn by Sabine, one dated 1892 showing the layout of the house before he began his restoration and another showing his early thoughts on how the house might be restored. Fortunately he did not follow the latter plan. It is evident from the diary, e.g. 21 Jan 1890, that there was a master plan, but this has not survived. In 1914 Sabine did engage an architect, Owen Little, 5, Bedford Row WC, to design a gatehouse to Lew House. His recently discovered detailed plans for the gatehouse are also now held at the Devon RO. Gate pillars and an arch were assembled and preliminary work began including the erection of 3 pillars, and creation of 3 slit windows in the storeroom behind what is now the bar room of Lewtrenchard Manor Hotel. The gatehouse was never completed probably because of the household disruption caused by the First World War, the death of Grace in 1916 and Sabine's own advancing years.

12. **Baroness Burdett Coutts, 1880 September 7.** (1814—1906) Wealthy philanthropist and benefactor of Rajah Brook of Sheepstor. She was the daughter of Sir Francis Burdett and in 1837 she became the wealthiest woman in England when she inherited a fortune of nearly £2,000,000 from her grandfather, the banker Thomas Coutts. On 12 February 1881, at the age of 67, she shocked polite society by marrying her 27 year old secretary, William Lehman Ashmead Bartlett the American-born MP for Westminster. Her new husband changed his name to Burdett-Coutts.

13. **Kitt's Steps, 1880 September 9:** A waterfall on the R. Lyd near Lydford viaduct. *A Book of Devon*, p 2 'Kits Steps'. *White's Directory 1850*. 'Kitt's Hole,' implausibly said to be named after a woman who drowned there

14. **The Royal Society, Old Burlington House and General Sir Edward Sabine, 1880 September 9**: This account has significant inaccuracies: The Duke of Wellington died in 1852 but the Royal Society did not move into Old Burlington House until 1857. Sir Edward Sabine did not become President of the Royal Society until 1861, 9 years after the event recorded

15. **General Sir Edward Sabine, his wife, Eliza, and his mother-in-law, Mrs Leeves, 1880 September 9**: In *Early Reminiscences*, pp 269-270, Sabine tells the story of how, as a young army captain, Sir Edward had fallen in love with and become betrothed to a young woman who, during his absence on active service in America, married a Colonel Leeves, by whom she had a daughter Eliza. On Edward's return from the wars, Mrs Leeves gave a lame excuse for her infidelity. Following the death of Colonel Leeves, Edward resumed his courtship – but this time of Eliza, not her mother. He married Eliza who became his close associate in his geophysical researches. In time Mrs Leeves overcame her disapproval of her daughter's marriage and eventually came to live with the married couple. Edward Sabine was promoted Major General in 1859 and General in 1870. He was an eminent Polar explorer and geophysicist. Knighted in 1879 and President of the Royal Society 1861-71

16. **The epistle of Trinity Sunday Mass, 1880 September 12:** Revelations Chapter 4, verse 6: '*....and around the throne, were four beasts full of eyes before and behind*' Enough to scare any child!

17. **Fall out over ordination, 1880 September 12:** Letter from Sabine to his mother.

Wednesday
13 Ashley Place
Victoria Road[1]
Westminster
1857 (The year written in pencil, presumably at a later date and in an
unknown hand)

My dearest Mama
I am very sorry that I have hurt you by that letter of mine but it is not enough to have been sure of one place and the day almost fixed when I was to have gone and all my hopes built up on it, then to have it suddenly cut away from under me, then to have distinct <u>order</u> to go to Marlboro'[2] the day of going and the day of returning and everything settled railway exactness and then to have that when I had made up my mind to it (as to take a pill) suddenly changed then to hear of Watson's (which by the way was not a village school but in his house with his pupils) and then that not doing because I was not a <u>classic.</u>

Now to have to abide Marlboro' again for a month! Perhaps hanging on as a burden to Uncle Fred[3] without being able to do anything for him – I

---

[1] Actually Victoria Street not road
[2] As assistant master
[3] **Frederick Bond**, then headmaster of Marlborough Grammar School

always thought a fortnight a long visit but a month I am sure would be tiresome to him. I really do not want to get myself in opposition to Papa as you seem to think (Uncle Fred has forwarded your letter) but it makes my heart sick to think of a year of insupportable indolence with only the Voluntary[1] to read for and that is a mere trifle. I know several of the subjects already.

You seem to be so afraid of my not getting a gentleman's situation but I don't care three straws for it being a gentleman's place so long as I can be doing something which will fit me hereafter for H. orders. I thought that a middle school[2] would be best for that but I think this (missing word, possibly ' **idea**') of going to Mr King's parish[3] would be better and I should have time to get a little experience before entering it, for the curate with whom I should live is not coming for a month in which time I should visit the ragged schools of London and go down sometimes when the college lectures are given and do odds and ends of work.[4]

Here I know some only poor clerks, some trades people who put one to shame they come from their work perhaps only in the evening and then go off to teach in a night school they have themselves started and which they themselves support, and that is not all they give all they can moreover towards the burials of the poor and provide bier, palls and everything for them for about a quarter of the price that undertakers would charge and go out in turn themselves with the coffins to the cemeteries.

If Papa will let me I should stay on here in London and shall only have my board to pay for, this month I should be leaving my work,[5] after that

---

[1] **The Voluntary:** The Voluntary Theological Examination, preparation for which was given by a series of lectures by the Lady Margaret Professor of Theology in Cambridge and which at this time was increasingly required by the bishops from those seeking to take Holy Orders.

[2] **Middle School:** A middle school in the mid-19th century was a school for the children of middle class children. Although others would follow, in 1857 when this letter was written the only middle schools of Anglo-catholic persuasion were those established by Nathaniel Woodard so it is evident that his father's ultimatum probably did no more than persuade Sabine which of two attractive options to choose.

[3] **Mr. King's parish:** Sabine was referring to St. Georges-in-the-East, Wapping, of which Mr Bryan King was rector, which was much troubled by riots. The Rev. Charles Lowder of St Barnabas, where Sabine was working and staying, had established a mission at nearby Wellclose Square, Wapping. Mr King's wife was the sister of Fardell, a student friend of Sabine's at Cambridge. *Early Reminiscences*, chap. 14; *The Church Revival*, chapter 10

[4] Probably one of the schools established by the mission at St Georges-in –the-East. See below.

[5] St Barnabas

going into Mr King's parish and the curate and I would live together and do what we could. I should then get some practical knowledge which is worth years of theoretical study. The expense would not be more than I would live at home for the journey and all included. I have spoken to Col. Sabine about it he did not like my tying myself down for a year or two for fear of my health giving way, but saw no objection to my going there until the end of June[1] to see how I liked it so as to leave whenever I got tired or not well or anything of the kind.

What good will being in the Brit Mus. do towards my going into orders and yet you suggest that. Uncle Sabine proposes my going as a travelling companion with someone abroad, but that would only make me more unsettled in my habits than ever. Whatever it is it must be a matter of time about orders, if Papa refuses to let me go for years then I must wait for years and prepare for years that is all.

You must excuse dear Mama all my bitterness in that unfortunate letter, (not available) but I had not recovered[2] the degree which is a terrible strain on the nerves and then all this miserable bother afterwards only made me worse and nearly drove me to desperation. What you say of the dons I do not think is fair. I am quite confident if you were to ask any of them that they would give me a very good character in my college. I will tell you what gave me great comfort just lately and would not have repeated it but to show you that you are rather too harsh upon my conduct at college which you judge as if it had been of consummate wickedness. Of course I have not been free from blame but I have not done wrong willingly and believe I have led a far better life (such as it was) at college than I do at home. At first the men used to say most unkind and wicked things about me and it made me so unhappy (that was my first year) that I was almost in despair, they used to show me such contempt and men I had known would stare at me and then walk away without taking the slightest notice of me. Well I know that at a wine last term[3] one of the freshman brought up my name and said he thought I was a hypocrite or else and they were the fastest men in college to shut him up directly and said they would not allow a word to be said against me.

I would not have told you this little matter, which small as it was gave me intense pleasure as I did not know till I heard it just as going away that the men in college had ever changed their opinion about me so I had always shunned them as much as possible, but that I wish to show you (and you are the only person I would repeat the little incident to) that the stricture

---

[1] June 1857
[2] 'recovered from' in modern English usage
[3] Presumably Michaelmas

on my college behaviour is hardly <u>just</u>. As for my reading I never could have got mathematical honours.

I know I am the last person to under rate my abilities as you know pretty well, but I know perfectly well what I can do and what I cannot.
I have done as well in my degree as it was possible for me to do. If I feel that I am not suited for H. orders at the end of June if papa will only let me try what the work is like before putting my foot irrevocably into it I will freely give it up and set about something else.

Perhaps it may prove as treacle to stop the shop boy and cure so that he never touches it again when once he has had his fill.
With best love to all
Your affect. son
Sabine B-G.

N.B. Why on earth did you tell Margaret[1] my opinion about Mr Marsh,[2] I thought at least you might have kept that back. I dread now giving any opinion upon any matter as a burnt child dreads the fire.

(The following lines are written down the side of this page.)
I have seen Charley but shall not go near the Gardiners[3]

I don't like Sam and so had better keep away.

Comment: This is one of the most important Baring-Gould family letters in the Devon Record Office. The content and the hurried way in which it is written without any date and with limited regard for grammatical correctness all suggest it was penned hastily, at a time of considerable distress and tension between himself and his parents.

The entry in *'The Diary of Sabine Baring-Gould'* for 12 Sept 1880 would suggest this letter was probably written just before Easter 1857 (Easter Day was 12 April) and shortly before leaving S Barnabas Pimlico soon after Easter, at his father's insistence. This letter could well have been the trigger for his father's decision. It has proved impossible to find the precise date on which Sabine came down from Cambridge having taken his degree as the relevant records are missing from the Clare College

---

[1] Sabine's sister, Margaret.
[2] The Rev. Theodore Marsh, Margaret's future husband.
[3] **The Gardiners:** Sabine's paternal Aunt Margaret Baring-Gould married Rawson Boddham Gardiner, described by Sabine in *Early Reminiscences*, page 110, as *'ugly'* and *'disagreeable.'* Their son, Samuel, is described there as an historian *'with a marvellous memory for dates and facts.'*

archives, but the diary entry for 12 Sept 1880 suggests this could be
around February 1857.

The address Ashley Place is close to the junction of Victoria Street and
Vauxhall Bridge Road and has been verified as the residence of Sabine's
great uncle, Colonel Edward Sabine. This was some ¾ mile from, and
within easy walking distance of, St Barnabas, Pimlico. The diary suggests
his parents were unaware of his exact whereabouts and Sabine had used
Colonel Sabine as a go-between.

Sabine was deeply resentful of the way in which his father had ordered
him hither and thither with all sorts of suggestions for what his parents
saw as suitable employment to take him away from what they regarded as
disreputable and inappropriate. It is known from Sabine's diary, 12
September 1880 that, on coming down from Cambridge, his father had
told Sabine that if he went ahead with ordination, as he wished, he would
not inherit the estate. In *Early Reminiscences* Sabine writes
euphemistically that he *slipped away* from Lew. Whatever the manner of
his going, it is probable that he left Lew House in great distress and anger
after failing to reach any agreement with his father on his future. Sabine
travelled to London where he called on the Rev. Charles Lowder at St
Barnabas Church, Pimlico. Lowder, the best known of the slum priests,
founded the Society of the Holy Cross and was a prominent member of
the Tractarian movement of which his father did not approve. Sabine was
increasingly drawn to the Tractarians during his time at Cambridge and
had already stayed at St Barnabas during vacations and undertaken unpaid
employment in the choir school. He now took up this work again, staying
in the Priest's House. He did not let his parents know where he was but
was prevailed upon by Lowder to keep in contact with them through his
uncle, Col. Edward Sabine. In both Diary and Reminiscences his uncle is
described as a General and President of the Royal Society but this
advancement and honour came after the events of 1857. He was promoted
Major General in 1859 and General in 1870. He was an eminent polar
explorer and geophysicist; knighted 1869 and President of the Royal
Society from 1861 to 71.

The diary supports the view that this letter was written after Sabine had
been at Pimlico for up to two months, was running out of funds and
needing to sue for peace with his parents.

His parents would almost certainly have been aware of the Rev. Bryan
King and the troubles at St Georges-in-the-East from newspaper reports
and his father would never have agreed with the suggestion that Sabine go
there *for a year or two.*

It is of note that even the intrepid polar explorer, Col Sabine, was concerned that his nephew should not undertake such stressful work for more than a couple of months for fear it would affect his health.

Sabine's parents are unlikely to have been moved by his graphic description of the fine work carried out by the mission in the slums of Wapping. Sabine was patently deeply distressed by their refusal to take heed of his wishes and, in addition to fury at his father, this letter also reveals a sense of betrayal by his mother who, in a postscript, he accused of not respecting confidences about his sister's marriage in May that year. His concerns for that marriage, echoed in his diary, (5 Jan 1881) were prophetic as the marriage must have failed at some point. (See explanatory endnote 30) Sabine was also stung by accusations that his poor degree reflected indolence or worse.

Sabine was at pains to demonstrate to his mother the high level of stress and despair he had experienced throughout his whole time at Cambridge as a result of perceived hostility from other students, in the hope that this would at least soften her heart, if not his father's. It is tempting to speculate why other students might have behaved in a hostile way towards Sabine but it was probably for no other reason than that he stood out and was picked on because of his earnest manner, pious attitudes and behaviour. It is not surprising that parental accusations of bad behaviour cause him so much distress.

It is reasonable to conclude that, whatever Sabine may have believed, his parents must have been greatly troubled by his disappearance in London. They would probably have viewed his behaviour as wilfully disobedient and irresponsible and would not have understood this early manifestation of their son's steadfast dedication to idealised goals.

The eventual solution to this impasse was achieved with the help of the Rev. Charles Lowder who found Sabine a paid teaching appointment with the Woodard Schools at New Shoreham. Sabine's father would have been uneasy at this appointment but would have regarded it as a respectable establishment. It is unlikely that Edward was aware of the full extent of Dr Woodard's commitment to the Tractarian movement and the problems created there by a somewhat furtive use of the confessional by the chaplain in his dealings with the boys. This had at least the tacit approval and encouragement of Dr Woodard.

Importantly, it is evident from subsequent correspondence with his mother that contact with his parents was re-established and the serious rift with them rapidly patched up if not healed.

18. **The Rev Charles Fuge Lowder, 1880 September 12:** 1820—1880.
Founder of the *Society of the Holy Cross*, a brave, upright, and some
would say, almost saintly man. He was a leading player in the catholic
revival in the Church of England and endured much hostility at St
Barnabas, Pimlico and St Georges in the East, Wapping. He was at one
time suspended from his appointment as curate at St Barnabas because of
his adherence to ritual in the sacrament. He has been described as the
greatest of the London slum ritualist priests.

19. **Canon John Sharpe, 1880 September 12:** 1810—1903. Sharpe was a
member of a wealthy North of England family, the son of the Rev.
Samuel Sharp, vicar of Wakefield and one of a long line of influential
clerics. He is said to have been the leading high churchmen in the North
of England and was an able and powerful figure in Horbury society.

20. **Conies: 1880 September 17:** Conies are rock rabbits. Proverbs 30:26:
     *The conies are but a feeble folk, yet they make their houses in the
     rocks.*
Also quoted in *Church Revival*, p.68 to describe the weak response of the
bishops to the Gorham judgement of 1851.

21. **Archbishop Frederick Temple, 1880 September 17 and 1882
February 27:** Despite Sabine's dismissive comments, Temple, 1821-
1902, is described in Wikipedia as *one of the best loved holders of the
title of Archbishop of Canterbury.* Born in the Ionian islands, he was the
son of Major Temple, who after serving as Lieutenant Governor of Sierra
Leone, retired to Devon where his son entered Blundell's school,
Tiverton. His appointment in 1869 as bishop of Exeter, where he
remained until 1885, was described by Pusey, the leading Anglo-catholic
priest, as *the most frightful enormity ever perpetrated by a prime minister.*
His status as a broad church man and headmaster of Rugby school were
also probably significant influences on Sabine's judgement of Temple.
The origin of his curious accent is unclear.

22. **Maternal aunts: Emily, Frances (Fanny) and Marianne (Kate) Bond,
1880 September 27 October 22 and 10 December:** Sabine's maternal
aunts were significant figures in his life. His brother Willy was lodging
with Kate and Fanny at 4 Colleton Crescent, Exeter during the early
stages of his terminal illness. Fanny lent Sabine money during the farming
crisis of the late 19th century. Kate attended at the death of both Sabine's
mother in 1863 and, many years later his sister Margaret in 1903. Kate
visited Sabine in Freiburg and toured the Tyrol with him in 1881. Finally
Sabine spent the Christmas of 1922 in Exeter with Kate when she was 92
years of age and he was 88.

23. **Pluto, 1880 November 21:** An account of this fairground act, with identical phrases, appears in a letter to Gatrill said to be dated 16 Nov1877 and quoted in full in *Further Reminiscences* p 96. The only reasonable explanation is that the letter was actually written on 16 November 1880 on which date the family certainly visited the fair, and not 1877. It was not unusual for Sabine to omit the year when dating a letter. It is likely that the year was omitted from this letter and that when Sabine wrote his reminiscences he incorrectly assumed the year was 1877.

24. **Frau Wilhelmine von Hillern, 1880 December 5:** 1836—1916, daughter of the German authoress, Charlotte Birch-Pfeffer. She began her career as an actress in 1853 but retired from the stage on her marriage to judge Hermann von Hillern in 1857. She published her first novel in 1875. *Geier Wally,* her most successful novel, is a German classic. See also *Further Reminiscences* pp 85-6

25. **Rous Lench Court, 1880 December 6:** Rous Lench Court, Rous Lench, 10 miles E of Worcester, was the 16th C seat of the Rous family. Purchased from them in 1876 by the Rev. William Kyle Westwood Chafy who modernised the house and laid out new gardens. Presumably this is Sabine's Chafy-Chafy.

26. **William Baring-Gould, 1880 September 12 andDecember 10**: Sabine's brother Willy, b 25 October 1836, is said to have been his mother's favourite but descriptions of him by his great nephew, Bickford Dickinson, in his very readable biography *Sabine Baring-Gould*, emphasise Willy's unreliability and his failure to repay debts. Similarly Cicely Briggs, a great-grand niece, in her often inaccurate and overly critical brief biographical account of Sabine in *The Mana of Lew*, concentrates on Willy's good looks, his indolence following recovery from a 'mild' nervous breakdown, and the possibility that he fathered several illegitimate children in Lewdown. She probably relied on nothing but rumour for that claim. There is no doubt, from a passing comment in the diary on 5 January 1881 that Willy did get into bad company and he probably was something of a lady's man, but Dickinson and Briggs both wrote in ignorance. It is evident from the diary that both Sabine and his father kept the truth to themselves. Willy was very gravely ill both mentally and physically. Sabine had Willy formally admitted to a private asylum in Witham, Essex on or very soon after the physician there, Dr Tomkins, wrote a letter to Sabine on 7 May 1875. This letter is held in the Baring-Gould archive at the Devon Record office. Willy remained in hospital until his death on 21 Feb 1880 and therefore could not have been involved in the scandals with the tenant of Lew House in 1876 as suggested by Cicely Briggs. The death certificate shows that Willy suffered from General Paralysis of the Insane. Today this is known to be caused by syphilitic infection of the brain. In the late 19th century there

would be no such certainty about the cause, but reasonable certainty of the diagnosis and total certainty about the outcome. Today the advanced stages are never seen because the disease is eminently curable.

27. **Miss Linda Dietz 1880 December 25:** All the transcriber has been able to glean about this English actress, who was evidently also an impresario, is a photograph found on a website devoted to corsetry:

28. **Deutschesfamilienblatt 1880 December 26 and 1881 March 19**: Mehalah was published in *Deutschesfamilienblatt Vol. II,* weekly 2 Jan to 22 Jul 1881. Below is the front page of the issue of this family magazine that featured the first instalment of the German translation of *Mehalah*

Fig. 42 Deutches Familienblatt: Mehalah title page

29. **Admiral Sir Edward Belcher, 1881 January 5:** Sabine's comments contrast sharply with those in a brief biography at the Belcher Foundation: Here, Admiral Sir Edward Belcher (1799—1877) of the British Royal Navy is described as one of the most capable naval commanders of his era. A war hero, explorer, scientist and writer, he is said to have been a wise, generous, and merciful man who was deeply devoted to the welfare of the men under his leadership!

30. **Margaret's Unfortunate Marriage 1881 January 5**: Sabine gives no hint of problems in Margaret's marriage in his published work. It is evident however from a letter written to Margaret by Sabine that underlying the words *unfortunate marriage* was a great depth of feeling: The letter is quoted here in full:

Dear Margaret

You have made a great muddle. Mary[1] is going to marry Mr
Dickinson, Leila[2] a Mr Carver.

You are also in great mistake about Arthur.[3] He has had nothing to do
with your money except instructing a broker ....[?] withdrawing £100 at
your wish from some investment and it was paid over by the broker to
the Colchester bank in your name and you used it. The money never
even passed his hands. As to £300 invested in the Banbury and
something[4] Railway that pays dividends, neither Arthur nor I have ever
had the securities you put them in the hands of Mr Robinson,[5] and I
absolutely refused to have to do with any of your money when you
wanted to be rid of the responsibility. Whether you ever got rid of him
when you were in that queer condition among those queer people from
which you were removed to Earl's Court, I cannot say. You were not
then accountable for your acts. You had then even pawned your jewelry
[sic] for the tickets were found about in your room.
Yours t'ly
S. Baring Gould
Lew Trenchard
N. Devon
Nov. 24/92

Comment: Dealing, as it appears to do, with payments from the estate
this letter is surely to Sabine's sister, Margaret, who married Theodore
Marsh rector of Cawston in Norfolk. It is patently not to his daughter
Margaret and there were no other Margarets towards whom the Lew
Trenchard estate would have a responsibility in 1892.

This letter implies that at some time Margaret had become mentally
unbalanced while living in unusual circumstances from which she was
removed. It is possible she was admitted to an asylum in Earl's Court,
London. There was a private asylum for young ladies at Earl's Court
House (known as *Mrs Bradbury's Establishment for Ladies only
nervously affected*) in the early 19th century but this had closed by 1870. It
is possible the asylum continued elsewhere under another name but was
still referred to as 'Earl's Court,' but no trace has been found. Margaret's
episode of mental unbalance could not have occurred before 1872, as
Sabine would not have had financial responsibilities towards members of

---

[1] Mary: Sabine's eldest daughter.
[2] Leila: Sabine's half-sister
[3] Arthur: Sabine's half-brother
[4] Presumably Sabine was referring to the Banbury and Cheltenham Railway.
[5] The identity of Mr Robinson is not known. Possibly someone with whom
Margaret had an emotional attachment.

the family before inheriting the estate. In any case as late as 1871 he wrote to his father to say that he had asked Margaret and her husband to stand sponsor at the baptism of his son, Edward. It can be inferred from the letter that Margaret's marriage was probably in serious trouble. Keith Lister's enquiries during his researches for his biography of Sabine found no trace of Margaret's existence at Cawston. She does not appear in the parish register and there is no mention of her in the obituary of her husband who died at Cawston in 1905 and is buried there. There is no written material about Margaret at Cawston and she is not buried there.

It is known from an insurance policy held in the *personal and family box* in the Baring-Gould archive at the Devon Record Office that in 1882, Margaret, then aged 45, was living in *The Wells, Ripon, Yorkshire*. In a Post Office savings book also held there, her address in 1885 is given as *3 Park Row, High Road Knightsbridge* and withdrawals were made at the *Sloane Street Post Office* —both addresses not very far from Earl's Court. Her death certificate throws further light. She died on 13 December 1903 at 10 Harsnett Road, Colchester, Essex at the age of 66. On the certificate she is described as wife of Theodore Marsh Clerk in Holy Orders. The cause of death is given as cirrhosis of the liver 4 years, dropsy 4 months and exhaustion. Her maternal aunt, M R *(Kate)* Bond of 4 Colleton Crescent was in attendance at the death. In 1903 aunt Kate was aged 73. Presumably Aunt Kate would have given details of the death to Sabine and possibly have returned the letter and other personal possessions to him. Sabine made a brief note of his sister's death in the 1903 entry in the Family Bible but gave no details. It is not known if he attended the funeral.

From all the above it can be inferred that Margaret had been separated from her husband for several years before her death. Patently Sabine approved of neither the company she had kept nor her behaviour. From the tone of the letter it is probable that her mental health problems were seen by Sabine as self-inflicted. The diagnosis of cirrhosis of the liver brings to mind the possibility of chronic alcoholism as a possible cause of the cirrhosis and a possible factor, together with marital failure, in the causation of both her mental illhealth and her financial problems.

31. **Joseph Whitworth, 1881 January 5**: Joseph Whitworth has been described as the father of precision engineering and, around the 1850s, his famous engineering firm was exporting sharpshooters to the Confederate army during the American Civil War

32. **Sir Augustus Henry Glossop Harris, 1881 February 14:** 1852 —1896; a larger than life figure, Harris was an actor, impresario and dramatist but perhaps best known as the manager of Drury Lane theatre and *the father of pantomime.*

33. **Hans Thoma, 1881 March 24:** Born Bernau in the Black Forest 1839. After a brief apprenticeship painting clock faces, studied at the Karlsruhe academy; eventually achieved recognition after an exhibition at Munich in 1870. Appointed Director of the Karlsruhe academy in 1899 and then professor at the Karlsruhe Academy. Died in 1920

34. **George William Wilshere, 1st Baron Bramwell, 1881 April 4:** (1808—1892), An eminent judge known for his controversial writing in eg *The Times*. Only on his retirement in 1881 was he elevated to the peerage. Sabine's anecdote in the diary was thus topical and therefore his claim in *Further Reminiscences, p 34,* that the story was picked up on his honeymoon tour in 1868 cannot possibly be correct.

35. **Cough Mixture, 1881 May 18:** A puzzling script given in drachms. It seems that either Sabine or his source did not know, could not read or could not remember the quantity of either *morphine syrup* or *codeine syrup*, one being represented by a gap the other by a question mark. *Aqua lauro. arab.* does not mean anything in itself, but might be an old rendering of *aq. laurocer.* ie cherry laurel water. As the dose is a casual *'take a sup'* it is likely the *muscilag. gum arab.* ie *muscilag. of acacia* was intended as a bulking agent. The final two words are baffling. They appear to read *copsa uto.* The nearest possible logical reading is *coque utend* ie 'use boiled' but there is no good reason for such an instruction. It would be an effective cough mixture but if given today would certainly carry the *do not drive or operate machinery* instruction!

36. **Gallitrap, 1881 November 9:** Site of a dressing floor and changing room for the nearby Lew Trenchard manganese mine. Situated on the bank of the river Lew near its confluence with the Cory Brook. Various possible meanings have been suggested. Sabine in *Early Reminiscences* pp 253-4, improbably suggests a *'gallows trap;'* and this is repeated and elaborated in *Henderson's Folklore of the Northern Counties of England to Northern Borders* 1866, p 239, Sabine's note 32. Sarah Hewitt in *The Peasant Book of Devon Speech* , 1892 suggested it was a mystic sign as used by a white witch. In recent times one local Devonian suggested it was a tumbledown structure; another thought it was nothing more than a sluice gate ie gully trap. Finally the existence of at least two other gallitraps in Devon both on the site of stone and slate sluice gates suggested this to be the most likely derivation. No such sluice gate is to be found now at the Lew Gallitrap but the presence of a leat and the need for water to wash manganese ore makes it likely that in the early 19th century there could have been a sluice gate here.

37. **Zitta, 1881 November 14:** No story entitled *Zitta* has been found in issues of *Deutschesfamilienblatt* for the years 1882/3. However in

*Tablette Biographique; Société de Gens de Lettres: Homme du Temps.
Sabine Baring Gould.* 1885, Paris, the following entry appears:
> *"Zitta" - this last work, from a translation authorised by the
> author, has already appeared in "Independance Belge", under
> the title "Etelka."*

In Roger Bristow's bibliography *Etelka* is entered as a French translation
of Sabine's novel *Cheap Jack Zita.* As this English novel was not
published until 1893 this is patently incorrect, but it does suggest a
connection between the two novels. See the entry for 29 January 1892
where Sabine writes that he had 'began *"Cheap Jack Zitta."'*

38. **James Piers St. Aubyn, 1882 February 1**, 1815 —1895, Victorian
architect and member of a prominent Devon family of landowners. He
built unimpressive Gothic churches and 'restored' many more. Apart from
Sabine, many others, including John Betjeman, have deplored his
restorations as brutal.

39. **John Coleridge, 1882 February 20:** father of Samuel Taylor Coleridge
who said that his *grandfather was a bastard brought up on the parish.*
Edward Coleridge was Samuel Taylor Coleridge's brother. Edward
Coleridge would not want to own up to his father or grandfather being
illegitimate, while Samuel Taylor Coleridge probably preferred to see his
grandfather, rather than his idealised father, as the bastard.

40. **Staverton Bench Ends, 1882 March 1 and 10 June 1882:** These four
bench ends were restored and used at St. Peter's Church Lewtrenchard.
The choughs were replaced by the images of rabbits and birds copied by
Sabine from old bench ends at the old church Boscastle. See also John
Hunwicke, *Lew Trenchard Church, Fr Sabine Baring-Gould's
reconstruction of the church, bench ends…Gould monuments, Devon and
Cornwall Notes and Queries, 2007*

41. **Prisoner of Orchard, 1882, June 24**: *The little dark room* at Orchard
was destroyed in recent years during restorations, but is still remembered
by the Yeo family of Orchard as 'the prison' without knowing the reason.
The brother of Mrs Yeo was Charles Luxmoore who was incarcerated for
4, not 16, years as reported by Sabine. John Nicholson Vowles leased
Lew House from Sabine's father Edward. The trial of Mr Yeo was
reported in the *News of the World* 3 Aug 1851. John Yeo was sentenced
to 6 months prison despite a strong plea for mercy by the jury. The
newspaper account suggested that Mr Yeo had been acting in good faith.

42. **Dockacre walking sticks, 1882 July 3**: Dockacre House, Launceston,
and the walking sticks appear as the fictitious house Dolbeare in *John
Herring*, chap. 8, *A Musical Walking Stick.*

43. **John Bright's Bottom, 1882 October 6**. John Bright, statesman and orator, 1811-1889. In *Early Reminiscences* p 286, this epigram was said by Sabine to have been heard at the table of Squire Blencowe of 'The Hook,' when Sabine was visiting from Hurstpierpoint. The two versions differ. The attribution of the epigram in the diary to a phrase in an 1882 speech by John Bright in opposition to Gladstone's government makes the origin claimed in *Early Reminiscences* less likely. However, John Bright's career was long and it is possible that the epigram was in circulation for many years and was heard by Sabine on both the occasions mentioned by him. This would also account for the many differences in the two versions

44. **Strain Oil, 1882 October 14:** *Oil of brick,* otherwise known as *oleum lateritium,* is based on either linseed or olive oil. Made by using hot bricks, hence the name. *Oil of Spike* is lavender oil. *Oil of Pelis* cannot be identified. Pellis is the Latin name for skin and it has been suggested that, as the other ingredients are relatively innocuous, *Oil of Pellis* might be an early name for such as methyl salicylate, gaultheria, wintergreen oil or sweet birch oil. These all have the same warming action to the skin required for the relief of muscular strain. Although unusual this recipe for strains is not as bizarre as that provided by the white witch Marianne Voaden, in *Devon Characters and Strange Events Series 1*, p 77.

45. **Abbotskerswell, 1882 November 26:** In 1954, the Devon historian WG Hoskins also found this medieval statue of the Blessed Virgin Mary attractive and thought the 16th century church house a good example of its kind.

46. **Edward Gould, Dunning and the Calendar, 1883 February 26:** *Further Reminiscences,* p 77; *Devon Characters and Strange events series 2* in *'John Dunning,'* pp 218-220; *Old Country Life* pp 48-51. In *Old Country Life* Edward is thinly disguised as Edward St. Pierre, while Dunning appears as himself.

47. **Wright of Derby, 1883 May 11:** Joseph Wright, 1734-1797, English portrait and landscape artist, described as the first artist to capture the spirit of the industrial revolution and noted for his use of *chiaroscuro,* emphasising the contrast between dark and light.

48. **Quarry lake, 1883 September 29:** It is evident from a 1906 OS map that the water course feeding the lake was underground for much of its course in the garden of Lew House and entered the lake 50 yards further east than the present waterfall. It is not known when the change was made, possibly 1928 when Walter Sarel made changes to the garden for Edward and Marion Baring-Gould.

49. **St Mark's Eve, 1884 January 26:** April 24th. Up to the 19th century there was a widespread English superstition that anyone sitting in a church porch around midnight on St Mark's Eve would see the souls of all those in the parish who were to die in the following 12 months. Sabine drew on this superstition in chapter 8 of his Dartmoor novel *Urith*. See also *Further Reminiscences*, p 125

50. **Dr Budd of North Tawton, 1884 January 26:** This anecdote appears in *Further Reminiscences*, p 127. The Budds were a famous family of medical men. The most notorious was Dr John Wreford Budd of Plymouth to whom a chapter was devoted in *Devon Characters and Strange Events series 2*, pp 50-367. Drs Samuel, William and Christian Budd are all described in the chapter as 'of North Tawton' but, sadly, this anecdote does not appear there and therefore cannot be attributed to the right Dr Budd!

51. **Julian's little man, 1884 June 14:** This event appears in *Early Reminiscences*, p19. Here the date is incorrectly given as 1883. Also included there is Grace's memory of seeing a little man in her childhood, as recorded in the diary on 5 January 1881.

52. **Rose beds, 1885, January 6:** With no reference in the text it is not known for certain if this is a record of roses then existing or intended future planting – possibly both. But bearing in mind the related diary entries for 1884 and a clear description of planting roses in the spring garden in 1883 it seems likely this was a record of existing roses. More than 60 of the 91 roses listed here and in the entry for 1 October 1884 can be found in modern catalogues and books on roses. An exciting development at Lew House in 2006 resulting directly from this research was the replacement by the head gardener, Robert Stemson, of all the roses then in the terraced rose garden. with those roses mentioned in the diary that are still available. It is interesting to note that not only did Sabine write of planting roses in the spring garden on 1 Oct 1884, but on 13 March 1885 he also described creating a pixy well in the spring garden. The location of either the spring garden or the pixy well is not known. The present rose garden was created in 1928 by Walter Sarel for Edward and Marion Baring-Gould.

Table 1: Rose Bed Plantings found after the entry for 6 January 1885.

Bed Outside		S Bed	N Bed	Central Raised Bed		
		Climbing Cheshunt Hybrid				
Belle Lyonaise	Souvenir de Glior (?)	Cl. Mme Lombard	~~Triomphe de Rennes~~	Duke of Teck	Cl. Devoniensis	Marquise de Castallani
Cheshunt Hybrid	Jean Pernet	Bouquet d'or	~~Chas. Lefebvre~~	Céline Forrestier	Duke Albany	Reine Marie Henriette
Senateur Vaise (?)	Fruit tree	Duke of Connaught	~~Abel carmine~~ (?)	Etienne Levet	V--- (?) Duchess (?)	Triomphe de Rennes
La France	Rêve d'or	Cl. Belle Lyonaise	~~John Hopper~~	Etoile de Lyon	Red Gauntlet	Mme Levet
Vict. Verdier	Belle Lyonaise	Maréchal Niel	~~Mme Verdier~~	Homère	Beauty of Europe	Gloire de Bourg la reine
Pr. C de Rohan *Prince Camille*	Homère	Jean Soupert	~~Prince Camille de Rohan~~	Princess of Wales	Boule de Neige	Calte *Catherine* Mermet
Mme Rothschild	M van Houtte	Cl. Devoniensis	~~Maréchal Niel~~	SK Williams	Mme Bradley	Gloire de Cheshunt
Gl. De Dijon	Ctess of Gold	Dupuy Jamain	~~Abel Grand~~	Gl. De Lyon *(Lyonaise)*	Mme Gabrielle Luizet	Alba Rosea
La Rosiere *(Pr. C de Rohan)*	Mme Fropot (?)	Paul Jamain	~~Duke Edward~~ (?)	Marguerite de ------ (?)	Perle des Jardin	Mlle Gujine (?) Verdier
Fisher Holmes		Marie van Houtte	Dr Andry	Mme Falcot	-------- (?)	Devoniensis
Pride of Waltham		Brightness of Cheshunt	Marguerite Brassac	Q of Waltham	Niphetos	Marquise de Castallani
		Marie van Houtte	Paul Veron	Solfatare	Duke Wellington	Maréchal Niel
		Maréchal Niel (?)	La France	Mme Levet	Jules Finger	Chas Darwin
		Mouet (?) Plaisir	Egaria	Rubens	Countess of Oxford	Mme Margottin
		Baronne de Maynard	Céline Forrestier	Mme-----(?)	Mm Carol Kuster (?)	Baroness Rothschild
		Rêve d'or	Mme (Victor ? *in pencil)* Verdier	Mme Lombard	Henriette Maria	W A *(William Allen)* Richardson
		Françoise Michelin		Souvenir de malmady *(? la Malmaison)*	President	Mrs Jowett

Climbing Charles Lefevre

53. **Mowhay, 1885, March 13:** pronounced mooey in Devon dialect. A mow-frame – ie a slate hay store raised on staddle stones. The pixy well no longer exists and its location and that of the spring garden are not known.

54. **Old gatehouse, 1885, March 13:** From the preface to *Early Reminiscences*:

> *...in the reign of Henry III it [Lew House] passed by marriage to the family of Monk of Potheridge, and Lew became an appanage of the second son. There was then probably a gate-house, for on the bench-end giving a bust of Anthony Monk, beneath him is represented such an entrance, with pillars. The gate-house was pulled down later, and the pillars employed for the entrance to the stable-yard, till my father threw them down and buried them to form the foundation of a set of pig-styes.*

It is possible that the pigstyes are those to be found in the model farmyard behind Lew House. At present the lower courses are buried in 1 foot of debris. The presence there of the pillars has yet to be confirmed. Sabine was desirous of having his own gatehouse and in 1914 commissioned architectural plans for one. Work actually started on the gatehouse but the project was never completed partly because of the outbreak of World War One and partly due to a loss of interest following the death of his wife, Grace, in 1916 and his own advancing years.

55. **Willsworthy, 1885, March 14:** Willsworthy is the principal dwelling featured in the novel *Urith*. The ruined chapel is also featured there. See the diary entry for 28 August 1889; also *Old Country Life* pp 59-60, where the sketch and plan from the diary are both reproduced with some enhancement.

56. **House of the De la Coombes, Combebow, 1885 March 16:** All that now remains of the house are a few grassed over mounds, but much of the fine old avenue of limes is still to be seen and is worth a visit.

57. **Hunting songs, 1888 March 16:** *Bellever Day* with some changes, appears in *Old Country Life*, pp 327-8. In a *Book of Devon*, pp 204-5, Sabine explains Bellever Day as an end of season festival week of hare hunting. *The Lamerton Hunt Song,* with slight changes, was published by Patey and Willis (no date given) as *The Lamerton Hunt Song. Words Written and Music composed by the Revd. S. Baring-Gould. Price 1s/-.* This is a waltz tune for voice with piano accompaniment and, as such, suitable for a Hunt Ball.

58. **Songs of the West lectures, 1889 September 7:** A letter to Mr Quick, librarian to the Tavistock Subscription Library, dated Jan 13, 1889 and

now held at Lew House suggests that a lecture was planned in the upper room of the Tavistock Subscription Library earlier in the year:

> *Dear Sir, The programme will do excellently. I hope to have the first part of my book out in time for the lecture. Can you manage someone to try to sell copies for me in the room, during the lecture. The parts are 3/- each, only part 1. is or will be ready, to subscribe before publication – for the whole set of 3 – 7/6, but on publication each part is 3/-*
>
> > *I remain*
> > *yours truly*
> > *S Baring Gould*
>
> *No need advertising in the Plymouth papers. I shall lecture there later on the same subject.*

No other record of this lecture is known to exist.

59. **Scarlet Fever and Bude, 1890 October 11**: Sabine describes this outbreak in an illuminating article *Our Scarlet Fever Outbreak*, that appeared 8 years later in *The Church Monthly* vol. xi Jan to April1898. This gives valuable insights into the Baring-Gould household and personalities. For a detailed analysis see R J Wawman, *Transactions SBGAS*, vol.5, 2005, 60-67

60. **The Turk and the Tory, undated.** [After the entry for 1890 November 15]: This poem, expressing fury at the then Prime Minister, Benjamin Disraeli over the Balkan Atrocities, was sent to William Gladstone, with slight changes and a covering letter on 23 Sep 1876. **The Tory War Cry:** This poem in a similar vein is found, with variations, in Plymouth notebook 2, and as 'an unpublished poem' from the 'Killerton MSS' in *Now the Day is Over* by H Kirk-Smith, 1997. Kay.

61. **Der Lindenbaum, undated.** [After The Turk and the Tory. See note 60]: – the linden tree. Sabine has muddled the title with the first line, which is *Am Linden vor der Thore* - which translates as 'the spring (or fountain) by the gate.'

62. **Furnace, 1891 December 24:** The remains of the furnace are to be found in northeast corner of the field opposite Lew House stable yard and between the Churchyard and Lew Hill, which is the route of the old road towards Lewdown Crossroads. There is no evidence of an orchard there now. The purpose of this furnace is unknown. Suggestions include charcoal burning, preparation of lime, or, intriguingly, the preparation of the cement invented by Sabine's father, Edward, as a by-product of Lewtrenchard slate quarry. This was used in the erection of the parapet as described in *Early Reminiscences* p 248. See also the diary entry for 1 December 1885 and 31 May 1896.

63. **Teck and Queen Mary, 1892 January 14:** The Duke of Clarence died on
14 January 1892, but Sabine's visit to Teck was not wasted. *Teck and its
Duchy, Chambers Journal* 30 Jan 1892; *In the land of Teck, The Graphic*
6 Feb 1892. In 1903 Princess May (Mary) married the Duke of Clarence's
brother, the future King George V, and on 10 July in that year Sabine's
articles on Teck appeared in Wedding editions of *The Illustrated London
News* and *The Graphic*, which also published the poem *'The Sprig of
May.'* The events are all briefly recalled in *Further Reminiscences* p 252.
It is of interest to note in an entry in the family bible for 1910, that Sabine
also visited Teck in June of that year while in a letter dated 29 September
of 1910 Sabine wrote the following in a letter to his daughter Mary: *I went
up to town on Monday to see the Duke of Teck, and found him very
pleasant.* Presumably the visit and audience reflect the Dukes favourable
view of Sabine's writing on the Duchy and his family.

64. **Visit to South of France, 1892 February 29:** Reported in some detail in
Further Reminiscences, chapter 19 *'Les Eyzies.'* See also *The Deserts of
Central France*; *Cliff Castles and Cave Dwellings*; Sabine's novel *Noémi.*

65. **Konx Ompax Abracadabra: One of two undated entries between 15
Aug 1892 and 15 August 1894.** See also explanatory note 66.
Footnote 1: No meaningful translation seems possible for the title. *Plop,
call a truce – Abracadabra* might be a flippant magic incantation to the
gods. What follows is as literal a translation of the text as could be
achieved by Greek scholar, Mrs Pam Hunwicke
Footnote 3: At this point the text appears to be unfinished. There is no
evidence of a page missing from the diary. Was this piece copied by
Sabine from a document or monument? Did he only have a fragment? Did
he compose this piece himself? To what does the passage refer? Could it
be about an ancient monolith such as the menhir re-erected at Lew Mill in
1880 or to some ancient structure on Dartmoor or in France? What is the
purpose of the curious title? Why is the passage entered in the diary
without any introduction or other commentary? Neither the diary nor
Sabine's published work provide any answers.

66. **The Rev. H. F. Sheppard, One of two undated entries between 15 Aug
1892 and 15 August 1894:** See explanatory note 65. Fleetwood Shepherd
was Sabine's friend and close musical collaborator in the early phases of
the collection of the folk songs of the West Country

67. **Ardoch Lodge, 1895 January 01:** Sabine's exasperation with his
stepmother over the plans for Ardoch lodge are also revealed in a letter
written in 1893 to his daughter, Mary in which he made the following
comment:

> *Poor Granny has been impatient for plans of Ardoch and estimates.
> The estimates were £715 and we have had to cut my plans down but*

she cannot expect a palace for £400. I do not think she has the faintest idea of the cost of building.

68. **Arthur Baring-Gould, 1895 June 16:** 1866 – 1955, Sabine's half-brother, and 32 years his junior. Although, as Sabine's curate, Arthur in some ways came to know him quite well, his attempt at a brief and unpublished biography was disappointing. *Further Reminiscences,* pp 112-113.

69. **Arson at Portgate, 1896 May 31:** The shop of Mrs Jane Tubb was in the dwelling opposite the Harris Arms on the old A30. This event is reported in *A Book of Devon,* p 112-3, with names and location changed. It also appears in *Devon Characters and Strange Events Series1 White Witches, p* 82-3.

70. **Barbara and Laurence Burnard, 1899 November 4:** Barbara and Laurence did marry in 1901 and in a letter to his son Edward on 16 June 1902 Sabine appeared to change his opinion on Barbara:

> *Barbara has been however greatly improved by her marriage. Her expression from being supercilious is changed, and she looks sweet. She has turned into an exemplary house-keeper as particular as her mother about all being kept nice and orderly, and keeps accounts in a most praiseworthy manner and is very particular about balancing them.*

Laurence was the son of Robert Burnard, Sabine's good friend and collaborator in their study of Dartmoor antiquities. The marriage is briefly mentioned in *Further Reminiscences* p 270

71. **Memorial inscription, undated, immediately following the end of the diary:** This is possibly a draft inscription. It suggests the intention to create a memorial over a vault at St Peters Church Lew Trenchard. However there is no known vault covering this period and the location of the remains of those in the inscription is not known. The closest match for the inscription is the Victorian brass memorial tablet in the chancel of the church.

72. **Charm, undated, on the last page of the ledger:** In *Devon Characters and Strange Events. White Witches, p 77,* the following, almost identical, charm for staunching blood is attributed to Marianne Voaden of Bratton Clovelly:

> *Recite: Jesus was born in Bethlehem, baptized in the river of Jordan. The water was wide and the river was rude against the Holy Child. And he smote it with a rod, and it stood still, and so shall your blood stand still. In the name, etc. Repeat thrice.*

73. **Alt Kirche Congress, Cologne, Bible 1872:** Attended by overseas delegates including the bishops of Ely and Lincoln. The Bishop of Lincoln was Christopher Wordsworth, whose *Theophilus Anglicanus* had been influential in Sabine's religious development. The Vatican Council decrees of 1869 and 1870 on Papal infallibility caused so much concern in some members of the Roman Catholic Church that they came together with a schismatic Dutch Church at the 2nd congress of *'Old Catholics'* in Cologne in September 1872. This attracted members of the Catholic wing of the Anglican Church who favoured neither the Church of Rome nor Protestantism. However it soon became apparent that the threat of Papal infallibility was far worse than the reality and the *'Old Catholic'* Church, although still in existence, has since then remained small and without influence.

74. **Wax seal, Bible 1897:** A fragile envelope addressed to the Rev C Baring-Gould, then rector at Lew Trenchard and bearing the traces of 3 post marks for Gt. Eversden, for Cambridge and for London, is in the possession of Merriol Almond and now held at the Devon Record Office. The date for the London postmark is 3 July 1858. The envelope contains a fragile red wax impress matching the plaster coat of arms in the Ballroom. The inscription on the envelope is as follows:

> *Impress of a white cornelian seal found in bog at Gt. Eversden. It was offered by the rector to E Baring Gould for 30/- but he declined to have it. It can not now be traced. SBG.*

The handwriting is undoubtedly Sabine's. See also *An Old English Home*, p 50 chimneypiece; p93-95 ceiling

Fig. 43 Wax Impress of Gould Coat of Arms

75. **Lewtrenchard Holy Well, Bible 1913:** The earliest information to be found on the Holy Well of Lewtrenchard is an entry in the parish register made in 1830 by the curate Caddy Thomas. He wrote that

*the Holy Well behind the church has been re-erected and
formerly its water was used for the font.*

Eighty years later Sabine Baring-Gould also wrote in the Parish register:

Holy well re-constructed Easter week 1913.

His entry for 1913 in his Family Bible included the comment

Built Holy Well in the Glen.

In 1922 he wrote in his *Early Reminiscences*, p 247, that

*Lew House had been quarried out of rocks about the Holy Well
in the Glen.*

The Glen is the valley of the stream that arises near Down House and flows
through the woods to the north of Lew House and eventually feeds the Quarry
Lake. Early attempts by local historians to locate the well in these woods were
unsuccessful but what they did find were the remains of a woodland garden. No
documentary evidence for a garden in the Glen has been found, but Julian Gibbs
of the National Trust and officers of the Devon Gardens Trust are of the opinion
that this was a typical Edwardian Garden. This would suggest that the woodland
garden was created about the same time as Sabine rebuilt the Holy Well in
1913, in which case it may well have been deliberately created as a beautiful
and peaceful setting for the well. Grace was crippled with arthritis at this time;
correspondence suggests that Sabine was concerned that she be encouraged to
take as much exercise as possible but that she was not easy to motivate. There is
reason to believe that Grace enjoyed walking in the Glen. It is possible that
Sabine saw the creation of a garden in the Glen as a way of enticing Grace to
take exercise. Perhaps he also thought that Grace would benefit from the
curative properties of the Holy water. In 2007 *The Friends of the Forgotten
Garden of Lewtrenchard* was established with the aim of restoring the garden
and finding the location of the Holy well. A 1914 photograph of the well in its
woodland location, an 1884 OS map showing the location of a spring, and the
finding of a promising waste pipe in this area led to excavations which
uncovered the plinth and basin of the well and thus confirmed this as the
original location. It seems likely the garden had a very short life and that the
onset of World War I, followed by the death of Grace contributed to its early
abandonment. A letter from Walter Sarel to Gertrude Jekyll referred to the
building in 1928 of the present rose garden at Lew House for Sabine's son
Edward and his wife Marion, while a letter written in December 1991 by
Edward's son 'Teddy' Baring-Gould to Sabine's granddaughter, Cicely Briggs,
confirms that in the process of building the rose garden,

*the "wishing well" at one end of the rose garden was moved
there from the "Glen" in the woods far behind the house.*

The stonework of the rose garden 'wishing well' is identical to that shown
in the 1914 woodland photograph of the Holy well.

76. **Getting Under Sabine's Skin, reference 102: Family Letter, Grace
   Baring-Gould to Mary Dickinson, probably 1909:**

Lew House
June[1]

My dearest Mary

When can you and Harvey come and stay with us. I am sorry I cannot ask
the dear boys, but Papa does not seem able now to bear the noise of
children at table, it is different if they are in the nursery, I am sure you
will understand my darling, I thought you would be hurt if I asked you
and not the boys, now you know the only reason why you have not been
asked lately, you may be quite sure there is nothing else, I have wanted to
write and tell you ever so long the reason but have kept putting it off, but I
could not any longer, please write and tell me you understand I cannot
bear that you should feel hurt or slighted in any way Phyllis said Grannie
had said something to her about it, she did not say anything to me.[2]

I hope dear Arscott's arm is getting on, Mrs Sperling told me about it last
week when they came back, poor dear you seem to have had a worrying
time altogether.

Have you heard that Joan has a little daughter, we had a telegram from
Bill on Friday,[3] both doing well, I am so thankful it is safely over, I
suppose we shall hear soon.

Aunt Kate[4] was with Grannie for a few days last week, she is not looking
at all well, poor dear she has too much to do, Aunt Emily[5] is much the
same, but her nurse has been ill so that had given her extra bother, they
are going away next month so I hope the rest and change will do her good.

With loads of love

Your ever loving mother

---

[1] Joan was married in October 1907. She, her husband and child returned to
England in the summer of 1910, therefore this letter must have been written in
either June 1908 or June 1909. In June 1908, Sabine wrote to Mary and said that
Joan and Bill Priestley may have to return to England early as his mother was ill;
he made no mention of a child. Joan's eldest daughter, Joyce was born 10 June
1909. Therefore the letter must have been written in 1909

[2] The entries in the family bible for 1908 and 1909 do not suggest any particular pre-
occupation to explain why Sabine, then in his mid-70s, should have been reluctant to
have his three grandsons, Arscott, aged 16 in 1909; Edward, 14; and Bickford, 9, to
stay. Neither was there any significant building in progress at Lew House. Presumably
at that age the children were too old to banish to the nursery and may well have been
too boisterous for Sabine who may have found that they intruded on his studies. What
is particularly evident from this letter is the extent of the distress and unhappiness of
Grace at this situation, whatever the cause, and her inability to influence the situation.

[3] Grace's daughter, Joan and her husband Bill Priestley, then resident in Bombay.

[4] Presumably aunt Kate Bond, of 4, Colleton Crescent, Exeter, then aged 78

[5] Probably Emily Sabine, daughter of Sabine's uncle Charles Baring-Gould.

Appendix B: 'Where to Find'

Contemporary Personal and Family Incidents

Page	Date	Event/Memoir
1880		
32	29 Jun to 3 Jul	Left E. Mersea for Lew.
	30 Jun	Daisy's serious illness
39	11 Jul	Barbara baptised
41	17 Jul	Daisy and Mary unwell
45	24 Jul	Edward laid foundation stone of staircase wing
48	9 Aug	To Belstone Tor with Mary, Edward and Arthur and Rev. W Lukis
52	19 Aug	Tea dance with Arundells at Kelly with Grace
54	30 Aug	To Eversfield with Grace. Carriage upset. Deja vu
55	2 Sep	Monument to Beatrice
60	11 Sep	Lucky white heather for Grace
	12 Sep	Daisy tearful at Trinity Sunday Mass
66	24 Sep	To the Glennies at Plymouth with Grace for 3 days
	26 Sep	Barbara unwell
67	9 Oct	Prepared for departure to Freiburg
		Edward tearful at prospect of leaving Lew
69-70	22—25 Oct	Journey to Freiburg
69	23 Oct	Daisy's bronchitis
	24 Oct	Moved by High Mass at Strassburg
70	3 Nov	Daisy and Barbara ill. Bewailed bronchitis, the family curse
	8 Nov	Mary, Daisy. Edward and Veronica to school
71	16—18 Nov	Freiburg Fair with children. Pluto the fire-eater. Thrifty Edward's generosity
82	25 Dec	Christmas with the von Hillerns.
1881		
91	12 Feb	Death of Uncle Charles
92	15 Feb	Arrived Lew Trenchard
		Problems with Uncle Charles' son, Charlie
	19 Feb	Uncle Charles' funeral
98	1 Apr	*'I am very much like a buoy'*
99	2 Apr	Cheap china from Freiburg
1881		
103	5 May	Aunt Kate Bond arrived
104	7—13 May	Excursions in the Black Forest
	16—18 May	Ramble in Black Forest
105	18 May	Daisy had bronchitis again
		Countess Kearney's recipe for cough mixture

Page	Date	Event/Memoir
105	5 Jun	11 days in the Tyrol with Kate Bond
		At Nassereith commissioned window for Lew
		Kate Bond a prude?
106	10 Jun	Kate Bond left
106	29 Jun 1881	Sent Bishop of Exeter his presentation to Lewtrenchard
	6 Jul	Travelled to England
	19 Jul	Instituted by Bishop of Exeter
	20 Jul	Inducted at St Peter's Lew Trenchard
	2 Aug	Family to Laufenburg, they on holiday, he to write.
	22 Aug	Children 'happy as the day is long'
	3 Sep	Return to Freiburg
	5 Sep	Mary and Daisy to school at Institut
Wasmer		
107	*8 Sep*	*Edward (Sabine) to board with Herr Baader*
	10 Sep	Leaves Freiburg. Waved goodbye to Mary, Edward and Daisy.
		Tale of a mislaid perambulator
108	12 Sep	6 Keppel Street London
	15 Sep	*To E Mersea to send luggage to Lew*
109	20 Sep	Went to Lew
	8 Oct	Grace and children arrived
	1 Nov	Birth of Diana Amelia
	2 Nov	A crimson umbrella
110	5—9 Nov	Local burglaries.
1882		
112	1 Jan	Diana Amelia baptised
116	7 May	Preached at Starcross asylum
120	24 Jun	Newspaper report of Kelly College speech
129	1 Aug	Mary, Edward, Margaret returned home from Freiburg
	3 Aug	Prize giving at Kelly College
130	24 Aug	Lew Trenchard School Treat and Service
1882		
132	21 Nov	Pengelly's 100th Court at Lew. Edward dined with the farmers. 4th heir to accompany Pengelly
1883		
135	29 Jan	Visit to Lloyd Worth of Worth
136	11 May	Felicitas born
137	29 Sep	Grace opened quarry lake
		To Continent with Gatrill
1884		
138	5 Jan	Death of *dear friend* Lloyd Worth.
		Life is a series of bitter disappointments
140	19 May	With Grace to stay with the Thynnes at Kilkhampton
141	7 Jul to 22 Aug	To Germany with Gatrill

Page	Date	Event/Memoir
1885		
143	5 Jan	Funeral of dissolute Russell Pasley
149	20 Aug	Birth of Henry
149	29 Sep	Marriage of Alex Baring in Paris as Grace moved house.
151	1 Oct	Lew House at last
		Grace *A general in the house*
151	2 Nov	All Souls Day. Mass at Lew Trenchard
151	9—11 Nov 1885	Bishop of Exeter at confirmations in St Peter's
1886		
153	12 Jun to 14 Jul	To Germany
	15 Jul	Masons idle in his absence
155	12 Aug	Grace and children to Bude
	23 Aug	Waited up for partying girls. Ghostly laughter
156	28 Aug	Grace and children returned from Bude
1889		
159	Jan	Bronchitis
	4 Feb	To Italy
	8 Feb	Bronchitis
	11 Feb to 30 Mar	Genoa, Rome, Florence and home
160	17 Jul	'Put down' letter to Daisy's suitor
161	15 Oct	*Dear Edward'* left home for America
	5 Nov	Mary thrown while hunting
1890		
165	18 Jan	Bronchitis
1890		
	21 Jan	No work on Lew House in 1889 because funds low. Borrowed £500 from bank.
		Gloomy fears of not returning from continental trip. Onus on Edward to complete SBG plans for Lew
166	27 Jan	Influenza at Guildford. Felicitas also very ill at Lew
166	12 Feb to 30 Apr	Italy and Provence
168	7 Aug	Grace to Bude
	11 Aug to 11 Oct	Scarlet fever attack. Vera, Henry, Julian, servants
1891		
171	20 Aug	Edward home. A peal of bells!
172	27 Aug	Children and Miss Biggs to Port Isaac
		Yet another 'put down' letter for Daisy's suitor
	29 Aug	Gummed in letter to Edward from Julian at Port Isaac
174	24 Dec	Trewartha. Drama at Redmoor Bog
1892		
177	29 Feb to 4 Apr	South of France
179	Undated	Mary engaged to AWH Dickinson

Page	Date	Event/Memoir
	Undated	Account of Mary's marriage. Sabine's concerns over Dunsland and marriage settlement
1894		
185	15 Aug	Death of Pengelly
	20 Aug	Baby Grace anecdotes
		Pengelly's early duties
186	18 Oct	Harry away to school
186	25 Dec	Daisy, Vera, Willy and Edward at Communion
1895		
186	1 Jan	All children dined at Lew. First and last time
		Severe winter
	1 Mar	Children have measles
187	16 Jun	Half-brother Arthur welcomed as curate
	18 Jun	Edward engaged - but is Marion a churchwoman?
	20 Sep	Two stories of family history
1896		
187	27 May	Vera laid ballroom foundation stone
		Vera's malapropisms
1897		
190	1 Feb	Edward and new wife arrived. Peal of bells
	2—17 Feb	Fatted calf celebrations. Several dinners and a ball.
191	18 Feb	Edward, Marion and Julian left
	20 Feb	Julian sailed
	25 Jul	Bad cold. Lost voice
	2 Aug	Post Bridge to recuperate
	12—19 Aug	John ill and nearly died
1899		
191	4 Nov	Laurence Burnard asked for Barbara's hand
	10 Nov	Sabine's unfinished reply. 'Butterfly' Barbara

Personal Memories

Page	Date	
1880		
42	19 Jul	Memories of death of Beatrice
60	12 Sep	Death of Rev. Lowder lead to recollections of Pimlico, Hurstpierpoint, ordination, conflict with parents and Willy. Engagement to Grace. Plans to be a missionary.
73	1 Dec	Early married life at Dalton
		A thief in the night
		A shot in the night
		A round of beef
		Pea Soup
		Dalton v E Mersea

Page	Date	Event/Memoir
78	8 Dec	My father's face
79	10 Dec	Father's death
		Brother Willy's mental illness and death
		(Included the only mention of brother Drake in the diary. Even his death in 1887 is not mentioned here or in the family bible entries)
1881		
84	3 Jan	Father's personality and relationship with children
1881		
90	24 Jan	Mother's personality.

Personal Finances

1880		
69	22 Oct	Farmers cannot pay rents. Lew House let for 5 years at £200 pa. Borrowed £1000. Will live cheaply on the continent to recoup. Net income from Lew £2.
70	29 Oct	Freiburg lodgings. 4 rooms, all found ex. wine, fuel and paraffin: £1 a day
81	12 Dec	Angry at book sales affected by poor reviews when *sore distressed for money*
1881		
83	1 Jan	Net income from Lew Estate £60. Laments arrears
104	14 May	Diocesan surveyor's report of dilapidations at Mersea
107	8 Sep	Edward's boarding costs at Freiburg £50 pa. Schooling extra.
1890		
165	21 Jan	Laments inability to build in 1889. No money. Borrowed from Bank.

Relatives

1880		
38	5 to 14 Jul	Sir George Young stood for parliament. Stayed at Lew.
66	27 Sep to 2 Oct	Aunts Fanny and Emily Bond, Mrs Glennie to stay
76	7 Dec	Little Aunt Harriet
77	8 Dec	Unctuous Uncle Alexander
1881		
85	5 Jan	Edward and Sophia set up home in Manchester to keep Willy out of bad company (1857)
92	15 Feb	Uncle Charles's personality
93	23 Feb	Frank Bond and his bride

Page	Date	Event/Memoir
1885		
149	29 Sep	Marriage of Alex Baring-Gould

Gould Family History

1880		
32	4 Jul	History from 1626 to death of Madam Gould 1786
43	20 Jul	Grandfather William's extravagances. Sabine lamented loss of Pridhamsleigh. Dreamt of buying it back. 'I will strain every nerve'
53	29 Aug	Gould and Baring livery
57	5 Sep	Family mottos and history 1649 onward
65	19 Sep	Sale of Staverton property by grandfather
1882		
116	8 May	Family portrait at E Ogwell Rectory, Staverton
	17 May	More on Staverton portraits
129	4 Jul	Grandfather's waste of money gambling and standing for parliament. Could have spent on buying Coryton. Sabine dreamt of acquiring Coryton one day. More on Edward Gould of Pridhamsleigh
1883		
135	26 Feb	More on Edward Gould, 'The Scamp'
136	11 May	Three stories of Old Madam from old servant Maria Beere
138	1 Dec	Verses on name 'Gould'
1884		
143	28 Dec	Family portraits by Joshua Reynolds
1885		
147	16 Mar	Lord Donnington letter on Gould portraits

Lew House and Estate

1880		
39	12 Jul	Renewal of staircase wing
45	22 Jul	Planted trees on estate
45		Planting failures
1880		
47	8 Aug	With Mr Lukis, antiquary, to Galford Down and the Lew Mill menhir
48	9 Aug	Began to rebuild porch
51	16 Aug	History of staircase wing Lew House
52	19 Aug	Erected the menhir at Lew Mill
56	3 Sep	History of dining room at Lew House
	5 Sep	Colour blind architects and other cautionary tales

Page	Date	Event/Memoir
64	15 Sep	Harvest festival. Gifts to Church
	16 Sep	Planting on the Lime Quarry Ramps
65	20 Sep	Planted more trees
67	2 Oct	Planted apple trees
1881		
109	29 Oct	Planted trees on lime quarry ramps
1882		
112	1 Jan	Drained fields
112	1 Jan	Aunt Emily's memories of panelling in old drawing room.
		Church furnishings
113	1 Feb	Moved the road behind Lew House
115	28 Feb	Grandfather's destructive restorations at Lew Mill Dower House and Orchard. Pengelly's memories of Lew Mill.
116	1 May	Began the Ramps Cottage
1883		
134	20 Jan	Planted trees
137	29 Sep	Grace cut last turf to create Quarry lake Planted on lime quarry ramps
1884		
141	1 Oct	Roses in garden and greenhouse
		Fruit trees
		Piped water to Lew House 1875/6
		Improvements to cottages and Wooda
		Drained marshes
		Andromeda and the Dolphin
1885		
144	undated	Planting of rose beds
145	13 Mar	Pixy well in Spring garden
148	20 Aug	Portrait of W Petty
152	12 Nov	Removal of parapet at Lew House
	1 Dec	Restoration of drawing room
1885		
153	4 Dec	Fireplace in dressing room
1886		
153	5 Jan	Granite window in drawing room
153	1 May	Old stone work in Lew House. 1682 doorway from Waddlestone.
154	11 Aug	More work on drawing room
155	24 Aug	Granite fireplace
156	28 Aug	More restoration work
	4 Oct	Another granite fireplace

Page	Date	Event/Memoir
1889		
159	30 Mar	Restoration at Lew Mill
161	29 Aug	Extension to 'Brent Tor View' on Lewdown
1890		
165	21 Jan	Commenced gallery in 1888. No money for building in 1889. Borrowed from bank
167	21 Jul	Restoration of dining room
168	26 Aug	Re-organised drainage for Lew House
1891		
170	Undated	Bemoaned delay in work on Lew House because of necessary work elsewhere on the estate
171	5 Mar	Planted trees
171	14 Apr	Y-cottages. Foundation stone laid by Henry
174	24 Dec	Cottages at the Y near completion Extensions to 'Rampenstein' Planted 600 apple trees
1892		
178	24 May	Newspaper cutting: Half yearly rent audit
1894		
185	1 Oct	Extensions to back wing of Lew House
186	18 Oct	Extensions to back wing of Lew House
1895		
186	1 Jan	Disclaimed responsibility for Ardoch Lodge design
	1 Mar	Cold winter. Work recommenced after a month. Roof off E Wing
1896		
187	27 May	Vera laid foundation stone for ballroom
188	31 May	Discoveries during renovation for ballroom
189		More history of Lew House and alterations by father and grandfather
1899		
193	Undated	Inscriptions for family monuments?

Local Characters and Anecdotes

Page	Date	Event/Memoir
1880		
54	29 Aug	The memories of Maria Beere, servant
55	31 Aug	The story of Dawe, the carpenter.
56	5 Sep	Scandal at Haine
60	12 Sep	Fresh scandal at Haine
1882		
122	24 Jun	The prisoner of Orchard
1883		
134	20 Jan	Stag Hunt at Lewdown

Devon families, churches and houses etc

Page	Date	Event/Memoir
1880		
44	22 Jul	Mr Radford and Lydford Gorge. Derogatory comments deleted
		The upstart Newtons of Millaton
		The misfortune of Capt. Luxmore of Witherdon
45	26 Jul	Staverton. Extracts from the registers
		Gift to Church
	27 Jul	Dartington registers
		Broadhempston memorials
46	28 Jul	Totnes registers
46	29 Jul	Ashburton registers
52	27 Aug	The confused swans of Reginald Kelly of Kelly.
63	13 Sep	The death of Capt. Carew
64	14 Sep	Lord Devon's unfortunate marriage
66	27 Sep	Thornton-West of Exeter
1881		
111	12 Nov	Working on new edition of *Visitation of Devon*
		Harris not Mohun-Harris
	13 Nov	Sale of Witherdon
1882		
112	1 Feb	'Restoration' of churches at Peter Tavy, Whitchurch, Virginstowe, Dunterton. Jacobstow, Maristowe, Broadwood Widger and Morwenstowe.
113	20 Feb	To Trecarrel, near Launceston with John Northmore
		What connected the Coleridges and Northmores?
114	27 Feb	The Pennells and Davys of Medland
116	1 Mar	Havock at St James, Okehampton
		Old Staverton bench ends rescued
117	17 May	Coat of Arms at Upcot, Broadwood
117	10 Jun	Boscastle bench ends
120	24 Jun	Hurdwick House
121		Wringworthy, Mary Tavy
		Well Town, Boscastle
131	2 Oct	Carvings at Fulford House, Crediton
132	21 Nov	'Restoration' at Sheepstor
		Longstone House
133	26 Nov	Registers at Woolboro', Newton Abbot, Bovey Tracey, Chudleigh, Abbots Kirswell
1883		
135	17 Feb	Kingsbridge registers
1884		
140	20 May	Wellcombe church and Holy well

Devon Clergy Anecdotes

Folklore, ghost stories etc

Page	Date	Event/Memoir
104	18 May	Haircuts for the Oberreid crucifix. Use in *Zitta*
1882		
128	3 Jul	A bundle of sticks at Dockacre
		The Tresmarrow skull
1884		
139	26 Jan	At Broadwood Widger
		Jack O'Lanterns
		Blue flames
		A ghostly kerchief donor
		The spiritual St Christopher of the R Wulf
		The church at midnight on St Mark's Eve
		A posthumous child cures diphtheria
141	14 Jun	Julian and another little man
155	23 Aug	A ghost in the avenue at Lew?
		Disembodied laughter at Lew
156	24 Sep	A fearful figure at Lew
1896		
187	8 Feb	A sacrifice at Meavy to 'the Good Folk'
188	31 May	Ill-wishing and arson at Portgate
1897		
193	4 Oct	Charm for staunching blood and a cure for rheumatism

Antiquities

1880		
48	11 Aug	Planned line of stones on Down Tor
52	16 Aug	Planned Harter Tor with Lukis
53	28 Aug	Lukis planning line of stones on Staddon Moor

Writing and Associated Events

1880		
81	12 Dec	Received bundle of reviews of 'repulsive' *Mehalah*. Mehalah written when 'depressed and embittered' by reviews of *Germany*. Income from these books.
1881		
96	19 Mar	£35 from Smith and Elder for *Mehalah*. Reviews earning from writing. Invited to write a novel of the Black Forest in German to be serialised in *Deutsches Familienblatt*

Page	Date	Event/Memoir
98	1 Apr	Offered £100 by Skeffington to write two vols of village sermons and one of sermons for saints' days. Also a book on Germany for Samson Lowe. Will write English and French versions of the Black Forest novel
100	6 Apr	German rights to *Mehalah*
101	18 Apr	Newspaper cuttings on *Mehalah*
106	11 Jun	Writing Black Forest novel *Zitta*
	22 Aug	Finished sermon outlines and 32 chapters of *Zitta*
	3 Sep	Finished village sermons for Saints' days and *Zitta*.
	5 Sep	Sold French translation of *Zitta*.
112	14 Nov	Sold *Zitta* for £200. French translation by Countess Kearney £50
1882		
112	1 Jan	Countess Kearney's translation refused. She wanted £25
131	10 Oct	Series of Church Songs
133	26 Nov	Started *John Herring* 1 Nov. Written 12 chapters
134	21 Dec	24 chapters of *John Herring*
1883		
136	24 Mar	Finished *John Herring*
136	25 Mar	*John Herring* to publishers
	14 Apr	Offered £100 for copyright
137	29 Sep	£100 for *John Herring* £40 for *Margery of Quether*
1884		
138	18 Jan	*Seven Last Words* £15. Reprint of *John Herring* £25. *Margery of Quether* £14
142	28 Dec	List of work published in the year. *Church songs*
1885		
143	3 Jan	Offered £400 for *Court Royal*
		Reviewed earnings from publications
1885		
145	24 Feb	Finished *Gaverocks*
	11 Mar	Began Bratton Clovelly novel. What to call it?
148	20 Aug	Finished Red Spider
		Sold *The Gaverocks*, *Red Spider,* and *Eve*
1886		
153	11 Jun	Dramatisation of *Mehalah* at the Gaiety Theatre. Disliked final scene. He will write a new final scene!
155	22 Aug	Finished *Richard Cable*
	24 Aug	Unable to sell historical and mythological articles. Angry outburst against '*loathed*' novel writing
157	4 Oct	£50 for *Little Tu'penny*
	16 Oct	£350 from Chamber for *Richard Cable* serial

Page	Date	Event/Memoir
	22 Oct	£400 from Smith and Elder for *Gaverocks*, £350 for *Richard Cable* after Chambers
1889		
161	28 Aug	Finished *Urith*. '*Poor stuff*'
	29 Aug	Sent *Urith* to Cornhill – refused
1890		
166	20 Feb	Portraits of the Emperors in Rome
	8 to 30 Apr	To Nice and Provence to write a book on Provence for Messrs Allen
167	16 Jun	Finished and sent off book on Provence
	2 Jul	Began *In the Roar of the Sea*
169	15 Nov	Two 1876 poems gummed in. *The Tory War Cry* and *The Turk and the Tory*. Associations with Gladstone
170	Undated	Music for *Church Songs*
1891		
170	5 Mar	Finished *Tragedy of the Caesars*
171	30 Mar	Began *Curgenven*
174	4 Sep	Finished *Curgenven*
	24 Dec	Serial rights *Mrs Curgenven of Curgenven* for £300
175	26 to 30 Dec	To Teck. Marriage of Duke of Clarence for Graphic
1892		
175	4 to 6 Jan	To Ely fens for *Cheap Jack Zitta* (sic)
	11 Jan	Poem: *The Sprig of May*
177	29 Jan	Began *Cheap Jack Zitta*
178	16 Apr	Finished *Cheap Jack Zita* (sic)
179	15 Aug	Began *Queen of Love*. Finished 30 Oct. 47 days
1894		
186	18 Dec	Finished *Broom Squire*. Started *Guavas*, half way through, resumed *Broom Squire* after visit to Thursley for dialect
1896		
187	27 May	Began *Perpetua* 21 Apr. Finished 14 May. Finished copying 30 May
190	15 Oct	Began *Domitia Longina*. Finished *A Study of S Paul*

Dealings with Frau von Hillern over English Translation of her play Geier Wally

Page	Date	Event/Memoir
1880		
75	5 Dec	Comment on Frau von Hillern, her family and work
82	15 Dec	Saw the dramatised version of Fr v H's novel *Geier Wally*

Page	Date	Event/Memoir
	25 Dec	Started to translate *Geier Wally* for English Stage.
	26 Dec	Unaware of German translation of *Mehalah*. Blames F v H. He had shared profits for translation of *Arzt der Seele (Ernestine)*
1881		
90	23 Jan	Translating *Geier Wally*. Negotiated between F v H and Miss Linda Dietz who will buy the play and take the lead part. He to receive 1/3 of F v H's earnings.
91	12 Feb	Saw F v H
	13 Feb	Saw F v H
	14 Feb	Saw Miss Dietz in London
93	28 Feb	Worked on play. Dined at Dietz's
1881		
	1 Mar	Finished play to Miss Dietz. Learnt that Fr v H planned to cut him out of the deal
94	4 Mar	Legal case against F v H
96	18 Mar	Chilly meeting with F v H
	22 Mar	F v H clever and unscrupulous. Suing **him**!
98	31 Mar	His case again
100	14 Apr	Meets F v H's lawyer. Sabine threatens an injunction
	18 Apr	Lawyer again
102	23 Apr	Unsatisfactory agreement. Ended contact with F v H
102	23 Apr	Bad behaviour of F v H's daughters at Mersea

Folksongs

1889		
161	17 Sep	Lectured on *Songs of the West* at Plymouth
	19 Nov	Lectured at Plymouth
	20 Nov	Lectured at Launceston
162	5 Dec	Lectured at Bristol
	7 Dec	Interview on *Songs of the West* in *The Globe*
1890		
167	31 May	Lectured at Royal Institution, London
	7 Jun	Lectured again
167	14 Jun	Lectured again
1897		
182	3 Dec	'Fingal Baring-Gould.' Gummed in Letter from Fleetwood Sheppard out of context and date.

Miscellaneous Anecdotes

1880		
51	15 Aug	Primitive Methodist sermon

Freiburg Anecdotes and Characters

Page	Date	Event/Memoir
103	1 May	The von Zieglers and the King of Bavaria
		Who is Countess Kearney?
107	*5 Sep*	*Capt. Festing's tips for farmers*

Miscellaneous entries

1880

52	28 Aug	*'To the memory of Mistress Maguire...'*
		Church window, Beaumaris (Anglesey)

1882

130	*23 Aug*	*Recipe for Cider Cup (Excellent, used New Year 2005)*
132	*14 Oct*	*Recipe for 'strain oil'*

1883

138	10 Dec	Unattributed verse

1884

138	20 Jan	Two Devon sayings

1886

154	15 Jul	Gatrill's Boathouse riddle

1888

157	7 Sep	Two hunting songs. *The Bellever Week* and *The Lamerton Hunt Song*

1893

181	Jan	*Konx Ompax Abracadabra* A page of obscure Greek handwriting.

Appendix C: Family Trees

THE MONKS OF POTHERIDGE[1]

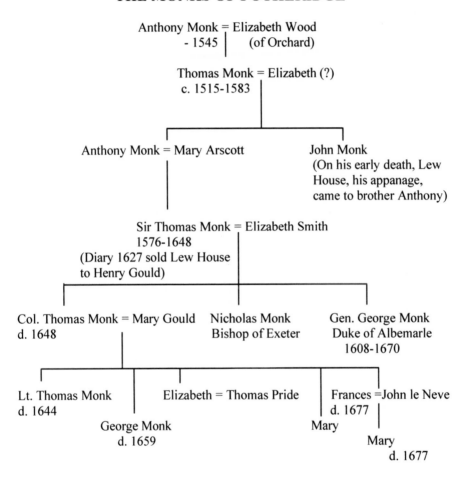

Anthony Monk = Elizabeth Wood
- 1545   (of Orchard)

Thomas Monk = Elizabeth (?)
c. 1515-1583

Anthony Monk = Mary Arscott   John Monk
                                      (On his early death, Lew
                                      House, his appanage,
                                      came to brother Anthony)

Sir Thomas Monk = Elizabeth Smith
1576-1648
(Diary 1627 sold Lew House
to Henry Gould)

Col. Thomas Monk = Mary Gould   Nicholas Monk   Gen. George Monk
d. 1648   Bishop of Exeter   Duke of Albemarle
                                                     1608-1670

Lt. Thomas Monk   Elizabeth = Thomas Pride   Frances =John le Neve
d. 1644   d. 1677
              George Monk   Mary
              d. 1659   Mary
                                                             d. 1677

---

[1] Based on information in the diary, p 1-2; also in *'Early Reminiscences'* chapter 1
and in *'Lew Trenchard, the Manor House, the Church and Baring-Gould'* by S
Gordon Monk.

THE GOULDS AND BARING-GOULDS

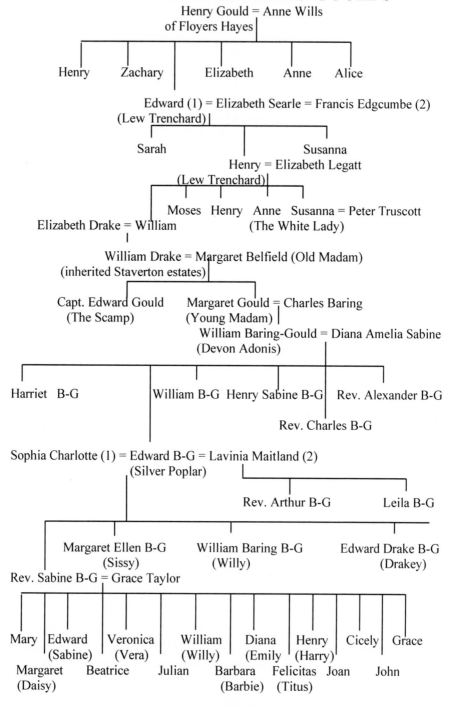

Henry Gould = Anne Wills
of Floyers Hayes

Henry   Zachary   Elizabeth   Anne   Alice

Edward (1) = Elizabeth Searle = Francis Edgcumbe (2)
(Lew Trenchard)

Sarah   Susanna

Henry = Elizabeth Legatt
(Lew Trenchard)

Moses Henry Anne Susanna = Peter Truscott
Elizabeth Drake = William   (The White Lady)

William Drake = Margaret Belfield (Old Madam)
(inherited Staverton estates)

Capt. Edward Gould   Margaret Gould = Charles Baring
(The Scamp)   (Young Madam)

William Baring-Gould = Diana Amelia Sabine
(Devon Adonis)

Harriet B-G   William B-G Henry Sabine B-G   Rev. Alexander B-G

Rev. Charles B-G

Sophia Charlotte (1) = Edward B-G = Lavinia Maitland (2)
(Silver Poplar)

Rev. Arthur B-G   Leila B-G

Margaret Ellen B-G   William Baring B-G   Edward Drake B-G
(Sissy)   (Willy)   (Drakey)

Rev. Sabine B-G = Grace Taylor

Mary Edward Veronica   William   Diana Henry Cicely Grace
     (Sabine) (Vera)   (Willy)   (Emily) (Harry)
Margaret   Beatrice   Julian   Barbara Felicitas Joan   John
(Daisy)   (Barbie) (Titus)

Appendix D: Maps

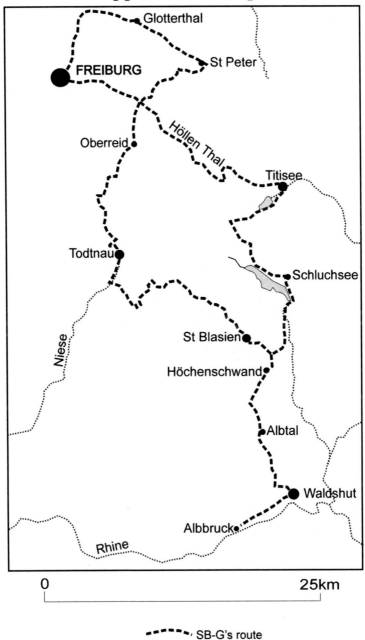

SB-G's route

Map 1. Excursions around Freiburg and to the Black Forest. 1881: 7,12,16 to 18 May.

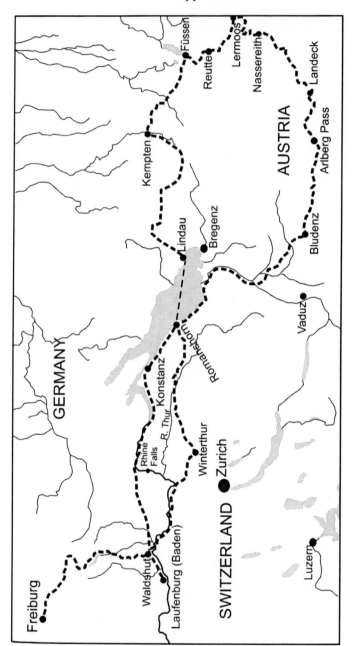

Map 2. Tour of the Tyrol with Kate Bond. 1881: 25 May to 5 June

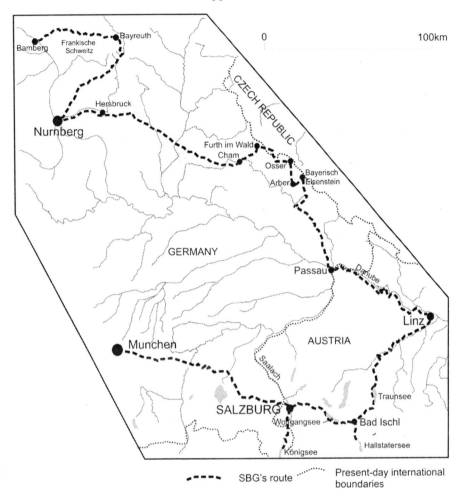

Map 3. Bavarian Tour with Gatrill. 1883. Dates not given.
See entry for 29 Sep. 1883

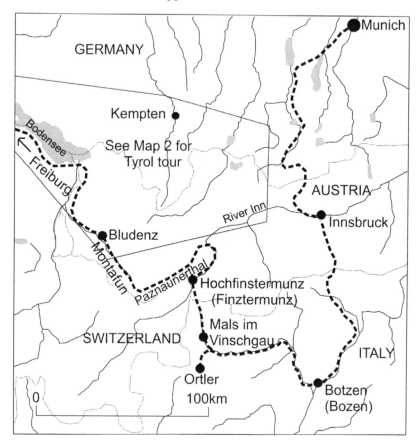

------- route taken by SBG

.... Present-day international boundaries

Map 4. Southern Tyrol Tour with Gatrill. 1884. 7 July to 22 August

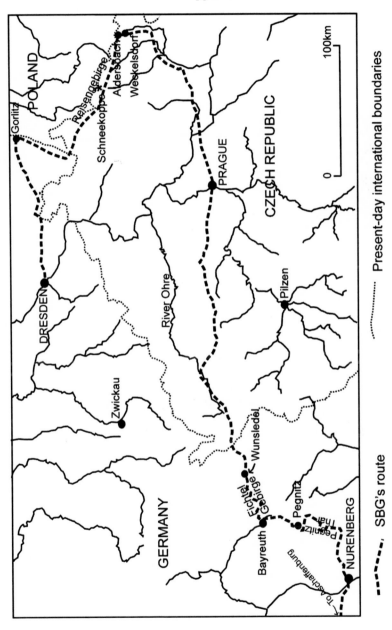

Map 5. Tour of Eastern European. 1886: 12 June to 14 July

.... Present-day international boundaries

- - - - SBG's route

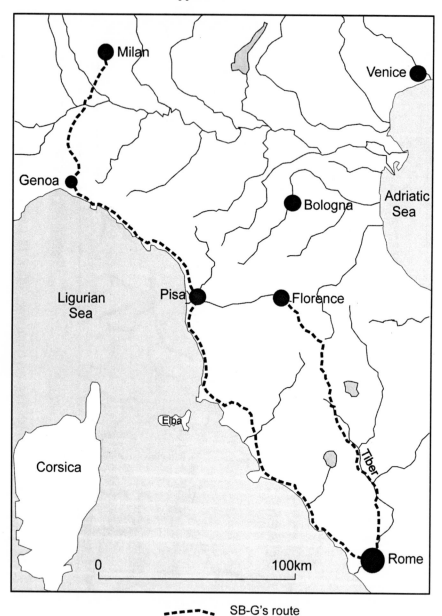

Map 6. Tour of Italy. 1889. 4 Feb. to 30 March

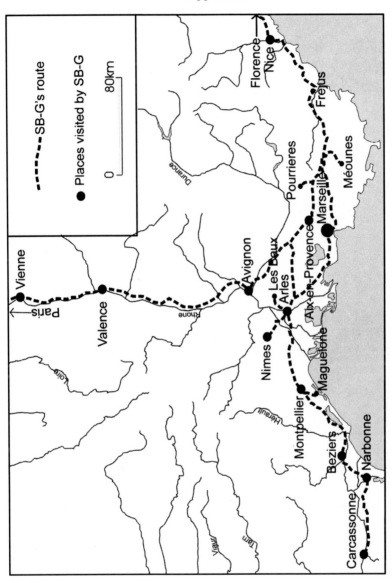

Map 7. Tour of Provence [Troubadour Land] 1890 8 to 30 April

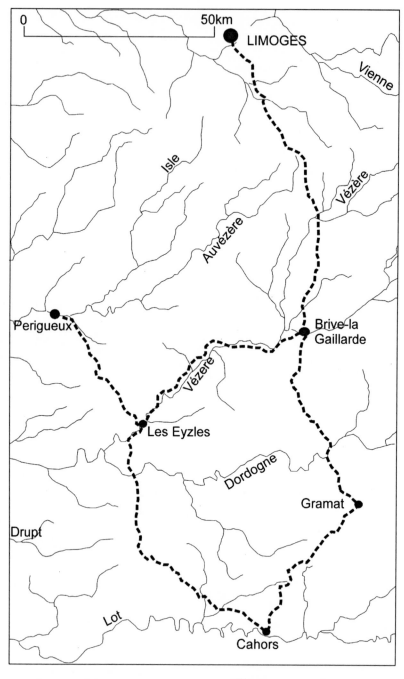

● Localitiesvisited by SBG   ▬ ▬ ▬ ▬   SBG's route

Map 8. Tour of the Dordogne. 1892: 29 Feb. to 4 April

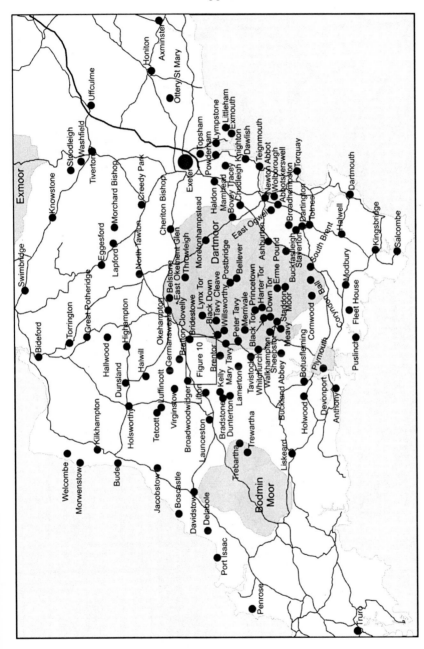

Figure 9. Localities in Devon and Cornwall mentioned by SB-G

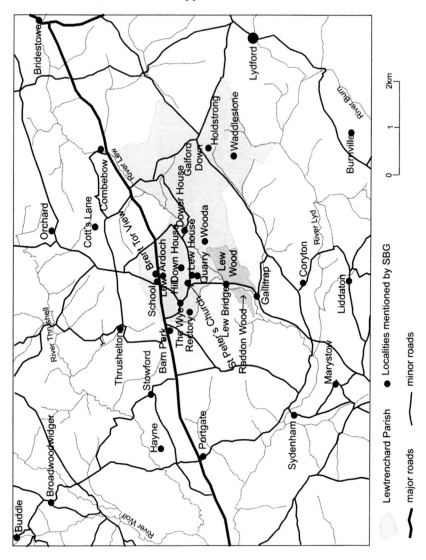

Map 10. Localities in and around Lewtrenchard mentioned in the Diary

Indexes

Index 1:
Names of all people mentioned in the Diary

Index 2: Names of all members of the
Clergy mentioned in the Diary

Index No. 3: Devon and Cornwall
Place Names in the Diary

Index No 4: Lew Trenchard Place Names

Index No. 5: British Place Names (other than Devon and Cornwall)

Index No. 6: Continental Place Names

Lightning Source UK Ltd.
Milton Keynes UK
23 January 2010

149025UK00001B/59/P